Economic Growth and Valuation of the Environment

Economic Growth and Valuation of the Environment

A Debate

Edited by

Ekko C. van Ierland

Professor of Environmental Economics and Natural Resources, Wageningen University, The Netherlands

Jan van der Straaten

Assistant Professor, Department of Leisure Studies, Tilburg University, The Netherlands

Herman R.J. Vollebergh

Assistant Professor of Public Economics, Erasmus University Rotterdam, The Netherlands

Edward Elgar

Cheltenham, UK • Northampton, MA, USA

Published by
Edward Elgar Publishing Limited
Glensanda House
Montpellier Parade
Cheltenham
Glos GL50 1UA
UK

Edward Elgar Publishing, Inc.
136 West Street
Suite 202
Northampton
Massachusetts 01060
USA

A catalogue record for this book
is available from the British Library

Library of Congress Cataloguing in Publication Data

Economic growth and valuation of the environment : a debate / Ekko C. van Ireland, Jan van der Straaten, Herman R.J. Vollebergh, editors.
p. cm.
Includes bibliographical references and index.
1. Economic development — Environmental aspects. 2. Sustainable development — Environmental aspects. I. Ireland, E. van (Ekko van) II. Straaten, Jan van der. III. Vollebergh, Herman R.J.
HD75.6D43 2001
363.7′05—dc21 2001040186

ISBN 1 84064 432 X

Printed and bound in Great Britain by MPG Books Ltd, Bodmin, Cornwall

Contents

List of figures

List of tables

List of contributors

Giles Atkinson, CSERGE, London, UK

Wilfred Beckerman, Emeritus Professor at Balliol College, Oxford, UK

Bart de Boer, Statistics Netherlands, The Hague, The Netherlands

Herman E. Daly, Professor at the University of Maryland, USA

Rob B. Dellink, Environmental Economics and Natural Resources Group, Wageningen University, The Netherlands

Paul Ekins, Professor at the University of Keele, UK

Salah El Serafy, former World Bank and Secretary of the UNEP/World Bank Group on Environmental Accounting for Sustainable Development, Washington, DC, USA

Sylvie Faucheux, President of the European Society of Ecological Economics, Université de Versailles-Saint Quentin en Yvelines, France

Sarah Fleisher Trainor, University of California, Berkeley, USA

Reyer Gerlagh, Institute for Environmental Studies, Vrije Universiteit, Amsterdam, The Netherlands

Robert Goodland, World Bank's Environmental Adviser, Washington, DC, USA

Kirk Hamilton, Environmental Department World Bank, Washington, DC, USA

Marjan W. Hofkes, Institute for Environmental Studies, Vrije Universiteit, Amsterdam, The Netherlands

Roefie Hueting, Statistics Netherlands, The Hague, The Netherlands

Ekko C. van Ierland, Professor of Environmental Economics and Natural Resources, Wageningen University, The Netherlands

Huib M.A. Jansen, Institute for Environmental Studies, Vrije Universiteit, Amsterdam, The Netherlands

Richard B. Norgaard, Professor at the University of California, Berkeley and President of the International Society for Ecological Economics, USA

Martin O'Connor, Université de Versailles-Saint Quentin en Yvelines, France

David Pearce, Professor at University College, London and CSERGE, London, UK

Astrid J. Scholz, University of California, Berkeley, USA

Jan van der Straaten, Department of Leisure Studies, Tilburg University, The Netherlands

Harmen Verbruggen, Professor of International Environmental Economics at Vrije Universiteit, Amsterdam, The Netherlands

Herman R.J. Vollebergh, Erasmus University, Rotterdam, The Netherlands

Acknowledgements

The publishers wish to thank the following who have kindly given permission for the use of copyright material:

Elsevier Science Publishers for article: 'Three persistent myths in the environmental debate', Roefie Hueting, *Ecological Economics*, **18**, 1996, pp. 81–8.

The New York Times for article: 'Europeans begin to calculate the price of pollution', Marlise Simons, *The New York Times*, Sunday 9th December 1990.

1. Valuation of nature and the environment

Ekko C. van Ierland, Jan van der Straaten and Herman R.J. Vollebergh

INTRODUCTION

The debate on valuation of nature and the environment, green national accounting and economic growth is a classic and important topic in environmental economics.[1] Discussion on the definition and meaning of national income began at the beginning of the twentieth century with the work of King (1919) and Pigou's famous *The Economics of Welfare* (Pigou, 1920). As is well known, Pigou was well aware of the pitfalls of equating income with welfare. King also argues that the two are different, because in a modern society higher income would always be accompanied by economic losses due to an increase in scarcity of elements of nature, relevant for human society. Furthermore, he claims that 'modern' production was only possible by using depletable resources such as coal and iron.

It took until after World War II before King's argument regained momentum in the debate on how to set up a system of national accounts. Fabricant (1947) argued again that the depletion of natural resources should be taken into account as a cost component in the system. Economists like Denison (1947), however, argued that this was unnecessary because nature and the environment would be infinite resources which could be used without restriction. The way in which the national accounts were set up clearly reflects the latter, by then the most commonly held view on the relation between growth and the environment.

Although after 25 years this issue returned vividly as never before, the importance of the environment for the system of national accounting was never entirely outside the scope of economists. For instance, in the then well-known macroeconomic textbook of Dernburg and McDougall (1963), one finds a full-length discussion about the inclusion or exclusion of environmental losses in the system of national accounts. In their view it would make sense to subtract for example the costs of water pollution caused by a paper mill from the national product. However, they had serious doubts on whether such corrections could be operationalized. They also refer to the views of the Department of Commerce who see 'its measure of national product as a measure of productivity'.

The debate renewed at the end of the 1960s when serious concerns grew about pollution and the exhaustibility of resources. Especially Mishan's classic contribution *The Cost of Economic Growth* (Mishan, 1967) induced a lot of discussion. He also challenges the traditional way to measure welfare or utility through the concept of national income, because of its failure to include the deterioration of the environment. Like King and Fabricant before, he claims that economic growth, measured as the rise in national income over time, is a misleading indicator of the true development of welfare. An appropriate indicator of welfare should also include utilities or disutilities not measured by the traditional concept of income.

Now, again, 30 years later, the basic question of how corrections of national income should be made, if made at all, remains still unresolved. Like King, Fabricant and Mishan, several scholars are still convinced that correction for environmental deterioration is necessary, but opinions tend to differ on how exactly such corrections should be made. Some, like Hueting, argue that these valuation exercises should also explicitly account for future generations and their rights on particular environmental services. This suggests that the concept of a sustainable or green national income is also the appropriate form of the green national product. Others, like El Serafy (1992) and Pearce, Hamilton and Atkinson (Chapter 9 of this book), also think it would be useful to include natural assets and their services in the national accounts, but only by using current accounting prices.

At the same time, other scholars still believe that such corrections are not necessary anyway (see, for instance, Beckerman, Chapter 7 of this book). Basically, following the argument of Denison, they argue that the income concept behind national income, although limited in several respects, still provides the best measure for welfare and growth. Welfare is the flow of utilities as experienced by the current generation. Therefore, welfare should reflect the value of those living at a particular date, and existing prices reveal their preferences in the best way. Correcting these values with other, less certain values of non-marketed goods and stocks of environmental capital is judged unreliable or uninformative.

There are many questions involved in the debate on green accounting and economic growth, such as why and how to put a value on environmental stocks and flows. One crucial distinction is between conceptual and operational issues (Mäler, 1991). *Conceptual* issues deal with questions such as whether income is an appropriate welfare measure, and if so, how environmental assets and services are related to this measure. A closely related issue is whether, and if so in what way, one should account for the welfare of future generations. Another classic issue is whether household defensive expenditures, that is expenditures for measures individuals undertake in order to reduce the impact of environmental damage, should be included in final demand, or, instead, should be deducted. A final issue is whether the value of the stocks of environmental and natural resources should be included or not.

Operational issues are always at stake if one considers it appropriate to include environmental assets and their services more explicitly. For instance, in order to compute a green national income one has to find ways to calculate changes in value of environmental assets. However, neither ecology-economy feedback mechanisms nor their monetary values are easy to recover. Moreover, if one is willing to include some notion of sustainability the question is which particular specification one has in mind. Furthermore, even if one does not agree that a correction of national income is a useful device, one might favour some sort of monitoring system for environmental resources. For instance, integrated assessments, combining environmental and traditional economic indicators, like the National Accounting Matrix including Environmental Accounts (NAMEA) system also ask for specification of what has to be measured, and how.

This book presents a set of papers on these issues honouring in one way or another the important contributions of Dr R. Hueting to this debate. Roefie Hueting was one of the first economists working at a leading Statistical Bureau who recognized the importance of the role of the environment for the national accounts. In *New Scarcity* (originally published in Dutch in 1974 and published in English in 1980), he systematically reviews the welfare theoretic underpinnings of the problem. The basic premise behind his work is that if it is plausible that economic growth, or the growth of production, contributes positively to welfare, and if this growth is impossible without loss of environmental functions, then an adequate indicator of welfare should count with both sides of the coin. This implies that a green national income will always be lower than the traditional national income as long as this loss of environmental functions is perceived as a welfare loss (at the margin). Starting from this premise, Hueting always insisted on the importance to operationalize his ideas on alternative indicators for welfare.

This chapter summarizes the papers collected in this book and shortly discusses the issues raised in each paper. We do not aim to provide a summary of the current state of affairs on green accounting, nor do we claim any comprehensiveness with respect to the current views on this subject. Our aim is to present the scientific debate on these topics by means of the chapters in this book. Most chapters were presented on the international symposium

Valuation of Nature and the Environment at the Royal Netherlands Academy of Arts and Sciences in Amsterdam in 1999. We grouped them together in four headings: Setting the stage (Part I), Reflections (Part II), Green Accounting (Part III) and Conclusion (Part IV). The remainder of this introduction closely follows this division.

PART I SETTING THE STAGE

Hueting and de Boer set the stage explaining their views on sustainable national income (SNI). Hueting has always been convinced that conventional measures of national income fall short as a welfare measure because they neglect the deterioration of the environment. In contrast, estimates of a SNI do reflect the trade-off between (growth of) income and the environment as two of the most important pillars of (subjective) welfare. At the *conceptual* level Hueting's claim rests on two central positive statements: (1) there exist strong preferences for the environment that cannot be fully expressed through market and budget mechanisms; (2) (at the current margin) more production implies less environment and vice versa. Together these statements imply that a sustainable national income will always be below a conventionally measured national income.

Crucial to his *operational* concept of a sustainable national income is the concept of environmental functions. These functions are descriptions of vital roles of the environment for humanity, like the production of oxygen and the supply of basic minerals. Thus one might think of these functions as providing basic services or commodities for which demand and supply exist. Supply in this context means human activities that improve a particular function. Monetary estimates for such activities are derived through a rather complicated assessment, called a 'demand and supply method' for valuation of environmental functions.

In Chapter 3, which contains a reprint of the paper *Three persistent myths in the environmental debate*,[2] Hueting clearly presents his views on environment and employment, economic growth and the cost of environmental protection.

Ekins' contribution provides some relevant background information. He discusses a number of topics currently dealt with in environmental economics, which are closely related to Hueting's contributions, in particular his concept of environmental capital and its relationship with sustainability and national accounting. An important point of departure for Hueting is the importance of environmental capital for wealth creation. This is shared by most (environmental) economists Ekins argues, as is clear by the now widely accepted four-capital model of wealth creation. The model includes: (1) ecological (or natural) capital; (2) human capital; (3) social and organizational capital; and (4) manufactured capital. Ecological capital provides the environmental functions mentioned before. In particular, it provides resources for production, the absorption of waste, and the basic context and conditions within which production is possible at all.

How to deal with environmental functions is one of the central issues in the debate on sustainability. Ekins claims that strong sustainability '(to be distinguished from very strong sustainability) is greatly to be preferred as the *a priori* position', because 'in keeping natural capital distinct from other types of capital, one would like to know natural capital's particular contribution to welfare, distinguishing between its contribution to production (through resource provision and waste absorption) and its services that generate welfare directly'. According to Ekins, however, a political judgement is needed to decide whether an environmental function should be used sustainably or not. Therefore he disagrees with Hueting who argued with Reijnders that 'sustainability is an objective concept to the extent that natural science is objective' (Hueting and Reijnders, 1998). Safe minimum standards are proposed not only in the context of endangered species, but also for a wider range of environmental issues that are characterized by chronic uncertainty, and possible irreversibility and immoderate losses.

Ekins also discusses the issue of environmental sustainability and national accounting. He criticizes several attempts to account for the negative ecological consequences of human activities in the national accounts, such as deductions from net domestic product (NDP) for imputed environmental costs as well as attempts to calculate sustainable national income based on a modelling approach (like the paper by Verbruggen et al. in Chapter 11 of this book). He defends, however, a somewhat different approach based on an estimate of what he calls the 'sustainability gap'. This gap is calculated, both in physical and monetary terms, by identifying the difference between actual pressure on the environment and levels required for sustainability and estimating its monetary value.

PART II REFLECTIONS

The contributions grouped together in the second part of the book reflect on several important presumptions behind the concept of a green or sustainable national income (SNI). First, Daly focuses on the premise of the existence of a demand curve for environmental functions. This leads him to reflect on one of the basic premises of economics in general, which is the notion that value stems from private subjective preferences. He argues that Hueting is led by the logic of practical problem solving to the introduction of what Daly calls a 'perpendicular' demand curve. This perpendicular social demand curve would be an expression of the objective value of sustainability. However, any postulation of such objective value entails a rejection of the central dogma of modern economic theory that all value arises from private subjective preferences. Hence Hueting's notion reveals a logical 'difficulty'.

Daly also argues that this difficulty arises because of the dogma of 'the omission of purpose and objective value from our cultural worldview'. This we should regret because only the belief in a reality of objective value can save us: with such a belief we can genuinely reason and escape from physical force or psychological manipulation deciding which preferences dominate. Unfortunately, both the value-free world of a non-purposeful biology and the subjectivistic world of economics prevent such notions to develop. Indeed, this dogma is coherent with, and likely to be derived from, the exclusion of purpose from science. Therefore, in his words, 'to attain purpose of using the biosphere sustainably we will first have to reclaim purpose itself from the dark shadow'.

In their contribution Norgaard, Scholz and Trainor also stress the importance of common or shared values, called 'sustainability ethic'. They argue that 'achieving sustainability is proving difficult precisely because a sustainability ethic is not widely shared'. Traditional, especially utilitarian, ways of evaluation do not achieve sustainability. According to the authors, however, utilitarianism has become increasingly dominant. This is unfortunate while utilitarianism would fail in a number of respects when it comes to the valuation of environmental problems. The authors discuss six interrelated challenges that would make 'apparent the need for valuing processes that account for values pluralism in environmental valuation and decision making'. Their claim is that additional ways of thinking about values should be incorporated more openly, implicitly suggesting that this would also improve the *outcomes* of the policy process.

Beckerman takes a radically different position. He claims that it is both impossible and unnecessary to have a theory of intergenerational justice. This claim challenges the basic assumption behind much of green accounting. This assumption is that changes in the stock of natural resources are often negative, and that depletion of this stock means that we are storing up problems for future generations. Indeed, this is one of the basic positive assumptions behind Hueting's claim that conventional estimates of economic growth overstate the true underlying net growth rate of welfare ('utility').

The structure of Beckerman's argument is simple. First, he claims that any coherent theory of justice implies conferring 'rights' on people that give a special status to certain of their interests. However, unborn people cannot be said to have any rights, because it makes no sense to attribute a property, like an interest, to a non-existent entity. Thus, it follows that the interests of future generations cannot be protected within the framework of any theory of justice. Instead we should search for a different ethic, basically related to some wider concept of morality.

This different approach changes the relative importance that we should attach to our various moral obligations to future generations. It brings the issue in the realm of theories of distributive justice (see Rawls, 1971). Here it is the distribution of some basic scarce resource between generations, which is important. Beckerman claims that this scarce resource is *not* the environmental resource, which he restricts to energy resources only. Our real obligations to future generations are related to basic human rights. Respect for these rights would ask for the bequeath of a more 'decent' society in terms of respect for such rights.

PART III GREEN ACCOUNTING AND SUSTAINABLE NATIONAL INCOME

The contributions in this part of the book reflect the current variety of views on green accounting and national income, both conceptual and operational. El Serafy, first of all, pays tribute to Hueting's contributions to ecological economics, in particular to his claim that using uncorrected national income data to guide economic policy is tantamount to steering society by the wrong compass. Next he explains in detail to what extent his own views differ from Hueting's. The main difference, according to El Serafy, is that his own perspective is less ambitious. Instead of focusing on national accounting as an instrument for estimating *welfare*, he proposes to correct gross national *product* (GNP).

In fact, El Serafy elaborates on the interesting dilemma mentioned in the first section between theoretically justified adjustments of gross domestic product (GDP) and practical or operational solutions. Although he does not consider Hueting as impractical, on the contrary, El Serafy believes that practical solutions should take for granted the existing procedures to estimate national product. Any approach that builds upon some form of shadow pricing, such as Hueting's demand and supply method for environmental services, would be too far away from the approximations and short cuts of the accountants, and also requires data not available to them. His own suggestion to calculate sustainable *income* by estimating value added by 'keeping capital intact' does not entirely solve this problem because 'environmental capital is different in nature from produced capital, and its decline or degradation sometimes requires a different treatment in the accounts'.

As a final issue El Serafy also discusses the policy context of measuring and using such adapted estimates of income. As far as the perceived importance of such adapted measures is concerned, in particular in relation to the United Nations System of National Accounts (SNA), he is not very optimistic. In fact, he argues, since the debate on the SNA in the early 1990s (UN, 1993) 'the unadjusted conventional measurements have persisted as the only "valid" ones available for macro-economic analysis', while not even a clear guidance was formulated with respect to the environmental adjustments, probably because they are not perceived as necessary anyway. Undoubtedly, the reluctance to adjust measures of GDP downward due to losses in environmental capital could be explained by the fact that such adaptations are not in the interest of politicians.

In a provocative chapter, Pearce, Hamilton and Atkinson contribute to the debate by arguing that shadow pricing is essential for the concept of 'sustainable GNP', while Hueting has stated that 'the construction of shadow prices that are directly comparable with market prices, a prerequisite for a theoretically sound correction of national income, is mostly not possible' (Hueting, 1991). Next, they test Hueting's own alternative of a 'sustainable GNP' by evaluating whether it overcomes his anticipated problems of finding shadow prices for environmental functions.[3]

First, they emphasize that government targets for sustainability, which might be used in calculating sustainable GNP, cannot be considered to reflect individuals' preferences. If this were the case, there would be no reason to bother about valuing the environment, because the government targets would be the correct targets by definition. Second, it would be incorrect to use the cost of achieving the sustainability target for establishing the 'green' GNP estimate. They claim that in this manner costs are becoming identical to benefits, implying that the benefit–cost ratio for achieving the sustainability targets is always unity. Finally, even for an environmental problem like acidification, where sustainability targets are available in terms of well-defined critical loads, the cost of reaching these targets would be far in excess of the marginal benefits. Therefore Pearce et al. consider the 'distance to targets' approach, according to them implicit in the Hueting analysis, suspect.

As a theoretically correct alternative they propose to estimate a green *net* national product, by correcting GNP for capital depreciation, resource extraction (in excess of its natural growth and valued at the unit resource rental), and pollution (in excess of natural assimilation and valued at the marginal social damages from pollution). Results of this method, including investment in human capital, are reported for a number of African countries in World Bank (1999). They show tremendous differences in ratios for gross savings and *genuine* savings.

In short, Pearce et al. acknowledge the logic of Hueting's approach, but emphasize their strong preference for shadow pricing, inclusive of non-market valuation. They recognize that many problems are still present in shadow pricing and that the results so far are not satisfying and should be improved. But this would only be a matter of time and resources. In other words, Pearce et al. remain optimistic about the applicability of cost–benefit analysis and valuation methods for finding useful (macroeconomic) indicators for sustainability.

In their chapter, Faucheux and O'Connor develop a 'structural perspective' on sustainable development in order to compare current views. Their perspective should allow for classification of what they think are two typical families of 'environmentally adjusted gross national product'. The chapter discusses the typical methods, model frameworks and empirical estimation procedures that correspond to each family. They introduce the concept of the 'monetization frontier' to demarcate two zones of natural wealth as revealed by the respective methods. One side is the valuation of resources and assets from the point of view of their potential conversion into commercially priced goods and services (trees into wood products, for example). The other side values these assets from the point of view of their roles as in situ services as sites, scenery, scientific interest and ecological life support in complement to human economic activity.

This generates two types of indicators – 'weak' and 'strong' – and they relate to these different roles of natural capital, and, as such, respond to distinct policy questions. According to the 'weak' approach, indicators are obtained through making subtractions from the conventional GNP, seeking to jump from GNP as a measure of one period's output level to an 'environmentally-adjusted' estimate of 'national net savings' and, from there, to an estimate of the *net* national product as an indicator of prospects for sustainable future welfare levels relative to the current level of consumption. The 'strong' approach, by contrast, creates signposts about prospects for reaching simultaneous economic and ecological sustainability goals. They exploit statistical estimation and modelling procedures for quantifying the long-term economic performance potential while respecting environmental pressure threshold criteria whose purpose is to ensure environmental quality, ecosystem integrity and resource renewability requirements.

Faucheux and O'Connor claim that, applied to their respective domains, the two approaches are complementary. The problem with the 'weak' recipes, which have a strong reliance on restrictive theoretical conditions, is that they do not yield indicators that are robust for evaluation of long-term sustainability prospects. The 'strong' approaches based on scenario frameworks of investigation, however, are inevitably speculative but nonetheless more robust for long-term policy guidance. The reason for this interesting conclusion is that Faucheux and O'Connor claim that they are anchored differently in science and policy quality considerations: (1) avoiding 'misplaced concreteness'; (2) integrating the hypothesis of the non-substitutable functional importance of natural systems as life support; and (3) providing also for the ethical preoccupation for human coexistence in a world of diversity and natural richness.

The final contribution to this part of the book, by Verbruggen, Dellink, Gerlagh, Hofkes and Jansen, can thus be seen as an example of the second type of recipe. Verbruggen et al. present the results of their study on alternative calculations of an SNI for the Netherlands according to the approach advocated by Hueting. The study has been commissioned by the Ministry of Economic Affairs and the Ministry of Housing, Spatial Planning and the Environment of the Netherlands.

First, they describe the methodology for establishing this SNI and some of its complications. The study uses a comparative static general equilibrium model that includes very detailed cost estimates for reducing a large number of emissions. If end-of-pipe technologies are insufficient, changes in economic structure and a reduction of economic activities in specific sectors are required. Detailed results are presented, both at an aggregated level and at the sectoral level. Although much scepticism exists about the possibilities of calculating SNI, their study provides detailed insight into: (1) the complications that have to be faced when calculating such an SNI; (2) the type of results obtained; and (3) the sensitivity for changes in sustainability standards, and for assumptions on international trade.

The study shows that for a rather long trajectory, the costs of reaching such sustainability standards are relatively modest. However, if the sustainability standards are viewed as revealing current preferences for the environment (implying pollution reduction levels in a range between 60–100 per cent), the change in income is tremendous: the SNI might be as much as 62 per cent lower than current national income (depending on the variant of the approach used). It really can be considered to be a milestone that these results are now available, and that Hueting's method is now tested in practice, well documented and available for further scientific debate and analysis.

PART IV CONCLUSION

The book closes with two concluding chapters. First, Goodland shows his great respect for Hueting's work with a detailed description of his contributions to economic science and policies, which aim at sustainability. Finally, Hueting reflects on the contributions presented in the book in order to clarify his views and to avoid possible misinterpretations.

This book shows that the debate on green national accounting is far from resolved and can be expected to be continued. The basic difference of opinion between Fabricant and Denison shortly after World War II is still apparent. This certainly applies to current accounting practices in the different countries. Although gradually more physical indicators describing both stocks and flows of environmental quality and its changes have become available, the question whether this should also lead to adaptations in the national accounting practice to compute a green national income or national product is still unresolved. Indeed, one can still observe a wide diversity of opinion towards this particular topic across the contributions of this book. The implicit controversy in the chapters of Hueting and Beckerman are illustrative in this respect.

Hueting suggests to compute a green national income based on shadow prices derived from sustainability indicators. Beckerman, however, still does not see any need to adapt current practice. Their controversy focuses on the question whether national income has any meaning in terms of measuring *welfare* or not. Welfare, according to Beckerman, can be anything that an existing population considers important, and he claims that no convincing reasons exist why the (intertemporal) value of environmental resources should be relevant in this context. Therefore such a claim implies a *normative* statement in his opinion. In contrast, Hueting starts the other way round. He claims that it is unlikely that generating income is possible without environmental deterioration. Therefore, according to his own view, he starts from the *positive* statement that trade-offs in welfare maximization are unavoidable, and any indicator of welfare should account for these facts.

So this controversy illustrates the important philosophical issue that facts and values are not always as clearly separable as had been thought once.[4] The chapter of Norgaard et al. illustrates this point as well, though in a somewhat different way. We agree with their basic claim that there exists a world of difference between collecting relevant information and acting upon this information when it comes to public policy making. Often, claims in favour of correcting national income or national product are closely related to the idea that politicians or policy-makers base their decision on strict economic arguments, in particular on the assumption that a higher level of income would also imply a rise in welfare. However, it is not entirely clear why a proper measurement of welfare including environmental degradation, if available, would also lead to a better quality of decision making by politicians. These are very different issues, and it seems useful to distinguish them carefully from each other.

Indeed, it is hard to deny that in general a relationship exists between higher levels of income and the provision of public goods, like education and health services. With respect to environmental quality the story is much less clear. One might agree with Hueting that income growth usually implies a deterioration of environmental quality, in particular if one starts from a pristine environmental capital stock. However, the relationship between development and environmental deterioration is not always as clear-cut as it seems. The dimensions of the environmental capital stock are so many and complicated that it is hard to find a proper way to measure and aggregate all the changes in the quality of this stock. The still growing recent research on environmental Kuznets curves, although concentrating usually on emissions only, confirms a mirror of scattered and sometimes even contradictory information (De Bruyn, 1999; Ekins, 2000). Although it still seems safe to start from Hueting's basic claim that a trade-off between income growth and environmental quality exists, this is not necessarily true for ever.

What is even more disturbing is that the trade-off from the past could very well reflect existing preferences. As early as 1960 even Mishan argued that 'as we become richer, surely we shall remedy all social evil'. This was indeed a firm belief behind the build-up of the post-war welfare state in most Western countries. In turn, however, this build-up has been facilitated by high growth rates. Higher tax revenues – necessary to finance growing welfare expenditures – are more easily enforced if people's after-tax incomes are growing. Therefore most political parties considered a high growth rate as a lubricant for this problem, and environmental sacrifices were considered as unimportant.

Of course, preferences cannot be considered as a static phenomenon as the gradual approval of the importance of environmental commodities reveals. Indeed, more authors now seem to be of the opinion that adaptations of the traditional measurement of national income is important and useful than, say, before the famous Brundtland Report in 1987. However, if it is true that policy only reflects current preferences, while each generation's preferences depend on existing (environmental) capital stocks (so-called endogenous preferences), this raises serious doubts on any analysis based upon intertemporal welfare comparisons. Of course, one can still *assume* that a government is serious if it reveals its long-run environmental policy goals, like the Dutch government in its famous National Environmental Policy Plan from 1989, and use them to calculate an adapted green national income. The same holds for calculations based on even stronger standards derived from (current) natural and ecological information on thresholds and irreversibility of environmental functions.

However, it is hard to see why politicians should also act upon such calculations. Indeed, politicians foster existing preferences and interest at the time they decide, and it is hard for them not to be swayed by the issues of the day. The Netherlands is a good example. When environmental policies came on the political agenda at the end of the 1960s, due to changes in public opinion and the rise of environmental pressure groups, there was a strong tendency to found these policies on cost–benefit analysis. In the second wave at the end of the 1980s attention shifted towards 'sustainability indicators', like those explicitly mentioned in the Dutch National Environmental Policy Plan in 1989. Often, these indicators were derived from existing scientific evidence on environmental or health risks. Nowadays, when it has become gradually clear that some of the goals originally set for 2010 can be reached only at extremely high costs, politicians start to think again in terms of sacrificing environmental goals in favour of other interests again. One wonders whether calculations of a green national income would change anything to that.

We hope that this book on economic growth and valuation of the environment and Hueting's important contributions to these particular topics foster further scientific insights in the academic issues involved. Moreover, we hope that it contributes at the same time to deciding which indicators of welfare, or which types of satellite accounts are most suitable for fulfilling the needs of policy-makers. In any case the book reveals that this topic will continue to be on the agenda of both the scientific and the policy community.

NOTES

1. These issues were discussed in honour of Dr Roefie Hueting at the international symposium 'Valuation of Nature and the Environment' at the Royal Netherlands Academy of Arts and Sciences in Amsterdam, The Netherlands, April 1999. The support of the Ministries of Foreign Affairs, Economic Affairs, Housing Spatial Planning and the Environment, various provinces, the Central Bureau of Statistics and various NGOs for organizing the symposium is kindly acknowledged.
2. Reprinted from Ecological Economics, Vol. 18, R. Hueting *Three persistent myths in the environmental debate*, 1996, pp. 81–8, with permission of Elsevier Science.
3. Although Pearce et al. disagree at many points with the views of Hueting, both criticize the Costanza et al. (1997) study on valuing global ecosystems functions. The use of marginal values to estimate the total value of these functions is clearly not in line with Hueting's concept of functions of ecosystems and their economic value.
4. Interestingly, both authors refer to the famous essay by Robbins (1938). See, however, Dasgupta (1993, pp. 5–9) for a discussion of the philosophical issues involved in the similar, though somewhat more general context of what he calls *destitution*. This is an extreme form of ill-being of a person and for which deteriorated environmental capital can certainly be held responsible in some circumstances.

REFERENCES

Costanza, R., R. D'Arge, R. de Groot, S. Farber, M. Grasso, B. Hannon, K. Limburg, S. Naeem, R. O'Neill, J. Paruelo, R. Raskin, P. Sutton and M. van den Belt (1997), 'The value of the world's ecosystem services and natural capital', *Nature*, 387, 15 May, 253–60.

Dasgupta, P. (1993), *An Inquiry into Well-being and Destitution*, Oxford: Clarendon Press.
De Bruyn, S. (1999), *Economic Growth and the Environment, an Empirical Analysis*, Amsterdam: Tinbergen Institute, Vrije Universiteit.
Denison, E.F. (1947), *Studies in Income and Wealth*, vol. 10, Conference on Research in Income and Wealth, New York.
Dernburg, T.F. and D.M. McDougall (1963), *Macro- economics: The Measurement, Analysis, and Control of Aggregate Economic Activity*, 2nd edn, New York: McGraw-Hill Book Company.
Ekins, P. (2000), *Economic Growth and Environmental Sustainability: The Prospects for Green Growth*, London, UK and New York, USA: Routledge.
El Serafy, S. (1992), 'Sustainability, income measurement and growth', in Robert Goodland, Herman Daly and Salah El Serafy (eds), *Population, Technology and Lifestyle: the Transition to Sustainability*, Washington, DC: Island Press, chapter 5.
Fabricant, S. (1947), *Studies in Income and Wealth*, vol. 10, Conference on Research in Income and Wealth, New York.
Hueting, R. (1991), 'Correcting national income for environmental losses: a practical solution for a theoretical dilemma', in R. Costanza (ed.), *Ecological Economics, the Science and Management of Sustainability*, New York: Columbia University Press, pp. 94–213.
Hueting, R. and L. Reijnders (1998), 'Sustainability is an objective concept, commentary', *Ecological Economics*, 27, 139–47.
King, W.J. (1919), *The Wealth and Income of the People of the United States.*
Mäler, K-G. (1991), 'National accounts and environmental resources', *Environmental and Resource Economics*, 1, 1–15.
Mishan, E.J. (1967), *The Cost of Economic Growth*, London: Penguin Harmondsworth.
Pigou, A.C. (1920), *The Economics of Welfare*, London: McMillan and Co.
Rawls, J. (1971), *A Theory of Justice*, Oxford: Oxford University Press.
Robbins, L. (1938), 'Interpersonal comparison of utility', *Economic Journal*, December.
United Nations (1993), *Integrated Environmental and Economic Accounting* (interim version), Handbook of National Accounting (Studies in Methods, Series F, no. 61), New York.
World Bank (1999), *World Development Indicators 1999*, Washington, DC: World Bank.

PART ONE

Setting the Stage

2. Environmental valuation and sustainable national income according to Hueting

Roefie Hueting and Bart de Boer*

1 INTRODUCTORY OVERVIEW

The notion of what some now refer to as the sustainable national income according to Hueting (SNI, see Verbruggen et al., Chapter 11, this volume) has a relatively long history that goes back to the mid-1960s. Most of the work has appeared in print. In this chapter we therefore restrict ourselves to our main lines of argument, referring the reader back to earlier publications where appropriate. Such a procedure is necessary, experience has taught, for our treatment of SNI involves concepts and insights from diverse fields of research, and for a proper overall understanding there must be careful elaboration of each. What is *terra incognita* for one reader may be self-evident to another, however, and we have therefore structured this chapter in a way that allows us to concentrate on the key steps of our approach while retaining the quality of our argument, at the same time allowing the reader to decide which sections are relevant to him or her and which can be skipped over. To assist the reader, in this introduction we will therefore briefly summarize the basic principles and their consequences before substantiating them in subsequent sections. The most important principles are the formal concept of welfare and the concept of competing functions.

On the road to the SNI, a series of theoretical problems had to be solved, notably with regard to environmental valuation. The solutions found follow from the principles adopted, and are thus consequences thereof. Arranging the principles and their consequences in fact provides an overview of the chapter. This procedure has allowed us to restrict the scope of Section 8 (Conclusions) of this chapter to the status of the SNI according

* The authors like to thank Jeroen van den Bergh, Thomas Cool and Lucas Reijnders for their useful comments and suggestions, and Nigel Harle for translation.

to Hueting within so-called general growth theory and the reasons for the pronounced differences between this SNI and estimates of other green national incomes, based on other principles and assumptions.

One further introductory note is in order. In Hueting (1974a) and later publications it is consistently argued that one problem is unresolvable: establishing shadow prices for environmental functions and, consequently, correct prices for goods produced and consumed at the expense of those functions. The strategy adopted to get round this problem in fact constitutes a crucial element in estimating an SNI as well as other green national incomes.

1.1 Principles

1. In our approach to SNI we are engaged in statistics, a science of the past, not in forecasting the future. Concerns about future generations, which are justifiable, are recognized as being an important element of the preferences of the current generation (see Section 2). In observing and measuring the past, it is relevant to take these preferences into account; doing so is obviously backcasting, not forecasting.
2. We remain within the traditional methods of the System of National Accounts (SNA), but provide another national income figure, the SNI, for use alongside the standard figure. Our figure is based on assumptions regarding preferences that differ from the assumptions implicitly made when standard national income (NI) figures are used as one of the indicators for welfare, namely that the current package of goods and the state of the environment perfectly reflect the preferences of the economic subjects, implying that the current path of the economy is optimal. The latter is questionable (see Principle 3, iv). Changes in the volume of NI are nonetheless still taken universally as the key indicator for economic success. The main purpose of the SNI research is to improve the statistical information about our economic success (increase in welfare).
3. Estimation of SNI rests on four pillars.
   i. The formal or indifferent concept of welfare, as introduced probably by Rosenstein-Rodan (1927) and elaborated further by Robbins ([1932] 1952) and particularly by Hennipman (1940, 1962, 1995), from which it follows immediately that if there exist strong preferences for the environment, conservation measures will lead to a decline in the NI and an increase in welfare (Hueting, 1974a; see Section 3). Thus, when strong preferences for sustainable use of the environment are assumed, as is the case when constructing the SNI, satisfying these preferences has a positive effect on welfare, borne

of the knowledge that future generations will have freer disposal over the functions of their physical surroundings, which outweighs the negative effect on welfare due to the resultant decline in instantaneous consumption. As Hueting (1996) emphasizes, this assumption can be neither proved nor refuted on empirical grounds.

ii. The concept of possible uses of our physical surroundings, referred to as environmental functions, or simply functions. Competing functions are economic goods (Hueting, 1969, 1970a, 1970b, 1974a; see Section 4).

iii. The position that sustainability is an objective, scientific concept that must be clearly distinguished from whether or not there exist preferences for such. This implies that it is indeed possible to establish sustainability standards, even though these may sometimes be bracketed within high margins of uncertainty. Standards for sustainability must thus be sharply distinguished from subjective preferences for attaining such standards, or for not doing so.

iv. The position that there exist certain 'blockages' (or 'barriers') as a result of which preferences for environmental conservation are *incapable* of being fully expressed through the market and budget mechanisms; see Section 5.2. This justifies making assumptions about preferences that differ from those underlying NI figures, when used as an indicator of economic success (see Principle 2 and Section 5.2).

4. For the valuation of environmental functions or losses of function (which amounts to the same thing) data are required on both preferences (demand) and costs (supply). Data on the costs of restoring and maintaining vital functions can, in principle, always be obtained. Preferences for such measures can be only very partially estimated, however, because of the existence of blockages (see Principle 3, iv). This is particularly true of preferences for maintaining vital environmental functions for the future, that is for sustainability. Making assumptions about preferences for the present and future availability of functions is therefore inescapable (see Section 5.2).

1.2 Consequences of the Principles

1. *The SNI according to Hueting is the maximum net income which can be sustained on a geological time scale, with future technological progress assumed only in the development of substitutes for non-renewable resources, where such substitution is indispensable for sustaining environmental functions, in turn essential for sustaining income.* The modelling exercise to estimate the SNI can only be consistent if the vast

majority of the subjects in the model are assumed to have an absolute preference for sustainability. This SNI concept is theoretically sound as well as operational, although it involves considerable statistical effort. Its theory is in line with so-called general growth theory (see Sections 5.3, 5.4 and 6).

2. When applying the concept of 'environmental function', the distinction between weak and strong sustainability cannot be made: non-renewable resources must gradually be substituted by other elements of our physical surroundings, whereas substitution of a large class of renewable resources is impossible, particularly life support systems, including ecosystems. Economically speaking, we find no essential difference between renewables and non-renewables: the only thing that matters is that their functions must remain available (see Section 7).
3. The environment is defined as the non human-made elements of our physical surroundings, on which elements we are entirely dependent and which can be described as a collection of possible uses or functions. In accordance with standard theory, producing is defined as adding value by labour. Goods can be produced solely by using and changing the environment. This process has an exclusively positive effect on welfare, and consequently adds exclusively positive value to our surroundings, as long as functions are not rendered scarce in the same process. When functions start to compete, however, they become scarce and their price rises from zero to an ever-greater positive value, which constitutes an impoverishment, and consequently an increase in costs. On this view it follows that in moving from NI to SNI or some other green national income *only* negative corrections can be made, and no additions (see Section 5, up to 5.1).
4. Maintaining a record of the SNI leads to greater awareness of the effect of asymmetric bookkeeping of environmental functions on the NI (see Section 5, up to 5.1).
5. We seek the maximum net national income at which the environmental functions are sustained. This implies that the functions must be sustained above or at the approximated minimum levels that nature can support and that the sacrifices required to attain the associated sustainable development path are minimum. (An SNI calculated with future function levels chosen as high as possible will probably be zero; see Section 6.6.) The goal, consistently, is to ensure that possible (potential) future uses of the environment (that is functions) are not lost. Future generations then retain their freedom of action *vis-à-vis* these functions, although we explicitly assume that they exercise this freedom while remaining on a specific, namely sustainable production and consumption path.

6. Because the bulk of national income is generated by those production (and consumption) activities that are most burdensome to the environment, a shift from environmentally burdensome to less burdensome activities will have a negative effect on the volume of NI (Hueting, 1981; Hueting et al., 1992). Calculation of this effect is a three-step process: (1) capital goods are reallocated as part of the optimization embodied in effectuating the necessary shifts among production activities; (2) the production possibilities frontier is assumed to be curved 'around' the origin; (3) prices are used that arise after internalization of the costs of the required elimination measures (including the levies to induce direct shifts) when making the step from standard to sustainable national income; see Section 6.4. Shifts from meat to beans, say, or from car to bicycle or plane to train are the most essential solutions from the environmental angle and also the most plausible (see 'Three myths', Chapter 3, this volume). However, the sectoral subdivisions available at Statistics Netherlands (CBS) are not yet sufficiently detailed to simulate this effect in the model, so that the effect is not yet visible in the result (see Verbruggen et al., Chapter 11, this volume). We hope to improve the approximation at a later stage. For the time being, less essential and less plausible shifts have been incorporated.
7. The SNI according to Hueting is defined such that adjustment of the NI in the successive years of investigation is based on the technology of the year in question, including technology that is operational but not yet on the market. This precludes the risks of extrapolated technological progress subsequently proving unattainable (precautionary principle). An inevitable exception is substitution of non-renewables (see Section 7 and note 6). This position implies that SNI may be expected to increase over time.
8. The difference between NI and SNI is a monetary measure for the *distance* between the current and the sustainable development path.
9. Sustainability standards for environmental pressure are – in theory – the levels of environmental pressure on the sustainable development path that is associated with the SNI and that includes both the economy and the environment. These standards reflect the regeneration capacity of the environment with respect to the various forms of environmental pressure and, with the exception of those relating to the consumption of non-renewables, are constant.
10. In practice it is and will probably remain unfeasible to compute the sustainability standards, the costs associated with attaining these standards and the SNI in a theoretically consistent manner, that is with a single, comprehensive, dynamic environmental-economic

model. Instead, the standards are calculated with the aid of environmental models and the SNI according to Hueting with a general economic equilibrium model. This requires introduction of additional rules as well as several *ad hoc* choices. The principal rule is the assumption that sustainability is guaranteed if human activity and the resultant environmental pressure do not accelerate the extinction of biological species at the global level. Because of these rules, the practical sustainability standards for environmental pressure and the practical SNI are probably lower than their theoretical counterparts were they to be computable.

11. As a very rough estimate of sustainable world income Tinbergen and Hueting (1991) arrive at a figure of 50 per cent of current world income. The provisional results of the study on an SNI for the Netherlands are of similar magnitude (Verbruggen et al., 2001). This means that roughly half our present production and consumption depends on unsustainable use of the environment.
12. We are concerned here with a comparative, static exercise in which time plays no role. A transition to a lower, sustainable level of economic activity free of shock to the social fabric will require considerable time. The transition route to a sustainable level must itself also be sustainable, that is involve no irreparable damage to vital environmental functions (see Section 6). The quest for such a route would be the obvious sequel to the present SNI study. Assuming a preference for sustainability, welfare will increase by pursuing this route as rapidly as possible.

2 SOME ARGUMENTS FOR AN SNI

Economic growth, defined as increase of production as measured in the standard national income, enjoys top priority in the economic policies pursued by every country of the world. The economic success of government policy and even success *tout court* is measured primarily against the yardstick of production growth. In doing so, we are steering by the wrong compass, however, for production growth – that is to say, a decrease in the scarcity of man-made goods – is accompanied by an increase in the scarcity of environmental goods. This is not a new phenomenon. Hueting (1974a) provides a brief historical survey, which includes Plato (about 400 BC) on erosion, Juvenal (about AD 100) on noise nuisance in Rome and Erasmus (around 1500) on the unhygienic conditions prevailing in European cities, with their open sewers and waste-strewn streets. In earlier ages it was a local phenomenon, though, which proceeded slowly. The world still had only a small population, moreover, and space was abundant: if need be people could simply move on. According to Tinbergen, even in the 1930s the environment did not play any substantial role in the economy, and it was consequently ignored when the System of National Accounts was established (Hueting, 1974a; Tinbergen and Hueting, 1991). Since about the middle of the twentieth century environmental degradation has become a global phenomenon, with pressure on the natural environment increasing rapidly, together with production and population, the doubling rates of which have declined markedly, showing up as a veritable explosion on long-term time charts.

The twentieth century can be characterized by a phenomenon entirely new in the history of humankind. Humanity is capable of destroying its civilizations and perhaps even the human species as such. This may be through nuclear war and the ensuing nuclear winter, but it may also be by way of an insidious process that eats away at the very foundations of our existence: the vital functions of our physical surroundings. Over the past few decades, the latter possibility has been the subject of a wealth of literature that has signalled the very real risks being posed to future generations by our actions here and now. One of the first reports to review the issue was the Study of Critical Environmental Problems (SCEP) *Man's Impact on the Global Environment* carried out by the Massachusetts Institute of Technology (Wilson et al., 1970). As the main threats to life on earth the study identifies climate change and large-scale disturbance of natural ecosystems. According to Odum (1971) the impact of the extinction of biological species, particularly predators, on life on earth can only be established with certainty after the 'point of no return', that is after recovery of equilibrium is no longer possible. This whole process is occurring at breathtaking speed, when viewed on an evolutionary time scale. There is a high risk of irreversible effects occurring, and the further the process continues the more difficult and of longer duration recovery will be. According to *The Limits to Growth* (Meadows, 1972), if population and production continue to grow, catastrophes are probably inevitable. Hueting (1974a) provides a synopsis of these publications.

The principal justification for an SNI lies in the following: there are solid, rational grounds for being concerned about the conditions under which our children's children will have to live if we maintain current levels of production and consumption, because of the cumulative nature of many of the processes involved. In particular, a wide variety of poorly degradable toxins and greenhouse gases are accumulating in the environment and human encroachment on undeveloped land – the main cause of species extinction – continues apace. In the now decades-long debate on growth and the environment, there are two diametrically opposed opinions. Given continued gross economic growth, that is per capita production and consumption multiplied by population, some hold that the situation will improve, others that it will deteriorate. We ourselves hold the latter position (Tinbergen and Hueting, 1991; Hueting, 1996). Ultimately, though, the response of ecosystems, life support systems and other natural processes to human activity is unpredictable, and will always remain so, as will the potential – or otherwise – of future technologies to alleviate the environmental impact of an ever-growing volume of produced, material goods. We see the future as a race between environmental technology and production growth, the outcome of which cannot be predicted (Hueting, 1997).

In such discussions concerning what is possible and what is not possible in the future, the SNI appears to provide a welcome *statistical resting point*. The SNI is defined as the maximum attainable level of production and consumption, using the technology of the year under review, whereby the vital functions, that is possible uses, of the physical surroundings remain available forever. In this approach, sustainability is formulated as the maintenance of vital environmental functions *ad infinitum* (Hueting and Reijnders, 1996a, 1996b, 1998). The difference between the standard and the sustainable national income reflects the *distance*, expressed as costs, which must be bridged in order to attain sustainability; this is our debt to future generations. Any politics concerned with safeguarding the foundations of human existence should surely give first priority to bridging this gap, and then wait and see whether, and how much, production growth then results.

As elaborated in Section 4, from the perspective of preferences there exist as many shadow prices for environmental functions as there are possible assumptions about demand for uses of the environment, that is for environmental functions; *ergo*, there are also as many 'green' national incomes, but only one of them is the SNI.[1] Given the future perils stemming from our activities now, sustainability is viewed by many as the crux of the environmental problem (IUCN et al., 1980; World Commission on Environment and Development, 1987; IUCN et al., 1991). The SNI points the way for application of the so widely recommended precautionary principle. This principle asserts that, given the inherent unpredictability of the future and the real risk of human activity having unprecedented effects, that activity should be governed by avoidance of such effects. When informing people on the issue of environment and growth, economists, in particular, have a responsibility that is of a different order than that involved in informing them on any other issue, because the possible consequences of misjudgement are of an entirely different order.

Among other possible green national incomes the SNI consequently enjoys a special status. To this may be added that in some regions in the south the future already appears to have begun: many thousands have already lost their lives or livelihoods as a result of floods, droughts and poisoned water resources, the result of neglecting the importance of nature's functions for humanity. This is obviously not to say that calculation of one or more green national incomes alongside the SNI would not contribute substantially to the information flow.

In the SNI study the estimate for the Netherlands is seen as an indicator for what is occurring at the global level. The picture is growing clearer as an SNI is calculated for more nations. In the Dutch case, the extent of the measures required to achieve sustainability is determined by and proportional to the contribution of the Netherlands to global environmental pressure (or to regional pressure in the case of regional problems). With an import and export quote of around 50 per cent, the Netherlands is solidly interlinked with the rest of the world and the environmental degradation occurring there. Importation of tapioca livestock feed and tropical hardwood, to take but two examples, has serious environmental consequences in the respective countries of origin. The Netherlands is one of the most densely populated countries in the world and is among the nations with the highest per capita production. In the study *The Ecological Footprint* (Wackernagel and Rees, 1996) the Netherlands scores high: the 'ecological footprint' of the Netherlands is almost 15 times higher than its land mass warrants. Conversely, the Dutch are exporting their – or rather the world's – environmental resources for a price below sustainability costs, as the exporters of tapioca and hardwood are doing with their environment. As a worked example, the Netherlands does not seem such a bad choice.

Right from the start, it has been argued that an income corrected for the environment should be estimated alongside rather than instead of the standard national income (Hueting, 1967, 1974a, 1974b). The latter course would, in the first place, disrupt a key macroeconomic time series that is employed for a wide variety of other purposes besides estimating production growth. Second, a green national income derives its informative value precisely from establishing the *distance* from the standard national income, measured in terms of costs. As is familiar, a national income, standard or green, is itself a meaningless figure: only when a comparison is made over time, or with other incomes, does meaningful information arise (see, for example, Hueting et al. 1992).

3 THE FORMAL OR INDIFFERENT CONCEPT OF WELFARE

The view now accepted by the mainstream of economic thought is that the phenomena arising from scarcity together form a logical entity, irrespective of the end for which the scarce means are employed. This is referred to as the formal or indifferent concept of welfare, a term probably introduced by Rosenstein-Rodan (1927). What he wrote can be summarized as follows. The subjective state of welfare or the total economic utility that people endeavour to achieve in their economic activities is a quantity determined purely formally. It encompasses all that has been striven after, to the extent that scarce goods have had to be used for achievement thereof, irrespective of (indifferent to) whether such pursuit springs from egoistic or altruistic, from ethical or unethical motives, from 'real' or 'imaginary' wants.

It was Robbins ([1932] 1952) and Hennipman (1940, 1943, 1962, 1995), among others, who elaborated the formal concept of welfare and formulated its consequences for economic theory. For these authors, the subject matter of economics is demarcated by the criterion of scarcity. According to Hennipman it is therefore logical and consistent to interpret welfare, the end and result of economic activity, as the overall satisfaction of wants pursued or obtained by means of economic goods or, more precisely, as the balance of the positive utility over the negative utility caused by external effects or productive efforts. In Hennipman's view economic activity can serve all kinds of ends. The ends themselves are meta-economic and are not for economists to judge. They cannot be derived from economic theory, nor are they amenable to it, but must be taken as given, as data. In the same vein, Robbins writes: 'There are no economic ends as such; there are only economic problems involved in the achievement of ends'.

Maximizing or even just increasing the social product (NI) should therefore, in Hennipman's view, no longer be considered a necessary end that can lay claim to logical priority. All those objectives aspired to by economic subjects that conflict with that end belong logically and in their entirety to the domain of economic policy. If preference is given to those objectives, he writes, this does not mean a sacrifice of welfare on the strength of 'non-economic' considerations, as it is still frequently represented, since economic goods are then being utilized in accordance with the wants of the subjects and thus to the benefit of their welfare.

Proceeding from the work of these authors, Hueting (1974a) posits the following. All economic activity is aimed at the satisfaction of wants, and consequently the term economic growth can mean nothing other than increase in welfare, defined as the satisfaction of wants derived from our dealings with scarce goods. Welfare is not a quantity that can be measured directly 'from outside'; it is a category of individual experience. It is for this reason that the statistician focuses in practice on charting trends in factors that *can* be measured and that can plausibly be argued to have an influence on welfare. These factors will not generally be strictly proportional to welfare but must at any rate satisfy the condition that they tend consistently in the same direction as the welfare they are indicating, positive or negative. The following welfare-influencing factors can be distinguished: (1) the package of goods and services produced; (2) scarce environmental functions; (3) time, that is leisure time; (4) the distribution of scarce goods, that is income distribution; (5) the conditions under which scarce goods are acquired,that is labour conditions; (6) employment, or involuntary unemployment; and (7) future security, to the extent that this depends on our dealings with scarce goods, and specifically the vital functions of the environment.

These factors are often in conflict with one another, although this is not always the case. For scarce goods it holds by definition, however, that more of one is less of another, for a good is scarce when something else has to be sacrificed in order to obtain it (sacrificed alternative, opportunity cost). The days when environmental functions were free goods are gone. All other things remaining equal (including technological state of the art), more production therefore means less environment and vice versa. When, in the margin, for whatever motive, preference is given to the environment over production and a government proceeds to impose controls on production processes and consumption habits that lead to a smaller volume of goods and services produced, there will be an increase in the overall satisfaction of wants obtained by means of scarce goods. *A decrease in production will then lead to greater welfare.* It is therefore misleading to identify growth of national income with an increase in welfare, economic growth and economic success, as is still common practice even today. This terminology is fundamentally erroneous in its implications, to the detriment of the environment, and it should therefore be outlawed, in much the same way as discriminatory language against women.

4 THE CONCEPT OF ENVIRONMENTAL FUNCTION

The notion of possible human use of the environment or 'environmental function' was introduced by Hueting (1969, 1970a, 1970b). In all, 16 basic functions of nature for humanity are distinguished; these include oxygen production, waste removal, gene pool for improving and creating crops and livestock, supplier of medicines (vaccines, antitoxins), supplier of natural products (timber, fish, skins, ivory and so on), hydrological regulation, erosion prevention and maintenance of biological equilibrium. The economic value of these functions is determined in an approach comprising, *inter alia*, the following elements: (1) estimate of expenditures on replacing the function (replacement costs) when the latter falls short of existing wants due to overload (up to this point it was a free good with zero value); (2) estimate of expenditures on measures to compensate for loss of the function (compensation costs); (3) estimate of expenditures incurred in going ever further to enjoy nature, such as travel expenses. This approach underwent substantial modification between 1970 and 1974, as discussed in the next paragraph. We mention the approach adopted in 1969, since this came to lead a life of its own and is still being used today.

In Hueting (1974a, 1974b) a fundamentally different approach is taken, the principles of which have not changed since. Compared with the 1969 approach the differences are as follows.

First, use is now made of a supply and a demand curve, because in any process of valuation preferences (demand) and costs (supply) are inseparably linked (see Section 5). The supply curve is made up of the (rising) costs of the at-source measures required to eliminate the environmental burden, leading to restoration of functions. These are termed the 'elimination costs'. One of the reasons for this choice is that the functions (or services) provided by ecosystems, say, cannot in fact be replaced, or only temporarily so. Restoration of functions by means of elimination is always possible, however, as long as the functions have not been irreversibly damaged of course (as in the case of species extinction, for example). The demand curve is made up of the expenditures actually made as a result of loss of function(s). These can be seen as revealed preferences for the various environmental functions. In conventional demand analysis, the researcher hypothesizes a utility function and derives the demand function from maximizing utility subject to income. Unknown parameters then are estimated using econometric techniques. Here, however, revealed preferences are used directly. Perhaps a term 'revealed demand curve' would be more suitable. But for the sake of brevity we will continue to use the shorter term. Anyway, the revealed preferences include the following: expenditures on measures to compensate for loss of function, including, *inter alia*, the replacement costs of the 1969 approach; expenditures on restoring damage due to loss of function (floods due to forests losing their 'hydrological regulation' function, for example); and expenses incurred in travelling ever further to enjoy nature. To a limited extent, but specifically not for the most essential functions, willingness-to-pay and similar estimates are also taken on board as revealed preferences, thereby avoiding double-counting (Hueting, 1974a, 1989, 1992b, 1995).

Second, in discussions among the multidisciplinary team that one of us had meanwhile formed at Statistics Netherlands for setting up environmental statistics and for adjustment of the standard national income for environmental losses, it proved impossible to satisfactorily demarcate the concept of 'nature' for statistical purposes. This resulted in a definition of 'environment' as the non-human-made physical surroundings, or elements thereof, on which humanity is entirely dependent in all its doings, whether they be producing, consuming, breathing or recreating. These physical surroundings encompass water, soil, air, natural resources, including energy resources, and plant and animal species. It is true that our observable surroundings are largely human-built. However, houses, roads and farm crops are the result of two complementary factors: labour and elements of the physical surroundings as here intended. Our crops, for example, have been bred or manipulated from genetic material taken from natural ecosystems; this material was not created by human beings and sooner or later we shall most probably have to fall back on it. We therefore continue to be dependent on the functions of the physical surroundings as here intended, including the functions of 'gene pool' (or: 'gene reserve'), 'habitat for biological species', 'water as raw material for drinking water', 'air for the physiological functioning of human beings, animals and plants', 'soil for cultivating crops' and the many functions of non-renewable natural resources.

Producing is defined, in accordance with standard economic theory, as the adding of value. This value is added to the physical elements of our environment. In this process one good is transformed into another in order to satisfy wants. The values are added by labour, that is hands and brains, with the brains guiding the hands, so that we are concerned ultimately with two factors: labour (technology) and environment. Thus, both consumption goods and capital goods embody a combination of the physical elements of the environment, on the one hand, and labour, accumulated or otherwise, on the other. In this view, labour and environment are the two factors with which humanity has to make do in securing a desired level of consumption. If environmental functions are lost we are left literally empty-handed. Environment and labour are thus complementary. Annual production as measured in the standard national income is therefore accompanied by a *physical flow of goods*. Put differently, regardless of whether the products are actually physical, in production and consumption there will always be an interaction with the physical environment and consequently always a physical burden on that environment. This environmental pressure is, obviously, a form of environmental use.

All this may seem obvious, but apparently it is not so to everyone. In the first place, production is still frequently taken to mean material welfare, a confusing *contradictio in terminis*, and the environment, immaterial welfare. Second, in recent publications on environmental valuation the distinction is neglected between the *possibilities* offered by the environment for direct use (for example breathing), for production and for consumption on the one hand, and the addition of value(s) to the environment, that is production, on the other (de Groot, 1992; Costanza *et al.*, 1997; Nentjes, 1997;

Opschoor, 1997). These authors establish the value of an environmental function such as 'water as a habitat for fish' on the basis of the market value of fish, for example, thereby ignoring the fact that economically speaking a fish swimming is not the same good as a fish caught. The difference is brought about by the value added by labour. The value added for catching fish (fishermen, making ships and nets) has nothing to do with the value of functions (determined by the labour required to safeguard the function and the preferences for that); see Section 5. If the fish would remain in ample supply at the current level of catch and the current pollution level and so on, the function 'water as habitat for fish species' would not be scarce and would have a value equal to zero, because no opportunity costs would have to be spent to safeguard the function. The fish, in contrast, would still realize its value added, its price, on the market. The market reflects only this value added and precisely *not* the value of the environmental function. By 'environmental services' these authors do not mean the *possibilities* of catching fish, cropping timber and so forth: the possible uses or functions which may or may not get lost, and restoration and maintenance of which requires sacrifices (opportunity costs). Rather, they take such 'services' to be the fish and timber themselves. How environmental functions are to be valued will be discussed in the following section.

When use of one function is at the expense of another or the same function, or this threatens to be so in the future, there is competition of functions. As an illustration, once certain water pollutant thresholds have been exceeded, use of the function 'dumping ground for waste' may come to compete with the function 'drinking water'. In the case of overfishing, similarly, the function 'habitat for (one or more) species or ecosystems' comes to compete with itself, because overfishing may lead to extinction of a number of species, and the function may consequently get lost; many species and ecosystems of which they were a part, in other words many functions, have indeed already been lost. The function 'soil for cultivating crops' may be damaged by unsustainable use of the function 'supplier of timber', leading to loss of the function 'hydrological regulator' and subsequent erosion; it may also be in conflict with itself, when unsustainable farming methods lead to erosion and salinization of the soil. The many functions of natural resources that threaten to get lost as a result of exhaustion of the resource are in competition with themselves.

Competing functions are *by definition* economic goods. If, at a given level of technology, use of function A is at the expense of use of function B, greater availability of function B will lead, one way or another, to reduced availability of function A; conversely, more of A will lead to less of B. An alternative will always have to be sacrificed (opportunity costs) and consequently both A and B are scarce – and consequently economic – goods.

Here, 'use' obviously also includes passive use such as designation of an area as a nature reserve, which thereby excludes other uses, following recognition of the right of other species to exist; the sacrificed use, or sacrificed alternative, constitutes the opportunity cost. Competing environmental functions, defined as economic goods, form the theoretical backbone of the SNI and its estimation.

In this way the environment, and environmental losses, acquires a central place in economic theory, in contrast to an approach whereby these losses are viewed as external effects. The subject matter of economic theory can then be formulated as follows: the problem of choice with regard to the use of the scarce, alternatively applicable, dead and living matter of our physical surroundings for the satisfaction of classifiable wants. Or, very briefly: arranging the dead and living matter of the environment according to our preferences. This is argued in Hueting (1974a) and, more extensively, in Hueting (1992b, 1995). One of the arguments can be stated succinctly as follows. In the literature external effects are defined, briefly, as unintended side-effects outside the market affecting third persons, non-market parties; for a more extensive definition, see Hennipman (1968). However, when a road is built through a nature reserve, or a sewer to a river, estuary or sea, and all citizens make equal use of the road or sewer, the same citizens nonetheless lose important functions, in part or *in toto*, and such decisions are often made intentionally, in full awareness of the consequences.

The availability of environmental functions is the degree to which those functions can be used for a given end. This depends on two factors: one objective and measurable, the other subjective and not directly measurable. *On the one hand*, the availability of functions depends on the quality, quantity and spatial extent of environmental elements such as water and soil, which are largely amenable to measurement in physical units, and on the likewise measurable functioning of systems, including, specifically, ecosystems and life support systems,[2] or in other words on the state of the environment. Through (over-) use of a certain function the state of the environment may be altered, leading to reduced availability of other functions or of the same function: competition between functions. Whether this happens, and to what extent, depends on the preferences of the economic subjects. The availability of functions is thus also dependent, *on the other hand*, on subjective preferences, which are not directly measurable. In Hueting (1974a) this is expressed in a system of coordinates with on the horizontal axis the availability of functions expressed in terms of a physical variable (parameter) and on the vertical axis the preferences and costs associated with restoration and maintenance of functions (see Section 5). *In this way the relationship is established between subjectivist economic theory and the measurable physical environment, or ecology.*

Three categories of competition between functions are distinguished: spatial, quantitative and qualitative. Spatial competition occurs when the amount of space is inadequate to satisfy existing wants, or threatens to be so in the future. For example, in many residential areas there is inadequate space to allow transport systems to operate and at the same time children to play in the street. Use of space for a wide variety of purposes, be it roads, agriculture or urban development, is at the expense of the function 'space for the existence of natural ecosystems'. Spatial competition is probably the main cause of species extinction, through loss and fragmentation of habitats. Everything points to this process continuing in accelerated tempo unless drastic measures are taken. Conservation of natural species is a key criterion for estimating the SNI according to Hueting (see Section 7).

In the case of quantitative competition, it is the amount of matter that is deficient or threatens to be so in the future. We are here concerned with natural resources such as oil, copper and groundwater, which are exhaustible and non-renewable on a human time scale or which cannot increase in quantity, such as water.

With qualitative competition, it is always one and the same function, the function 'dumping ground for waste', or much more accurately: 'addition or withdrawal of species and matter' that is in conflict with other possible uses such as 'drinking water', 'physiological functioning' and 'habitat for species'. The introduction of agents into the environment (water, soil and air) or their withdrawal from it, in the course of a given activity, alters the quality of these environmental media, and as a result other uses of them may be disturbed or rendered impossible. Here, an 'agent' is defined as an abiotic or biotic element or amount of energy (in whatever form) introduced into or withdrawn from the environment that can cause loss of function. Thus, agents may be chemical substances, plants, animals, heat, ionizing radiation and so on.

Competition between functions is a manifestation of the finite nature of the environment, and to trace this competition in appropriate matrices is to expose the underlying conflicts. This has been done by Hueting (1974a). The conflict proves to lie almost entirely in the use of environmental functions for production and consumption, and growth thereof, in the here and now, at the expense of other desired uses and of future availability of environmental functions, including those functions necessary for production and consumption. In other words, the conflict boils down essentially to a question of sustainable versus unsustainable use of environmental functions. An elaboration for the use of the functions of a rainforest has been published by Hueting (1991).

For a proper understanding of the economic aspects of the environment it is instructive to compare the concepts outlined above with the concepts traditionally used in economic theory. This is no more than a metaphorical exercise, however, as the two categories of concepts are ultimately incompatible. Thus, some functions of the physical surroundings can be seen as consumption goods. Examples include: 'air for physiological functioning (breathing)', 'water as raw material for drinking water' and 'swimming water'. Other functions can be viewed as production means, such as 'water for irrigating crops' and 'gene pool for breeding and modifying crops and livestock'. However, 'normal' consumption goods and production means have to be reproduced over and over again, while environmental functions remain, in principle, freely available. Only if they come to compete, with each other or with themselves, for example if certain thresholds are exceeded, does their continued availability require a sacrifice. Finally, what was termed 'the non-manmade physical surroundings' in Hueting (1974a) is now often referred to as 'natural capital'. This, too, is instructive, but once again there is an anomaly: 'normal' capital goods wear out, but natural (or environmental) capital does not, in principle. Below, we shall use the two terms synonymously, however.

These differences in terminology make no difference when it comes to the valuation method elaborated in Section 5. After all, capital goods derive their value from the value of the consumption goods they are used to produce, and thus ultimately from preferences for these goods. Similarly, environmental capital, or the physical surroundings, derives its value from the value of its possible uses, the environmental functions, and thus from preferences for these functions. The elimination measures are of course always aimed at conserving water, air, soil, ecosystems, and so on, and thus at natural capital as the vehicle of the functions.

5 DEMAND AND SUPPLY METHOD (DSM) FOR VALUATION OF ENVIRONMENTAL FUNCTIONS

In Hueting (1974a, 1992a, 1992b, 1995) and Hueting et al. (1992, 1998) the view is defended that there can in principle be only one method for the valuation of environmental functions and their loss. It is argued that what are presented as different valuation methods are in fact valuation techniques that form parts of this one method. The method may yield widely varying results, however, mainly because assumptions must generally be made regarding preferences (the demand side). If these assumptions are made explicit, environmental valuation can yield comprehensible and valuable information. If they are not, as is all too frequently the case, the widely varying results will probably not be taken seriously by serious people. On the cost (supply) side there may be differences too, but these are generally made 'automatically' explicit in the presentation of cost estimates; here, the degree of difference is less dramatic. This position has been further elaborated by Hueting and de Boer (2001), in a parable of a carpenter who measures the area of a room, using different methods, with results varying by a factor of 10, 50 and more, as is the case with the various methods currently in sway for valuing the environment. The reasoning can be summarized as follows.

Environmental functions start out as free goods, available in abundance with regard to existing wants and consequently of zero value. The emergence of competition between functions marks a juncture at which functions start to fall short of meeting existing wants. The availability of functions or, in the terms of the SNA, their volume, decreases from 'infinite' (abundant) to finite (shortfall). Use that was initially free comes to require the sacrifice of an alternative. As a result, the shadow price of environmental functions rises, and with it their value, defined as price times quantity, from zero to positive. A *new category of scarce goods* has come into being. As the availability of environmental functions declines further, their shadow price continues to rise. This real increase in price and value reflects an increase in scarcity and thus a rise in costs or in other words: a decrease in wealth. After all, a rise in real prices reflects an impoverishment or, in terms of the SNA, a decrease in volume. A decrease in real prices reflects an increase in wealth or, in terms of the SNA, an increase in volume. The concept of 'volume' has two aspects, quantity and quality; in the elucidation below, for the sake of brevity we shall consider only the former.

Increases in volume are the result of increases in labour productivity, due in turn to technological progress: a greater volume of goods can be produced per unit labour, and the real price per unit product consequently falls. Conversely, a decline in volume results from a decline in productivity, measured in terms of produced goods, which is what follows from internalizing the costs of the measures taken to restore unaccepted loss of environmental functions (see Section 5.1). From this it follows that, in the view presented here, any adjustment of national income for losses of function will comprise only subtractions, and no additions. This is for a simple reason: losses of function are not written off when they originate, so restoration (and compensation, and so on) may not therefore be written on. In other words, the availability of the functions has not changed in comparison with the original situation, neither has welfare (assuming constant preferences). Ignoring this observation would result in asymmetric entries, rendering inter-year comparison less reliable. Environmental functions fall outside the SNA (Tinbergen and Hueting, 1991). As long as these are free or virtually free goods (see above), neither can they indeed be entered in the accounts, because their shadow price is zero, or approximates zero. In the

SNA, and in fact throughout the economy, it holds that the sum total of values (added to the physical surroundings; see Section 4) equals the sum total of revenues equals the sum total of costs. Evidently, this holds likewise for environmental functions. Because the environment falls outside the SNA, however, so too do losses of function (costs) as well as the restoration and maintenance thereof (revenues). The unrecorded losses of function (costs) can be incorporated in the national income by way of entering the opportunity costs required for restoring that part of the loss of function that is not accepted; what loss is deemed unacceptable depends on the preferences (see Section 5.1). In this way a 'green' national income comes into being alongside the standard national income. In accordance with the aforementioned basic rule, the revenues in the form of restoration of functions are equal to the costs of restoration, but remain invisible, because the environment remains outside the system. These *are* recorded in physical terms, however; see Figure 2.1 in Section 5.1. We shall return to this point in Section 6.4.

As long as one form of use of our physical surroundings is not hampering another, an insufficiency of labour (intellect) is the sole factor limiting sustained production growth. As soon as one use is at the expense of another, though, or threatens to be so in the future, a second limiting factor is introduced. Labour is then not only reducing scarcity, but is also creating new scarce goods: formerly free, or less scarce, environmental functions. Similarly, consumption is then not only satisfying wants, but is also cancelling out such satisfaction. Labour and consumption, besides having a positive effect on welfare (more produced goods), also have a negative effect (diminished environmental functions). These losses are not entered in the SNA, nor in the majority of cost–benefit analyses (CBA). Over and against the unentered costs stand the revenues (more produced goods), which *are* entered. The question arises: what is the result on balance?

In the view presented here, the answer is given in four steps, in which the calculation is gradually built up, without suggesting any sequence of calculation. The first two steps constitute a partial approach and are described essentially in Hueting (1974a). Additions introduced in later publications are included in the following brief review. The third step embodies a macro-approach based on environmental economic growth theory as developed by Stiglitz (1974), Hartwick (1977, 1978) Dasgupta and Heal (1979) and others. Step four is the setting up of a system of reliable, and thus reasonably detailed, interlinked environmental economic models with which to carry out valuation based on the principles deduced in the previous steps. The third and fourth steps have been elaborated and discussed in a number of internal Statistics Netherlands papers, correspondence with colleagues and several publications (de Boer et al., 1994, 1995, 1998; Brouwer and O'Connor, 1997).

The basic point of departure is the same for all four steps. If there are no preferences for a good, its value is zero, irrespective of how important, or even indispensable, that good may be for humankind. If a good can be obtained without sacrificing an alternative, its value is likewise zero. In valuing environmental functions, both preferences and costs must be quantified. These are therefore two inseparably linked elements of the valuation of environmental functions and their loss. This is why the method is known as the demand and supply method, or DSM, a name adopted only late on in its development (in 1996). Valuations that are, ultimately, estimates of only preferences (demand) or costs (supply) are here viewed as techniques forming part of the single valuation method presented here.

With respect to the economics of the environment we are concerned almost always with the choice between produced goods and environmental functions. If valuation is to be of use in making such choices, the two categories of goods must be expressed in the same unit. For environmental functions this requires the construction of shadow prices comparable with the market prices in which produced goods are expressed, that is shadow prices without a consumer's surplus. To establish the total economic value of the two categories, given by BCGR in Figure 2.1, which does include the consumer's surplus, requires very extensive survey campaigns, for both categories. Overall, the results of such an exercise are of dubious reliability. This holds particularly for the vital necessities of life such as food, drink and medical care, for the intramarginal utility of these goods includes the utility of the first slice of bread, the first sip of water and the saving of a life (Hueting, 1974a). It holds in equal measure for the vital environmental functions (Hueting, 1989, 1992b, 1995; Geurts et al., 1994; Hoevenagel, 1994a, 1994b, 1994c). In practice, therefore, we consider it necessary to define value as (shadow) price (marginal utility) times quantity, determination of which requires data on both preferences and costs.

5.1 Valuation on the Basis of Revealed Preferences and Known Elimination Costs

As a *first step* in the chain of reasoning, the line is taken that all preferences for environmental functions can be expressed in the marketplace or, as a complement to this, be discovered by means of surveys. On a system of coordinates function availability is recorded on the horizontal axis, in physical units, with the preferences and annual costs of the measures to restore functions being plotted on the vertical axis (see Figure 2.1). Two cost curves are constructed. The figure shows that the reduction of the costs plotted on the one curve constitutes the benefits accruing from the increase of costs plotted on the other. The aim, now, is to find the minimum total cost, or in

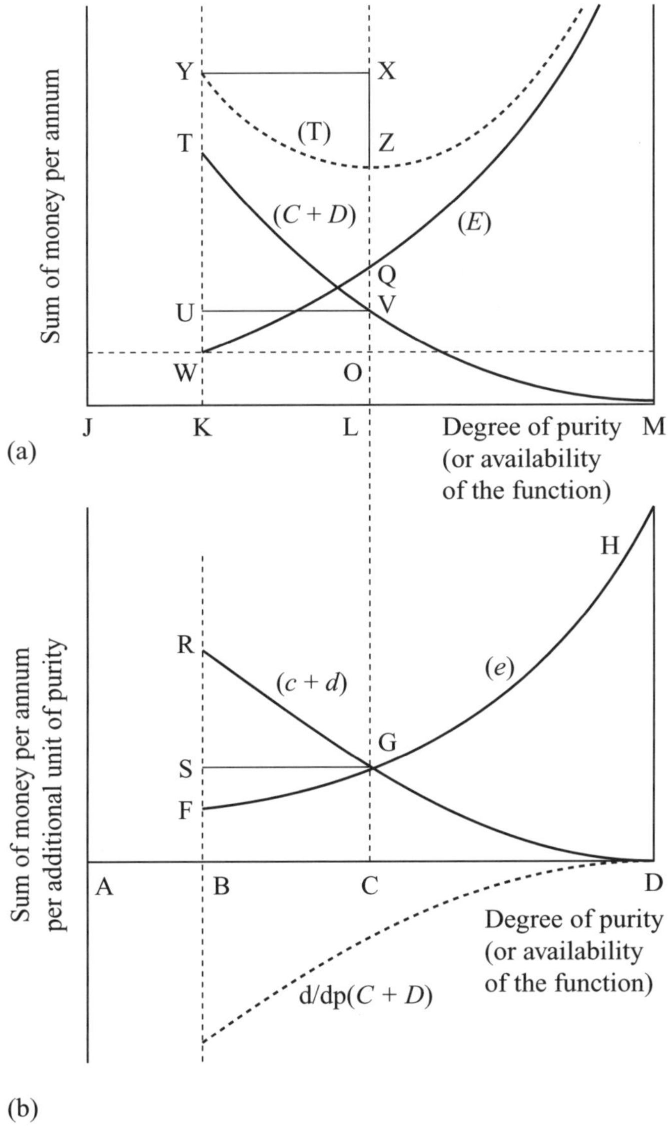

Figure 2.1 *Costs of elimination and revealed preferences for an environmental function: (a) total curves; (b) marginal curves. (E)=elimination costs, (C+D)=compensation and (financial) damage costs, (e)=marginal elimination costs, (c+d)=marginal compensation and (financial) damage costs. Taken from Hueting (1974a)*

other words the point where the difference between benefits and costs is maximum.

The first of these two cost curves consists of the sum total (without double counting) of all expenditures, actually made or yet to be made, by whatever party, resulting from loss of environmental functions and of the expenditures that people state they are willing to make to regain these functions (willingness to pay and to accept surveys, that is contingent valuation). As stated in Hueting (1974a, 1989, 1992b, 1995), surveys prove to yield unreliable results for precisely the most vital functions. The costs actually incurred fall into four categories: (1) expenditures on measures to compensate for loss of function, such as the raising of dykes as a result of disruption of various functions regulating hydrology and climate, or on preparing drinking water as a result of overuse of the function 'dumping ground for waste'. These are the compensation costs; (2) expenditures, actually made or yet to be made, relating to damage, such as housing damage and harvest losses caused by flooding due to loss of the function 'hydrological regulation' of forests and soil, and production losses and medical costs ensuing from, say, loss of the function 'air for physiological functioning'. This is the financial damage; (3) travel expenses incurred in going ever further to enjoy naturc; (4) Ricardian rent paid via the price of raw materials.

All these amounts can be interpreted as expressing revealed preferences for the original functions, so that the negative first derivative of the cost curve built up from these amounts can be seen as a collective demand curve for environmental functions (see Figure 2.1): the first derivative lying in the fourth quadrant is reflected to the first quadrant [$-(\mathrm{d}/\mathrm{d}p)(C+D)=+(c+d)$, where the symbol p represents purity]. For category (2) this is based, strictly speaking, on the assumption that those suffering damage through loss of a function are prepared to pay at least the amount required to restore that damage in order to achieve restoration and lasting availability of the function in question. The curve has the same shape as a normal demand curve. With decreasing availability of the function, progressively more compensation measures must be taken and progressively more financial damage occurs: the price (and thus the marginal utility) increases.

The second cost curve is built up from expenditures on measures, to be taken by whatever party from the year of investigation onwards, which increase the availability of the original functions. This can only be achieved by eliminating the cause of loss of function and, where necessary and feasible, by neutralizing the accumulated impact of earlier environmental burdening *in situ*. For this reason this curve is referred to as the elimination cost curve (or abatement cost curve). The measures involved thus eliminate the source of the loss of function, that is the environmental burden, permitting partial or complete restoration of the function in question. They are, of course, arranged in order of increasing cost per unit of environmental burden eliminated. The measures consist of: (1) technical measures, including process re-engineering, redesign and developing and applying (renewable) substitutes for non-renewable resources (for example solar energy, glass fibre); (2) direct shifts from environmentally burdening to less burdening activities (reallocation); (3) a shrinkage of economic activity, with employment remaining unchanged (more leisure time); and (4) a decrease in the size of the population. No pronouncement is made as to the time frame within which these measures are to be implemented, as will be clear from their nature. Whether, and to what extent, they are indeed implemented depends on the preferences, in other words on the position of the demand curve. The cost curve to emerge from this procedure may be considered as a supply curve, because the measures act to make available, or supply, environmental functions. From how the curve is built up it follows that it is a collective supply curve. The sum of the elimination costs is equal to the sum of the prices of the production factors that must be withdrawn, by a variety of routes, from the production of consumption goods and budget goods in order for functions to be restored. The curve rises progressively from bottom left to top right. The further a function is to be restored, the more efficient the measures must be. This is generally accompanied by progressively rising (marginal) costs per unit avoided environmental burden.

As we move further up along the elimination cost curve, we automatically move further down the curve of compensation and other costs: as the original functions once again become more available, the necessity of such expenditure decreases. It is this reduction in compensation and other costs that constitutes the benefits accruing from the expenditures made on elimination measures. By summing the two curves a U-curve is obtained (see Figure 2.1). The minimum of this U-curve reflects the position of optimum function recovery, for here the total social costs are minimum while the difference between total benefits and costs is maximum. The minimum of the U-curve corresponds to the point of intersection of the first derivatives of the two curves, that is of the marginal supply and demand curve. This point of intersection would reflect the shadow price that we are seeking and that can be compared directly with the market prices, *provided* all preferences for environmental functions were reflected in the demand curve constructed as described above. The shadow price (CG in Figure 2.1) simultaneously determines the value of the environmental function as well as the costs of the unaccepted function loss. The residual function loss, recorded in physical terms, *is* accepted: the associated increase in production (which is entered in the national accounts) is valued more highly. Like any price, the shadow price of an environmental function is an indication of its marginal utility.

To value is to compare. In economics, there is no such thing as an absolute value; a good can only be worth more or worth less compared to another good. Because what is always at stake is a conflict between the environment and produced goods, as we have seen above, the value BCGS (or BCGF; see below) in Figure 2.1 gives us precisely what we need for making the inevitable choices involved in this conflict. At the same time, shadow prices that can be compared directly with market prices are also a necessary precondition for adjusting the standard national income for environmental losses. BCGS (or BCGF) comprises no consumer's surplus, for example, just like market values. Other conceptions of the valuation of environmental functions exist, however, and these will be discussed below.

Now consider Figure 2.1 again. The shadow price (partial, see above), directly comparable with the market price of a produced good, equals CG. The cost that must be incurred to achieve the optimum, and thus the value of the function, is given by BCGF, corresponding with the line OQ. BCGF simultaneously indicates the value of the function, comparable with the market value of produced goods. As stated in Section 4, value should be shadow price times quantity, or in other words the area of BCGS. In Hueting (1974a), from which Figure 2.1 is taken, the producer's surplus was neglected. This is not essential, however (Hueting and de Boer, 2001). Now, the total value or benefits is equal to the increase in monetized total utility as one moves from B to C = BCGR = line section TU. *This thus includes BCGF as well as BCGS.*

FGR = monetized net increase of utility gained as the availability of a function increases from B to C = line section ZX. This net increase equals the total increase in utility BCGR minus the costs BCGF. This must always be a positive number, because there is a change from suboptimal to optimal.

Further on in the aforementioned exposition of Hueting (1974a) a second step is made: the demand curve $(c+d)$ in Figure 2.1 moves to the right and is then termed $(c+d+x)$; x is not shown in Figure 2.1. If x is large (but unknown; *ergo* x) and $(c+d)$ is situated far below $(c+d+x)$, then the bulk of FGR (after neglecting the producer's surplus) consists of what can be called the consumer's surplus, although we would rather refer to FGR as 'net benefit' or, because x represents an assumption about preferences for a function, as 'meeting an assumed demand'.

Erroneously, some authors (for example, Costanza et al., 1997; Opschoor, 1997) refer to FGR as 'the value'. Erroneously, because net increase in utility after reallocation (of resources and capital goods) and value are of course two entirely different things, while it is clearly 'value' that these authors are after. Certainly, comparison of FGR with costs may be a useful tool for deciding whether or not to go ahead with a given project – if a reliable demand curve is available, that is, for that is often not the case. But that 'value' is a very different concept can be readily understood with reference to a produced good with a very low consumer's surplus and a high price; few people will hold that surplus to be the value of the good.

5.2 Extension with Assumed Preferences for Environmental Functions

The *second step* in the reasoning behind our method is the following. It can be plausibly argued, for a variety of reasons, that preferences for environmental functions can be expressed only very partially through the market and the political process (mainly the budget mechanism) (see Section 1, principles 2 and 3, iv) and that questionnaire-type surveys cannot provide reliable answers when it comes to the most vital functions, that is those on which the lives of future generations are dependent (Hueting, 1974a, 1989, 1992b, 1995; Bateman and Turner, 1992; Geurts et al., 1994; Hoevenagel, 1994a, 1994b, 1994c; de Boer et al., 1995). As an example of compensation costs (as revealed preferences) there is no point in creating new forests or lakes so long as the process of acidification has not been halted by elimination measures, because without elimination at the source the process will acidify the newly created forests and lakes. Erosion-driven soil loss cannot be compensated. Much of the damage resulting from loss of functions will take place in the future; cases in point are damage due to disruption of climatic stability and to the loss of the functions of natural ecosystems such as rainforests and estuaries. No financial damage or compensation expenditures can therefore arise in the present. Choosing a discount rate, for instance the market interest, for calculating the net present value of future damage boils down to making an assumption about preferences for future environmental costs and benefits (Hueting, 1991). This does not, therefore, resolve the basic problem of preferences being unknown. We cannot base ourselves on observed individual behaviour, furthermore, given the working of the prisoners' dilemma. In practice, individuals do not switch to environmentally sound behaviour, because they doubt whether others will do the same, as a result of which the effect is thought to be negligible while the individual concerned causes him or herself detriment. The same holds at a meso- and macro-scale. If one company takes measures to protect the environment but others do not, it will price itself out of the market. If a given country adopts measures and others do not follow, that country will suffer damage, while the effect of those measures will be insubstantial. Finally, there is a lack of information, for example about the complex nature of life support systems and the relation between safeguarding the environment, employment and growth (see Three myths, Chapter 3, this volume). *All these aforementioned factors, which make it impossible and very difficult respectively to fully express preferences for environmental functions, we shall call blockages (or barriers).* These blockages play an important role in Section 6.

The shadow prices we are seeking thus remain largely unknown. This has two consequences. First, the value (or relative scarcity or marginal utility or correct price) of the goods produced and consumed at the expense of scarce environmental functions remains likewise unknowable; this value differs from product to product, moreover (Hueting, 1974a). Second, we cannot escape from making *assumptions* about the urgency of the preferences for present and future availability of environmental functions (for example Hueting et al., 1992, 1995a, 1995b, 1998; Hueting and Bosch, 1994). This obviously holds in equal measure for cost–benefit analyses as well as for adjustments of national income for environmental loss. *When making such assumptions, the optimum described above is once again valid, as is the shadow price that is directly comparable with market prices, and this optimum is again located at the point of intersection of the supply and demand curves.*

In practice, an assumption regarding preferences can take the form of standards for the availability of environmental functions. We can imagine certain situations in which such is indeed the case. If there is some kind of 'survival minimum' for the function, the demand curve will become very steep near the minimum. It makes no difference, in principle, whether this minimum is below or above the current level of the function. If prices are high, however, the demand curve must bend towards the vertical axis, because it is impossible to sacrifice more income (goods) than is produced. The further to the right the urgently desired level lies, therefore, the shorter the vertical section of the curve will be. If it is plausible that the steep section of the curve will intersect the supply curve (marginal cost function), the demand curve can be replaced by a simple standard at the point of the urgently desired function level; this does not affect the outcome. Something similar holds if the demand curve is simply not well known but a reasonable assumption can be made about the position of the optimum and thus also of the optimal level of the function. That function level then becomes the standard. A special case arises if preferences for consumption and use of the environment in the future are far more urgent than those for consumption and use of the environment now (see the discussion of sustainability, below). In theory, the optimal function level is a characteristic of the sustainable path that can be found by optimizing a dynamic macroeconomic model; in practice, however, this is a calculation that is well nigh impossible to perform. Fortunately, the position of the optimum can be estimated (see third step in Section 5.3).

From the above it follows that there are as many values for environmental functions as there are assumptions regarding preferences and, *ergo*, as many green national incomes, too. We understand 'green national income' to mean the national income in a situation in which preferences for environmental functions and produced goods are fulfilled as satisfactorily as possible. By this we mean that welfare is limited only by the technological state of the art in the year for which calculations are being made, and not by the aforementioned blockages; these are assumed to have been entirely overcome.[3] We thus base our calculation of an SNI on the assumption of preferences existing for the continued availability of vital environmental functions; an SNI is therefore a special case of a green national income. As long as the assumptions are made clear and explicit, the ensuing valuation exercise can yield valuable and comprehensible information.

5.3 Generalization in Dynamic Environmental Economic Theory

As a *third step*, the theory presented above is generalized in a macroeconomic sense by taking a systems approach. This step is necessary because the measures occurring in the calculation of green national income cause such a large change in the pressure on the environment that all variables change as a result, including the prices of market goods, budget goods and environmental functions. In other words, the *ceteris paribus* condition of the previous steps no longer pertains. The applied systems approach starts from the notion that all relevant interacting processes in society and the environment can, at least in principle, be modelled as mathematical relations between variables that can be combined in one comprehensive model. Meadows (1972), Solow (1974), Stiglitz (1974), Weitzman (1976), Hartwick (1978), Dasgupta and Heal (1979), Mäler (1991), Asheim (1994), Pezzey (1994) and Vellinga and Withagen (1996) are among those who have led the way in this approach.

This step leads to a generalized model of an economy consisting of a series of production activities and groups of consumers, each using both short-lived and long-lived (that is capital and durable) goods and services and each using the environment. These actor groups apply technical measures to reduce pressure on the environment and slow down or halt its deterioration. These measures require labour, capital goods, matter and energy flows. Outputs and consumption activities are dependent on all these inputs.

The assumption that (partly assumed) preferences are fulfilled in the best possible way, given the other data, relations and assumptions of the model, is often formalized in economics as the concept of all people maximizing their welfare. A person's welfare is not a physiological or psychological quantity amenable to direct measurement, but a theoretical internal model variable in which the products and environmental functions the person uses are weighted according to his or her (estimated or assumed) preferences. In calculating a person's welfare, allowance is made for the fact that the weight someone assigns to a product or function is influenced by the available quantities of all other goods and functions. The calculation of an individual's welfare from the quantities of products and environmental functions that he or she uses and wants to use in the future is described in a mathematical relation called the individual welfare 'functional'. It follows that individual welfare merely reflects the ranking of the combinations of products and functions considered in order of their desirability to the person in question. Consequently, all individuals are assumed to maximize their welfare.

We simplify matters and consider society as a whole, maximizing so-called social (or collective) welfare, or welfare in short, which reflects the ranking of the packages of products and functions that are used by the sum total of individuals in a society. Like individual welfare, social welfare is of course not directly measurable.[4] When the model is solved and the model variable called welfare is used as an outcome, it cannot therefore be anything but a welfare *indicator*.

As both present and future product flows and function levels are weighted in the welfare indicator, this is sometimes referred to as 'intertemporal welfare' as opposed to 'instantaneous welfare'. These terms may be confusing. 'Intertemporal' welfare at any given time may instantaneously rise (because people 'feel' instantaneously better) if a future risk is judged to have become smaller than it was. Here, 'instantaneous' denotes an aspect of 'intertemporal' welfare. From now on, however, we shall distinguish 'instantaneous welfare' in any given year from welfare in the general sense in that year; this may be somewhat inelegant, but it is in accordance with the literature. Instantaneous welfare at a particular moment in time is the result of weighting all product flows and functions levels that are *used at that moment*, provided this weighting can be isolated from the intertemporal weighting. Welfare in the general sense is in that case the result of the weighting of the instantaneous welfare levels in the present and all future moments, that is intertemporal weighting.

Like welfare, production output is described as non-linearly dependent on inputs. Though it is questionable whether all non-linearities in the production functions hold in the long run, the general form is non-linear.

In general the model is dynamic, as it describes the effects of changes of economic and environmental stocks on other parts of the system. Economic stocks consist mainly of capital goods and durable consumption goods, while environmental stocks are quantities or concentrations of environmental resources and levels of pollutants, biota, available land and so on. The magnitudes of these stocks are so-called state variables and how they develop in time largely determines the solution of the model. The processes described by the model influence how these stocks vary, thereby producing patterns of inertia that are characteristic of the model. One result is that realistic model solutions as responses to sudden man-made changes are always gradual, and therefore always follow continuous *paths* in the space of the state variables (state space). Each set of assumptions concerning the representation of real processes in the model, parameter values and input data produces a path. Welfare is maximized by determining the ways in which controllable human actions depend on time and this process selects one optimal path for each set of assumptions, parameters and input data applied. For our purpose, it suffices to plot such a path in terms of certain characterizing variables, such as a welfare indicator, or benefits and costs, just as Figure 2.1 presents these variables for different static (that is time-independent) situations.

Several of the aforementioned authors have sought welfare indicators that can be related to national income. De Boer et al. (1995, 1998 and in preparation), Brouwer and O'Connor (1997) and Zeelenberg et al. (1997) have reviewed their efforts. We shall elaborate this subject in Section 6.

5.4 Practical Model System

In the previous section the calculation procedure is described in generalized terms, proceeding from standard economic theory. For such a calculation to be reliable, a large dynamic model is required that comprises all the relevant processes in both the economy and the environment. Welfare must be maximized within this complex model, yielding an optimal path, in our case a sustainable path. This appears to be an impossible task, given the capacities of standard computing hardware and software. We therefore opt for an approach using a set of interlinked models rather than one all-embracing model; this is our *fourth step*. The economic activities of production and consumption are represented in one model, and additional models constructed for each of the various environmental problem areas. Ideally, information should then be transferred back and forth between the models in a process of iterative exchange. To avoid tedious iterations with the total model set, we have reduced these interactions to one-way information flows, that is to one-time operation of each model for a given period. This means that the overall optimum, that is the optimal path, can be calculated only approximately, as opposed to the case with the theoretical comprehensive model. We have opted to achieve a reasonable approximation by assuming that the optimal function levels of the theoretical model (see Section 5.3) can be formulated in words and/or roughly quantified. It is further assumed that the levels of the state variables of the environment (quantities, qualities such as concentrations, space) corresponding to the assumed optimal function levels can be estimated, at least to within some range, on the basis of expert opinion or by using appropriate standards for the state of the environment. These standards are then entered as constraints in the model of each environmental problem, and standards for allowable environmental pressures (emissions and so on) are then derived by iteration. These pressure standards may be functions of time. However, the pressure levels associated with overall sustainability must be capable of being maintained forever and therefore these (constant) levels are independent of time (see Sections 6.5 and 6.6). The standards are then entered as constraints in the economic model. In this step it is decided which technical measures, which direct production shifts and which levels of production shrinkage and population reduction are to be taken to arrive at the standards and, subsequently, what national income results from these actions at the time of interest, that is the year of investigation.

6 INS AND OUTS OF A GREEN AND A SUSTAINABLE NATIONAL INCOME CALCULATION

Four main subjects are reviewed in this section. First, it is explained that each different set of assumptions regarding preferences for environmental functions and blockages preventing their expression forms a specific case, for which the model (or model set) computes an optimal development path of the economy and the environment. Second, we show that two significant *welfare indicators* and a *green national income* can be calculated for each path, and how they are related. Third, we argue why we opt for green national income as a practical welfare-related indicator. Finally, we focus on a special case: sustainable national income.

We work towards these goals by discussing a series of cases of increasing relevance to our problem: (1) preferences for environmental functions are unimportant because functions are abundant; (2) functions are scarce and preferences are such that the optimal path (computed by the model) approximates the actual path; (3) preferences for the environment are stronger than in the second case, but there are blockages preventing their full expression; (4) preferences are as strong as in the third case, but the blockages have been overcome; and (5) the special form of the last case in which preferences for sustainability are general and dominant. These cases are considered in Sections 6.1 to 6.5, respectively.

This staggered approach also enables several other issues to be explained: the difference between the welfare indicator on the actual and the optimal path; the difference in national income on the two paths, that is the opportunity costs; the part played by technical measures, production shifts and other measures in these costs; the prices to be used in calculating these costs; the nature of sustainability; and the existence of feasible transition paths to – for instance – sustainability. We shall discuss only the main features of these issues, referring for details to the literature as appropriate. De Boer et al. (forthcoming) gives a mathematical exposition of the argumentation.

6.1 Environmental Functions not Scarce

Consider an imaginary country (or a real country in the distant past) where people value the present and future availability of environment functions, but where these functions are abundant. The situation is then relatively simple. As explained in Section 5.3, a welfare indicator can in theory be calculated using a model of the economy including its interaction with the environment. This indicator, which we shall call v, depends in this straightforward case only on present and future consumption of man-made goods and services. Welfare must, of necessity, be maximal in both the actual and the model economy. The actual and the model path consequently roughly coincide. If the model is 'correct', therefore, maximization of its welfare indicator will result in a model solution, or model path, that approximately reconstructs the actual development of the economy in this imaginary country. In particular, this means that the quantities of selected groups of man-made goods consumed in a series of historical years should be 'adequately' approximated by the model's consumption variables over these years. As a by-product, the welfare indicator is calculated in a fashion entirely consistent with the adopted assumptions on preferences.

In this case several convenient simplifications can be made. Calculation of the welfare indicator including the future (in the welfare 'functional') generally involves the use of different discount rates for different consumption goods. These rates may even depend on the length of the period between the future and the present year, that is on time. If *the same discount rate* is used for all consumption goods, the welfare indicator *on the optimal path*, in this case the current path of the economy, may be written as a sum of various kinds of terms. The consumption of produced goods (c) in the year of investigation is represented by the instantaneous welfare term, evaluated for that year. The consumption of products in the future is represented by the increases in the stocks of produced capital goods in the present year (dk/dt), each stock change weighted with its own 'welfare shadow price'. Additional terms occur if parts of the model are explicitly dependent on time, that is on time-dependent influences from outside the model ('exogenous' or input variables), such as a climate variable or a measure of technological progress. Some of these time dependencies can be avoided by making the influence an 'endogenous' variable, that is by extending the model such that the influence is the result of an internal process. The corresponding terms in the welfare indicator formula then disappear, being incorporated in other terms. Other time dependencies are often assumed away. We therefore concentrate on the terms due to immediate and future consumption, expressed in the consumption flows c and the rates of change of the capital stocks dk/dt, respectively.

A monetary welfare indicator proportional to the welfare indicator v can be computed by dividing the latter by the marginal welfare of some marketed product in the year of investigation. The outcome is entirely arbitrary, as it depends on the arbitrary reference level and units of the welfare indicator itself and the arbitrary choice of market good. Consequently, this result cannot be compared with national income. If there were a unique way of doing this, one would obtain the macroeconomic equivalent of such monetary welfare measures as the 'real economic value' and consumer's surplus of a good. We assume this to be impossible and follow the literature in that the term in c, the instantaneous welfare function, is linearized. Thus an approximate welfare indicator is obtained in which the flow of each consumption good and the change of the stock of each capital good is represented by a separate term. Replacing the marginal welfare coefficients in all the terms by the prices arising from the model exercise (which approximate the market prices) yields an approximate monetary welfare indicator or 'monetary welfare measure', which we denote as w. We call these prices shadow prices. It is important to note that, as a result of linearization and expression in market prices, the macro-equivalents of the consumer's surpluses have disappeared from both the immediate consumption terms and the stock change terms of the welfare measure. The respective terms of this measure still constitute the contributions of present and future consumption to welfare in a given year. These terms now sum to the macro-totals of *consumption* plus *net investments*, in other words to *net national product* (or income): y on the model's optimal path (Weitzman, 1976). As a formula: $w=p(c+dk/dt)=y$. This model-calculated national income is a good approximation of real standard national income as calculated in the national accounts, provided the model and its optimal path are fair approximations of the present economy and its development. This implies that the prices are 'real' prices, insofar as they are free of inflationary or deflationary tendencies.

6.2 Relatively Weak but Perfectly Expressed Preferences for the Environment

In a more realistic case than the last, the production and consumption of goods leads to direct or delayed damage to environmental functions, which consequently become scarce. Here, however, only moderate preferences for environmental functions are assumed, to such a degree that the model's optimal path (*'business as usual'*, *b* in Figure 2.2) is a fair approximation of the current economic and environmental path (*'actual'*, *a*). Although there are blockages preventing full expression of these preferences (see Section 5.2), these are assumed to have a negligible effect. The national income computed by the model under the assumed preferences is formally a green national income, but is in this case a good approximation of standard national income; see Figure 2.2.

If the same discount rate is taken for all consumption goods and all environmental functions in the welfare function, the welfare indicator *v* calculated for this optimal path may be broken down into terms, as indicated in Section 6.1. Some of these terms may be explicitly time-dependent (see above). Some of the latter may now also stem from environmental sub-

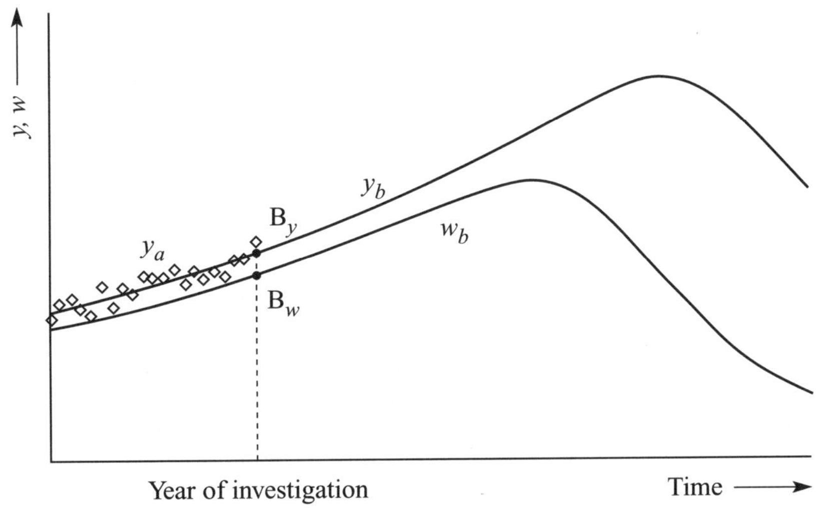

Figure 2.2 *Standard national income (y_a) as measured in the System of National Accounts and its approximation and extrapolation on a 'business as usual' path (y_b) as computed with an environmental economic model with relatively weak but assumed unblocked preferences for the environment, for a fictitious case; w_b is the welfare level on the 'business as usual' path. The collapse appears earlier in w_b than in y_b, because in w_b the future is taken into account, not in y_b. The points B_y and B_w indicate the levels of national income y and the welfare measure w in the year of investigation*

models. Both are again not discussed. Now the available quantities of both produced goods and environmental functions contribute to the welfare indicator. The available levels of consumption goods (c) and environmental functions (φ) in the year considered (the year of investigation) both contribute to the instantaneous welfare term. The rates of change of the modelled stocks, namely of stocks of produced capital goods (dk/dt) and of levels of environmental functions ($d\varphi/dt$), appear in the welfare indicator as well. Each change rate is weighted with its own factor that can be expressed in terms of marginal welfare. These stock changes represent the safeguarding of the consumption of produced goods in the future and the deterioration of the future potential for using the environment, respectively.

Having linearized the instantaneous welfare term in the welfare indicator v, we can once again obtain an approximate monetary welfare measure w, following the procedure described in Section 6.1. However, w now consists of the weighted sum of the available quantities of consumption goods (c) and environmental functions, and the rates of change of both the stocks of produced capital goods and the levels of the environmental functions; the weights are the *monetary shadow prices* (see Section 6.1). The expression for the welfare measure can be rearranged in such a way that the equality to net national income plus environmental terms becomes apparent. The latter are the contributions to welfare of available environmental function levels (φ), their rates of change ($d\varphi/dt$) and several cost terms (these costs do not cover all elimination, restoration and compensation costs and financial damage; for the sake of brevity we refer to de Boer et al. (forthcoming). The terms expressed in the function levels and the associated costs stand for the immediate use of environmental functions, as the term in c stands for the immediate consumption of products. Likewise, the terms in dk/dt and $d\varphi/dt$ stand for the consumption of products in the future and the use of functions in the future, respectively. The latter term, consisting of the changes in environmental stocks, weighted with shadow prices, is analogous to the net investments term expressed in dk/dt and is therefore often referred to as the rate of change of 'natural capital'.

After these simplifications, the shadow prices of the produced goods (c,k) used in the indicator are the model's market prices of those goods. As the model's *business as usual* path (b) is an approximation of the actual development (a), the model's market prices are in this case approximately equal to the real market prices. Consequently, the model's national income approximates standard national income as provided by the national accounts. If net national income is increasing at the expense of the environment, the shadow prices of the declining environmental function levels φ are positive and increasing, because the functions are becoming scarcer.

The derivatives of the function levels with respect to time, $d\varphi/dt$, are often negative because the functions are frequently on the decline, but their shadow prices are positive; see Section 5.3. This approach is proposed by Repetto et al. (1989, 1991), Mäler (1991), Landefeld and Carson (1994a, 1994b), Hamilton (1995) and probably several other authors.

It may well be realistic to assume relatively weak preferences for the environment and to accept the correspondingly small difference between the monetized welfare measure and national income, as has been done in this case. This choice means assuming that people are either not aware of the possibility of serious losses of environmental functions in the future, or do not care. From Section 5.2 it follows that stronger preferences for environmental functions are equally plausible. Cases built on this assumption are elaborated below.

6.3 Strong but Poorly Expressed Preferences for the Environment

In this case, people are assumed to have stronger preferences for environmental functions than appear from the actual development of the economy; yet the model is considered realistic. This discrepancy is explained by the existence of blockages in society that prevent people's preferences for environmental functions from being completely expressed in their actions, as discussed in Section 5.2 and referred to briefly in the introduction of Section 6. These blockages can be modelled as additional constraints on welfare optimization. The resulting optimal path is the '*business as usual*' path (*b*) that was also found as the optimal solution of the case presented in the former section, but which may now be referred to as the *'blocked path'*. Again, it approximates actual economic development and might be extrapolated into the future as an economic forecast (Figure 2.2). In this case, however, the national income associated with the path is *not* a green national income, because society's preferences for the environment are not expressed completely and immediately. We nonetheless prefer the procedure for calculating path *b* presented here (strong preferences, blocked expression thereof), because it allows us to keep the assumption on preferences the same, which allows this path to be compared with that from which our indicator is taken. This latter path is introduced in the next section.

6.4 Strong and Perfectly Expressed Preferences for the Environment; Absolute Optimum

The blockages preventing people from expressing their preferences for the environment in their actions can probably be overcome by a persistent, dedicated and broad policy, of which price instruments and awareness-raising are important constituent components. This may well be a lengthy process. Subsequently, social, production and consumption processes must be adapted to match the preferences. These adaptations will take the form of technical measures, production shifts, production shrinkage and measures to reduce population, as discussed in Section 5.1. Implementation of these measures will, again, take considerable time. Once the measures are in place the various pressures on the environment will be reduced. After delays that may again be substantial for some environmental processes, the state of the environment will return to more stable levels that under the assumed preferences form an optimal mix with the consumption and investment packages.

As the indicator we seek should be as transparent as possible, we make it independent of assumptions regarding the dynamics that determine the time lags in the adaptations just discussed. We assume – in a manner of speech – that these adaptations are started and completed all at once in the year of investigation. The result is an unfeasible 'leap' from the blocked path *b* to the unfeasible path *s* on which the assumed *strong preferences for the environment are perfectly and immediately expressed*, so welfare is absolutely maximum, given the technical possibilities at the present and as expected in the future (Figure 2.3). Despite the unfeasibility of the leap, this path is of great interest because it has a strong signal value, as a statistical orientation point or 'beacon' to head for when devising (environmental) economic policy, since it indicates the direction of perfect fulfilment of assumed preferences for the environment. The national incomes associated with the paths of this type are the *green national incomes* corresponding to the assumed (unblocked) preferences.

The stronger the assumed preferences for the environment, the lower the resulting green national income will be. It goes without saying that the green national incomes resulting from unblocked preferences are lower than the green national incomes resulting from blocked preferences. An example in which weak and blocked preferences for the environment are assumed is the analysis of Mäler (1991). The path of which 'our' SNI is a characteristic is one of the unblocked paths discussed here. This SNI path distinguishes itself from the other unblocked paths because adjustment of the standard national incomes in the successive years of investigation is based on the technology available in the respective year of investigation. This precludes the risk of extrapolated technological progress subsequently proving unattainable, with the attendant possibility of a collapse at some time in the future; see y_b in Figure 2.3. The SNI according to Hueting is lower than the other green and sustainable national incomes and the unfeasible 'leap' is therefore greater – and substantially so. This is because the

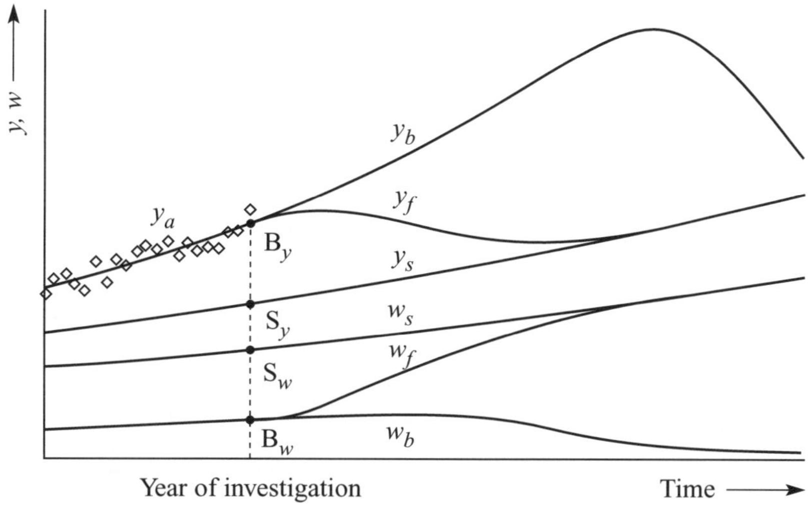

Figure 2.3 *Actual standard national income observations (y_a, fictitious example) compared with the net national income (y) and a welfare indicator (w) on three optimal paths, calculated with a dynamic environmental economic model. The blocked path (index b) approximates the actual path (index a) by assuming incomplete expression of preferences for the environment. These preferences are assumed to be completely expressed on the unfeasible unblocked path (index s) and the feasible unblocked path (index f). The points B_y and B_w indicate the levels of national income y and the welfare measure w on the blocked path b in the year of investigation; S_y and S_w are the corresponding points on the unfeasible unblocked path s*

path to which this SNI belongs does not involve cheaper solutions to environmental problems being anticipated in the future, as with the other *s*-paths, so that the opportunity costs are higher. Nonetheless, this path is not the lowest conceivable, for – entirely in line with the notion of sustainability – this path is concerned solely with maintaining vital environmental functions. Noise nuisance (function: ‘silence as freedom from noise’) is thus not included, for example, to the extent that it does not damage health, because noise does not accumulate and does not therefore undermine the living conditions of future generations. The situation is shown in Figure 2.6.

The path *s* is found in theory by assuming that the blockages of the preferences have been overcome (that is have disappeared) and by optimizing the sizes of the modelled stocks in the year of investigation along with the measures that need to be taken in later years to maximize welfare.[5] The stocks in the modelled production, consumption and social processes consist of capital goods, durable consumer goods, employment allocation and population size. The differences between these stocks on the blocked path *b* and the unblocked path *s* in a given year are caused by the *measures*

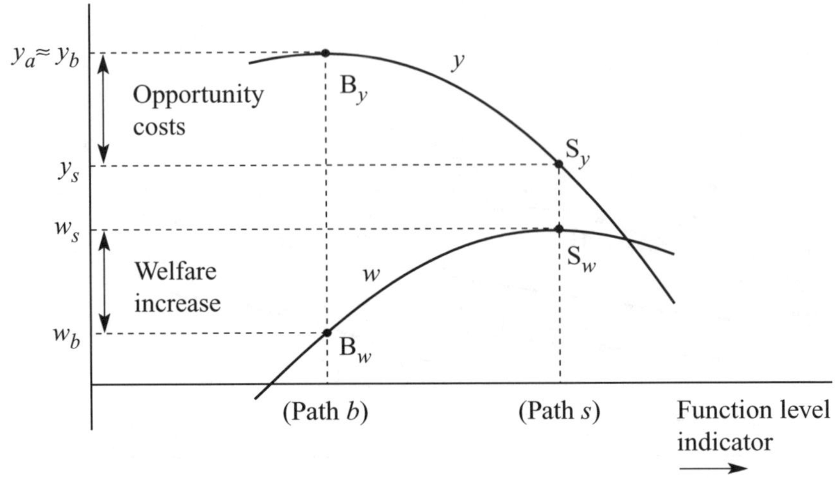

Figure 2.4 *Net national income (y) and the welfare indicator (w) in an (historical) year of investigation on the blocked optimal path (b) and the unfeasible unblocked path (s); y_a is the observed standard national income in that year. The points B_y, B_w, S_y and S_w correspond to those in Figure 2.3*

available in that year, required to reach *s* from *b* outright in that same year. The consequence of the assumption of blockages being overcome from the year of investigation onwards is that technology on path *s* in the year of investigation must be the same as on path *b* in that year.

In theory, the environmental stocks at each point on path *s* are the result of welfare maximization, as mentioned above. In practice, standards are derived or set for these stocks and related pressure standards are derived; the measures are selected on the basis of cost minimization; see Section 5.4.

As just stated, welfare on path *s* is greater than on any other path. Figure 2.4 illustrates this point. The welfare indicator *v* and its monetary approximation *w* have the properties discussed in Section 6.2. Under the simplifying assumptions discussed there, the monetary welfare measure *w* is again equal to national income on the path, plus terms due to the immediate use of environmental functions in the year of investigation, plus terms due to their use in the future. The environmental terms take the form of the modelled environmental stocks and their rates of change, respectively, both valued at the model's marginal prices, analogous to market prices, plus the costs of elimination and restoration measures, to the extent that these directly increase environmental function levels. The costs are a negative term of course. On the unblocked path *s*, the total term for future use of the environment, expressed in the rates of change of environmental stocks, is greater than on the blocked path *b*, while the total term for immediate use is probably of the same order of magnitude on both paths. Future use of the environment gains in importance if stronger preferences for the environment are assumed. On path *s*, the welfare indicators *v* and *w* are dominated by future use of the environment; this group of terms is related to the elimination costs. If these costs decrease with time, through technological progress, for example, *both* the welfare indicators *and* national income increase, and vice versa. Comparing paths in any one year, however, for instance in the year of investigation, shows that national income decreases while welfare increases, and vice versa (Figure 2.4). This can be explained using the terms of the monetary welfare measure, as was done in Section 6.2.

Note that the time axis in Figure 2.3 might be a bit difficult to grasp. What is primarily relevant is the welfare evaluation by the current generation at the year of investigation. Here we see the jump increase in welfare (from point B to point S) when the infeasible leap to sustainability is made. The time axis shows a feasible evolution towards sustainability in the course of time, indicating a step-by-step decrease in national income accompanied by a step-by-step increase of welfare as the sustainable situation is approached. At each moment in time, welfare of course depends upon the complete 'future' development following that moment. The time axis of the graph is useful to show that the choice for the SNI is consistent over time. It may be repeated that some preference schemes could show a drop in welfare if the switch is made, but the assumed preferences underlying the SNI lead to a rise.

6.4.1 Welfare measure versus green national income

Unfortunately, the simplifying assumptions under which the welfare indicators behave so obligingly do not always apply. More important, the comprehensive dynamic environmental economic model required to perform a sufficiently realistic calculation is so complex that we are obliged to use a set of coordinated models instead of one comprehensive model, which, strictly speaking, makes welfare maximization impossible (see Section 5.4.) Consequently, standards for function levels cannot be obtained from the optimum but have to be approximated; see Section 5.4. Although it is, in principle, feasible to subsequently calculate the monetary welfare indicator *w* using the solution of this model system, this is still a complex task, while it probably cannot be checked whether the presented indicator really represents the maximum for the calculated path.

Another problem stems from our goal, which is to include the environment in national income in order to make this a more complete welfare indicator and one that can be compared with standard national income. This indicator consists of standard national income plus appropriate environmental terms. Comparing the values of this indicator on the blocked

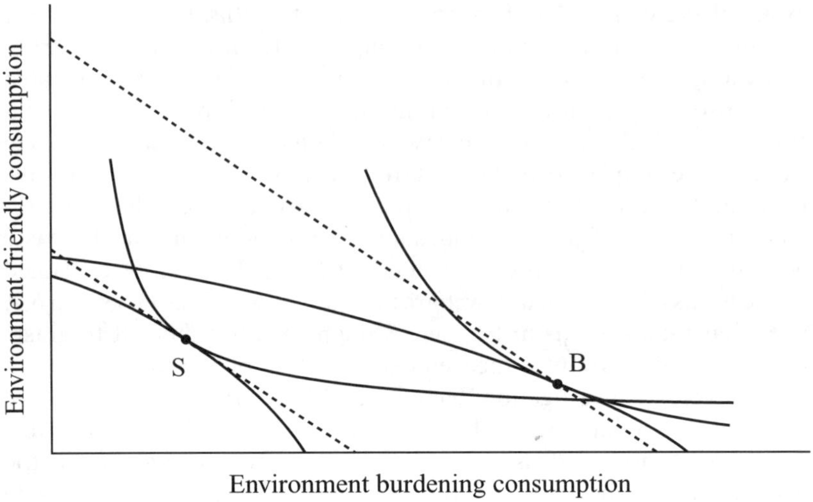

Figure 2.5 *The optima B and S discussed in the text as calculated by an environmental economic model under the assumptions made on preferences and blockages. In point B, approximating the actual situation in the study year, blockages prevent key preferences for the environment from being expressed. In S, these blockages are overcome. The (convex) indifference curves through these optima reflect the different forms of the welfare functional under the respective conditions. Each optimum lies on a different boundary of production possibilities (concave lines), determined by the availability levels of environmental functions. The dashed lines indicate the levels of consumption at both optima, using the prices at the optimum with blockages overcome (point S); these levels represent the standard national income (through point B) and the green or sustainable national income (through point S). Lines of constant income through both optima using prices of the optimum with blockages in effect (point B) are not drawn*

path *b* (w_b) and the unfeasible unblocked path *s* (w_s) is obviously not the same thing as comparing national income on both paths. Standard national income on the actual path *a* (y_a) or its modelled approximation on path *b* (y_b) can best be compared with national income on path *s* (y_s), that is with the green national income corresponding with the assumed preferences. Green national income y_s is lower than standard national income y_b, because of the opportunity costs of the required measures (see Figure 2.5). Welfare increases as a result of the 'leap' from path *b* to path *s*. Comparing the two paths *b* and *s* at any given time, a decrease in national income is found to be accompanied by an increase in the welfare indicator. The comparison shows the gap between the two paths in terms of the opportunity costs; this is a very important measure in practice, which is relatively easy to explain. This discrepancy (decrease versus increase) does not exist on the optimal path, because there the mix of environmental functions and produced goods is optimal.

These considerations lead us to the conclusion that the calculation of a green national income as proposed by Hueting (1974a) and Hueting et al. (1992, 1995a, 1995b) is the best practicable approach for our present purpose.

6.4.2 Prices with and without measures

The theory discussed above makes clear that the welfare indicators v and w for path b or s at a given instant in time are expressed in shadow prices valid for the same path and the same instant (see Section 6.1). In other words, v_s and w_s on the 'indicator path' s are expressed in the shadow prices arising *after* implementation of what were referred to in Section 5.1 as elimination and compensation measures and subsumed under the headings technical, shift, shrink and population. Above, however, the welfare indicators v_s and w_s were abandoned in favour of green national income, that is national income on the unfeasible unblocked path s (y_s). In comparing (approximated standard) national income on the blocked path b (y_b) and (green) national income on path s (y_s) in the year of investigation, the comparison must be between points B and S in Figure 2.5.

Bearing in mind the close relation between the welfare indicator and national income, there are now grounds for concluding that this comparison of real income should be done on the basis of the prices arising *after* implementation of the measures (point S in Figure 2.5). The prices resulting after internalization of the costs of the measures (including levies) reflect the relative importance of the environmental functions better than the prices in the actual situation on path b: the 'new' price ratios are those on the sustainable path s. Shifts to more environmentally friendly production, particularly, are weighted more appropriately in this way, provided the model used computes all relevant production shifts.

This point can be elucidated as follows. It follows from Hueting (1981) and Hueting et al. (1992) that the bulk of national income growth is generated by industries that cause the greatest losses of environmental functions, both in production and in consumption. The increase in productivity in these industries, measured in terms of goods produced, is much greater than elsewhere in the economy, so the real prices of these products decrease strongly (see Section 2.5) and, with them, the price ratio between environmentally burdening and less burdening products. As a result, any shift to environmentally friendly products has a negative impact on the volume of national income (Hueting et al. 1992). This impact can be approximated by weighting using the (new) prices on path s, in which the costs of function restoration are internalized; as a result, the real prices of environmentally burdening products increase, as does the price ratio between environmentally burdening and friendly products. The latter price ratios reflect the situation on the sustainable path better than the price ratios on the actual

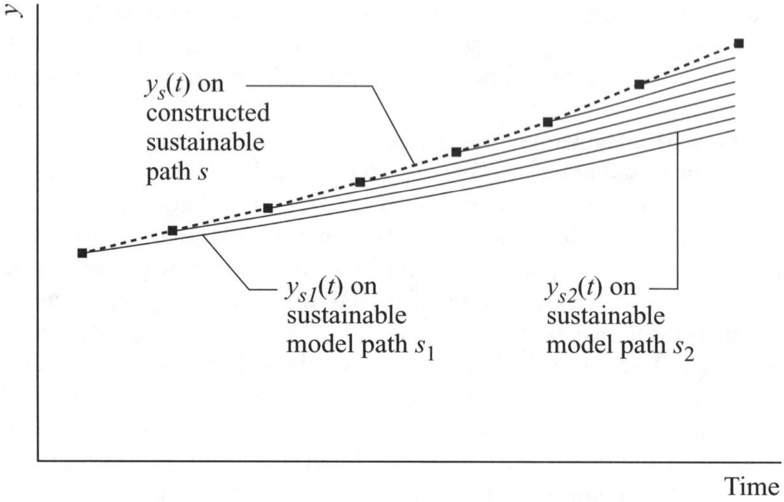

Figure 2.6 *Construction of the unfeasible sustainable paths and the corresponding sustainable national income y_s. In the calculation of the sustainable national income according to Hueting, technological progress is ex ante assumed zero on each model path. Consequently national income on these paths $y_{s1}(t)$, $y_{s2}(t)$ and so on are constant and their graphs are horizontal lines. National income on the ex post constructed sustainable path s, however, may still rise due to technological progress*

path. This clarifies and improves the original concept of calculating the cost involved in production shifts.

6.5 Strong and Perfectly Expressed Preferences for the Environment; Feasible Optimum

As indicated in Section 6.4, adaptation of the modelled stocks in production, consumption, social and environmental processes to 'removal' of the blockages may take a long time. From this perspective, large instantaneous changes in these stocks are unfeasible. If this restriction is respected, welfare maximization results in a feasible unblocked path *f*, which starts in the actual situation as observed in the year of investigation. In that year the stock variables in the environmental and the production and consumption parts of the model have the same values on path *f* as on the blocked path *b*, and consequently approximately the same values as in reality. The first part of the feasible unblocked path *f* is a *transition* phase, in which measures are being implemented, environmental functions are recovering, national income is falling and welfare is rising. This transition is followed by a more stable phase in which these variables are more or less consolidated; in this phase the path comes to approximate the unfeasible path *s*, which obviously becomes feasible by that time. In Figure 2.3, path *f* is assumed to approach path *s* asymptotically.

The feasible unblocked path is included in Figure 2.3 for clarification because it is a vital element of understanding the indicator, especially when the indicator is presented to the public. Calculation of the feasible unblocked path is obviously not part of our research effort. Nonetheless, an indication of how such a path can be constructed is given in de Boer (1999) for the case of global warming. The standard is illustrated by comparing it with a feasible unblocked emission path. A dynamic model of the factors blocking preferences is not available, and so these blockages are assumed to be overcome outright in the year of investigation. The storage of carbon and heat in the oceans enables the feasible greenhouse gases emission path to lag centuries behind without causing losses of function that would otherwise prevent the long-term, optimal, stable emission value from being reached.

6.6 Strong and Perfectly Expressed Preferences for Sustainability; Absolute Optimum; SNI

This is a special case of that discussed in Section 6.4. Thus, we again assume that the blockages on preferences are overcome outright and that the measures required to reach the preferred path *s* are all implemented at once in the year of investigation, in an unfeasible 'leap', so to speak. In this case, though, we assume absolute preferences for sustainability, which we define loosely as the minimum availability of *vital environmental functions* that can be sustained forever in the future, either at a *constant* or at an *ever-increasing* level. In theory 'the future' is infinite, but in practice we limit it to the time span in which the influence of geophysical processes on the environment is unlikely to exceed human influence, say several millennia or longer. Moreover, we proceed from the special form of the definition that is limited to minimum *constant* levels of environmental functions; these represent our 'sustainable levels'. By 'absolute preferences for sustainability' we mean that people's preferences for the sustained availability of environmental functions far exceed their preferences for the availability of consumption goods or environmental functions in the year of investigation, or in any other isolated year.

The theory discussed in the previous sections can be applied to the problem of sustainability. See, among others, Stiglitz (1974), Dasgupta and Heal (1974, 1979), Hartwick (1977, 1978), Pezzey (1994) and Gerlagh (1999); Zeelenberg et al. (1997) provide a short overview. This theory indicates that an absolute preference for sustained availability of environmental functions implies sustained availability of consumption goods. The reverse statement, that an absolute preference for sustained availability of consumption goods implies sustained availability of functions, can probably be proven, because production is impossible in the absence of environmental functions. Although these two statements look very similar, they reflect the fact that sustainability can be defined in several ways, leading in turn to differences in the ensuing paths *s*. In every definition of sustainability, a distinct group of variables directly influencing welfare or directly related to welfare is kept constant forever: the welfare indicators *v* or *w*, environmental function levels, levels of actual use of the environment, flows of consumption goods, aggregate consumption, or net national income. Sustaining one of these variables at a maximally attainable level is at the expense of the other variables, although these are sustained as well. This trade-off also occurs if a group of variables, such as function levels, use levels or consumption flows, are sustained at maximally attainable levels. This requires multi-objective optimization, leading to a set of possible outcomes (paths). However, welfare maximization under assumed absolute preferences for sustained instantaneous welfare, or for sustained aggregate consumption, or for sustained national income, leads to a unique and different result each time, namely a maximum feasible sustainable level of, respectively, instantaneous welfare, aggregate consumption, or national income. The model solution is a different *sustainable path* (*s* again) for each of these cases. The function levels remain constant on each sustainable path, despite the fact that this was not explicitly assumed as the goal of the preferences, but these levels are in general different for each sustainable path. All model variables on such a sustainable path remain constant, it should be added, with the notable exception of stocks and extractions of non-renewable resources. Their function levels are sustained as well, however; see Section 7.

Sustainable function levels can therefore be found in theory; they follow from the process of welfare maximization in a comprehensive environmental economic model, under the assumption of strong preferences for sustainability. By adopting a specific definition of sustainability, we arrive at unique function levels. We define sustainability as the solution (path) of the environmental-economic model in which national income is maximal and is sustained at that level forever, under constant technology, employment and population. This national income is the SNI as defined in Section 1.2, point 1 under 'Consequences of the Principles'. The model then should indeed show that the functions are sustained above or at the minimal levels that nature can support (see Section 1.2, point 5 under 'Consequences of the Principles'). The goal, consistently, is to ensure that *possible* (potential) future uses of the environment are not lost. Future generations can then decide for themselves whether they wish to step up their level of usage. This approach thus involves minimum sacrifice (in terms of income, that is consumed goods) for the present generation.

In practice, as explained in Section 5.4, the comprehensive environmental-economic model required to compute maximum welfare and the corresponding sustainable function levels is far too complex to perform such optimization, even more so because a sustainable optimal path is not only an optimum but a limit case as well. Studies using simple environmental economic models that do allow for such optimization (Pezzey, 1994; Gerlagh, 1999) give us the following grounds for a simpler – and therefore feasible – one-way computation procedure. First, the sustainable levels of use of environmental functions may be interpreted as the regeneration capacities of nature for these types of use. Second, in theory these sustainable levels constitute the sustainability standards to be applied in the practical calculation using linked models (Section 5.4). Third, no attempt has yet been made to derive realistic standards from simple environmental-economic models, but if one were to do so, these standards would probably turn out to allow higher activity levels (and therefore a higher SNI) than the standards we establish in our practical approach. The difference is due to the use of optimization in the simple models on the one hand and the application of the precautionary principle, some additional plausible assumptions and the more detailed environmental models of the practical approach, on the other. This approach is explained in Section 7.

Within the theory discussed up to now, it appears to be possible to find a sustainable path at a low enough but still positive rate of technological progress: vital environmental functions are maintained and (real) production and consumption increase without ever collapsing. Generally, technology on the sustainable path s progresses more slowly than on the blocked path b. For each year of investigation an optimal sustainable path is found ($s_1, s_2, \ldots, s_n$), starting in that year with technology equal to that on the unblocked path b, but with diverging technology in all later years. Only the level of y_s at the starting point of each path is taken as 'SNI' for the respective year of investigation. For later years of investigation, new sustainable paths with ever-higher levels of y_s at their starting points will most probably be found, as a result of technological progress. Connecting the starting points of the sustainable paths *ex post* yields the realized development of the sustainable national income or 'SNI' (as well as the realized developments of the other model variables under sustainability). This process is elucidated in Figure 2.6.

This procedure may be theoretically sufficient to arrive at a sustainable income, but it involves the risk of the theory proving erroneous, in that the projected technological progress needed to preserve the environmental functions may in the long run not be realized and a collapse may occur at some time in the future. Compare y_b with y_s in Figure 2.3. While some of the authors mentioned in this section accept this risk or just acknowledge it without taking the consequences, others, like the present authors, deem the risk too high. We therefore consider it appropriate to calculate the sustainable national income for each year of investigation (n) under the assumption that technological progress on the corresponding sustainable path (s_n) is *zero* (except for non-renewable resources; see Section 7). As before, connecting the starting points of the sustainable paths s_n *ex post* yields the realized development of sustainable national income y_s as we advocate it (SNI according to Hueting). It may rise in the course of time, as a result of actually realized technological progress, not anticipated in the model paths $s_1, s_2, \ldots, s_n$.

6.7 Basic Assumptions for Practical Calculation of SNI

Hueting et al. (1992) give a number of basic assumptions required for practical estimation of a country's SNI. See also Verbruggen et al. (2001) elsewhere in this publication. We mention the most important of these here; some have already been discussed.

- The transition to sustainable activities is made in every country in the world simultaneously and in the same way. This prevents the transfer of burdening activities from one country to another. In the model (Verbruggen et al., Chapter 11, this volume), an approach is taken in which the sustainability costs of import and export turn out to be approximately equal, thus meeting a proposal of ours.
- Sustainability standards for environmental pressures are set for the region in which they affect functions, that is national, regional or global. A given country's contribution to meeting a regional or global standard is proportional to its contribution to regional or global pressure.
- Transition costs are not taken into account. The SNI is associated with the calculated sustainable path, which runs at a certain distance from the current path and does therefore not involve any *transition* to the sustainable path. Therefore the costs of destruction of existing capital goods and the formation of new capital goods, for instance, are not included in the SNI. However, the costs of eliminating effects that have accumulated in a long period, such as soil pollution, *are* included as costs, likewise distributed over a long sanitation period.
- The employment rate is kept constant. Normally environmentally friendly producing and consuming requires more labour, because attaining a given end, for example raising crops or bridging a

distance, requires with environmental protection much more labour than without (see 'Three myths', Chapter 3, this volume). However, just now we keep constant all variables that are not relevant for the main issue.

- Technology is kept constant, except where technological progress is necessary to sustain environmental functions, that is in the development of substitutes for non-renewable resources (see Sections 6.6 and 7).

7 SUSTAINABILITY STANDARDS

As we saw in Section 5.4 as well as Section 6.6, assumptions regarding preferences for the availability of environmental functions allow for a one-way approach involving the application of standards. Similarly, assumed absolute preferences for sustained availability of functions can take the form of sustainability standards for these functions. The demand curve of Figure 2.1 is then replaced by a vertical line; see Figure 2.7.

Under such preferences for sustainability, the optimal function levels are sustained forever and the green national income to be calculated is turned into the (maximally attainable, *ad infinitum*) sustainable national income. As it is difficult to estimate or even quantify these levels, it is assumed that their existence is guaranteed by two slightly more practical conditions, which must both be satisfied in the present and in the future. The first is that the extinction of biological species at the global level may not be accelerated by human influence; see below. This condition puts certain demands on the state (quality) of the environment. The second condition is that any changes in the state of the environment may have only a minor, acceptable impact on human health. Health is generally described in the modern literature as a state of well-being extending beyond the mere absence of illness. Nonetheless, most 'maximum acceptable risk' levels in force for environmental state variables are construed with the aim of preventing illness. Be this as it may, both the species condition and the human health condition impose bounds on the acceptable variation in the state of the environment, however imprecise. Generally, the limits set for different environmental problems have to be tuned to each other in order to avoid combinatorial (synergetic) effects, leading to negligible risk levels instead of maximum acceptable risk levels (Beek, 1995). From these limit values, *sustainability standards* for the various forms of environmental pressure can then be derived as discussed above, that is with the aid of environmental models, and subsequently the sustainable national income can be calculated by imposing these standards on the economic activity model (see Section 5).

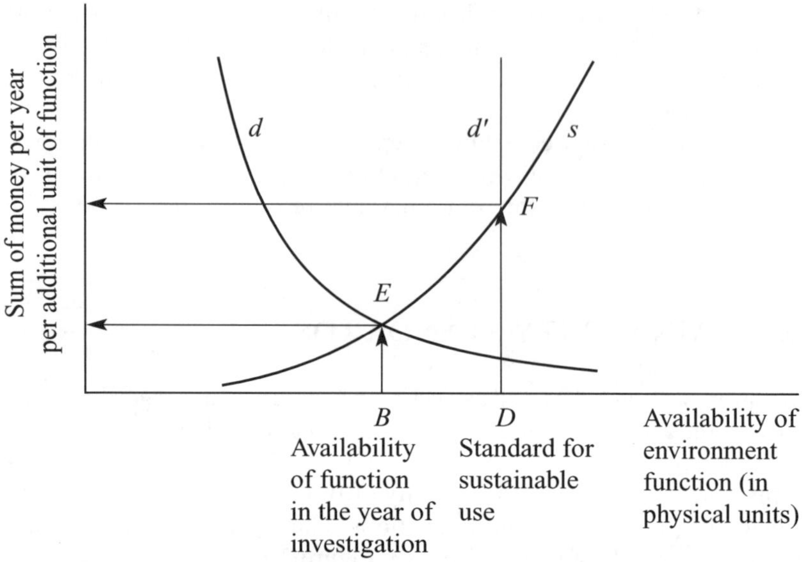

Figure 2.7 *Translation of costs in physical units into costs in monetary units:* s*=supply curve or marginal elimination cost curve; d=incomplete demand curve or marginal benefit curve based on individual preferences (revealed from expenditures on compensation of functions, and so on; d' ='demand curve' based on assumed preferences for sustainability; BD=distance that must be bridged in order to arrive at sustainable use of environmental functions; area BEFD=total costs of the loss functions, expressed in money; the arrows indicate the way via which the loss of environmental functions recorded in physical units is translated into monetary units. The availability of the function (B) does not need to coincide with the level following from intersection point (E)*

Figure 2.8 presents an overview of the practical calculation procedure used at present.

We hold that sustainability standards can be scientifically established. See Hueting et al. (1992) and Hueting and Reijnders (1998) for several examples and Bosch (1994), de Boer and Bosch (1995) and Dellink and Van der Woerd (1997) for a number of quantified standards. Thus sustainability, defined as the situation in which vital environmental functions remain available *ad infinitum*, is an objective concept, to the extent that the natural sciences can be deemed objective (Hueting and Reijnders, 1998). As Costanza and Patten (1995) and Hueting and Reijnders (1998) have argued, in the context of the interaction between human activity (loosely referred to as 'the economy') and the environment, criteria for sustainability are to be regarded as assumptions. Scientifically, therefore, it can only be established *ex post* whether the measures taken to fulfil these criteria, or standards, were indeed adequate.

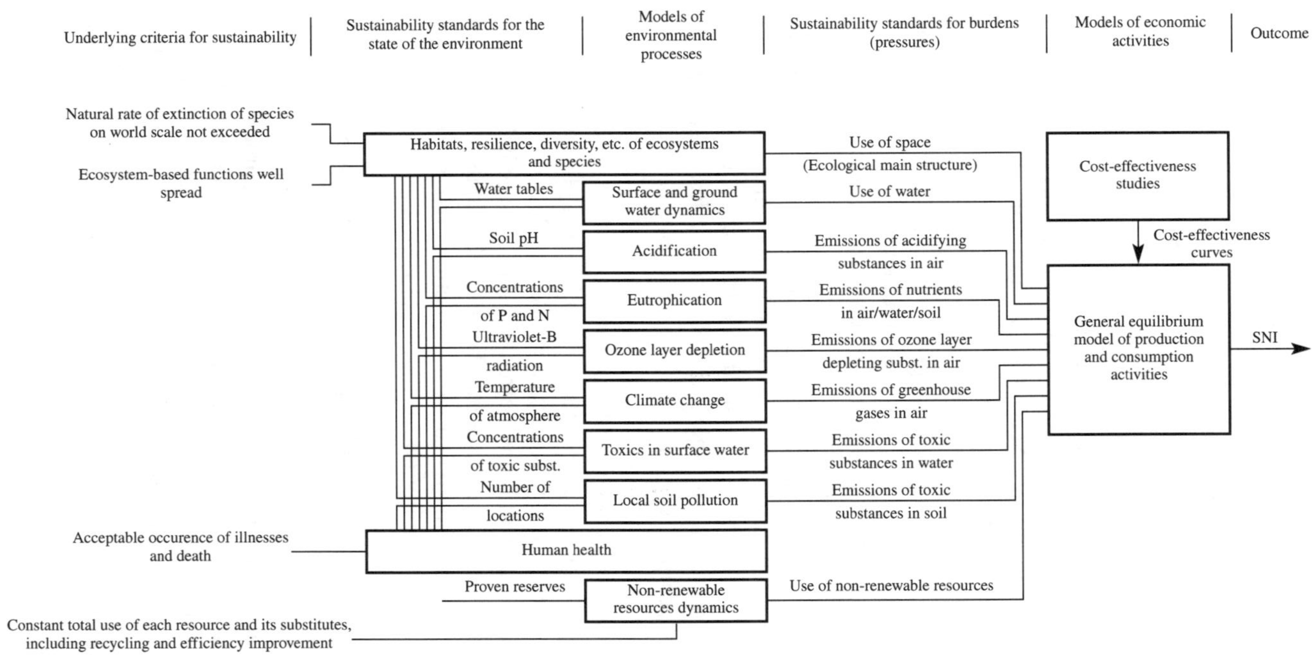

Figure 2.8 *Main steps in the calculation of the SNI (simplified). Blocks represent models of (sets of) processes, lines represent (sets of) variables. Calculation order is from left to right, unless arrows indicate otherwise. Crossover effects between environmental problem areas (themes) are not shown*

As argued earlier, the availability of environmental functions depends on the quality, quantity and spatial capacity of the environment (or physical surroundings or environmental capital), which is after all the vehicle or carrier of these functions. Environmental functions remain available for as long as this environmental capital (in a broad sense, see pp. 28–9) remains intact. Sustainability standards can thus relate to the qualitative, quantitative and spatial aspects of the physical surroundings, and environmental models then used to translate these standards into standards for human activities: emission or withdrawal of substances, heat, species, and so on into or from the environment (see Section 4), for example, or land use, or use of raw materials such as crude oil or copper. State variables are related to pressure variables using environmental models. The elimination measures mentioned in Section 5.1 reduce the pressure variables to the permitted or sustainable level of environmental burdening. In doing so, a distinction is made between renewable and essentially non-renewable (that is very slowly forming) resources.

Sustainability aims to maintain the functions of environmental capital provided by nature (in a broad sense, see pp. 28–9). As rightly pointed out by Goodland, this definition of sustainability goes beyond 'sustainable yield', a notion that is current in fishery and forestry circles. Sustainability applies to aggregate natural capital, not just to a few species of fish or timber trees (Goodland, 1995). In the case of forestry, for instance, it includes biodiversity, ecosystem integrity, water source and water moderation values and contributions to geochemical cycles (including the carbon cycle) and climate. Apart from this, a level can be established above which a (plant or animal) species can be harvested sustainably (see below). Thus there is obviously a level, defined as a number of individuals of a species, below which the species is threatened with extinction; arriving below that level is unsustainable, remaining above that level is sustainable. Together with the condition that harvesting a species should not disrupt the ecosystem of which it forms a part (see Odum, 1971), this yields the sustainability standard for the species.

In establishing sustainability standards, we have taken as the basic point of departure the natural regeneration capacity of the environment: as long as this remains intact, environmental functions will remain available. The following examples illustrate how this quantity and the acceptable, that is sustainable burden can be established. It can, for instance, be established that the rate of erosion of topsoil may not exceed the rate of formation of such soil due to weathering. Similar consumption standards can be set for other natural resources. With respect to how sustainability relates to species, then, the standard holds that the rate of human-induced extinction should not exceed the rate at which new species come into existence. This boils down to preserving all the species still alive today, for it is assumed that during the past several thousand years conditions have been such that, leaving aside drastic human intervention for the moment, the number of new species must certainly have at least equalled the number of species lost to extinction (Raup, 1986; Hawksworth, 1995). However, in contrast to the situation prior to human intervention, the rate at which natural species are becoming extinct is today at least a factor 10000 higher than the rate at which new species are evolving (Raup, 1986). In the absence of drastic human intervention, the quantity and quality of renewable natural resources such as groundwater or biomass (including wood) generally show a substantial degree of constancy. In the absence of human intervention, environmental capital is thus characterized by a substantial degree of constancy or even increase.

With regard to pollution, too, criteria can be established. Acid precipitation, for example, should not exceed the neutralizing capacity of the soil. Likewise, there should be no exportation of risks to future generations through pollution of groundwater that is to serve as a source of drinking water for those generations. In many cases, the accompanying environmental burden can be determined with great accuracy. There is a wealth of data on the rate at which new fertile soil is naturally formed and on the neutralizing capacity of natural soils, and these data enable a precise indication to be given of the admissible environmental burden due to erosion and acid rain (Reijnders, 1996). In other cases we have insufficient knowledge to make firm pronouncements. For example, at present we can do no more than give a rough indication of the conditions under which plant and animal species are able to survive (Hawksworth, 1995; de Boer, 1979). On the basis of the best available global circulation models it can be calculated that worldwide emissions of carbon dioxide must be reduced drastically to achieve stabilization of the global warming process, but an exact percentage cannot be given (de Boer, 1996). Similarly, shortcomings in our toxicological knowledge mean that we cannot fully analyse the risks associated with polluted groundwater. However, this does not detract from the fact that improved scientific knowledge can lead to a more precise establishment of standards for sustainability.

All in all, it is feasible to establish scientifically the environmental burden that is 'admissible' on the basis of the objective of sustainability. Hueting and Reijnders (1999) describe how the precautionary principle can be employed if there are uncertainties and inadequate knowledge in the context of sustainability.

In the case of very slowly forming natural resources such as crude oil and copper, which are to all intents and purposes non-renewable, 'regeneration' can take three forms: efficiency improvements, recycling and, over the longer term, substitution of one form of environmental capital by another that can provide the same functions. Familiar examples of substitution include solar power and glass fibre for crude oil and copper wire, respectively.

This can be expressed as follows in a numerical value. Sustainability of non-renewable natural resources means that in a given period only as much may be withdrawn from the stock as substitutes for the resource are expected to be developed in the long run as well as new potential for recycling and conserving the resource (improvement of efficiency). In this way the functions of a resource available in the year of investigation are maintained at the same levels in the future. In practice this can be worked out by, for instance, taking from a period in the past the quantity of possible uses (for example heating, transportation, and so on expressed in effective energy) that has become available through efficiency improvement, substitution and recycling and then assuming that the relative rates of efficiency improvement, substitution and recycling will be the same in the future.[6] There follows from this a maximum permissible annual rate of extraction that can be used as a sustainability standard. In a formula: $e(t_0) \leq r(t_0).S(t_0)$, in which $e(t_0)$ is the extraction rate in year t_0, $r(t_0)$ the relative rate (or rate coefficient) of reduction of consumption of the resource (resulting from substitution, and so on) at *a constant level of activities*, and $S(t_0)$ the stock in year t_0 (Tinbergen, 1990).

This formula is applied at the global level. Standards for individual countries can be subsequently derived by applying the general rule, given in Section 6, that a country's share in meeting the global standard should be equal to its share in total extraction.

In practice, the factor $r(t_0)$ is determined mainly by efficiency improvements, as substitution and recycling have still made only a very minor contribution in recent years. The aforementioned assumption that the line recording use of the resource in the past can be continued into the future with, basically, a constant annual rate of efficiency improvement, implies that as time progresses the same material output can be achieved at a fraction of current resource use. In a study on the development of energy efficiency, Tinbergen (1990) found a practical value of 1.67 per cent for this improvement rate. From this it follows that in 60 years' time the *present level of production* can be achieved with 37 per cent and in 315 years' time with 0.5 per cent of current fossil fuel consumption: $S(315) = (1-0.0167)^{315} \times S(0) = 0.005 \times S(0)$. Such enormous efficiency improvements (63 per cent and 99.5 per cent, respectively) seem rather unlikely. In the context of sustainability, 315 years is a very short time. The probability that humankind will sooner or later have to manage without the functions of the non-renewable natural resources, if no substitutes are found, is comparable to the certainty that humankind will sooner or later have to manage without the functions of the soil in those areas where the degree of erosion is higher than the rate of soil formation.

Because efficiency improvements alone are thus inadequate to achieve sustainability, it has been proposed that, in the calculation of SNI, additional measures must be taken for the development of substitutes (Tinbergen and Hueting, 1991). We here adopt this proposal, applying the following procedure. For each resource, statistical data are used to establish the rate at which substitution (the ultimate solution) has taken place over the past 10 to 20 years and the annual cost this has entailed. It is then calculated how long it would take, at this rate, to completely replace the resource (1). Next, it is calculated how long it will take for the resource to be depleted, at the *current* level of production (2). Then (1) divided by (2) yields a rough approximation of the required 'acceleration factor' for the development of substitutes in time for them to replace the functions of the resource when it is depleted. This factor multiplied by the statistically established annual cost of substitute development yields the sum that needs to be reserved for this purpose.

The figures thus found can be no more than rough estimates, of course. In the context of non-renewable natural resources, though, this is an approach that does justice to the principle of sustainability, which is the point of departure of our estimates. Our approach would be comparable with that of Solow (1974), Hartwick (1977, 1978) and others, if the latter were to exclude unfeasible substitution of renewable resources by other resources and by capital (see below), that is if they were to abandon their faith in the extreme areas of formal production functions.

When using the concept of environmental function, the only thing that matters in the context of sustainability is that vital functions remain available. What does the conservation of vital functions imply for the distinction between renewable and non-renewable resources and for the distinction between strong and weak sustainability?

As for renewable resources, functions remain available as long as their regenerative capacity remains intact. Regeneration in relation to current use of 'non-renewable' resources such as crude oil and copper that are formed by slow geological processes is close to zero. 'Regeneration' then takes the form of efficiency improvement, recycling and, in the final instance, developing substitutes. The possibilities for this are hopeful (Reijnders, 1996; Brown et al., 1998). So, economically speaking, there seems to be no essential difference between the two types of resource: sustainability is attained if their functions remain available.

Advocates of 'weak sustainability' take the line that all elements of the environment can ultimately be substituted by man-made alternatives, implying that restoration of lost elements can be postponed in anticipation of cheaper substitutes provided by future technologies. However, the life support systems (see note 2) of our planet, on which a number of vital functions depend, are not substitutable at all (Lovelock, 1979; Roberts, 1988; Reijnders, 1996). The same holds for most of the functions of natural ecosystems, especially in the long term (see, for example, the remark on the function of 'gene pool' in Section 4). Consequently, there can be no such thing as 'weak sustainability' for the functions of these systems.

Advocates of 'strong sustainability' hold it to be impossible for humanity to substitute many of the elements of the natural environment. In its strictest form, however, this implies that stocks of non-renewable resources should remain fully intact, an unrealistic aim, as already discussed. Consequently, strong sustainability for non-renewable resources seems to be impossible.

In conclusion, there seems to be only one kind of sustainability, whereby non-renewable resources must gradually be substituted by other elements of our physical surroundings in order to guarantee the availability of functions, and substitution of a large class of renewable resources is impossible, particularly life support systems, including ecosystems.

The question is often asked whether sustainability standards should be applied locally or globally. This depends on the scale at which the functions in question should be substituted. For instance, preservation of the function 'soil for growing crops' requires local application of the standard for erosion (the erosion rate may not exceed the soil formation rate; see above), because exceeding the standard at one place cannot be compensated by remaining under this standard elsewhere. Crude oil, on the other hand, is a global resource, so in this case the sustainability standard, effectuated through efficiency improvement and substitute development, should be applied worldwide.

8 CONCLUSIONS

1. The SNI according to Hueting is the maximum net income which can be sustained on a geological time scale, with future technological progress assumed only in the development of substitutes for non-renewable resources, where such substitution is indispensable for sustaining environmental functions, in turn essential for sustaining income. This can only be realized if a vast majority of the subjects have an absolute preference for sustainability. The concept is theoretically sound as well as operational, although it involves considerable statistical effort. Its theory is in line with so-called general growth theory.

2. The pronounced quantitative differences between the SNI according to Hueting and other green national incomes can be traced back largely to different views *vis-à-vis* the position of the optimal path of the economy and thus to different assumptions regarding the strength of preferences for the environment and the associated question of recognition, or otherwise, of the blockages referred to in Section 5.2. Authors such as Repetto et al. (1989, 1991) and Mäler (1991) assume that preferences for the environment are fully expressed in actual expenditures on compensation for and elimination of loss of function and in the financial damages incurred as a result of such loss. According to these authors, then, society is on the optimal path and there are no blockages on preferences for the environment. The standard national income is then corrected for the aforementioned costs, to the extent that these are actually incurred by government and private households. By applying this correction, a better measure is obtained of changes in the volume of scarce goods, being one of the factors influencing welfare. Others, such as Stiglitz (1974), Hartwick (1977, 1978), Asheim (1994), Pezzey (1994) and Pezzey and Withagen (1995) recognize that the optimal path is a sustainable path if strong preferences for sustainability are assumed. Comparison of the sustainable national income associated with this path with the standard national income associated with the actual path is hampered by the fact that the paths are calculated using different welfare functions, however. We therefore consider it more logical to consistently assume preferences for the environment to be strong enough for the optimal path to be sustainable. In our perspective, the existence of the suboptimal path in the real world is explained by the blockages preventing these preferences from being expressed; this in contrast with the sustainable path, where these blockages have been overcome. The pronounced differences in outcome are thus explained mainly by major differences in assumptions regarding preferences for the environment, with other theorists either denying the existence of blockages or, if blockages are indeed recognized, assuming far weaker preferences for the environment than we do. In our interpretation, the latter holds *inter alia* for El Serafy (1989, 1995). Under the assumption of strong preferences for sustainability, application of the theory of such authors as Stiglitz, Hartwick, Pezzey, Asheim and Withagen will yield an SNI of similar magnitude as the SNI according to Hueting.
3. If the underlying assumptions are rendered explicit, environmental valuation and green accounting can yield valuable and comprehensible information. If they are left undeclared, these disciplines will become discredited because of the incomprehensibly wide range of quantitative outcomes they yield.

NOTES

1. In calculating the SNI, often choices must be made because of existing scientific uncertainties (see Hueting and Reijnders, 1999). From both the preference side and the cost side, a whole spectrum of outcomes can result, from which a choice must be made for the purpose of presentation.
2. Life support systems are understood as the processes that maintain the conditions necessary for life on earth. This comes down to maintaining equilibria within narrow margins. The processes may be of a biological or physico-chemical nature, or a combination thereof. Examples of biological processes include the carbon and nutrient cycles, involving the extraction of such substances as carbon dioxide, water and minerals from the abiotic environment during biomass creation, and the return of these substances to the abiotic environment during biomass decomposition. Examples of physico-chemical processes include the water cycle and regulation of the thickness of the stratospheric ozone layer. As the examples show, there is interaction between the processes, with the possibility of equilibrium being disturbed. The water cycle, for example, may be disturbed by large-scale deforestation.
3. Another, frequently employed definition of green national income is the monetary welfare measure corresponding with the assumed preferences and is related to the green national income as we define it. We shall return to this point later.
4. From a systems theory point of view, personal or social welfare is 'observable' in most models, that is, it can be reconstructed from the model's input and output variables, like an individual's or society's actions, respectively. Therefore, 'observable' welfare can also be reconstructed from data on these variables. In reality, data are only available for actually measured (observed) environmental economic development and therefore only allow reconstruction of the small section of the welfare 'functional' in the neighbourhood of the data. The result of this 'functional' is still an ordinal quantity, reflecting the fact that it cannot be directly measured.
5. The unblocked path can be thought of as a rough approximation of the course economic development would have hypothetically taken if society had overcome its blocked preferences at the (likewise hypothetical) moment in the past when the environmental functions grew scarce, with technological development following the actual historical course, which is hypothetical indeed.
6. This involves an assumption about technological progress in the fields of substitutes and recycling. This exception to the point of departure that the estimation should be based on the technology that is operational in the year of investigation, or shortly thereafter, is the only way to arrive at a sustainability standard for non-renewable resources. The only other option, to pass on stocks untouched to future generations, is unfeasible and also makes no sense, because this would then have to be carried through *ad infinitum*.

REFERENCES

Asheim, G. (1994), 'Net national product as an indicator for sustainability', *Scandinavian Journal of Economics*, 96, 257–65.

Bateman, I.J. and R.K. Turner (1992), *Evaluation of the environment: the contingent valuation method*, Centre for Social and Economic Research on the Global Environment, GEC Working Paper 92–18.

Beek, M. (1995), *De risico's van normen. Een overzicht van de methodiek en afgeleide (eco)toxicologische risicogrenzen ter onderbouwing van Streef-, Grens- en Interventiewaarden*, Rijkswaterstaat, Rijksinstituut voor Integraal Zoetwaterbeheer en Afvalwaterbehandeling, Lelystad, Werkdocument 95.097X.

Boer, B. de (1996), 'Calculation of sustainable national income in the

Netherlands: some results', paper prepared for the workshop *Valuation Methods for Green National Accounting: a Practical Guide*, organized by The World Bank, UN Statistical Office and Ecological Economics, Washington, DC, March 20–22.

Boer, B. de (1999), 'Sustainability standards', in H. Verbruggen (ed.), *Interim Report on Calculations of a Sustainable National Income according to Hueting's Methodology*, Institute for Environmental Studies, Vrije Universiteit, Amsterdam.

Boer, B. de, M. de Haan and M. Voogt (1994), 'What would net domestic product have been in an environmentally sustainable economy? Preliminary views and results', in *National Accounts and the Environment*, papers and proceedings from a Conference, London, England, 16–18 March, Statistics Canada, Ottawa, Canada.

Boer, B. de, and P.R. Bosch (1995), 'The greenhouse effect: an example of the prevention cost approach', paper prepared for the 2nd meeting of the London group on *National Accounts and the Environment*, Washington, 15–17 March.

Boer, B. de, R. Brouwer and C. Zeelenberg (1995), *Milieu en Nationaal Product in de Economische Groeitheorie*, Centraal Bureau voor de Statistiek, Voorburg.

Boer, B. de, R. Hueting and M. de Haan (1998), 'Green accounting in The Netherlands', paper presented at the workshop *From Research to Implementation: Policy-Driven Methods for Evaluating Macro-Economic Environmental Performance (Greenstamp)* at Eurostat, Luxembourg, 28–29 September, European Commission, DG XII, Brussels.

Boer, B. de et al., forthcoming, *Theoretical and Practical Steps Towards a Sustainable National Income*, Statistics Netherlands, Voorburg, The Netherlands.

Boer, P.J. den (1979), 'Het overleven van soorten', *Intermediair* **15** (48), 7–13.

Bosch, P.R. (1994), *Energiedragers*, draft report, Statistics Netherlands, Voorburg, The Netherlands.

Brouwer, R. and M. O'Connor (1997), *Methodological problems in the calculation of environmentally adjusted national income figures*, Study for the European Commission, Directorate General XII, Contract No. EV5V-CT94-0363, Brussels, 2 volumes.

Brown, L.R., C. Flavin and H. French (1998), *State of the World 1998*, W.W. Norton, New York.

Costanza, R. and B.C. Patten (1995), 'Defining and predicting sustainability', *Ecological Economics*, (15), 193–6.

Costanza, R. *et al.* (1997), 'The value of the world's ecosystem services and natural capital', *Nature*, 387, 15 May.

Dasgupta, P.S. and G.M. Heal (1974), 'The optimal depletion of exhaustible resources', *Review of Economic Studies*, Symposium Issue, 3–28.

Dasgupta, P.S. and G.M. Heal (1979), *Economic Theory and Exhaustible Resources*, Nisbet/Cambridge University Press, Welwyn/Cambridge.

Dellink, R. and F. van der Woerd (1997), *Kosteneffectiviteit van Milieuthema's*, Instituut voor Milieuvraagstukken, Vrije Universiteit, Amsterdam.

El Serafy, S. (1989), 'The proper calculation of income from depletable natural resources', in Ahmad, Y.J., S. El Serafy and E. Lutz (eds), *Environmental Accounting for Sustainable Development*, The World Bank, Washington DC.

El Serafy, S. (1995), 'Depletion of natural resources', in W. van Dieren, (ed.), *Taking Nature into Account: A Report to the Club of Rome*, Springer-Verlag, New York.

Gerlagh, R. (1999), *The efficient and sustainable use of environmental resource systems*, Proefschrift Vrije Universiteit, Thela Thesis, Amsterdam.
Geurts, P., R. Hoevenagel and A. van der Veen (1994), *Het domein van Contingent Valuation*, Faculteit Bestuurskunde, Universiteit Twente, Enschede.
Goodland, R. (1995), 'The concept of environmental sustainability', Annual Review of Ecology and Systematics, 26, 1–24.
Groot, R.S. de (1992), *Functions of Nature: Evaluation of Nature in Environmental Planning, Management and Decision Making*, Wolters Noordhoff.
Hamilton, K. (1995), *Pollution and Pollution Abatement in the National Accounts*, CSERGE, University College London and University of East Anglia, Norwich.
Hartwick, J.M. (1977), 'Intergenerational equity and the investing of rents from exhaustible resources', *American Economic Review*, **66**, 972–4.
Hartwick, J.M. (1978), 'Investing returns from depleting renewable resource stocks and intergenerational equity', *Economics Letters*, **1**, 85–8.
Hawksworth, D.L. (ed.) (1995), *Biodiversity, Measurement and Estimation*, Chapman & Hall, London.
Hennipman, P. (1940), *Economisch Motief en Economisch Principe*, Amsterdam.
Hennipman, P. (1943), 'Nut, nuttigheid en gebruikswaarde', *De Economist*, 433–8.
Hennipman, P. (1962), 'Doeleinden en criteria', in *Theorie van de Economische Politiek*, Leiden.
Hennipman, P. (1968), 'De externe effecten in de hedendaagse welvaartstheorie', *Economisch-Statistische Berichten*, 20 March.
Hennipman, P. (1995), *Welfare Economics and the Theory of Economic Policy*, Hartnolls, Cornwall.
Hoevenagel, R. (1994a), *The Contingent Valuation Method: Scope and Validity*, Vrije Universiteit, Amsterdam.
Hoevenagel, R. (1994b), 'An assessment of the contingent valuation method', in R. Pethig (ed.), *Valuing the Environment: Methodological and Measurement Issues*, Kluwer Academic Publishers, Dordrecht.
Hoevenagel, R. (1994c), 'A comparison of economic valuation methods', in R. Pethig (ed.), *Valuing the Environment, Methodological and Measurement Issues*, Kluwer Academic Publishers, Dordrecht.
Hueting, R. (1967), 'Welvaartsparadoxen', paper prepared for the National Centre of Administrative Studies, The Hague.
Hueting, R. (1969), 'Functions of nature: should nature be quantified?', paper prepared for the World Wildlife Fund.
Hueting, R. (1970a), 'Functions of nature: should nature be quantified?', *Economisch-Statistische Berichten*, 21 January (in Dutch).
Hueting, R. (1970b), *What is Nature Worth to Us*? A collection of articles from the years 1967–1970 (in Dutch).
Hueting, R. (1974a), *New Scarcity and Economic Growth*, Dutch ed, Agon Elsevier, Amsterdam, Brussel, (1974), English ed, North-Holland Publishing Company, Amsterdam, New York, Oxford, 1980.
Hueting, R. (1974b), 'A statistical system for estimating the deterioration of the human environment', Paper prepared for the *Symposium of the International Association for Statistics in Physical Sciences (IASPS)* at Harvard University, 10–20 August, 1971, in John W. Pratt (ed.), *Statistical and Mathematical Aspects of Pollution Problems*, Marcel Dekker Inc., New York.
Hueting, R. (1981), 'Some comments on the report "A Low Energy Strategy for the

United Kingdom", compiled by Gerald Leach et al. for the *International Institute for the Environment and Development (IIED)*, paper prepared for the *Working Party on Integral Energy Scenarios*, The Hague, 20 May.

Hueting, R. (1989), 'Correcting national income for environmental losses: towards a practical solution', in Y. Ahmad, S. El Serafy and E. Lutz (eds), *Environmental Accounting for Sustainable Development*, The World Bank, Washington, DC.

Hueting, R. (1991), 'The use of the discount rate in a cost–benefit analysis for different uses of a humid tropical forest area', *Ecological Economics*, 12.

Hueting, R. (1992a), 'Correcting national income for environmental losses: a practical solution for a theoretical dilemma', in R. Costanza (ed.), *Ecological Economics: The Science and Management of Sustainability*, New York, 1991. Also published in J.J. Krabbe and W.J.M. Heijman (eds), *National Income and Nature: Externalities, Growth and Steady State*, Kluwer Academic Publishers, Dordrecht, Boston, London.

Hueting, R. (1992b), 'The economic functions of the environment', in P. Ekins and M. Max-Neef (eds), *Real-life Economics*, Routledge, London and New York. Also published in L.L. Boyer (ed.), *Proceedings of the 5th International Conference on Underground Space and Earth Sheltered Structures*, Delft University Press, Delft.

Hueting, R. (1995), 'The economic functions of the environment – valuation of environmental effects', in *Evaluation of Environmental Effects of Transport*, Report of an International Roundtable organised by PTRC Education and Research Services Ltd., The Hague, 19–20 June, London.

Hueting, R. (1996), 'Three persistent myths in the environmental debate', *Ecological Economics*, **18** (2), 81–8, August.

Hueting, R. (1997), 'Groei van de produktie is gevaar voor milieu', *NRC Handelsblad*, 2 August.

Hueting, R., P.R. Bosch and B. de Boer (1992), *Methodology for the calculation of sustainable national income*, Statistics Netherlands, Voorburg, SDU/Publishers, The Hague, Statistical essays, M44. Also published as WWF International report, Gland, Switzerland, June.

Hueting, R. and P. Bosch (1994), 'Sustainable national income in The Netherlands: the calculation of environmental losses in money terms', D. Pearce and S. Vaucheux (eds), *Models of Sustainable Development: Exclusive or Complementary Approaches of Sustainability?*, Université du Pantheon-Sorbonne, Paris, pp. 43–56.

Hueting, R., P. Bosch and B. de Boer (1995a), 'The calculation of sustainable national income', *Occasional Papers and Reprints*, IDPAD OP&R 1995–2. Indo-Dutch Programme on Alternatives in Development IDPAD, New Delhi, The Hague.

Hueting, R., B. de Boer, P.R. Bosch and J. P. van Soest (1995b), 'Estimating sustainable national income', in W. van Dieren (ed.), *Taking Nature into Account: A Report to the Club of Rome*, Copernicus, Springer-Verlag, New York.

Hueting, R. and L. Reijnders (1996a), 'Duurzaamheid is een objectief begrip', *Economisch-Statistische Berichten*, 425–7.

Hueting, R. and L. Reijnders (1996b), 'Duurzaamheid en preferenties', *Economisch-Statistische Berichten*, 537–9.

Hueting, R. and L. Reijnders (1998), 'Sustainability is an objective concept', *Ecological Economics* 2.

Hueting, R., L. Reijnders, B. de Boer, J. Lambooy and H. Jansen (1998), 'The

concept of environmental function and its valuation', *Ecological Economics*, **27** (1), 31–5.
Hueting, R. and L. Reijnders (1999), 'Uncertainty and sustainability', *Ecological Economics*, **29** (1).
Hueting, R. and B. de Boer (2001), 'The Parable of the Carpenter', *International Journal of Environment and Pollution*, **15** (1), 42–50.
IUCN, UNEP and WWF (1980), 'World conservation strategy: living resource conservation for sustainable development', Gland, Switzerland.
IUCN, UNEP and WWF (1991), 'Caring for the earth: a strategy for sustainable living', Gland, Switzerland.
Landefeld, S. and C.S. Carson (1994a), 'Accounting for mineral resources: issues and BEA's initial estimates', *Survey of Current Business.*
Landefeld, S. and C.S. Carson (1994b), 'Integrated economic and environmental satellite accounts', *Survey of Current Business*, pp. 33–72.
Lovelock, J.E. (1979), *Gaia: A New Look at Life on Earth*, Oxford University Press, Oxford.
Mäler, K.-G. (1991), 'National accounts and environmental resources', *Environmental and Resource Economics*, **1**, 1–15.
Meadows, D.L. (1972), *The Limits to Growth, A Report for the Club of Rome Project on the Predicament of Mankind*, Universe Books, New York.
Nentjes, A. (1997), Personal communication.
Odum, E.G. (1971, *Fundamentals of Ecology*, 3rd edn, Philadelphia, PA, p. 223 *et seq*.
Opschoor J.B. (1997), *Correspondence with R. Hueting in 1997 and 1998*, available on request.
Pezzey, J. (1994), 'Theoretical essays on sustainability and environmental policy', Ph.D- thesis, University of Bristol, Bristol.
Pezzey, J. and Withagen, C. (1995), *Single-peakedness and initial sustainability in capital-resource economies*, Report, University College/Eindhoven University of Technology, London/Eindhoven.
Raup, D.M. (1986), 'Biological extinction in earth history', *Science*, 231, 1528–33.
Repetto, R. W. Margrath, M. Wells, C. Beer and F. Rossini (1989), *Wasting assets: natural resources in the national income accounts*, World Resources Institute, Washington DC.
Repetto, R. W. Cruz et al. (1991), *Accounts overdue: natural resource depreciation in Costa Rica*, World Resources Institute, Washington, DC.
Reijnders, L. (1996). *Environmentally Improved Production Processes and Products*, Kluwer Scientific Publishers, Dordtrecht.
Robbins, L. (1952), *An Essay on the Nature and Significance of Economic Science*, 2nd ed, London (1st ed 1932).
Roberts, F. (1988), 'Modern Cassandras', *Resource Policy*, 14, 306–7.
Rosenstein-Rodan, P.N. (1927), 'Grenznutzen', in *Handwörterbuch der Staatswissenschaften*, 4. Auflage, Vierter Band, Jena, p. 1195 *et seq*.
Solow, R.M. (1974), 'Intergenerational equity and exhaustible resources', *Review of Economic Studies*, Symposium, 29–45.
Stiglitz, J.E. (1974), 'Growth with exhaustible natural resources: efficient and optimal growth paths', *Review of Economic Studies*, Symposium, 123–37.
Tinbergen, J. (1990), 'Bepalen van omslagpunt is van essentieel belang', *NRC-Handelsblad*, 16 October.
Tinbergen, J. and R. Hueting (1991), 'GNP and market prices: wrong signals for

sustainable economic success that mask environmental destruction', in R. Goodland, H. Daly, S. El Sarafy and B. von Droste (eds), *Environmentally Sustainable Economic Development: Building on Brundtland*, United Nations Educational, Scientific and Cultural Organization, Paris. Also published in: R. Goodland et al. (eds), *Population, Technology and Lifestyle, The Transition to Sustainability*, Island Press, The International Bank for Reconstruction and Development and UNESCO, Washington, DC, 1992. Also published in: R. Goodland et al. (eds), *Environmentally Sustainable Economic Development: Building on Brundtland*, Environment Working Paper No. 46, The World Bank, Washington, DC, 1991.

Vellinga, N. and C. Withagen (1996), 'On the concept of green national income', *Oxford Economic Papers*, 48, 499–514.

Verbruggen, H., R.B. Dellink, R. Gerlagh, M.W. Hofkes and H.M.A. Jansen (2001), 'Alternative calculations of a sustainable national income for the Netherlands according to Hueting'; see Chapter 11, this volume.

Wackernagel, M. and W.E. Rees (1996), *Our Ecological Footprint*, New Society Publishers, Gabriola Island, Canada.

Weitzman, M.L. (1976), 'On the welfare significance of national product in a dynamic economy', *Quarterly Journal of Economics*, 90, 156–62.

Wilson, C.L. et al. (1970), 'Man's Impact on the Global Environment. Assessment and Recommendations for Action', Cambridge, Mass.

World Commission on Environment and Development (1987), 'Our Common Future', Oxford, UK and New York, USA.

Zeelenberg, K., B. de Boer and R. Brouwer (1997), *Sustainability in Growth Models*, Statistics Netherlands, Division of Research and Development and Division of Agriculture, Manufacturing and Environment, Voorburg, Research Paper No. 9744.

3. Three persistent myths in the environmental debate[1]

Roefie Hueting

1 MYTH 1: ENVIRONMENT CONFLICTS WITH EMPLOYMENT

The proposition that to preserve the environment we must sacrifice employment is probably the major obstacle standing in the way of a sound environmental policy. This is because the proposition overlooks the simple fact that the possible uses or functions of the environment (including natural resources) are scarce goods which require the use of production factors for their restoration, preservation and substitution. Of these, labour is the most important. For example, in the Netherlands more than 80 per cent of the net domestic product is labour income (including mixed income – that is income of industries that goes to private households). In macroeconomic terms, labour is the dominant cost factor. *A given amount of production and consumption requires more labour with environmental conservation than without*. The extra labour required is used to maintain scarce environmental functions.[2]

This conclusion can be elucidated as follows:

Human beings ultimately depend on three factors for survival and for the level of consumption that they want to attain:

- the possible uses, or functions, of their physical surroundings, the environment: water, air, soil, plant and animal species, space, and natural resources, including energy resources;
- 'hands and brains' – in other words, labour. And because the brain steers the hands, it is ultimately human ingenuity that counts;
- time.

Of course, capital is also a production factor. But capital goods are manufactured by labour, using elements of our physical surroundings: the environment. Ultimately, the environment, labour and time are the factors with which humans have to make do in obtaining what they need.

The environmental problem can be conceived as a process involving the steady substitution of time, or working hours, through depletion of the environment. For example, spraying herbicides requires less time than manual weeding. The point made in italics above can therefore be reformulated as follows: given the technology available at a given time, it takes more time, that is working hours, to attain a certain goal without depleting the environment than if the environment is depleted.

There is a continuous exchange between the time spent on work with that on leisure. Working hours are reduced either directly or by longer holidays and part-time work. On the other hand, there is an increase in working hours owing to the participation of women, and all kinds of small jobs on the side. Leisure and working hours can be substituted[3] once a basic level of self-support has been reached. So the point can again be reformulated as follows: *attaining a certain goal requires more labour with environmental conservation than without.*[4]

Travel provides a clear example of the exchange between time and the environment, both in production and consumption, and also of the potential for substituting time for work by time for consumption. A newspaper reporter can interview three international 'personalities' a week by travelling by airplane, and perhaps one by taking the boat or train. The same holds true for consumption: we can reach more distant places if we travel in ways that burden the environment than if we do so in environmentally friendly ways.

As a society,[5] we have the following three choices:

- *First Choice* From this day on we take the train to a nearby resort, instead of taking a plane halfway round the world to Bali. This means a lower level of welfare acquired from goods produced, because the new consumption pattern differs from revealed preferences. It also means a lower real national income, because activities with a capacity for producing a volume of goods that has increased to fabulous heights in recent decades are replaced by activities for which this capacity has increased only modestly, or not at all (see Section 2).
- *Second Choice* We continue going to Bali, but we do so by train and boat. This means an increase in travel time, less time for work and consequently lower consumption. A lower volume of national income accrues due both to the lower labour productivity of the transporters and to shorter working hours for the traveller.
- *Third Choice* We continue flying to Bali and accept the inherent loss of the environment.

With the current state of technology it is impossible to realize existing levels of production and consumption sustainably.[6] As long as this is the case, we can only increase our production and consumption (per time unit) at the expense of the environment (see also Section 2). The extra labour needed to save the environment is either directly or, on balance, the result of environmental protection.

Clean production and consumption require provisions and adaptations of all kinds. Examples include cleaning industrial or household waste water, integrated pest control in agriculture, sustainable exploitation of forests, and prevention of noise nuisance. Such provisions and adaptations require more labour *directly*.

In the case of activities that burden the environment being replaced by environmentally less burdensome activities, there is always a *positive balance* of additional labour and saved labour. Besides travel (see above) packing is a clear example. Disposable packaging and cutlery were introduced to reduce labour input in order to increase labour productivity. However, the ensuing loss of scarce environmental functions is not taken into account in the calculation of this productivity. If we buy eggs in a basket, milk in a jug and take-away Indonesian food in a rantang, we will certainly cause some loss of employment in the packaging industry, but at the same time we create more jobs in the service sector. This too results in a decrease in labour productivity: the same goal is reached with more working hours and more consumer time. In the past, the price mechanism forced out labour at the expense of the environment because the environment falls outside this mechanism. This labour will be drawn in again when we start taking the environment into account in whatever form by 'internalizing' it (again, given the available technology).

The absurdity of a perceived conflict between the environment and employment becomes particularly evident when we trace its consequences. If conservation of the environment were to be achieved at the expense of employment, then 'clean' production and consumption should require less time than 'dirty' production and consumption. Because labour is the dominant cost factor, as explained above, clean production would then be cheaper. From this it follows that there would then be no environmental problem! Everyone would then switch to these cleaner, cheaper production methods, forced to do so by the market. Thus, if merely one company were to switch to clean production, the rest would have to follow suit in order not to be priced out of the market.

The situation is presented upside down: the opposite of what we are being told is true. There is an environmental problem because clean production creates structurally more employment than dirty production. This makes clean products more expensive, and this is why we produce and consume in a way that burdens the environment.[7]

The environment is a collective good, and decisions about it can only be made collectively. If one company switches to production methods that meet national or global sustainability standards, while others do not follow suit, then higher costs will price that company out of the market, and dis-employ its employees. Therefore, the logical conditions under which regaining the availability of environmental functions that have become scarce goods creates rather than destroys employment must be made binding for the whole economy. Of the necessary preconditions the following are the most obvious:

1. Income has to be reduced in proportion to the costs of the measures required to conserve the environment. This precondition is completely logical. The extra labour required to restore and conserve scarce environmental functions is deployed to acquire non-market goods. Since income is nothing but a claim to produced goods (the sum of incomes equals the sum of goods produced), environmental measures come down to a reduction of (the growth of) the wage base. This outcome corresponds with an extremely simple datum. A good is scarce if one needs to sacrifice something else that one would like to have in order to acquire it. With scarce goods it therefore holds that more of the one entails less of the other. Thus, *ceteris paribus* (including the technology available at a given moment), more environment means less production and vice versa. The conflict is therefore apparently between the environment and production or its growth, rather than between the environment and employment.
2. Other countries must take similar measures to the same degree. This precondition is logical too, because otherwise firms from countries without protection measures can compete domestic industries out of the market.

It is difficult if not impossible to test the effects of the introduction of these conditions empirically. The environmental measures taken to date are marginal in relation to what has to be done to arrive at a sustainable use of the environment. Most measures only slow down the rate of deterioration, owing to the persistent and cumulative character of the burden. No government in the world accepts the unavoidable truth that, given the available technology, more environment means less production (and vice versa); so nowhere is reducing the wage rate taken in consideration.

However, the introduction of the necessary preconditions *can* be simulated and their effects *can* be tested with the aid of an econometric model. This has been done in the Centre for Energy-saving scenario (CE-scenario)

(Potma et al., 1983). A summary in English is given in Hueting (1987). In this study two contrasting scenarios are elaborated; one with business as usual and one giving top priority to saving the environment and resources. All variables that are not relevant to the problem are kept the same. In this way the effects of environmental protection on employment and production are isolated. In the environment scenario, wages are reduced in proportion to the costs of the measures taken, but similar measures in other countries are not assumed. Still, the outcome of this model study confirms what can be expected on the grounds of simple analysis: unemployment decreases[8] and production growth is checked (if the outcome of a model is not in conformity with the underlying theory, one of the two has to be reconsidered).

One of the underlying assumptions of the model study is that the demand for goods and services produced remains fully intact. For example, people have been travelling from time immemorial; they will not stay at home if car and air traffic decreases: they will go by train, boat or bicycle, even though they do not get as far per unit of time; the revealed preference for travel will not suddenly disappear.

The enormous concern voiced by governments and industry about environmental issues would lead one to expect major encouragement of research on the logical conditions under which two major issues of our time – unemployment and the environment – neutralize rather than reinforce one another. But nothing could be further from the truth. The abovementioned CE-scenario has been completely ignored.

Openly admitting this obvious fact and creating the logical conditions under which the problems of unemployment and the environment neutralize one another, would lead to a structural drop in labour productivity. This certainly checks the growth of production as measured in national income, and probably leads to a lower production level. With this conclusion we have now arrived at the heart of the environmental problem – growth of production.

2 MYTH 2: PRODUCTION MUST GROW TO SAVE THE ENVIRONMENT

Growth is at the heart of the environmental problem. Humans depend on the possible uses, or functions, of the environment for all their activities. Production growth, as measured in terms of national income, increasingly impairs environmental functions, including those that make life on this planet possible. This process, whereby the most fundamental scarce and consequently economic goods available to humans are destroyed, is generally called 'economic growth' and is identified with economic success. Growth defined in this manner receives top priority in every country of the world.

The identification of production growth with economic growth and economic success suggests that things go well economically only when production grows. This, however, completely contradicts economic theory. Economic theory by no means assumes that humans try to attain the highest possible production. Rather, it assumes that humans, in their dealings with scarce goods, try to attain the highest possible level of satisfaction of wants – in other words, welfare. In doing so, it is certainly not only goods and services produced for the market that are involved. The concepts 'production', 'money' and 'market' are absent in the definition of the subject matter of economics (see Hennipman, 1962, 1995; Robbins, 1952).

It follows that we can only speak of economic growth and economic success if there is an increase in satisfaction of our wants – that is, in our welfare. Welfare depends on many more factors than only production, and one of these is surely the environment. If, at the margin, we value the environment higher than production, and measures to preserve the environment lead to a lower level of production, then less production leads to greater welfare.

The identification of an increase in national income with economic growth and economic success masks economic development and perverts economic theory. National income measures the volume of production. An increase in national income, therefore, is an increase in production. The question then arises why years of pleading to call things by their proper names have led nowhere. Is it because the Western credo of progress has become ever more linked to production growth? If this is the case, then we are up against a deep-rooted, erroneous notion of progress that is threatening our planet.

The all-time low in reflections on the relationship between growth and the environment is the widespread proposition that production must increase in order to create scope for financing environmental conservation. There are two ways of elucidating why this proposition is perhaps the most dangerous ever invented. The first is to examine which activities contribute most to growth. The second is to examine what effects environmental protection has on production levels.

An analysis of the basic source material of the Dutch National Accounts (NA) (Hueting, 1981; Hueting et al., 1992)[9,10] shows that between one-quarter and one-third of the activities making up the national income do not contribute to its growth because it is difficult, if not impossible, to measure the development of productivity. These activities include production by the government, such as governing, the administration of justice, and most cultural activities, such as music and theatre. Another part of the activities contributes little to the growth of national income. The desired growth of at least 3 per cent a year expressed in official policy, which means doubling production every 23 years, must therefore be achieved by much higher growth percentages in the remaining activities. Unfortunately, these are mainly precisely those activities that cause the greatest environmental damage, owing to their use of space, soil and resources, and their pollution, in production or consumption. These activities include the oil and petrochemical industries, agriculture, public utilities, road construction and mining. Roughly 30 per cent of the activities, precisely the most environmentally damaging, generate about 70 per cent of production growth.

Moreover, according to Kuznets (1947, 1948), some of the activities included in the 70 per cent are complementary to those included in the 30 per cent. They are basically transaction costs. Kuznets argues that expenditure on these activities is of a cost character and should therefore be entered as intermediate deliveries. Entering them as final deliveries is double-counting, according to Kuznets. Examples include the expenditure invoked by the complexity of modern, urban patterns of living, such as expenditure on bridging greater distances between home and work, on banks, employment agencies, unions, brokerage houses and on legislation. Kuznets distinguishes three classes of such activities. A summary is given in Hueting (1980, 1992a).

The first way of testing the proposition 'growth is required to save the environment' yields the following result: the lion's share of the contribution to growth comes from the most damaging activities. We can now test the proposition by looking into the effect of environmental protection on growth.

Environmental conservation is a problem of shifting activities, in other words of re-allocation; it is not a funding problem involving a need to earn extra money to pay for it; macroeconomically, extra money can be earned only by extra production, which generally causes an extra burden on the environment (given the available technology, see above). Re-allocation in order to slow down the depletion of the environment and natural resources can be accomplished in two ways: by prescribing environmental conservation measures for production and consumption activities, and by direct changes in production and consumption patterns.

The first method, prescribing add-on provisions or changes in production processes, leads to real price increases. This is self-evident because extra production factors have to be factored in. A real price increase is identical to a decrease in the growth of national income. Stated simply, you can buy less for the same income. The ensuing check on growth is partially masked because, according to the current conventions of the NA, losses of scarce environmental functions (which are normal economic goods, see Hueting, 1980, 1992b) are not written off, but their restoration *is* written on, as far as it is financed by the government or private individuals. This is known as 'double-counting' or 'asymmetric-entering'. The effect can nevertheless be observed because nobody perceives the construction of a sewage treatment plant or the installation of a catalytic converter as an increase in his or her consumption.

Technical measures can often only put a brake on the rate of deterioration because of the persistent and cumulative character of environmental damage. In such cases, the only solution is to supplement technical measures by direct changes in production and consumption patterns.[11] A direct shift from environmentally burdening to environmentally friendly activities also checks growth, or might lead to a lower production level. This is because the accumulated capacity of the 30 per cent damaging activities to produce an annual volume of goods (the productivity) has increased gigantically over the past few decades, whereas this capacity has not increased, or only very little, in the more environmentally friendly activities. This is due partly to the fact that the depletion of the environment and of resources is not accounted for under the current conventions of the NA.[12]

Environmental measures lead to a check on growth, and growth apparently usually leads to further environmental deterioration. The widely held notion that 'growth is required to finance environmental conservation' thus proves to be extremely dangerous for the environment.

Safeguarding the environment in the long term requires that we shift our priorities from production growth to environmental conservation, and to wait and see to what extent production may then increase. This avoids the risks for future generations and is much cheaper in the long run: restoration is usually more expensive than preventing environmental loss. Such a shift in priorities would, furthermore, provide much better incentives for research into and application of environmentally friendly technologies than the current policy of focusing on production growth.

The combination of growth and environmental conservation is only possible in the case of technologies being invented that: (1) are sufficiently clean; (2) do not deplete energy stocks and other natural resources; (3) leave the soil intact; (4) leave sufficient space for the survival of plant and animal species; and (5) are cheaper than currently available technologies. This is scarcely conceivable for the entire spectrum of our activities. At any rate, such technologies are not yet available. Those who argue in favour of both growth and environmental conservation, or even for growth in order to save the environment, are therefore either blind to reality or are gambling on technologies that have neither been invented nor become operational, thus risking the basis of our existence.

3 MYTH 3: WE WOULD LIKE TO SAVE THE ENVIRONMENT, BUT IT IS TOO EXPENSIVE

We would love to save the environment, but it is too expensive. Of the three myths this may not be the most dangerous one, but it is certainly the most hypocritical. All fundamental solutions for safeguarding the environment are clearly much cheaper[13] than continuing the process that is threatening life on this planet.

For example: travelling by bicycle is much cheaper than driving the same distance by car. Heating one room, in combination with a sweater and an extra blanket, is much cheaper than heating the entire house. A vacation by boat or train is cheaper than a holiday flight. A diet combining some meat and beans is cheaper than eating lots of meat. Winter vegetables in winter are cheaper than summer vegetables in winter. Raising two children is cheaper than raising ten.

The burden on the environment is determined by the number of people, the amount of activity per person, and the nature of this activity. Because activities with little or no impact on the environment can be expanded, the shift to environmental sustainability comes down to adapting the number of individuals of our species and the kind of activities we engage in to the carrying capacity of our planet. This adaptation is extraordinarily cheap.

Of course, there is an economic sacrifice to be made; otherwise there would be no environmental problem. Most of us would love to make unrestricted use of the private car, are mad about eating meat, and prefer to have sex without a pill or condom. Recent initiatives to calculate a sustainable level of activities – the sustainable national income (Hueting et al., 1992) – will show a major difference with the standard national income. But if we unlink our credo of progress from the growth of our consumption, there is no reason at all to panic. In the first place, shifting to sustainability will not damage our health. On the contrary, environmentally friendly activities are usually healthier than those that harm the environment. Second, a sustainable level of activity by no means implies a return to the Middle Ages, as often claimed. The global national income is now four times higher than it was about 1950. Were living conditions then worse for most of the people in the world than they are today? A sustainable level of activity will probably be higher than that of 40 years ago. Thus, according to a rough estimate by Tingergen and Hueting (1991), global production and consumption will have to be halved in order to attain sustainable levels, thus to repay our debt to future generations.

4 EPILOGUE

Given a certain availability, the value (and the scarcity) of goods depends on preferences. For market goods, prices indicate their marginal utility relative to one another. Prices say nothing about the value of market goods relative to scarce environmental functions. The value of these functions can never be fully established, because the intensity of the wants for them (relative preferences) can mostly be determined only very partially or not at all. For losses of function that threaten the future, such as the extinction of species, it is impossible to do so (Hueting, 1980, 1992b). This is why the true value of goods produced and consumed at the expense of the environment is equally unknowable. In the conflict between production and the environment we therefore have to weigh two unknown values – not one known value against one unknown value. In doing so we can make assumptions about the preferences, such as the assumption that the economic subjects want to use the environment sustainably, and use estimated production costs of environmental functions (their elimination costs) and market goods (Hueting et al., 1995). That is not the subject of this chapter. Scarce environmental functions – the most fundamental economic goods at the disposal of human beings because they constitute the very basis of our existence – cannot be preserved as long as in any discussion concerning the weighting process the information on the key items – employment, growth and financial feasibility – is turned upside down.

NOTES

1. This is a rewritten version of a press presentation of 'Caring for the Earth, a Strategy for Sustainable Living', Rome, October 1991. (World Conservation Union, United Nations Environment Programme and World Wide Fund for Nature.)
2. Conventional labour productivity, whereby the loss of scarce environmental functions is not taken into account, is therefore declining.
3. The degree of substitution and its direction obviously depend on preferences. Decisions on this point can usually be made individually.
4. Whatever goal, whether travelling or producing meat.
5. Environmental functions are collective goods. Individual decisions are subject to the prisoners' dilemma. Within a given structure, one puts oneself at great disadvantage while the desired effect is estimated to be negligibly small because one doubts whether others will join the effort. This is why a choice can only be made collectively.
6. This appears from the study on sustainable national income. See Chapter 11, this volume.
7. The point is whether or not we want to 'pay' for environmental conservation in the form of re-allocating production factors for the implementation of technical provisions or in

the form of a direct shift from environmentally burdening to environmentally friendly activities. Examples: from car to bicycle, from a lot of meat to a little meat plus beans. There is no way to establish unambiguously what sacrifices we are prepared to make to preserve the environment (see Epilogue, Section 4).

8. Of course, seasonal, frictional and business-cycle unemployment are not influenced, nor the unemployment caused by the fact that labour productivity is lower than the legal minimum wage.
9. van der Ploeg (1994a, 1994b) implicitly arrives at the same conclusion with his distinction of the industry in a hard sector with a high growth rate in productivity and much pollution, and a soft sector with a low growth rate in productivity and little pollution.
10. The sectorial composition of the Dutch National Accounts does not differ appreciably from that of the UK nor probably from that of most other northern countries (see Hueting, 1981).
11. This appears from the study on sustainable national income, carried out by Statistics Netherlands.
12. The increase in volume, realized in the highly productive, environmentally burdening sectors is spread across society owing to demand and supply and many linking mechanisms. Thus, the volume produced by a hairdresser is not appreciably greater than that of his colleagues 40 years ago, whereas his real (deflated) income, or his claim to a volume of produced goods, has risen by a factor of four during that same period.
13. Cheaper in the ordinary everyday meaning of the word – that is, in the sense that less input of production factors is required. See note 7 and the text on p. 86, fourth full paragraph.

REFERENCES

Hennipman, P. (1952), 'Doeleinden en criteria der economische politiek', in J.E. Andriessen and M.A.G. Meerhaeghe (eds), *Theorie van de Economische Politiek*, Stenfert Kroese, Leiden.

Hennipman, P. (1995), *Welfare Economics and Theory of Economic Policy*, Edward Elgar Publishing Company, Brookfield, UK.

Hueting, R. (1980), *New Scarcity and Economic Growth*, North-Holland, Amsterdam; New York, USA and Oxford, UK.

Hueting, R. (1981), Some comments on the report 'A low energy strategy for the United Kingdom', compiled by Gerald Leach et al., International Institute for Environment and Development (IIED). [Prepared for the Working Party on Integral Energy Scenarios, The Hague, 20 May. Also published as: De relatie tussen produktiegroei en energiev verbruik, Maakt groeifanatisme blind? Economisch-Statistische Berichten, 24 June, pp. 609–611.]

Hueting, R. (1987), 'An economic scenario that gives top priority to saving the environment', *Ecol. Model.*, 38; 123–40.

Hueting, R. (1992a), 'Calculating a sustainable national income: a practical solution for a theoretical dilemma', in A. Franz and C. Stahmer (eds), *Approaches to Environmental Accounting*, Physica-Verlag, Heidelberg.

Hueting, R. (1992b), 'The economic functions of the environment', in P. Ekins and M. Max-Neef (eds), *Real-Life Economics*, Routledge, London–New York.

Hueting, R., P. Bosch and B. de Boer (1992), *Methodology for the calculation of sustainable national income*, Statistical Essays, M 44, Statistics Netherlands, Voorburg. [Also published as WWF International report, Gland, Switzerland.]

Hueting, R., B. de Boer, P. Bosch and J.P. van Soest (1995), 'Estimating sustainable national income', in W. van Dieren (ed.), *Taking Nature into Account*, Springer Verlag, New York.

Kuznets, S. (1947), 'National income and industrial structure', in *The Econometric Society Meeting*, 6–18 September. Washington, DC. Proceedings of the International Statistical Conferences, vol. V. Calcutta, undated, p. 205.

Kuznets, S. (1948), 'On the valuation of social income', in *Economica*, February/May.

Potma, T.G., H.Y. Becht, R. Hueting, and G.J. Zijlstra (1983), Het CE-Scenario, Een realistisch alternatief, Centrum voor Energiebesparing, Delft.

Robbins, L. (1952), *An Essay on the Nature and Significance of Economic Science*, Macmillan, London.

Tinbergen, J. and R. Hueting (1991), 'GNP and market prices: wrong signals for sustainable economic success that mask environmental destruction', in R. Goodland, H. Daly, S. El Serafy and B. von Drost (eds), *Environmentally Sustainable Economic Development: Building on Brundtland*, United Nations Educational, Scientific and Cultural Organization, Paris. [Also in R. Goodland, et al. (eds), 1992, *Population, Technology and Lifestyle: The Transition to Sustainability*, Island Press, Washington, DC; and in R. Goodland et al. (eds), 1991, *Environmentally Sustainable Economic Development: Building on Brundtland*, Environment Working Paper No. 46. The World Bank, Washington, DC.]

van der Ploeg, F. (1994a), Zachte sector van economie moet naar markt worden overgeheveld, NRC Handelsblad, 9 April.

van der Ploeg, F. (1994b), Scheefgroei in de economie, Milieuforum, February.

4. Key issues in environmental economics

Paul Ekins

1 INTRODUCTION

In this chapter I present what seem to me to be some key issues in environmental economics, referring to the main ways I think Roefie Hueting, and many other people, have contributed to the understanding of these issues. Inevitably I also draw on some of my early, and more recent, work (for example Ekins and Max-Neef, 1992; Ekins, 2000). Doubtless I will not mention many of Roefie's works that might be mentioned in this chapter. I may also overlook other contributions that have been so seminal to the way my thinking has developed that I now regard them as my own. I can only ask Roefie and any others who find this to be so to forgive me, in the knowledge that my principal concern in this chapter has been to try to get the ideas across rather than reconstruct their genesis.

It is Herman Daly who has consistently stressed the importance of 'pre-analytic vision' in any consideration of environment-economy relations (see, for example, Daly, 1996, p. 6), and Section 2 of this chapter sets out the pre-analytic vision on which the subsequent discussion is based. Section 3 introduces the idea of the environment as natural capital, which has played a fundamental role in much of the recent environmental-economics literature, and places it in the context of a four-capital model of wealth creation. Capital, of course, is a stock concept. One of Roefie Hueting's most important contributions to environmental economic analysis was to identify the flows from this stock as 'environmental functions', and this is the subject of Section 4, using which it is possible to introduce a rigorous definition of environmental sustainability, which is the subject of Section 5. Section 6 shows how standards of sustainability may be derived. Section 7 shows how the national accounting system may be extended to indicate the environmental sustainability or otherwise of current economic activities. Section 8 briefly considers the relationship between sustainability and economic growth. Section 9 concludes.

Throughout this chapter I have tried to draw attention to the contributions of Roefie Hueting to thinking about the various issues covered. Sometimes I have come to different conclusions from Roefie. Always, however, I have found his ideas pertinent and challenging.

2 CONCEIVING THE ECONOMY

In 1992 I put forward the perception that human life may be perceived as having four essential dimensions: the economic, social, ethical and ecological, and illustrated the perception as in Figure 4.1 (Ekins, 1992, pp. 86–8). I was encouraged that the tetrahedral presentation might have some merit when I came across what I have labelled Figure 4.2 in Serageldin (1994, p. 2), which suggested that the Environment Department of the World Bank, at least, was working from a similar conceptualization.

Figure 4.1 is intended to represent a regular tetrahedron with the four keywords at its corners. They are equivalent – there is no implied hierarchy in that one corner is drawn as an apex of the pyramid – any of the keywords could have been in this position. Each point of the space inside this pyramid can be imagined as having four coordinates corresponding to one of the dimensions. The closer a point to any particular corner, the greater the coordinate, meaning that the stronger is the influence of that dimension relative to the others. The corners themselves are the points of pure economy, society, ecology and ethics. It is as if each of these points radiates

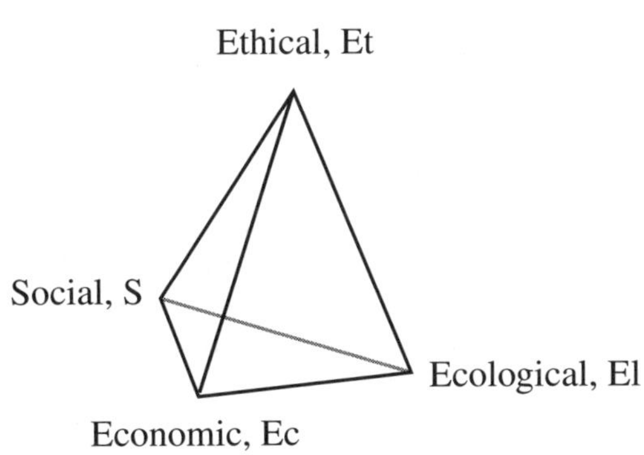

Figure 4.1 *Four-dimensional human space*

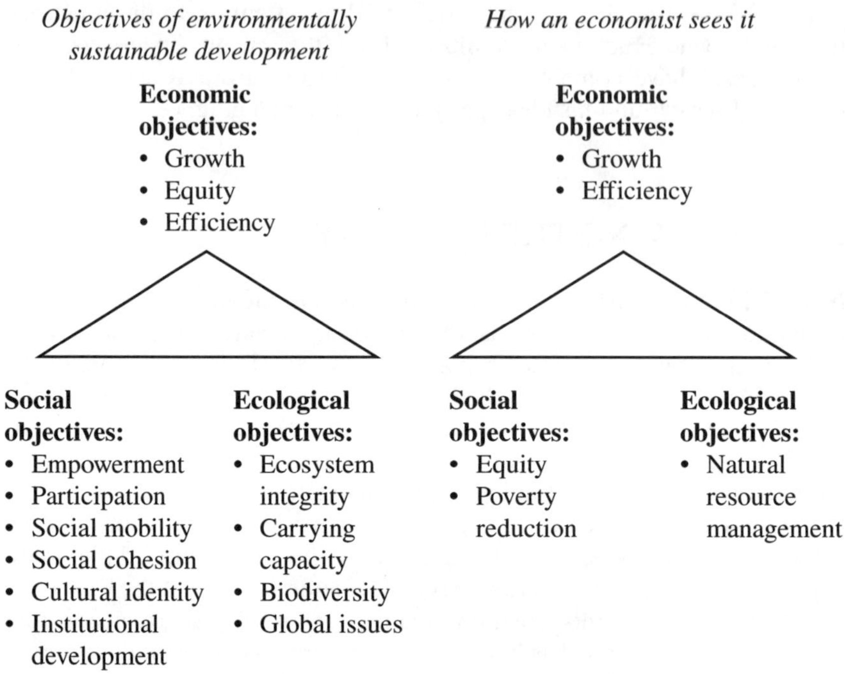

Figure 4.2 *Objectives of environmentally sustainable development*
Source: Serageldin (1994, p. 2)

an influence within the figure that diminishes in intensity with distance from the point. Each corner has a triangular plane opposite it, where the dimension represented by that corner is taken to have no influence, that is, its coordinate is zero. The point at the centre of the pyramid is where all the dimensions are equally influential or balanced.

It must be stressed that all that can be indicated in this way is the *relative* strength of the four dimensions. It says nothing about the intensity of those strengths. If one dimension is perceived as more influential, then *de facto* this diminishes the relative importance of the others, even though they may still be extremely important. Thus the pyramid's centre could equally apply to a condition of passionate ecological, social, ethical and economic commitment, or to one of total apathy. Conceiving of the space in this way allows it to be used for a rough and ready but quite insightful analysis of human affairs in many different ways. In Ekins (1992, pp. 87–8, 118–19) it is used to distinguish between various kinds of environmental concern and between different schools of economic thought.

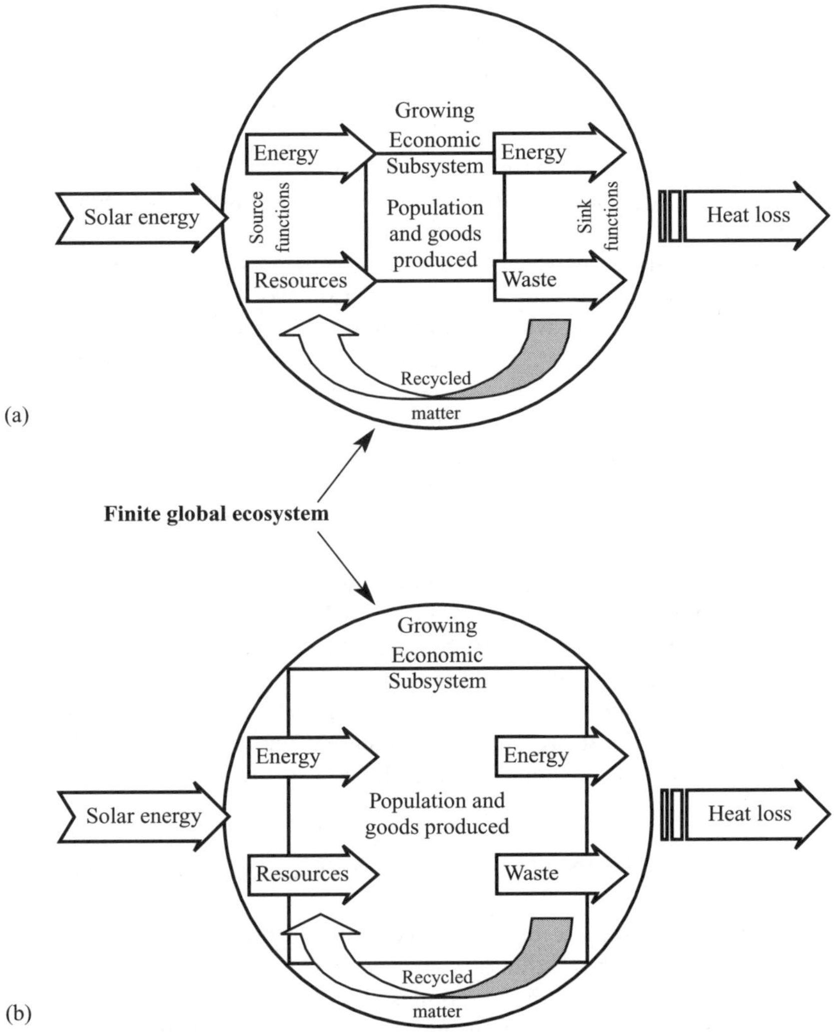

Figure 4.3 *The finite global ecosystem relative to the growing economic subsystem*
Source: Daly (1992, p. 5)

At all points on the surface of, or inside, the tetrahedron of Figure 4.1, with two exceptions, the economic and ecological dimensions interact. The exceptions are the planes ElEtS (where the economic dimension is absent) and EtEcS, where the ecological dimension is absent. Bizarre as it may seem to ecological economists, representations of the economy from which the ecological dimension is completely absent are by no means unusual. As Daly (1991, p. 33) has observed, all too often the economy is conceived as an abstract flow of exchange value between households and firms, and, through taxes and transfers, between these and governments. Social and ethical issues may be considered in such a framework, through such questions as: who should get what? Or, through what institutions should production and consumption be mediated? But issues of resources and environmental quality do not arise. This omission is rectified in the now celebrated diagram of Daly's shown as Figure 4.3, which emphasizes the ecological scale of the economy compared to the planetary ecosystem of which it is a subsystem. The top half (a) of Figure 4.3 shows natural resource inputs to, and physical waste outputs from, an economy which is relatively small compared to the global ecosystem of which it is a subsystem. The bottom half (b) shows the physical requirements of, and consequent wastes from, a much bigger economy. Daly (1991, p. 34) asks: 'How big should the subsystem be relative to the total ecosystem? Certainly this, the question of optimal scale, is the big question for environmental macroeconomics'. It is also an uncomfortable question because it is clearly reasonable and important, but no one can at present give a categoric answer to it. I shall argue later that the idea of sustainability may help in this regard.

3 THE ENVIRONMENT AS NATURAL CAPITAL

One way in which the ecological and economic dimensions of human life may be related is through the idea of *capital*. Capital is, of course, one of the fundamental concepts in economics, denoting the stock of assets that are responsible for wealth creation. As with the representation of the economy as an abstract flow of exchange value, mentioned earlier, the three conventional categories of capital: land, labour and (manufactured) capital, again seemed to do scant justice to the ecological and social dimensions of wealth creation. In order to remedy this I put forward in 1992 a four-capital model of wealth creation as in Figure 4.4 (Ekins, 1992, pp. 147–51), distinguishing between manufactured, human, environmental and social/organizational capital. Again the same idea seems to have commended itself to Serageldin and Steer (1994, p. 30), who write of the 'need to recognise at least four categories of capital', defined as in Figure 4.4.

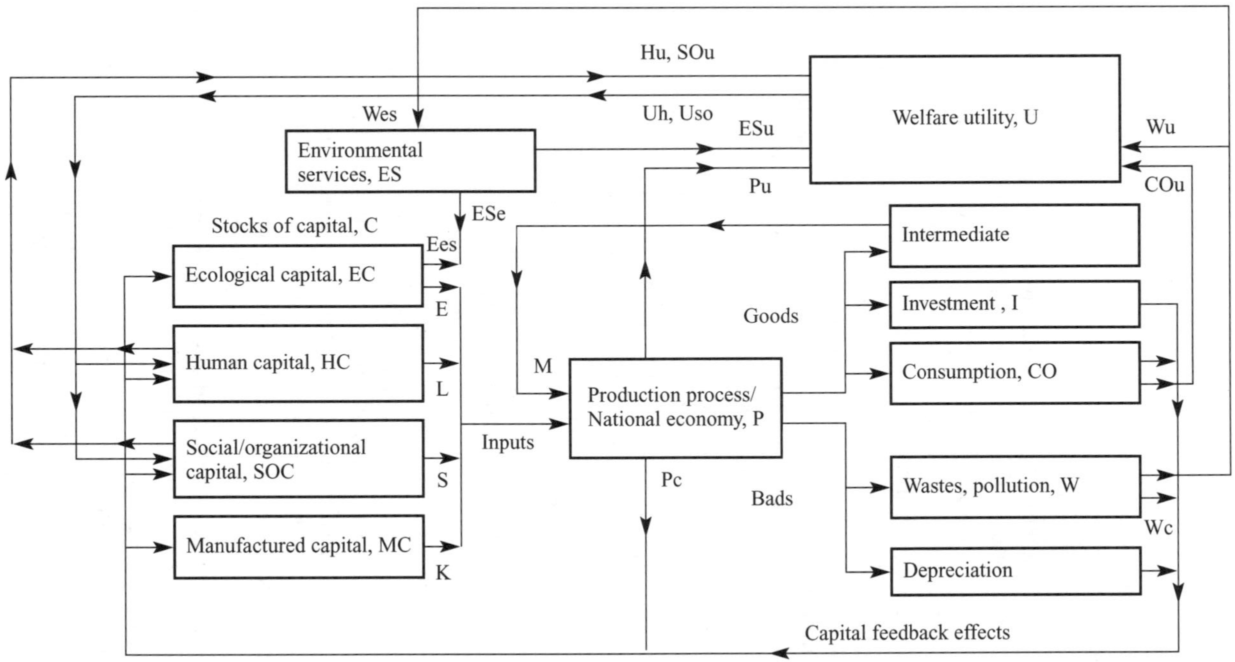

Figure 4.4 *Stocks, flows and welfare in the process of production*

In the conventional three-capital model of the economy, land, labour and manufactured capital are judiciously combined in an economic process that produces goods and services, some of which are consumed to give utility to the consumers, and some of which are invested to enhance the capital stocks (or make up for depreciation). In contrast, Figure 4.4 portrays four kinds of capital stock, each of which produces a flow of 'services': from the environment (*E*, *Ees*), from human capital (*L*), from social/organizational capital (*S*), and from manufactured capital (*K*), services that serve as inputs into the productive process, along with 'intermediate inputs' (*M*), which are previous outputs from the economy that are used as inputs in a subsequent process.

Manufactured capital comprises material goods – tools, machines, buildings, infrastructure – which contribute to the production process but do not become embodied in the output and, usually, are 'consumed' in a period of time longer than a year. Intermediate goods, in contrast, either are embodied in produced goods (for example metals, plastics, components) or are immediately consumed in the production process (for example fuels). Human capital comprises all individuals' capacities for work; while social and organizational capital comprises the networks and organizations through which the contributions of individuals are mobilized and coordinated.

Ecological capital is a complex category which performs three distinct types of environmental function (as categorized by Pearce and Turner, 1990, pp. 35ff.), two of which are directly relevant to the production process. The first is the provision of resources for production (*E*), the raw materials that become food, fuels, metals, timber, and so on. The second is the absorption of wastes (*W*) from production, both from the production process and from the disposal of consumption goods. Where these wastes add to or improve the stock of ecological capital (for example through recycling or fertilization of soil by livestock), they can be regarded as investment in such capital. More frequently, where they destroy, pollute or erode, with consequent negative impacts on the ecological, human or manufactured capital stocks, they can be regarded as agents of negative investment, depreciation or capital consumption. Either way, the wastes contribute to the capital feedback effects identified in Figure 4.4.

The third type of environmental function does not contribute directly to production, but in many ways it is the most important type because it provides the basic context and conditions within which production is possible at all. It comprises basic 'environmental services' (*ES*), including 'survival services' such as those producing climate and ecosystem stability, shielding of ultraviolet radiation by the ozone layer, and 'amenity services' such as the beauty of wilderness and other natural areas. These services are produced directly by ecological capital independently of human activity, but human activity can certainly have an (often negative) effect on the responsible capital and therefore on the services produced by it, through the capital feedback effects discussed earlier.

The outputs of the economic process can therefore, in the first instance, be categorized as 'goods' and 'bads'. The goods are the desired outputs of the process, as well as any positive externalities (incidental effects) that may be associated with it. These goods can be divided in turn into consumption, investment and intermediate goods and services. The bads are the negative effects of the production process, including capital depreciation and polluting wastes and other negative externalities, which contribute to environmental destruction, negative effects on human health and so on. Insofar as they have an effect on the capital stocks, the bads can be regarded as negative investment.

The necessity for a matter/energy balance on either side of the production process means that all matter and energy that feature as inputs must also emerge as outputs, either embodied in the goods or among the bads. On disposal of the former, therefore, all these former inputs are returned to the environment, to the stock of ecological capital, where they may have a positive, negative or neutral effect. The essential point is that, for matter, Figure 4.4 represents a closed system; for energy, inputs can be received from the sun, and heat can be radiated from the earth into space.

The major differences between the three-capital model and the four-capital model of Figure 4.4 can be summarized as follows:

- Land has been redefined as ecological capital, with the identification of its three key sets of environmental functions, resource provision, waste absorption and the direct provision of environmental services as discussed above.
- Wastes and pollution from the production process and consumption have been added. These affect utility directly (*Wu*, for example litter, noise) and through their mainly negative feedback into the stocks of environmental, human and manufactured capital. These feedbacks, *Wc*, can reduce the productivity of environmental resources (for example through pollution) and affect the ecological capital that produces environmental services (for example by engendering climate change or damaging the ozone layer); they can damage human capital by engendering ill health; and they can corrode buildings (manufactured capital). They can also affect environmental services directly (*Wes*, for example by reducing the beauty of natural areas).
- Labour has become the service delivered by an expanded concept of human capital, the formation of which Becker (1964, p. 1) defined as

'activities which influence future monetary and psychic income by increasing the resources in people'. Human capital can therefore be seen to include such aspects of labour power as knowledge, skills, health and motivation. Specifying human capital thus allows the model to recognize the direct relationships between human capital and welfare: a happy worker will be more productive (*Uh*); and a healthy worker will be happier as well as more productive (*Hu*).

- The addition of social/organizational capital reflects the considerable part played by institutions in wealth creation. The concept was first developed by Tomer (1973, pp. 267–81), and considerably expanded in his book *Organisational Capital* (Tomer, 1987). Whereas human capital is embodied in individuals, social/organizational capital derives from their ways of interacting. As with human capital, social/organizational capital has a direct relationship with welfare. Social structures (for example the family) are major determinants of welfare (*SOu*), while the welfare of individuals will affect the performance of social structures (*Uso*).
- It is explicitly acknowledged that utility is generated by many other aspects of life apart from consumption. Broadly these can be classified according to the four modes of experience identified by Max-Neef (1991, pp. 30ff.):

Being:	affected by the quality of the environment (*ESu*), the nature and level of wastes (*Wu*), and the quality of human capital itself (*Hu*);
Having:	derived from consumption (*COu*);
Doing:	derived from the work process (*Pu*);
Interacting:	derived from social and organizational structures as well as from the work process (*SOu*).

- Feedback effects are emphasized in Figure 4.4. One that has not yet been mentioned is the joint relationship between the stock of ecological capital (*EC*) and the environmental services (*ES*) deriving from it. In a stable ecosystem, *EC* and *ES* will tend to be symbiotically balanced. Another important feedback is that from the work process to the human and social organizational capital stocks (*Pc*), reflected in the emphasis that has been placed on 'learning by doing' (Arrow, 1962) and in the perception that work can 'deskill' workers (Braverman, 1974).
- The greater complexity of Figure 4.4. This is a disadvantage in terms of its tractability for formal analysis. However, more tractable models have undesirable limitations in their physical interpretation. It seems that the complexity of Figure 4.4 is necessary if the full contribution

of the environment to wealth creation and welfare is to be understood and its relationship to economic growth adequately analysed.

4 THE CONCEPT OF THE ENVIRONMENTAL FUNCTION

In Section 3, the key contribution of the environment to the human economy and to human life in general is perceived to be through the operation of a wide range of 'environmental functions'. This concept was first employed in economic analysis by Hueting, who defined it as 'possible uses' of the environment (Hueting, 1980, p.95). De Groot has subsequently defined them as 'the capacity of natural processes and components to provide goods and services that satisfy human needs' (De Groot, 1992, p.7). These 'natural processes and components' can in turn be identified as the stocks of and flows from natural capital (though De Groot does not use the term), which features as ecological capital in Figure 4.4 and in various definitions of sustainability and sustainable development (see, for example, Pezzey, 1992, pp.55ff.). De Groot identifies 37 environmental functions, which he classifies under four headings: regulation, carrier, production and information (ibid., p.15).

This classification is quite consistent with that used in Section 3, which grouped environmental functions under three headings: provision of resources for human activity; absorption of wastes from human activity; and provision of environmental services independently of or interdependently with human activity. The resource functions in the typology of Section 3 correspond broadly to De Groot's production functions, but also include some carrier functions. The waste absorption functions are included among the regulation functions; and the provision of services includes the information functions and some regulation and carrier functions.

One of Hueting's most telling insights was that, with the increase of the human population and the scale of its activities, the environmental functions are increasingly in competition with each other. It is worth quoting him in detail on this point:

> A conflict is being waged between growth of production and population on the one hand and the environment on the other. The new scarcity [the title of Hueting's book – PE] is manifesting itself in increasingly severe competition between the activities utilizing the various environmental functions; the use of an environmental function is at the expense of other functions or, to put it another way, leads to loss of function. The environmental functions now in short supply are economic goods. Deterioration of the environment may be defined as

> the occurrence of losses of function. The latter are regarded as costs (Hueting, 1980, p. x).

In a later article Hueting has written: 'Competing functions are economic goods, because they fully meet the definition of scarcity. Functions have been changed from free goods with an economic value of zero into scarce goods with an ever higher positive value. This increase in value is basically an increase in scarcity (costs) (Hueting et al., 1998, p. 31). Thus is environmental deterioration placed squarely in the field of economic analysis.

5 FROM ENVIRONMENTAL FUNCTIONS TO ENVIRONMENTAL SUSTAINABILITY

If we wish, or need, to choose between environmental functions on an economic basis, we need to value the functions. As Hueting (1980, Hueting et al., 1998) has stressed, this involves constructing supply and demand curves for the functions. In Hueting's own words: 'Supply curves reflect the costs of all kinds of measures needed to conserve and restore functions: opportunity costs. They can always be constructed, except for irreversible and actual losses. Demand curves can only very partially be constructed with the aid of data on expenditures on compensatory measure that replace a function, or financial damage etc.' (Hueting et al., 1998, p. 32). Elsewhere Hueting (1992a, p. 66) gives convincing reasons why the construction of full demand curves is not possible, because of the inadequacy of techniques of environmental valuation, especially contingent valuation. This situation led to another very fruitful insight, again as early as Hueting (1980) (or, in that work's Dutch edition, in 1974): that one way round the problem was to postulate a social preference for 'environmental sustainability', defined by some minimum standard, or level, of the environmental function, which allows the demand curve of the environmental function to be drawn as a perpendicular line to the horizontal axis at the sustainable level of the function.

Since this early insight of Hueting's, environmental sustainability has become an organizing concept for much environmental policy, not least because it is an integral part of the concept of 'sustainable development'. This, at least since the Brundtland Report of 1987 (WCED, 1987), has been one of the principal stated policy objectives of practically every government in the world. It therefore seems desirable to arrive at a reasonably clear conception of what sustainability, especially as it relates to the environment, may mean.

The basic meaning of sustainability is the capacity for continuance more or less indefinitely into the future. The past 20 years have seen a substantial accumulation of evidence that, in aggregate, current human ways of life do not possess that capacity, either because they are destroying the environmental conditions necessary for their continuance, or because their environmental effects will cause unacceptable social disruption and damage to human health. The environmental effects in question include climate change, ozone depletion, acidification, toxic pollution, the depletion of renewable resources (for example forests, soils, fisheries, water) and of non-renewable resources (for example fossil fuels) and the extinction of species.

As shown in Figure 4.4, the economic component of human welfare, or utility, derives from, *inter alia*, income and from the environment, which performs various functions, some of which contribute to production, and therefore income, others of which contribute to welfare directly. Income is generated by stocks of capital, including manufactured, human and natural (or ecological) capital. Natural capital also performs the environmental functions, which create welfare directly. For economic welfare to be non-declining, the stock of capital that generates it must be maintained (Pezzey 1992, pp. 14ff.). This implies in turn that, for economic sustainability, net investment, that is gross investment minus capital depreciation, must be positive.

There is then the issue as to whether it is the total stock of capital that must be maintained, with substitution allowed between various parts of it, or whether certain components of capital, particularly natural capital, are non-substitutable, that is they contribute to welfare in a unique way that cannot be replicated by another capital component. Turner (1993, pp. 9–15) identifies four different kinds of sustainability, ranging from very weak, which assumes complete substitutability, to very strong, which assumes no substitutability so that all natural capital must be conserved. The assumption of the former is implicit in the so-called 'Hartwick rule' (Hartwick, 1977), namely that, provided that the resource rents from the exploitation of exhaustible resources are invested in manufactured capital, per capita consumption can remain constant indefinitely over time. Very strong sustainability has been called 'absurdly strong sustainability' (Daly, 1995, p. 49) in order to dismiss it from practical consideration. Turner's more interesting intermediate categories are:

- Weak environmental sustainability, which derives from a perception that welfare is not normally dependent on a specific form of capital and can be maintained by substituting manufactured for natural capital, though with exceptions.
- Strong sustainability, which derives from a different perception that substitutability of manufactured for natural capital is seriously limited by such environmental characteristics as irreversibility, uncertainty

> and the existence of 'critical' components of natural capital, which make a unique contribution to welfare. An even greater importance is placed on natural capital by those who regard it in many instances as a complement to man-made capital (Daly, 1992, pp. 27ff.).

The point at issue is which perception most validly describes reality. Resolving this point should be an empirical rather than a theoretical or ideological matter. However, if weak sustainability is assumed a priori, it is impossible to show *ex post* whether the assumption was justified or not for the following reason.

The assumption underlying weak sustainability is that there is no essential difference between different forms of capital, or between the kinds of welfare that they generate. This enables, theoretically at least, all types of capital and the services and welfare generated by them to be expressed in the same monetary unit. In practice, there may be insuperable difficulties in performing the necessary monetization and aggregation across the range of issues involved, but the theoretical position is clear and strenuous efforts are being made to make it operational. But the numbers that emerge from these efforts can only show whether or not weak sustainability has been achieved, that is whether overall welfare has been maintained. They cannot shed any light on the question as to whether the assumption of commensurable and substitutable capitals was justified in the first place. In assuming away any differences at the start, there is no way of establishing later on whether such differences were important.

The strong sustainability assumption does not suffer from this severe defect in scientific methodology. In keeping natural capital distinct from other kinds of capital, it can examine natural capital's particular contribution to welfare, distinguishing between its contribution to production (through resource provision and waste absorption) and its services that generate welfare directly. The examination may reveal that in some cases the welfare derived from natural capital is fully commensurable with other welfare from production and can be expressed in monetary form, so that in these cases substitutability with other forms of productive capital exists, and the weak sustainability condition of a non-declining aggregate capital stock is sufficient to maintain welfare. In other cases the outcome of the examination may be different. The important point is that, starting from a strong sustainability assumption of non-substitutability in general, it is possible to shift to a weak sustainability position where that is shown to be appropriate. But starting from a weak sustainability assumption permits no such insights to enable exceptions to be identified. In terms of scientific methodology, strong sustainability is therefore greatly to be preferred as the *a priori* position.

There are other theoretical reasons for choosing the strong sustainability assumption, in addition to the practical reason of the sheer difficulty of carrying out the necessary weak sustainability calculations for complex environmental effects. Victor (1991, pp. 210–11) notes that there is a recognition in economics going back to Marshall that manufactured capital is fundamentally different from environmental resources. The former is human-made and reproducible in the quantities desired; the latter is the 'free gift of nature' and, in many categories, is in fixed or limited supply. The destruction of manufactured capital is very rarely irreversible (this would only occur if the human capital, or knowledge, that created the manufactured capital had also been lost), whereas irreversibility, with such effects as species extinction, climate change, or even the combustion of fossil fuels, is common in the consumption of natural capital. Moreover, to the extent that manufactured capital requires natural capital for its production, it can never be a complete substitute for resources.

Victor et al. (1994, p. 107) identify the elements of natural capital that are essential for life as we know it as water, air, minerals, energy, space and genetic materials, to which might be added the stratospheric ozone layer and the relationships and interactions between these elements that sustain ecosystems and the biosphere. Some substitution of these essential elements by manufactured and human capital can be envisaged, but their wholesale substitutability as assumed by weak sustainability, appears improbable, certainly with present knowledge and technologies. In fact, if the process of industrialization is viewed as the application of human, social and manufactured capital to natural capital to transform it into more human and manufactured capital, then it is possible to view current environmental problems as evidence that such substitutability is not complete. If our current development is unsustainable, it is because it is depleting some critical, non-substitutable components of the capital base on which it depends. 'Critical natural capital' may then be defined as natural capital which is responsible for important environmental functions and which cannot be substituted in the provision of these functions by manufactured capital.

The environmental sustainability of human ways of life refers to the ability of the environment to sustain those ways of life. The environmental sustainability of economic activity refers to the continuing ability of the environment to provide the necessary inputs to the economy to enable it to maintain economic welfare. Both these sustainabilities in turn depend on the maintenance of the requisite environmental functions, according to some classification as above. Which functions are important for which ways of life, and which economies, and the level at which they should be sustained, will vary to some extent by culture and society, although there are obviously basic biophysical criteria for human production, consumption and existence. Hueting and Reijnders (1998, p. 140) go so far as to maintain that 'sustainability is an objective concept to the extent that natural science is objective'. It may be true that natural science, perhaps allied to the precautionary principle, can indeed give unequivocal guidance as to whether an environmental function *is being* used sustainably. What it cannot do is say categorically, except with regard to those environmental functions that are universally agreed to be most fundamental to human life and health, whether particular environmental functions *should* be used sustainably. As with cost–benefit analysis, the idea of sustainability itself does not provide a means of side-stepping the need for political judgement.

Taking an a *priori* position of strong sustainability, for the reasons discussed earlier, *environmental sustainability is here defined as the maintenance of important environmental functions*. (This is very similar to Hueting and Reijnders' (1998, p. 140) definition, namely that 'environmental capital – defined as the possible uses, or functions, of the environment and natural resources – . . . should remain intact'.) The advantage of defining it in this way, rather than as the maintenance of natural capital *per se* (although the Hueting and Reijnders definition above seems to mix up environmental capital with the functions deriving from it), is that such a definition makes explicit the requirements of manufactured or human capital and technical change if they are to be full substitutes for natural capital. Manufactured capital is a substitute for natural capital if it performs the same environmental functions as the natural capital. It is clear that this is more likely to be the case when the natural capital performs a single resource function (for example as an energy source) than when it is multifunctional in diverse ways (for example a rainforest). Similarly technical change can only be said to compensate for natural resource loss when, through the new technology, a reduced quantity of natural resources can perform the same environmental functions. To the extent that manufactured capital and technical change do not fully perform the environmental functions of the natural capital they replace, then substitutability between them has not been complete and there has been a trade-off between them.

There will be cases when such a trade-off appears justified; environmental sustainability is not here perceived to require the maintenance of *all* environmental functions. But the loss of natural capital to date, combined with ignorance about the importance of what remains, together with threshold effects and irreversibilities that make unwelcome changes impossible both to predict and undo, argue for caution. As Perrings et al. (1995, p. 22) observe: 'Ecosystems typically continue to function in the short-term even as resilience declines. Indeed, they often signal loss of resilience only at the point at which external shocks at previously sustainable levels flip these systems into some other basis of attraction and so some other regime of behaviour'. It is because environmental unsustainability is fraught with uncertainty and possible irreversibility and large costs that the idea of aiming for a minimum environmental standard that will ensure the sustainability of environmental functions seems to be justified.

The idea of minimum environmental standards can be traced back to the classic work of Ciriacy-Wantrup (1952), which prefigured many of the current concerns of sustainability by his development of the concept of 'the safe minimum standard'.

First, Ciriacy-Wantrup (1952, pp. 38ff.) identifies the existence of 'critical zones' for many, especially renewable, resources, where such a zone 'means a more or less clearly defined range of rates (of flow of the resource) below which a decrease in flow cannot be reversed *economically* under presently foreseeable conditions. Frequently such irreversibility is not only economic but also technological' (ibid., p. 39) and, one may add with regard to extinguished species, biological. In the terminology being employed here, this means that the loss of environmental functions may be irreversible. The 'critical zone' concept is strikingly similar to that of the 'critical load' that is employed in modern environmental policy.

Then Ciriacy-Wantrup (ibid., p. 88) identifies the possibility of 'immoderate losses' arising from environmental degradation, with respect to which: 'One important objective of conservation decisions is to avoid *immoderate* possible losses – although of small probability – by accepting the possibility of moderate ones – although the latter are more probable.' A decision rule that would achieve this is the 'minimax' criterion, which involves minimizing maximum possible losses. The application of this criterion to resources characterized by critical zones leads Ciriacy-Wantrup (ibid., Chapter 18, pp. 251ff.) to recommend the 'safe minimum standard' (SMS) as an objective of conservation (what today would be called environmental) policy: 'A safe minimum standard of conservation is achieved by avoiding the critical zone – that is, those physical conditions, brought about by human action, which would make it uneconomical to halt and reverse depletion.'

Despite the fact that the SMS approach was addressed in a practical way at those environmental problems, characterized by chronic uncertainty, and possible irreversibility and immoderate losses, for which more conventional economic approaches based on cost–benefit analysis are either inappropriate or infeasible, it made little impact on the literature of subsequent decades. The next substantial reference is by Bishop (1978), who concludes his article, which focused on endangered species, with the observation 'it is worthwhile to note that problems of irreversibility and uncertainty are not limited to endangered species, that the SMS approach may be applicable to a wider range of resource issues' (Bishop (1978, p. 17).

Bishop (1993, p. 72) brings the SMS approach into the context of current environmental discourse by relating it to sustainability: 'To achieve sustainability policies should be considered that constrain the day to day operations of the economy in ways that enhance the natural resource endowments of future generations, but with an eye towards the economic implications of specific steps to implement such policies.' Here the SMS has been converted into a sustainability standard. In the terms previously discussed, those activities that entail the possibility of irreversible effects and immoderate costs are now identified as environmentally unsustainable.

The SMS approach overcomes the problems of valuing environmental damages by proposing that policies that constrain or transform human activities towards environmental sustainability should not be considered in a normal benefit–cost framework but one which seeks to achieve the sustainability standard in a cost-effective way. Sustainability is accorded this pre-eminence as a policy objective because of the importance of environmental functions for human welfare, and because of the irreversibilities and large costs that may be associated with their loss.

The problems of unsustainability arise, as has been seen, from chronic competition between environmental functions. Hueting (1980, pp. 98ff.) has distinguished between qualitative, quantitative and spatial competition:

- *Qualitative* excessive emissions lead to excessive concentrations which lead to unsustainable effects (the environment becomes qualitatively unable to perform certain functions).
- *Quantitative* excessive extraction leads to excessive depletion which leads to unsustainable effects (the environment becomes quantitatively unable to perform certain functions).
- *Spatial* excessive occupation (of space) leads to excessive congestion, which leads to unsustainable effects (the environment becomes spatially unable to perform certain functions).

What counts as an 'unsustainable effect' rather than a sustainable economic cost is a matter of judgement which, as noted earlier, can only partially be resolved by science. Ethics and the attitude to risk also play a significant role here. It is important that the basis of judgement is articulated clearly, especially as to who is responsible for the effects and who is bearing their costs, and differentiating the contributions played by science, ethics and risk acceptance or aversion.

In order to make the SMS approach operational, detailed sustainability standards will need to be formulated for all the important environmental functions that are perceived to be at risk from human activities, but some general principles for these standards can be posited with regard to the generic functions of resource use, waste absorption and life support. Daly (1991, pp. 44–5) has suggested four principles of sustainable development:

1. Limit the human scale (throughput) to that which is within the earth's carrying capacity.
2. Ensure that technological progress is efficiency-increasing rather than throughput-increasing.
3. For renewable resources harvesting rates should not exceed regeneration rates (sustained yield); waste emissions should not exceed the assimilative capacities of the receiving environment.
4. Non-renewable resources should be exploited no faster than the rate of creation of renewable substitutes.

These principles are among the rules that Turner (1993, pp. 20–21) has formulated 'for the sustainable utilization of the capital stock', the others of which are: correction of market and intervention failures; steering of technical change not only to increase resource-using efficiency but also to promote renewable substitutes for non-renewable resources; taking a precautionary approach to the uncertainties involved.

Of these rules, the correction of failures and the steering of technical change are more do to with achieving sustainability than defining standards for it; and in view of the complexity of applying the concept of carrying capacity to human activities, it seems desirable to express it more specifically in terms of those environmental problems that appear most pressing. Such considerations enable the Daly–Turner rules to be reformulated into a set of sustainability principles:

1. Destabilization of global environmental features such as climate patterns or the ozone layer must be prevented. Most important in this category are the maintenance of biodiversity (see below), the prevention of climate change, by the stabilization of the atmospheric concentration of greenhouse gases, and safeguarding the ozone layer by ceasing the emission of ozone-depleting substances.
2. Important ecosystems and ecological features must be absolutely protected to maintain biological diversity. Importance in this context comes from a recognition not only of the perhaps as yet unappreciated use value of individual species, but also of the fact that biodiversity underpins the productivity and resilience of ecosystems. Resilience, defined as 'the magnitude of the disturbance that can be absorbed before the system changes its structure by changing the variables and processes that control its behaviour' (Folke et al., 1994, p. 6) depends on the functional diversity of the system. This depends in turn, in

complex ways, not just on the diversity of species but on their mix and population and the relations between the ecosystems that contain them. 'Biodiversity conservation, ecological sustainability and economic sustainability are inexorably linked; uncontrolled and irreversible biodiversity loss ruptures this link and puts the sustainability of our basic economic-environmental systems at risk (Barbier et al., 1994, p. 41).

3. The renewal of renewable resources must be fostered through the maintenance of soil fertility, hydrobiological cycles and necessary vegetative cover and the rigorous enforcement of sustainable harvesting. The latter implies basing harvesting rates on the most conservative estimates of stock levels, for such resources as fish; ensuring that replanting becomes an essential part of such activities as forestry; and using technologies for cultivation and harvest that do not degrade the relevant ecosystem, and deplete neither the soil nor genetic diversity.
4. Depletion of non-renewable resources should seek to balance the maintenance of a minimum life expectancy of the resource with the development of substitutes for it. On reaching the minimum life expectancy, its maintenance would mean that consumption of the resource would have to be matched by new discoveries of it. To help finance research for alternatives and the eventual transition to renewable substitutes, all depletion of non-renewable resources should entail a contribution to a capital fund. Designing for resource efficiency and durability can ensure that the practice of repair, reconditioning, reuse and recycling (the 'four R's') approach the limits of their environmental efficiency.
5. Emissions into air, soil and water must not exceed their critical load, that is the capability of the receiving media to disperse, absorb, neutralize and recycle them, nor may they lead to concentrations of toxins that cause unacceptable damage to human health. Synergies between pollutants can make critical loads very much more difficult to determine. Such uncertainties should result in a precautionary approach in the adoption of SMSs.
6. Landscapes of special human or ecological significance, because of their rarity, aesthetic quality or cultural or spiritual associations, should be preserved.
7. Risks of life-damaging events from human activity must be kept at very low levels. Technologies that threaten long-lasting ecosystem damage should be foregone.

Of these seven sustainability principles, 3, 4 and, to some extent, 2 seek to sustain resource functions. 5 seeks to sustain waste-absorption functions; 1

and 2 seek to sustain life-supporting environmental services; 6 is concerned with other environmental services of special human value; and 7 acknowledges the great uncertainties associated with environmental change and the threshold effects and irreversibilities mentioned above. The principles are clearly an application of the SMS approach, but they seek to reinterpret it explicitly in the context of ensuring the sustainable use of important environmental functions.

The above sustainability principles should be applied together. For example, excessive fossil fuel use violates principle 1 on global warming, and on its own may lead to a perception that nuclear power should be deployed as a substitute energy resource. However, nuclear power is not compatible with environmental sustainability because it violates principle 7 on environmental risk. In this case acceptance of the sustainability principles suggests that the efficiency of energy use should be maximized, and safe renewable energy sources should be developed (as per principle 4), while, in the interim, CO_2 emissions from fossil fuels should be minimized (for example by switching to low carbon fuels) and the safety of nuclear power should be a prime concern. In this way, the principles give clear guidance how to approach today's principal perceived environmental problems. They may need to be supplemented as new environmental problems become apparent.

The sustainability principles are coming to be reflected in a number of international treaties, conventions and principles, including the Montreal Protocol to phase out ozone-depleting substances (1 above), the Convention on International Trade in Endangered Species and the establishment of World Biosphere Reserves to maintain biodiversity (2 above), the Second Sulphur Protocol to limit SO_2 emissions (5 above), and the Precautionary Principle, endorsed by the United Nations Conference on Environment and Development in *Agenda 21*, to limit environmental risk-taking (5 and 7 above). None of these international agreements was the outcome of detailed application of environmental evaluation techniques in a framework of cost–benefit analysis. They rest on a simple recognition that they represent the humane, moral and intelligent way for humans to proceed in order to maintain their conditions for life, and are argued for on that basis.

Interpreting the SMS approach as the setting of sustainability standards to ensure the sustainable use of important environmental functions offers a practical methodology to address those environmental problems where uncertainty, irreversibility or possible large costs make the use of benefit–cost analysis problematic. The methodology was applied in the formulation of the Second Sulphur Protocol. It was applied by the German Advisory Council on Global Change to recommend the necessary level of

CO_2 reduction to the First Conference of the Parties on Climate Change in Berlin (WBGU, 1995). Hueting et al. (1992, Appendix 2, pp.44–52) have also used the methodology to indicate how sustainability standards can be derived for 17 different environmental problems.

6 DERIVING STANDARDS FOR ENVIRONMENTAL SUSTAINABILITY

The different forms of competition (qualitative, quantitative, spatial) will need to be addressed by different kinds of standards.

6.1 Qualitative constraints

Qualitative competition comes about usually through emissions and wastes that cause pollution. It is important to emphasize that not all wastes or emissions cause pollution. They only do so when they exceed the extent to which the environment can absorb, neutralize or recycle them, or cause unacceptable health effects on humans. In the non-human bioeconomy there is no such thing as pollution. All emissions or waste products from one process are transformed into resources for another in a multitude of interlinked cyclical processes powered by the sun, which provides the necessary external energy input to decrease entropy in the biosystem overall, as life forms become increasingly varied and complex. Thus the qualitative constraints for ecosystems or natural processes are the relevant critical loads, while for humans they are defined by standards relating to human health.

In general for qualitative constraints, a standard can be set at each level of an impact from an unsustainable process:

1. effect, for example a tolerated level of sickness from pollution or disruption from noise;
2. concentration, for example maximum levels of pollutants in soil, water, air, organisms;
3. emissions, for example maximum emission levels.

6.2 Quantitative Constraints

For renewable resources the basic sustainability standard is clear: the definition of a minimum acceptable stock and then the definition and enforcement of a strictly sustainable harvest. For non-renewable resources, the situation is more complex and various methods can be employed in order to address explicitly the issue of how a non-renewable resource can be used 'sustainably', when all depletion of such a resource must bring closer its exhaustion. The approach of Hueting et al. (1992, p. 15) is to determine the maximum sustainable rate of depletion in any period, according to the improvements in use-efficiency, recycling or development of substitutes for the resource during the period in question. Where $r(t)$ is the total rate of such improvements, $d(t)$ is the rate of extraction (depletion rate) and $S(t)$ is the stock of the resource, they posit the equation

$$d(t) \leq r(t) * S(t) \tag{4.1^1}$$

In fact it is not clear that, when it is the sustainable use of the environmental function that is of concern, taking into account recycling, substitutes and end-use efficiency, $d(t)$ is actually the relevant variable. Rather it is the rate of waste disposal, $w(t)$, which indicates the loss of a resource from useful service. Ekins (2000, Appendix 4.1) derives a relation between w and the stock of the unextracted resource, S, the amount of the resource in current use, C, the level of renewable substitutes for the resource, R, the efficiency of use of the resource, e, and the proportional increase in R between two time periods, a. When the subscripts $_0$ and $_1$ indicate the quantities in two consecutive periods, sustainable use requires:

$$w_0 \leq (1 - e_0/e_1)(S_0 + C_0) + (a_0 - e_0/e_1)R_0 \tag{4.1}$$

If the increases in R are somehow incorporated directly into e, and if $w_0 = d_0$, that is as much resource is extracted as is disposed of, then this equation reduces to Hueting et al.'s Equation 4.1^1.

Another way of seeking to ensure sustainable use is to set a minimum life expectancy of the resource, L_{min}. Where d_1 is the depletion rate in period 1 from a stock level of S_1, then

$$d_1 \leq S_1/L_{min}$$

In Appendix 4.2 of Ekins (2000), where d_2 is the rate of depletion in period 2, and D_1 is the amount of the resource discovered in period 1, it is shown that, when operating at maximum depletion rates consistent with L_{min}

$$d_2 = d_1 \, [1 + (D_1 - d_1)/S_1] \tag{4.2}$$

The interpretations of sustainability given by Equations 4.1 and 4.2 are quite different. The effect of 4.1, strictly in accordance with the principle of strong sustainability, is to ensure that the stock of the given resource, together with any substitutes that may have been developed, maintain their capacity to perform the relevant environmental function at its current level. The disposal of the resource is only sustainable if technical advances enable the stock remaining (plus substitutes) to perform the same level of function as the initial stock. Discoveries, which add to the quantity of known stock, mean that the stock is able to maintain a higher level of environmental function than was originally thought, and it is this higher level that then becomes the standard for sustainability. Obviously, under Equation 4.1, if no technical advance takes place in a given period, and there is no further development of renewable substitutes for the resource, then, even if there are substantial discoveries, the sustainable level of resource consumption (disposal) in that period is zero.

Equation 4.2 interprets sustainability as the maintenance of the current level of environmental function for a certain minimum length of (finite) time. Discoveries increase the possible depletion rate by increasing the stock, that is the sustainable level of environmental function is not adjusted upward as in the Hueting method. With no discoveries, and operating at the maximum depletion rate consistent with the minimum life expectancy, this depletion rate will decline over time, according to the ratio of depletion in the previous period to the undepleted stock (as seen by setting $D_1=0$ in Equation 4.2). Technical advance does not enter into Equation 4.2. If it occurs, but depletion stays the same, then the consumed resources will have increased their productivity of useful services delivered. But this will not change the minimum life expectancy of the resource.

In terms of the strict maintenance of environmental functions over an indefinite time period, the Hueting et al. (1992) method would appear to be correct. For non-renewable resources, the level of environmental function depends only on the stock, whether discovered or not. As discoveries are made, so that the quantity of the known stock is revised upward, so is the level of function that needs to be sustained. Only recycling, more efficient use, or the development of (renewable and renewed) substitutes can add to the environmental function of a given stock, so that it is only by the amount of these advances that the stock can be sustainably depleted. Hueting et al. (1992, p. 15) advocate that an average rate of technical advance for an earlier period should be computed and applied to the present stock to estimate sustainable use rates. Clearly the estimation of advances in recycling, use efficiency and the development of substitutes across a wide range of non-renewable resources is a substantial statistical and methodological challenge.

The minimum life expectancy method, on the other hand, treats discoveries as windfalls which will either enable the stock to last longer or, at constant life expectancy, allow greater annual consumption. Here it is only the current level of environmental function that is to be sustained, and only for a definite period. With no discoveries, the sustainable level of depletion according to this decision rule would gradually decline. The minimum life expectancy method entails relatively simple calculations, requiring no information beyond discoveries, initial stock and depletion rates, which are already widely available.

These differences between the methods perhaps suggest that they are suited for different tasks. The method of Hueting et al. would provide a rigorous method for calculating the gap between current and sustainable depletion; the minimum life expectancy method would ensure that sudden resource shocks were avoided and would give guidance as to the resources most in need of the development of substitutes. The method of Hueting et al. was developed for a national economy; the minimum life expectancy method would need to be applied with regard to global resource stocks. Setting the minimum life expectancy for different resources would be somewhat arbitrary, but should perhaps be between 30 and 50 years, based on the time scale required for the development and diffusion of major new technologies, if these were needing to be deployed once a resource was totally exhausted.

How much of a non-renewable resource can be used sustainably is one issue; how receipts from that use should be accounted is another. Given that use of a non-renewable resource amounts to the liquidation of natural capital, it is clearly incorrect that all the receipts from such depletion should be accounted as income, as they are as present. El Serafy (1989) has proposed that the receipts (net of extraction costs) be divided into two streams, one representing current income, the other to generate a permanent income stream in the future equal to that consumed as income in the present. El Serafy calculated a formula by which this proportion can be computed, relating it to the discount rate and the life expectancy of the resource. The formula is:

$$I/R = 1/(1+r)^{n+1}$$

where I = that part of receipts to be considered as capital
R = receipts
r = discount rate
n = life expectancy of the resource

For the UK this formula has been applied to the depletion of the UK's North Sea oil and gas reserves by Bryant and Cook (1992) and, more recently, Vaze (1998). Using a discount rate of 5 per cent and the total of proven and probable reserves to calculate the lifetime of the resource, Bryant and Cook (1992, Table 1, p. 103) estimate the depletion cost from 1980–90 to be £44 billion (price year unspecified). Adding possible to proven and probable reserves (and therefore extending the resource lifetime and reducing the depletion cost), Vaze (1998, Table 4, p. 73) arrives at a total depletion cost for 1980–94 of £51 billion for a 3 per cent discount rate, and £21 billion for a 6 per cent discount rate (1990 prices).

It may be noted that, if the Hueting et al. method is an application of the strong sustainability principle, the El Serafy method is an example of the weak sustainability principle. The monetary receipts are divided into two parts, broadly a capital and income component, but there is no requirement for the capital component to be invested such that specific substitutes for the depleted resource are provided. To the extent that the capital component is so invested, of course, the strong sustainability principle will be being followed. The Bryant and Cook and Vaze calculations suggest that, since the beginning of extraction of UK oil and gas in the 1970s, by 1994 £20–50 billion should have been invested in the development of renewable energy substitutes had the UK Government been applying a strong sustainability rule. The lower figure is at least 50 times the amount that was actually invested by the Government in research, development and demonstration of renewables during this period. It goes without saying that an enhanced investment of this kind would have substantially accelerated the development of renewable substitutes for fossil fuels.

The Hueting et al. minimum life expectancy and El Serafy methods could be applied as alternatives or together, with their different implications summarized thus. The Hueting et al. method would give an indication of the gap between current activities and strong sustainability. The El Serafy method would guarantee to future generations a continuing flow of the resource in question but, depending on new discoveries, it could be a diminishing one. Reductions in sustainable depletion would be gradual. El Serafy's method could result in total exhaustion of the resource but should have ensured the development of a substitute or an equivalent income stream from another source. This would only be compatible with strong sustainability where the asset producing the income stream was a perfect substitute for the depleted resource.

Given that the whole notion of sustainable use of a non-renewable resource is somewhat contradictory, a case can be made for applying the methods together as appropriate and therefore benefiting from their different sustainability insights.

6.3 Spatial Constraints

The principal unsustainability effect from spatial competition is species extinction. Because of its irreversibility and the uncertainties involved, an appropriate standard would appear to be that no species be knowingly extinguished. This is the presumption underlying the US Endangered Species Act, and is rendered the more imperative by the fact that many extinctions are currently occurring, and many more undoubtedly will occur, as a result of processes already under way, which cannot be immediately halted (though for sustainability they must be over time). Other potentially unsustainable examples of spatial competition are waste-dumping and traffic congestion. Both these are likely to be much ameliorated by sustainability measures to reduce emissions and depletion, so it may not be necessary to formulate sustainability standards in these areas (although, the cost savings associated with dealing with these problems must be computed as far as possible and subtracted from the costs of the sustainability measures in the other areas.)

7 ENVIRONMENTAL SUSTAINABILITY AND NATIONAL ACCOUNTING

When the national accounts were being systematized in the 1940s, environmental issues had a low perceived importance, and the accounting structure adopted simply ignored environmental issues. This situation persisted well into the 1980s, as shown by the fact that the environment was practically ignored in Eisner's detailed 1988 survey (Eisner, 1988) of proposed national accounting extensions. Partly this was due to the lack of worked-out environmental adjustments for Eisner to include in his empirical review. But the virtual omission of the environment from the conceptual and methodological discussion also indicates the low profile this issue had among national income accountants at that time. The change of attitude in relatively few years has been striking, and restores the issue of the treatment of the environment in the national accounts to an importance it had in an earlier period of environmental awareness, the 1970s. Then, one of the fathers of national accounting had written:

> Pollution, depletion and other negative by-products of economic production were greatly accelerated because of the very rapid rise of total output. . . . Economic production, and the technology that it employs, may be viewed as interference with the natural course of events, in order to shape the outcome to provide economic goods to man. All such interference has potential negative economic consequences – pollution and the like – the more lasting, the higher the level of production technology as measured by its capacity to produce goods (Kuznets, 1973, p. 585).

Herfindahl and Kneese (1973, pp. 447–8) were confident about the implications of these 'negative ecological consequences' for the national accounts:

> The exclusion of the services of clean air, clean water, space etc. from the list of final goods probably is not the result of disagreement that the services provided by nature are a factor in true welfare, but rather of the judgment on the part of the income accountant that obtaining acceptable estimates for these values would be too difficult and costly. It is clear, however, that any reduction in the service flows of common property resources that is viewed as a loss of real product by consumers means that NNP overstates any increase in final product as compared with the total flow from the truly relevant and larger list of final goods and services. In the extreme case the 'true' service flow could actually decrease while NNP rises.

This situation can be considered in terms of the concept of ecological capital developed in Section 3. As was then seen, the economic functions of the environment include the provision of resources, the absorption and neutralization of wastes and the provision of other services independently of human agency. In the process of economic activity, resources can become depleted (and, in the case of non-renewable resources, are bound to become so) and the environment can become degraded through pollution or occupation (change of use). Exactly analogously to the consumption of manufactured capital, continuing depletion and degradation imply that the environment will in the future be able to fulfil its functions less effectively or not at all. Yet in many cases these functions are of vital importance to economic, and wider human, life. It is for this reason that current use of the environment is perceived as 'unsustainable': it cannot be envisaged to continue.

The calculation of gross national product (GNP) and National Income (net national product – NNP) give no inkling of this increasingly serious unsustainability, which is far more pronounced now than in the early 1970s, despite the fact that income in the Hicksian sense is defined as a sustainable quantity. This inconsistency in the accounts' treatment of the environment has been one of Hueting's most abiding concerns. In 1993 it led him to say, together with a Nobel Laureate economist who, like Kuznets, was among those responsible for the early development of the accounts, that 'society is steering by the wrong compass' (Tinbergen and Hueting, 1992, p. 52).

The overarching reason, then, for seeking to adjust the national accounts for environmental effects is to gain a clearer understanding of the contribution made to production and human welfare by the environment, and of the way the environment's ability to continue to make that contribution is being undermined by the scale and nature of economic activity. There are several possible responses to this situation. One is to redefine the production boundary of the national accounts to include all environmental services. According to Hartwick (1990, p. 292): 'It only makes economic sense to deduct economic depreciation from GNP for those stocks whose flows are priced appropriately in GNP. . . . (T)he correct approach would be to re-price the environmental services by appropriate scarcity or shadow prices and revise GNP upwards. Then any annual declines (increases) in the corresponding *stocks* should be valued and netted out (added to) GNP to obtain NNP.'

Faber and Proops (1991, pp. 225ff.) have shown how the pollution degradation services provided by the natural environment can be treated in the same way as the pollution abatement provided by economic investment. The 'real' national income, consisting of both natural goods and services and those produced by the economy would then be higher than the 'measured' goods and services recorded in the macroeconomic aggregates of the national accounts. Continuing pollution, which damaged the pollution degradation capability of the natural environment, and so reduced the services it could deliver, would then show up as a deduction from this 'real' national income. If investment in pollution abatement were to be diverted from other economic opportunities in order to take the place of these lost natural services, 'measured' output would stay the same, but there would in fact have been a real economic loss. If such a diversion were not to take place, the loss of natural services would be experienced as reduced environmental quality. In either case the loss of natural services has reduced 'real' output. This is of relevance to the correct treatment of pollution abatement, and other environmental protection, expenditures, in the national accounts, as will be seen below.

Faber and Proops (1991, pp. 228ff.) go on to extend this model to the depletion of natural resources, noting that such resources are a 'wealth asset . . . with the same status as labor and capital goods'. In other words natural resources are a form of capital as per the model of Figure 4.4. Faber and Proops consider that currently the national accounts measure the services from this capital at much too low a level, so that it is over-exploited, and 'real' national income is underestimated for this reason, too. However, it would also be possible to treat the depletion of natural resources as capital consumption in the same way as the depreciation of manufactured capital is treated.

This may be a theoretically appealing approach, but it is practically infeasible for all the reasons concerning uncertainty about and difficulties in valuing environmental functions discussed earlier. For practical reasons it seems preferable to continue to take the production boundary to be the human economy, with the current conventions of the national accounting system, but to treat any depletion of ecological capital due to economic activity as capital consumption and seek to deduct it from GDP to form an adjusted net domestic product (NDP). This was the approach recommended by the UN Statistical Division in its system of integrated environmental and economic accounting (UNSD, 1993, Bartelmus et al., 1993). The approach sticks resolutely to the treatment of the national accounts aggregates as measures of production and not welfare. In contrast to Hartwick (1990), Mäler (1991), Hamilton (1994) and Dasgupta (1995), it does not attempt to adjust GDP or any of the other national accounting aggregates in order to improve them as welfare indicators. Economic welfare is a complex and heterogeneous concept, including, at least, considerations of income, employment, working conditions, income distribution, leisure, health, environment and security (Hueting, 1992b, p. 257). Such a concept is never going to be adequately captured by adjustments to the national accounting framework.

Bartelmus et al. (1993, p. 108) have set out the three basic shortcomings of the national accounts with regard to the environment:

> National accounts have certain drawbacks that cast doubt on their usefulness for measuring long-term environmentally sound and sustainable economic development. For one thing they neglect the scarcities of natural resources that can pose a serious threat to sustained economic productivity. For another they pay only limited attention to the effects of environmental quality on human health and welfare. In addition, they treat environmental protection expenditures as increases in national product, which could instead be considered social costs of maintaining environmental quality.

One of the differences between the 1990s and the 1970s is that there now exist a number of quantitative estimates of adjustments that would need to be made to the national accounts for them to reflect environmental depletion and degradation. It is not possible to survey these estimates in this chapter, but the conclusions of the study by Repetto et al. (1989, pp. 2–3) are not unrepresentative, when they note that under the conventional system of national accounting:

> a country could exhaust its mineral resources, cut down its forests, erode its soils, pollute its aquifers, and hunt its wildlife and fisheries to extinction, but measured income would not be affected as these assets disappeared . . . (The) difference in the treatment of natural resources and other tangible assets confuses the depletion of valuable assets with the generation of income. . . . The result can be illusory gains in income and permanent losses in wealth.

To address the shortcomings identified by Bartelmus et al. (1993) in the national accounts' treatment of the environment, four specific purposes and intended outcomes of what has come to be called integrated environmental and economic accounting (IEEA) may be identified:

- To identify the scale of environmental protection expenditures that are made necessary by current processes of production and consumption. Such expenditures are a burden on the economy imposed by the modes and processes of economic production and consumption, but they also give some indication of the level of social importance attached to environmental protection. Domestic industrial expertise in environmental protection, which may result from stringent regulations related to it, may also be an important possible source of export earnings in a context where commitment to environmental protection is increasing worldwide.

- To make some assessment of the value of the ecological capital stock that has been degraded as a result of economic activity, in a given period. As already discussed, this is analogous to the perceived need to account for manufactured capital in the computation in the present national accounts of real (Hicksian) national income.
- To estimate the level, given current technologies and economic processes, of the maximum environmentally sustainable national income (ESNI).
- To give a quantitative estimate of the gap that exists, as a result of economic activity, between current environmental conditions and those which might be deemed sustainable. Without some estimation of such a 'sustainability gap', and how it changes over time, it is not possible to know whether 'sustainable development' is being achieved.

Each of these outcomes of IEEA may be related in some way to the aggregates of the economic accounting system, principally GNP and GDP, and will be briefly explored in turn.

7.1 Accounting for Environmental Defensive Expenditures

'The term "defensive expenditures" is commonly understood as the expenditures associated with the negative social and environmental impacts of economic production and consumption patterns.' (Brouwer and Leipert 1998, p. 1, footnote 1). The whole point of such expenditures is that they defend against negative externalities, *unwanted side effects of production and consumption*. The other defining characteristic of defensive expenditures is that they only act to offset, partly or wholly, the negative effects with which they are associated. At most they maintain the *status quo ante*, the social and environmental situation that existed before the economic activities with the negative effects, took place.

There is continuing debate as to how defensive expenditures should be dealt with in the System of National Accounts (SNA). It is clear that defensive expenditures are beneficial in themselves; they add to welfare, and some have used this fact to argue that they should be included in GNP and NNP, as at present (for example Mäler, 1991).

However, this is only part of the necessary argument. As was seen earlier in the work of Faber and Proops (1991), the 'real' output of the total economy-environment system comprises both economic and environmental goods and services. If the production of economic goods and services reduces the output of environmental goods and services (which is what 'a negative impact on the environment' means in economic terms), then 'real' output from the economic activity should be accounted net of this reduction. Alternatively, the economic goods that only serve to offset this reduction, to maintain the output of environmental goods at their level before the damaging economic activity took place, should not be included in the net output of the economy during the accounting period.

This characterization of the relationship between GNP and defensive expenditures illustrates an important point that is valid when considering any adjustment to the macroeconomic aggregates: the adjustment must be consistent with the interpretation being given to the aggregate and with the use to which it is being put. Thus if GNP is being used to represent the money flows through the economy, then clearly defensive expenditures should be included in GNP. If, on the other hand, GNP is intended to be interpreted as the net output of the economy during the accounting period, then defensive expenditures should be deducted from it, as, of course, should capital depreciation. Similarly, defensive expenditures should be excluded from any figures of net output that are being considered as a contribution to economic welfare. Such a treatment would appear to be consistent with the conclusions of EUROSTAT: 'In one sense it can be argued that environmental protection expenditures are aimed solely at maintaining the particular quality of the environment and avoiding its degradation. They would not therefore lead to real additional output and should be deducted from domestic product, (EUROSTAT, 1994, p. 20).

7.2 Making Deductions from GNP/GDP

The basic equation for the environmental adjustment of GDP to improve it as an indicator of production (as distinct from welfare), is put forward in UNSD (1993, p. 99), and is also described by its authors in Bartelmus et al. (1993) as follows:

$$\begin{aligned} &\text{GDP} - \text{consumption of fixed capital} = \text{NDP} \\ &\text{NDP} - \text{(imputed) environmental costs} = \text{EDP} \end{aligned} \tag{7.1}$$

where EDP = eco, or environmentally adjusted, domestic product (Bartelmus et al., 1993, p. 54; the validity of the equation is unchanged by substituting GNP, NNP and ENP for the equivalent domestic quantities.)

In Equation 7.1 the 'imputed environmental costs' are the costs of environmental depletion and degradation. With regard to depletion costs, insofar as they relate to marketed resources there is no problem in subtracting these costs from NNP, although there is still no final consensus as to the method of valuation that should be employed. Such subtraction is analogous to the treatment of the depreciation costs of manufactured capital.

The situation with regard to environmental degradation is not as straightforward, and the two methods of calculating the relevant costs may be considered in turn. Where NNP is regarded as a measure of welfare, then (marginal) damage costs are the theoretically correct measure to use to calculate the reduction in environmental services, and loss of welfare, due to environmental damage, to be subtracted from NNP. However, this procedure is problematic on two counts: first, as noted above, welfare seems too complex a concept to be adequately captured by NNP; second, it is not practically possible to estimate the damage costs in a way that yields figures robust enough (quantitatively or methodologically) to be combined with national accounting figures. These problems are so deep and intractable that they seem effectively to rule out the calculation of ENP by this route.

Turning to the second method, the calculation of the costs required to abate, avoid or restore environmental damage (sometimes collectively called maintenance costs), their subtraction from NNP, as UNSD (1993) suggests, seems of doubtful validity. GNP and NNP are aggregates of value added, income and expenditure (depending on which of the three equivalent ways has been used to calculate them) based on market values that pertain simultaneously in a fully interconnected economy. Maintenance costs are aggregates of hypothetical costs based on available technologies. Although measured in money terms, they are therefore a quite different kind of number to the macroeconomic aggregates which reflect the equilibrium prices in the economy.

The rationale for subtracting maintenance costs from NNP is that this would give an estimate for the level of economic activity that was feasible while maintaining environmental quality. If maintenance costs were small, this might be true because the actual implementation of the maintenance technologies would not significantly affect the prevailing economic conditions. But then ENP would not be materially different from

NNP. If maintenance costs were large, however, then their implementation could be expected to change every other price and quantity in the economy, as other economic activities adjusted to take account of the new imperative that was being given to environmental protection. Maintenance costs and NNP are incommensurably different kinds of numbers and subtracting the former from the latter would be statistically invalid.

Nor can the analogy with the subtraction of the depreciation of manufactured capital be used in this case. As Keuning (1996, pp. 13ff.) has pointed out, the depreciation of manufactured capital is a cost that has been taken into account by economic actors during the accounting period, and it relates to actual expenditures that have been made in the past. The prices and quantities that go into the construction of GNP and NNP can therefore be expected to have taken this capital consumption into account. None of this is true for environmental degradation, which will normally have been omitted entirely from firms' financial accounts (and from the national accounts, which is why an adjustment is being sought in the first place). Keuning concludes: 'The situation would have been completely different if a completely new cost item had been introduced at the company level. . . . The appearance of such a new cost item would have affected output prices' (Keuning 1996, p. 13).

To conclude, there would seem to be no way to arrive at a practical and robust estimate of EDP/ENP, as defined in Equation 7.1, simply by subtracting cost figures from the relevant macroeconomic aggregate. While such a procedure may be theoretically sound, whether NNP is regarded as an indicator of welfare or net production, in the former case there is no way to arrive at credible estimates of the damage costs, and in the latter case it is not valid to deduct the maintenance costs, which might be credible, from NNP. The best that can be achieved in terms of adjusted macroeconomic aggregates is a partial ENP, obtained by deducting from NNP the environmental defensive expenditures and the depletion costs that have been incurred during the period concerned. This may be expressed as a ratio (partial ENP)/GNP to give an indication of the extent of environmental defensive expenditures and resource depletion relative to economic activity overall.

ENP has been one interpretation of the often ill-defined concept 'Green GNP'. It should now be recognized that, if conceived in terms of making deductions from NNP, it is not an operational concept. Another interpretation of green GNP has been as an environmentally sustainable national income (ESNI), that is, the income that could be generated by an economy using currently available technologies while respecting constraints of environmental sustainability. The next section considers how an ESNI might be derived.

7.3 Modelling Environmentally Sustainable National Income

GNP is calculated from prices and quantities in the economy that take account of economic interactions and interconnectedness. Using the maintenance cost approach it is possible to define the least cost way of achieving environmental standards that are deemed to be compatible with environmental sustainability. This is the methodology formulated by Hueting et al. (1992), which 'is intended to supply information on the costs of measures required for bridging the distance between a sustainable level of activities and the level reached in a given year in the past. In so doing we encounter the burden that has mounted up in the environment over an often long period' (Hueting et al., 1992, p. 14).

Hueting et al. (1992, p. 7) believed that 'Comparison of this amount (the costs of the required measures) with the standard national income yields the sustainable national income', but in fact, as noted in the previous section, because they are static cost calculations, rather than being derived in the context of full economic interaction, they cannot simply be deducted from GNP. Rather, any calculation of green GNP (ESNI) using the costs of technologies that would have to be implemented to bring environmental performance within sustainability standards requires the implementation of these technologies to be simulated in the context of an economic model that contains these interactions and which projects the economic implications of progressively meeting the sustainability standards over time. Once the standards had been met, the model's economic output could be regarded as the ESNI, offering an estimate 'of the level and composition of environmentally respectful economic output that, for each accounting period being considered, may be feasible with currently known technology or under hypotheses about future technological innovation' (ECDGXII, 1997, p. 8).

Such modelling is a major undertaking, requiring integrated economy-energy-environment modelling that is disaggregated enough to enable the various technologies and environmental effects to be adequately modelled. However, there have been a number of modelling simulations of this kind, carried out with varying degrees of detail and sophistication. An early attempt was de Boer et al. (1994), who found that reducing the impacts across five environmental themes (climate change, ozone depletion, acidification, eutrophication, waste disposal) to sustainability levels reduced GNP by 64 per cent. However, as the study acknowledges, this is not a very realistic result, because it does not, in fact, model technical abatement measures at all, but reduces environmental impacts simply by reducing the activities that are responsible for them. Such a procedure gives very little insight into the economic implications of reducing environmental impacts by bringing about technical change over time. More satisfactory approaches to such modelling are taken by Faucheux et al. (1998), Meyer and Ewerhart (1998) and Verbruggen (elsewhere in this book), all of which permit more sophisticated economic adjustments in response to imposed environmental constraints, the costs of which are therefore much reduced from those obtained by de Boer at al. (1994).

7.4 Estimating the Sustainability Gap

Given an indicator of an environmental state or pressure that shows the current environmental position for some environmental issue, and a sustainability standard for the same indicator that shows a sustainable state, or the maximum pressure that is compatible with a sustainable state, with regard to that environmental theme, it is possible to determine a 'sustainability gap' ($SGAP_P$), in physical terms, between the current and a sustainable situation.

$SGAP_P$ indicates the degree of consumption of natural capital, either in the past or present, which is in excess of what is required for environmental sustainability. For the state indicators, the gap indicates the extent to which natural resource stocks are too low, or pollution stocks are too high. For pressure indicators, the gap indicates the extent to which the flows of energy and materials that contribute to environmental depletion and degradation are too high. $SGAP_P$ indicates in physical terms the extent to which economic activity is resulting in unsustainable impacts on important environmental functions.

$SGAP_P$ can give useful information as to the environmental impacts that need to be reduced, and by how much, but it does nothing to relate these impacts to the economic activities that are responsible for them, and which will need to be changed if the impacts are to be reduced. It would therefore seem desirable to link the sustainability indicators, and hence $SGAP_P$, to the national accounts, specifically by allocating the physical impacts responsible for the sustainability gap to the different sectors in the national accounts.

The sectoral disaggregation of environmental effects has been pioneered by the NAMEA (National Accounting Matrix including Environmental Accounts) system developed in the Dutch Central Bureau of Statistics. As described in Keuning (1996, pp.4–5), this system covers the depletion of three types of natural resources – crude oil, natural gas and wood – and five types of environmental degradation: the greenhouse effect, depletion of the ozone layer, acidification, eutrophication, generation of wastes (Keuning, 1996, pp.4–5). These environmental themes are related to seven aggregate economic sectors, which overall are responsible for generating the unsustainable environmental effects: agriculture, manufacturing (including oil refineries, chemical industries, basic metal industry, other manufacturing), electricity generation, construction, transport, services and other, and households. The NAMEA system has been recommended by the European Commission as the model for a European System of Integrated Economic and Environmental Indices (Keuning, 1996, p. 2). Sweden and the UK have also decided to adopt NAMEA as the organizing framework for their work.

The sustainability gap indicators represent the physical improvements in the state of, or the reductions in the pressures exerted on, various environmental media and resources that are required in order to comply with the relevant sustainability standard. The NAMEA matrix can allocate the pressures among the various sectors that appear in the national accounts, but in order for the sustainability gap indicators to be compared directly with economic activity and output, they need to be given a monetary valuation. Consideration of technologies of abatement/avoidance and restoration, by sector or with regard to different environmental media, enable, for each environmental theme, a series of cost curves to be built up, so that the cost of attaining each of the sustainability standards can be derived. These costs may then be aggregated to arrive at a full monetary figure for the sustainability gap ($SGAP_M$). Table 4.1 sets out the general schema, relating it to the normal input/output structure of the national accounts. In general abatement/avoidance costs are used to calculate the costs of reducing environmental pressures (for example emissions) to sustainable levels, while restoration costs are used to calculate the costs of restoring environmental states to sustainable levels.

Table 4.1 Matrix for the construction of the sustainability gap

	Economic sectors	Environmental impacts			
		Current	Sustainable	SGAP	
Economic sectors	Input/output tables	NAMEA pressure indicators			
Totals				**Physical**	**Monetary**[1]
Environmental quality		State indicators		**Physical**	**Monetary**[2]

Notes:
[1] Calculated using abatement/avoidance costs.
[2] Calculated using restoration costs.

Source: Ekins & Simon (1998, p. 161).

$SGAP_M$, of course, is identical to the Hueting et al. cost figure discussed in the previous section. However, for the reasons given earlier, it is not here envisaged that this cost is commensurable with GDP or the other national accounting product aggregates. Therefore it could not be subtracted from, say, NDP, in order to produce a 'sustainable income', or 'green GDP' figure. $SGAP_M$ also does not represent the amount of money that would have to be spent to achieve sustainability. The latter amount could only be estimated from whole-economy modelling using the $SGAP_M$ calculations, which would take account of economic feedbacks and interactions, as discussed in the previous section. Actually closing $SGAP_P$ would probably cost substantially less than $SGAP_M$, because of the economy's adjustment to the expenditures entailed. $SGAP_M$ is very much a static, partial equilibrium calculation, representing at a moment in time the aggregation of expenditures that would need to be made to reduce the various dimensions of $SGAP_P$ to zero.

However, $SGAP_M$ would still be an expressive indicator of the potential of an economy, at a certain moment in time, to achieve environmental sustainability. It would reflect both the physical distances from environmental sustainability and the economic possibilities of reducing those distances. Over time, $SGAP_M$ would decrease if either the physical sustainability gaps decreased, or new technologies, processes or materials were developed, which enabled those gaps to be reduced at lower cost in the future. $SGAP_M$/GDP, either in aggregate or for each environmental theme, would also be an interesting indicator with which to make inter-country comparisons of environmental efficiency, in much the same way as energy intensity (energy use/GDP) is currently used.

The concept of Hicksian income, and thence environmentally sustainable income, have been important organizing ideas for the methodologies of adjustment of the national accounts that have been developed, so it is a matter of some regret that no methodology can at present yield a convincing number for 'green GDP' in the current or past periods, or seems likely to be able to do so. However, as Young (1992, p. 12) points out, this may turn out to be just as well, because 'There is a risk that resource-modified accounting systems may develop a false sense of policy security by implying that all the environmental problems faced by the nation are being adequately dealt with'.

It may in any case be that the (partial EDP)/GDP and $SGAP_M$/GDP ratios, which can be calculated and which will be responsive to both economic growth and environmental policy, will fulfil the objectives of trying to calculate green GDP in the first place. For it is these numbers that monetarily represent, for the former, the relative economic burden of countering environmental degradation and some, at least, of the consumption of ecological capital; and, for the latter, a continuing failure to achieve standards of sustainability.

8 ENVIRONMENTAL SUSTAINABILITY AND ECONOMIC GROWTH

The relationship between economic growth and the environment remains among the most contested ground in the environment-economy discourse. At least since the publication of *Limits to Growth* (Meadows et al., 1972), a strong strand of opinion has held that indefinitely continuing economic growth is incompatible with environmental sustainability. Such a view has perhaps been particularly associated with Herman Daly (see, for example, Daly, 1996), but also with Roefie Hueting, through such quotes as the following: 'Saving the environment will certainly check production growth and probably lead to lower levels of national income. This outcome can hardly surprise. Many have known for a long time that population growth and rising production and consumption cannot be sustained forever in a finite world' (Tinbergen and Hueting, 1992, p. 56).

One of the confusions in the literature on this issue is caused by a failure to distinguish consistently between the growth in the economy's use of matter and energy (sometimes called its biophysical throughput) and the growth in economic output, measured in money terms, which is what is normally meant by economic growth. Clearly, in a physically finite world there is a limit to the amount of matter and energy available to the economy, especially considering the increase in entropy which (by the second law of thermodynamics) must arise from its use. However, the relationship between economic output (in money terms) and the flow of matter and energy associated with it is not fixed. Lecomber (1975) identified the three key effects that can reduce biophysical throughput, even as economic growth proceeds: changes in composition of output, substitution between factor inputs, and technical progress (more efficient use of the same input). If these three effects add up to a shift away from the resource or pollutant that is constraining economic growth, which is equal to or greater than the rate of growth, then the limits to economic growth are put back indefinitely. But, Lecomber (1975, p. 42) warns: '[This] establishes the *logical* conceivability, not the certainty, probability or even the possibility in practice, of growth continuing indefinitely. Everything hinges on the rate of technical progress and possibilities of substitution. This is perhaps the main issue that separates resource optimists and resource pessimists. The optimist believes in the power of human inventiveness to solve whatever problems are thrown in its way, as apparently it has done in the past. The pessimist questions the success of these past technological solutions and fears that future problems may be more intractable.' Lecomber looks for evidence in an effort to judge between these two positions, but without success. 'The central feature of technical advance is indeed its uncertainty' (ibid., 1975, p.45).

Ekins (2000) is an attempt to look again in detail at the evidence on this issue that was available to Lecomber and which has accumulated since. One fact that emerges is abundantly clear: whatever the 'logical conceivability', the economic growth that the world has experienced since 1975 has been anything but environmentally sustainable. In fact the environmental destruction that has been associated with it, and which continues, has been unprecedented and, at least since the Brundtland Report (WCED, 1987), is now widely recognized as among the principal challenges facing humanity.

Environmental policy is now making greater efforts to address this challenge, and it is clear that there are widespread opportunities for 'win-win' policies that correct distortions or inefficiencies in markets, and thereby increase economic output, while improving the environment: removing environmentally damaging subsidies, increasing the take up of already competitive, environmentally benign technologies, and ecological tax reform, are three examples that spring immediately to mind. Moreover, a wide range of less environmentally damaging technologies, such as those which exploit renewable energy sources, are being developed and may in time allow continuing economic growth with greatly reduced environmental damage. Von Weizsäcker et al. (1997) have written of factor four technological improvements in relation to the environment. Others believe that factor ten improvements are possible.

However, as Lecomber recognized, the essence of technical change is its uncertainty. No more certain is the ability of policy-makers, even when they have the will, actually to realize any win-win opportunities that may be available. Withdrawing subsidies, reforming tax systems and correcting market failures are anything but easy political options. Progress in these areas has certainly not been fast enough over the last 20 years to validate optimism that any theoretical compatibility between economic growth and environmental sustainability will in fact be achieved.

This continuing failure to make economic growth environmentally sustainable renders more serious another, perhaps even more fundamental, failure of economic management in recent decades: the continuing inability of capitalist market economies to thrive, or even survive, *without* economic growth. Theoretically, it should be possible at least for the richer countries to maintain, and perhaps even to reduce their output and consumption, without sliding into economic crisis and unemployment. Whatever the theory, the evidence suggests that societies cannot achieve this in practice. In fact there is very little evidence that economic recession leads even to environmental improvement, as would be expected if economic growth and environmental destruction were as inexorably connected as is sometimes asserted.

The danger is that, for as long as recession, or even a 'steady-state' economy, translate into economic crisis and unemployment, a society faced with a choice between economic growth and environmental sustainability will continue to choose the former. Eventually, of course, environmental degradation will make economic growth unachievable (that is, after all, what environmental unsustainability means), leaving the society to cope with both economic and environmental disintegration. One often senses that this awful possibility has never been far from the mind of Roefie Hueting during the 40 or so years that he has been working for the preservation of environmental functions, 'the most fundamental goods at the disposal of human beings because they constitute the very basis of our existence' (Hueting, 1996, p. 87).

9 CONCLUSION

This chapter has covered a lot of ground, much of which is covered in more detail by other contributors to this book. The range of issues discussed indicates the range of Roefie Hueting's contribution to ecological economic thought. It is, of course, much to be regretted that our societies have not as yet managed to use the insights of Hueting and others like him to 'solve' the problems of sustainable development, or even to reverse some of the most threatening trends of environmental unsustainability. But before such problems can be solved they must be understood, which is far from easy with such a complex problematique, which is rooted in the heart of the way our societies envision progress and, indeed, conceive of their existence. Hueting has contributed in a fundamental way to the generation of such understanding. What is now required, if the worst results of environmental unsustainability are to be avoided, is for people and their societies to act on it.

REFERENCES

Arrow, K.J. (1962), 'The economic implications of learning by doing', *Review of Economic Studies*, **29**, 155–73.

Barbier, E.B., J. Burgess and C. Folke (1994), *Paradise Lost? The Ecological Economics of Biodiversity*, Earthscan, London.

Bartelmus, P., C. Stahmer and J. van Tongeren (1993), 'Integrated environmental and economic accounting – a framework for an SNA satellite system', in E. Lutz, (ed.), *Toward Improved Accounting for the Environment*, World Bank, Washington, DC, pp. 22–45.

Becker, G. (1964), *Human Capital: A Theoretical and Empirical Analysis, with Special Reference to Education*, National Bureau of Economic Research and Columbia University, New York.

Bishop, R. (1978), 'Endangered species and uncertainty: the economics of a safe minimum standard', *American Journal of Agricultural Economics*, **60** (February), 10–18.

Bishop, R. (1993), 'Economic efficiency, sustainability and biodiversity', *Ambio*, **22** (2–3) (May), 69–73.

Braverman, H. (1974), *Labour and Monopoly Capital: The Degradation of Work in the 20th Century*, Monthly Review Press, New York/London.

Brouwer, R. and C. Leipert (1998), 'The role of environmental protection expenditures in a system of integrated economic and environmental accounting: theory, practice and future prospects', CSERGE Working Paper GEC 98-01, CSERGE, University of East Anglia, Norwich.

Bryant, C. and P. Cook (1992), 'Environmental issues and the national accounts', *Economic Trends*, 469, November, HMSO, London, pp. 99–122.

Ciriacy-Wantrup, S.V. (1952), *Resource Conservation: Economics and Policies*, University of California Press, Berkeley.

Daly, H.E. (1991), 'Elements of environmental macroeconomics', in R. Costanza, (ed.), *Ecological Economics: The Science and Management of Sustainability*, Columbia University Press, New York, pp. 22–31.

Daly, H.E. (1992), 'From empty world to full world economics', in R. Goodland, H.E. Daly and S. Serafy El (eds), *Population, Technology and Lifestyle: the Transition to Sustainability*, Island Press, Washington, DC.

Daly, H.E. (1995), 'On Wilfrid Beckerman's critique of sustainable development', *Environmental Values*, **4**, pp. 49–55.

Daly, H.E. (1996), *Beyond Growth: The Economics of Sustainable Development*, Beacon Press, Boston.

Dasgupta, P. (1995), 'Optimal development and the idea of net national product' in I. Goldin and A. Winters (eds) *The Economics of Sustainable Development*, Cambridge University Press, Cambridge, pp. 111–43.

De Boer, B., M. de Haan and M. Voogt (1994), 'What would net domestic product have been in a sustainable economy: preliminary views and results', in *National Accounts and the Environment*, Papers and Proceedings from a Conference, London, March, Statistics Canada, Ottawa.

De Groot, R.S. (1992), *Functions of Nature*, Wolters-Noordhoff, Groningen, The Netherlands.

ECDGXII (European Commission Directorate General XII) (1997), 'Methodological problems in the calculation of environmentally adjusted national income figures: final summary report', Report for ECDGXII on contract number EVSV-CT94-0363, July, Brussels.

Eisner, R. (1988), 'Extended accounts for national income and product', *Journal of Economic Literature*, **26** (December), 1611–84.

Ekins, P. (1992), 'A four-capital model of wealth creation' in P. Ekins. and M. Max-Neef (eds), *Real-life Economics: Understanding Wealth Creation*, Routledge, London/New York, pp. 147–55.

Ekins, P. (2000), *Economic Growth and Environmental Sustainability: The Prospects for Green Growth*, Routledge, London/New York.

Ekins, P. and M. Max-Neef (eds) (1992), *Real-life Economics: Understanding Wealth-Creation*, Routledge, London.

Ekins, P. and S. Simon (1998), 'Determining the sustainability gap: national accounting for environmental sustainability' in P. Vaze (ed.), *UK Environmental Accounts: Theory, Data and Application*, Office for National Statistics, London, pp. 147–67.

El Serafy, S. (1989) 'The proper calculation of income from depletable natural resources' in Y. Ahmad, S. El Serafy and E. Lutz, (eds), *Environmental Accounting for Sustainable Development*, World Bank, Washington DC, pp. 10–18.

EUROSTAT (1994), *SERIEE*, EUROSTAT, Luxembourg.

Faber, M. and J. Proops (1991), 'National accounting, time and the environment: a neo-austrian approach', in R. Costanza (ed.), *Ecological Economics: The Science and Management of Sustainability*, Columbia University Press, New York, pp. 215–33.

Faucheux, S., M. O'Connor and S. van den Hove (1998), 'Towards a sustainable national Income?' in S. Faucheux and M. O'Connor (eds), *Valuation for Sustainable Development: Methods and Policy Indicators*, Edward Elgar, Cheltenham.

Folke, C., C.S. Holling and C. Perrings (1994), 'Biodiversity, ecosystems and human welfare', Beijer Discussion Paper Series No. 49, Beijer International Institute of Ecological Economics, Stockholm.

Hamilton, K. (1994), 'Green adjustments to GDP', *Resources Policy*, **20** (3), pp. 155–68.

Hartwick, J. (1977), 'Intergenerational equity and the investing of rents from exhaustible resources', *American Economic Review*, **67** (5), 972–4.

Hartwick, J. (1990), 'Natural resources, national accounting and economic depreciation', *Journal of Public Economics*, **43**, 291–304.

Herfindahl, O. and A. Kneese (1973), 'Measuring social and economic change: benefits and costs of environmental pollution', in M. Moss (ed.), *The Measurement of Economic and Social Performance*, Columbia University, New York, pp. 441–508.

Hueting, R. (1980), *New Scarcity and Economic Growth*, North Holland, Amsterdam (Dutch edition first published 1974).

Hueting, R. (1992a), 'The economic functions of the environment,' in P. Ekins and M. Max-Neef (eds), *Real-Life Economics: Understanding Wealth Creation*, Routledge, London/New York, pp. 61–9.

Hueting, R. (1992b), 'Growth, environment and national income: theoretical problems and a practical solution' in P. Ekins and M. Max-Neef, (eds), *Real-life Economics: Understanding Wealth Creation*, Routledge, London/New York, pp. 255–63.

Hueting, R. (1996), 'Three Persistent Myths in the environmental debate', *Ecological Economics*, **18**, 81–8.

Hueting, R., Bosch, P. and B. de Boer (1992), *Methodology for the Calculation of Sustainable National Income*, Statistical Essay M44, Netherlands Central Bureau of Statistics, Voorburg/Heerlen.

Hueting, R. and L. Reijnders. (1998), 'Sustainability is an objective concept', *Ecological Economics*, **27** (2), 139–47.

Hueting, R., L. Reijnders, B. de Boer, J. Lambooy and H. Jansen (1998), 'The concept of environmental function and its valuation', *Ecological Economics*, **25** (1), 31–5.

Keuning, S. (1996), 'The NAMEA experience: an interim evaluation of the Netherlands' integrated accounts and indicators for the environment and the economy', paper presented to the International Symposium on 'Integrated Environmental and Economic Accounting in Theory and Practice', Tokyo, 5–8 March, mimeo, Statistics Netherlands, National Accounts Department, Voorburg.

Kuznets, S. (1973), 'Concluding remarks' in M. Moss (ed.), *The Measurement of Economic and Social Performance*, Columbia University, New York, pp. 579–92.

Lecomber, R. (1975), *Economic Growth versus the Environment*, Macmillan, London.

Mäler, K.-G. (1991), 'National accounts and environmental resources', *Environmental and Resource Economics*, **1**, 1–15.

Max-Neef, M. (1991), *Human Scale Development: Conception, Application and Further Reflection*, Apex Press, New York.

Meadows, D.H, D.L Meadows, J. Randers and W. Behrens (1972), *The Limits to Growth*, Universe Books, New York.

Meyer, B. and G. Ewerhart (1998), 'Multisectoral policy modelling for environmental analysis', in K. Uno and P. Bartelmus (eds), *Environmental Accounting in Theory and Practice*, Kluwer, Dordrecht, pp. 396–406.

Pearce, D. and R.K. Turner (1990), *Economics of Natural Resources and the Environment*, Harvester Wheatsheaf, Hemel Hempstead, Herts., UK.

Perrings, C., R.K Turner and C. Folke (1995), 'Ecological economics: the study of interdependent economic and ecological systems', Beijer Discussion Paper Series No. 55, Beijer International Institute of Ecological Economics, Stockholm.

Pezzey, J. (1992), *Sustainable Development Concepts: An Economic Analysis*, World Bank Environment Paper No. 2, World Bank, Washington, DC.

Repetto, R., W. Magrath, M. Wells, C. Beer, and F. Rossini (1989), *Wasting Assets: Natural Resources in the National Accounts*, World Resources Institute, Washington, DC.

Serageldin, I. (1994), 'Making development sustainable', in I. Serageldin and A. Steer (eds), *Making Development Sustainable: From Concepts to Action*, Environmentally Sustainable Development Occasional Paper Series No. 2, World Bank, Washington, DC, pp. 1–5.

Serageldin, I. and A. Steer (1994), 'Epilogue: expanding the capital stock' in I. Serageldin and A. Steer (eds), *Making Development Sustainable: From Concepts to Action*, Environmentally Sustainable Development Occasional Paper Series No. 2, World Bank, Washington, DC, pp. 30–32.

Tinbergen, J. and R. Hueting (1992), 'GNP and market prices' in R. Goodland, H.E. Daly and S. Serafy El (eds), *Population, Technology and Lifestyle: The Transition to Sustainability*, Island Press, Washington, DC, pp. 52–62.

Tomer, J. (1973), 'Management consulting for private enterprise: a theoretical and empirical analysis of the contribution of management consultants to economic growth in the United States', unpublished Ph.D. thesis, Rutgers University, New Brunswick, NJ.

Tomer, J. (1987), *Organizational Capital: The Path to Higher Productivity and Well-Being*, Praeger, Westport, CT.

Turner, R.K. (1993), 'Sustainability: principles and practice' in R.K. Turner (ed), *Sustainable Environmental Economics and Management: Principles and Practice*, Belhaven Press, New York/London, pp. 3–36.

UNSD (United Nations Statistical Division) (1993), *Integrated Environmental and*

Economic Accounting: Handbook of National Accounting, Studies in Methods, Series F, No. 61, Interim Version, UN Statistical Division, New York.

Vaze, P. (1998), 'Valuing the depletion of oil and gas reserves' in P. Vaze (ed.), *UK Environmental Accounts: Theory, Data and Application*, Office for National Statistics, London, pp. 61–73, reprinted from *Economic Trends*, Issue 510, August 1996, The Stationery Office, London.

Victor, P.A. (1991), 'Indicators of sustainable development: some lessons from capital theory', *Ecological Economics*, **4**, 191–213.

Victor, P., E. Hanna and A.Kubursi (1994), 'How strong is weak sustainability?', paper presented to the International Symposium 'Modèles de Développement Soutenable', 1 of Proceedings, pp. 93–114, University of Paris 1, published in S. Faucheux, M. O'Connor, and J. van der Straaten (eds), *Sustainable Development: Analysis and Public Policy*, Kluwer, Dordrecht.

Von Weizsäcker, E., A.Lovins and H. Lovins (1997), *Factor Four: Doubling Wealth, Halving Resource Use*, Earthscan, London.

WBGU (German Advisory Council on Global Change) (1995), 'Scenario for the derivation of global CO_2 reduction targets and implementation strategies', WBGU, Bremershaven.

WCED (World Commission on Environment and Development) (1987), *Our Common Future* (The Brundtland Report), Oxford University Press, Oxford/New York.

Young, M.D. (1992), *Natural Resource Accounting: Some Australian Experiences and Observations*, Working Document 92/1, February, CSIRO, Canberra.

PART TWO

Reflections

5. Roefie Hueting's perpendicular 'demand curve' and the issue of objective value

Herman E. Daly

1 INTRODUCTION

A logical difficulty encountered in the technical problem of correcting national income for the loss of natural functions has led Roefie Hueting into a fundamental conflict not only with orthodox economics, but also, surprisingly, with the dominant assumption of Western culture since the Enlightenment. That assumption of our modern culture is the rejection of teleology, of final causation or purpose, as a real and undeniable part of the world in which we live. I do not think that Roefie Hueting was seeking such a conflict – on the contrary I think it makes him uneasy. But Hueting is relentlessly logical and honest – characteristics that often lead one to situations of conflict. Furthermore, all of us are involved in that conflict whether we are aware of it or not. It is not just Hueting's problem. My task in this study is to explain more fully and give reasons for what I have just asserted. To do that I should begin with some words about the technical problem that has led to the philosophical confrontation.

2 THE TECHNICAL PROBLEM

The loss of natural functions, the 'New Scarcity' that Hueting (1980) has been a pioneer in identifying, explaining, and measuring, has traditionally not been recognized in national income accounting. Loss of environmental function has been an unmeasured reduction in both productive capacity and direct welfare. To account for this loss in true national income it is necessary to value natural functions in order to subtract the loss. This requires prices for natural functions, which in turn requires supply and demand curves. Hueting's supply function is the marginal cost curve of restoration of the natural function. His difficulty arises with the demand curve that is unknown because markets for many natural functions do not exist, and even if they did most interested parties (for example future generations, other species) are not allowed to bid in the market. The logic of income accounting requires the subtraction of the value of sacrificed ecological functions. But sacrificed functions cannot be valued in the same way as other goods and services because the demand curve cannot be defined – that is, cannot be defined in the same way as other demand curves, namely in terms of individual preferences expressible in markets. Hueting's resolution is a perpendicular 'demand curve', an expression of objective value, not individual preferences (Hueting, 1991) . The objective value is sustainability. This entails a rejection of the dogma that individual subjective preferences are the sole source of value, and introduces collective objective value as an additional source.

Roefie Hueting has been led by the logic of practical problem solving into a rather basic conflict with the dogma that all value arises from private subjective preferences. He needs a perpendicular demand curve at a level of environmental exploitation that is sustainable in order to determine prices proper for the calculation of sustainable national income. Income is by definition (Hicks, 1948), an amount of output such that its production during this year does not impair our capacity to produce the same amount next year. In other words, productive capacity must be maintained intact, there must be no net consumption of capital, either man-made or natural capital. Since we currently consume natural capital without deducting it, our calculation of national income is erroneous both by the quantity of natural capital consumed and by the price distortions caused by the drawdown of that natural capital. The condition of ecological sustainability has to be imposed in some way before one can calculate national income that is true to the very concept of income as sustainable production. So Roefie Hueting is led by standard economic logic to his imposition of a perpendicular demand curve at a sustainable level of exploitation of natural functions. It is not a gratuitous desire on his part to impose his personal preferences on the rest of the world. It is the honest national income accountant's professional duty to measure true income, not some amalgam of capital drawdown and production. Hueting appeals to the Brundtland Commission and other political bodies who have advocated sustainability as a social goal, in at least partial justification for his treating sustainability as an objective value.

He might also appeal more explicitly to the very concept of income. Strictly speaking the term 'sustainable income' is a redundancy because income is by definition sustainable. The very concept embodies the implicit purpose of prudential behaviour, of avoiding unplanned impoverishment by inadvertent consumption of productive capacity. National income is not a 'value-free' fact – it is a concept built around a prudential purpose. Its definition is not decided by aggregating individual preferences. If we did not have the purpose of avoiding capital consumption and consequent impoverishment (and, yes, of increasing wealth) there would be little reason to calculate national income in the first place. But practice has strayed far from theory, both because the purposive element in the concept has been forgotten, and the 'new scarcity' has been overlooked or denied. Consequently, what we currently call national income is decidedly unsustainable, necessitating the awkward pleonasm 'sustainable national income' for the corrected figure, in order to again convey the original meaning of income.

3 SOME CONFLICTS IN ECONOMIC PHILOSOPHY

To understand valuation we must pay some attention to the valuer – the valuing agent or self that is presupposed by valuation. Economists take this valuer to be the human individual. The market weights and aggregates individual valuations. Individual values, usually called preferences by economists, are taken to be subjective in the sense that, if they were objective, individuals could agree on them and enact them collectively. It is assumed that there is no objective value or standard for judging preferences. Values are by assumption reducible to subjective individual preferences. By motivating individual choices these subjective preferences become causative in the real world through the market. But they are not causative through collective action because they are assumed to lack the degree of objectivity necessary for the agreement presupposed by collective action.

Since the marginalist revolution economics has accepted a subjectivist theory of value – that value is rooted in utility conceived as the satisfaction of individual preferences. Diminishing marginal utility underlies the demand curve, which in combination with supply (based on increasing marginal costs) determines prices. Earlier in the history of economic thought value had been considered objective in the sense of being rooted in 'real costs', especially labour cost. Today some ecologists believe in an energy cost theory of value, so objective cost theories of value have not completely died out. Among economists, however, cost means 'opportunity cost', the best alternative benefit forgone. Thus the ultimate root of cost is the same as that of benefit – subjective preference, whether enjoyed or forgone. I am not objecting to opportunity cost, or to marginal utility. My use of the term 'objective value' in this chapter refers not to costs but to preferences – the notion of objectively good preferences. This notion has been rejected by economists who hold that preferences are purely personal and subjective. Moreover, any appeal to the concept of objective value in this sense is thought to be merely the veiled imposition of the speaker's personal preferences on everyone else. Indeed, this must follow from the dogmatic assumption that the only locus of value is subjective individual preference. If this is true then any claim on behalf of objective value can only be, at best confusion, and at worst an attempt to 'undemocratically' promote one's own preferences at the expense of others. Of course if the value of democracy, too, is simply a personal preference rather than an objective value, then it is hard to see why it should be privileged over non-democratic pursuit of one's own preferences. But for now my point is simply that the non-existence of objective value is an assumption, not a conclusion of rational argument or empirical investigation. It may have started out as a methodological assumption, but today it functions as an ontological axiom.

Hueting's perpendicular demand curve represents an objective concept of sustainability in two senses: first, that a sustainable level of aggregate resource use is objectively definable ecologically and subject to at least crude measurement; second, that sustainability so defined is itself an objective value whose authority over private preferences should be accepted by individuals and expressed by their democratic representatives. Surprisingly, even the objectivity of sustainability in the first sense seems controversial, and Roefie Hueting and Lucas Reijnders (1998) had to write an article countering the notion that the very concept of ecological sustainability is subjective. My concern here is with objectivity in the second sense – that sustainability, in addition to being objectively definable (at least as definable as the concept of 'money'), is a good thing – an objective value worthy of being a goal of public policy. If the objective value of sustainability conflicts with private subjective preferences, then too bad for private subjective preferences. As offensive as this last statement is to economists, most would accept that preferences for murder and robbery should be ruled out, presumably because they conflict with objective value. But they remain reluctant to rule out 'revealed preferences' for unsustainable levels of consumption, because they do not recognize sustainability as an objective value.

Others, including myself, have been led to the same conflict as Hueting, but from a somewhat different starting point. If, instead of measuring national income in a way that reflects sustainability, one is trying to design a policy for actually attaining sustainability in a market economy, one encounters the same problem. For example, the policy of tradable permits for depletion or pollution requires as a first step that total quantity extracted or emitted be limited to an amount that is sustainable. In this case it is the supply function that becomes a perpendicular at the chosen total quantity. Supply is decided socially by reference to the objective value of sustainability, and demand is left to the market. But demand is only allowed to determine the price that rations the fixed total quantity that has been set socially. Demand, subjective individual preference, is not allowed to influence quantity – it only determines the rationing price, subject to the total quantity that is set by the objective value of sustainability.

It is interesting that one approach leads to a perpendicular demand curve, and the other to a perpendicular supply curve. This difference in analytical representation deserves further reflection and explanation, but for present purposes I want to emphasize that both analytical adaptations represent the introduction of objective value, and therefore both conflict with the fundamental dogma that all value arises from subjective individual preferences.

Is it possible to go too far in granting monopoly rights to subjective individual preferences in the determination of value? The force of the preference dogma was recently brought home to me in a conversation with a young professor of environmental economics. He confided to me that personally he had a strong preference for sustainability, but since he doubted that sustainability was derivable from the individual preferences of the population, he could not justify devoting time and effort as a professional economist to furthering the idea. I was shocked by what he said. However, if all value really is reducible to subjective preference then his position is not unreasonable – except one wonders why he is so diffident about asserting his own preferences, unless he just happens to have a personal preference for diffidence rather than assertiveness.

Of course the same logic applies to all social goals – full employment, a just distribution of income, avoidance of inflation, and indeed also the promotion of aggregate economic growth. Many social goals cannot be derived from individual preferences, so more and more they are thought by young economists, who reflect the current university teaching, not to exist. Goals like full employment and distributive justice were recognized in an era in which the dogma of individual preference was not so well established, and they continue to command respect thanks to historical inertia and to our enormous capacity to believe contradictory things. But more and more I suspect that they will fall into the same orthodox disrepute as sustainability as we continue to try to live by the dogma of subjective personal preference, and its corollary, the denial of objective value. I believe that sustainability is an objective public value whose legitimacy does not derive from private subjective preferences any more than does democracy or justice. We do not submit the institution of democracy itself to a popular vote, nor do we allow free market participants to sell themselves into slavery even if that is their preference.

4 OBJECTIVE VALUE AND TOTALITARIANISM

While I believe that logic and honesty have driven Hueting to his perpendicular, I also believe that he is personally very uncomfortable with it, for a number of reasons. Not the least of these reasons is that he is a child of World War II. As a witness to the atrocities of Nazism, Imperialism, and Communism, Hueting is very sensitive to the evils that can result from totalitarian regimes that are only too willing to trample individuals in the name of collective and presumably objective values. Hueting worries that departure from the dogma of individual preferences would lead to a slippery slope that could end again in totalitarianism. One can certainly understand his concern. While I respect this fear, and the life experience that underlies it, I want nevertheless to suggest that it is the preference dogma that is today the broader path to totalitarianism, and that only a commitment to objective value can save us from it.

The argument has already been made by C.S. Lewis (1944) and I need only try to summarize it. A good place to begin is Lewis's statement, so shocking to modern prejudices, that 'A dogmatic belief in objective value is necessary to the very idea of a rule which is not tyranny or an obedience which is not slavery.'

Nothing could be more contrary to the dogma of subjective preference. Yet Lewis's logic is both simple and compelling. If you and I disagree in our purposes or preferences, and neither of us believes in objective value, then there is nothing that either of us can appeal to in an effort to persuade the other. I can only restate and clarify my preferences, and you can only do the same. I hope that once I have made my preferences clear to you, you will agree with them, and you hope the same about me. But that usually does not happen. Our different preferences or purposes have no authority beyond the strength of personal conviction with which we hold them. Once our differences have been made unmistakably clear the only resolution is coercion, either by physical force or psychological manipulation. Only if we accept the reality of objective value whose authority trumps our personal preferences is there any possibility of reasoning together and of being genuinely open to persuasion.

We may not agree in our perceptions of objective value either, but as long as we are trying to discern more clearly a reality whose existence we both recognize, there is reason for at least a modicum of patience, tolerance, and goodwill. But why should I be tolerant of your subjective preferences which have no more authority than mine, indeed none at all to me since I am by assumption guided only by my own preferences. If I happen to be the stronger or the cleverer I will have my way. It makes no sense to appeal to my 'moral sensitivity' unless we believe that there is something real to which we should be sensitive. A 'moral compass' implies the existence of objective value, a true magnetic north to lure the sensitive needle towards itself. If our individual moral compass needles point in different directions we can try to sensitize them by reasoning together, but we must sensitize them to objective magnetic north, not to our own subjective preferences. If we believe there is no magnetic north, then we should find an alternative use for our compass – such as throwing it at the cat.

5 THE BIG PHILOSOPHICAL ISSUE

In what follows I want to reconsider critically a major feature of our culture that provides the larger context for the economist's preference dogma: the separation of the world of private subjective preferences that make no truth claims and are therefore not cross-examined – from the world of purposeless efficient causation in which truth claims are both made and cross-examined (Newbigin, 1986). To put it paradoxically, how can it be that the only things that are supposed to have value in public discourse are 'value-free' facts?

Why has this assumption that all value is rooted in individual preferences become a basic dogma in economics? I suspect because it is coherent with, and likely derivative from, a larger cultural assumption that excludes purpose from science. If objective value exists then its attainment obviously constitutes a purpose, and the hallmark of modern science is the exclusion of final causation and the focus only on efficient causation. Purpose and value have been confined to the private subjective world of individual experience in which one person's experience or preference is as good as another's. In the public world of facts upon which agreement is expected and truth claims are made, efficient causation reigns, and purpose is not allowed. Our age is often called 'pluralistic' – but we are pluralistic only in the private realm of values and purposes. In the public realm of fact, pluralism would be considered irresponsible indifference to the truth.

Of course, purpose continues to exist in the private subjective world of individuals and is presumed by economists to be causative in the public world, as noted earlier. Even this degree of causative efficacy via purpose as individual preference is an embarrassment to many scientists who, consistent with the overall banishment of teleology from science, dismiss our conscious experience of individual purpose as an epiphenomenon, an illusion. Economists usually do not go this far, but they do try to confine purpose to the private subjective world of individuals and devote their efforts to explaining mechanistically how these individual actions, motivated by private preferences, give rise to public consequences, to definite prices and allocations under different market structures. This market allocation is usually taken as implicitly good, in the same way that democracy is considered good, although such goodness is impossible to demonstrate on the basis personal subjective preferences with no appeal to objective value. Some people like markets and some do not, some people have a preference for democracy and others do not – just as some people like apples better than oranges. If one insists on deriving all value from the private sphere of individual preferences, and to deny any notion of publicly objective value, then one must accept the consequences, however nihilistic.

The problem is that economists, and with them modern culture, do not believe in objective value. Modern culture believes passionately in objective facts in the public world of efficient causation from which purpose has been expunged, and allows purpose to exist only in the private world of subjective experience in which no truth claims are allowed. One person's purposes are as good as another's; but one person's facts have to stand up to public scrutiny. An attitude that, as just noted, would be considered irresponsible indifference to truth in the public realm of facts is considered humble tolerance in the realm of purpose. This is because, in our plausibility structure, purpose is considered less real than fact. Therefore discussing purpose is less serious than discussing fact – we can afford to be 'tolerant' about subjective matters, like dreams, that don't really matter. Besides, if we start taking objective value seriously we may end up with religious wars like we had before the Enlightenment. If purpose is, as many scientists claim, just an illusion, or if, as economists claim, one person's purposes are as good as another's, then it would indeed make sense not to pay too much attention to purpose, and that benign neglect would contribute to peace and tranquillity. Furthermore, the elimination of final causation from the study of nature has been enormously fruitful in physics, chemistry, and even biology. Why not apply the same philosophy to the study of everything, of all that is, including economics? This indeed is the current programme. The problem is that this programme is leading us to conceptual absurdity, political paralysis and ecological catastrophe – because it is founded on an inconsistency.

6 WHITEHEAD'S LURKING INCONSISTENCY

Alfred North Whitehead (1925) recognized this cultural contradiction back in 1925, and referred to it as the 'lurking inconsistency':

> A scientific realism, based on mechanism, is conjoined with an unwavering belief in the world of men and of the higher animals as being composed of self-

> determining organisms. This radical inconsistency at the basis of modern thought accounts for much that is half-hearted and wavering in our civilization . . . It enfeebles [thought], by reason of the inconsistency lurking in the background . . . For instance, the enterprises produced by the individualistic energy of the European peoples presuppose physical actions directed to final causes. But the science which is employed in their development is based on a philosophy which asserts that physical causation is supreme, and which disjoins the physical cause from the final end.

Whitehead went on to observe that, 'It is not popular to dwell on the absolute contradiction here involved'.

Biologist Charles Birch (1990), a keen student of Whitehead, has written an insightful book entitled *On Purpose* in which he begins to come to grips with Whitehead's lurking, radical inconsistency, which Birch restates as follows: 'The central symbol of ecological thinking in this book is purpose. It has become the central problem for contemporary thought because of the mismatch in modernism between how we think of ourselves and how we think and act in relation to the rest of the world'. Economics involves both thinking about ourselves and thinking and acting in relation to the rest of the world, the environment, thus neatly straddling the two poles of the lurking inconsistency.

In the emerging transdiscipline of ecological economics many of us, including sometimes Roefie Hueting, have spent the last decade criticizing economists for their neglect of the embeddedness of the economy in the larger ecosystem, and for their (our) ignorance of ecology in general. It has been the economist who needed correction and the ecologist who supplied it. I think this was, and still is, entirely necessary. However, as we try to develop policy on the basis of that theoretical understanding, it seems that ecologists are not only becoming less helpful, but also something of an obstacle. Why is this? I think Whitehead gives us the clue in the quotation above.

The enfeeblement of modern thought, noted by Whitehead, is evident today in the environmental movement, especially as it is promoted by biologists and ecologists, at least by their most visible representatives. Their science and philosophy is mechanistic. No final causes or purposes are permitted into their neo-Darwinian world of efficient causation by random mutation and natural selection. This mechanical process, over long time periods, is held to explain not only the evolution of all living things from a common ancestor, but also, in some versions, the emergence of the common ancestor itself from the 'primordial chemical soup'. For human beings in particular, random mutation and natural selection are thought to determine not only such characteristics as eye colour and height, but also intelligence, consciousness, morality and capacity for rational thought.

Powerful though it is, the neo-Darwinist explanation nevertheless faces severe difficulties even in the realm of mechanism. But leave those aside. My point is that it is obviously inconsistent to declare the world void of purpose, and then exempt one's self from that declaration by urging some policy in pursuit of – guess what? – a purpose! The manipulator (policy-maker) credits him or herself with the very capacity for purposeful action in pursuit of objective value that he or she denies to the manipulated (the rest of the world). Herein lies the broad path to totalitarianism, alluded to earlier.

7 PURPOSE AND VALUE

We, and perhaps higher animals in general, directly experience purpose, and within limits, act in a self-determining manner guided or lured by purpose. If we are part of nature then so is purpose; if purpose is not part of nature then neither, in large part, are we. However, the immediate reality of final cause and purpose that we all directly experience, must, in the mechanist's view, be an 'epiphenomenon' – an illusion that itself was selected because of the reproductive advantage that it chanced to confer on those under its influence. The policy implication of the dogma that purpose is not causative in the world is *laissez-faire* beyond the most libertarian economist's wildest model. The only 'policy' consistent with this view is, 'let it happen as it will anyway'. It is odd that the illusion of purpose should be thought to confer a selective advantage while purpose itself is considered non-causative – but that is the neo-Darwinist's problem. Economists do not go so far as to declare purposes illusory, but, as we have seen, they attain nearly the same result by confining them to the realm of private subjectivity exempt from the discipline to which public claims of objective truth are submitted. If one person's preferences are as good as another's, and preference is the ultimate source of value, then there is really nothing for us to talk about. There remains, however, a great deal for us to fight about.

But, economists do vigorously affirm at least one public purpose, one apparently objective value. That purpose is of course aggregate growth in GDP. It is thought to be derivable from individual preferences by the (invalid) argument that more and more preference satisfaction by more and more individuals must necessarily result from aggregate growth in GDP. But the 'New Scarcity' (remember the subtitle – 'more welfare through less production') means that GDP growth has unmeasured costs that might be growing faster than the measured benefits (usually taken as GDP itself). So the inference is unwarranted. However, even an unworthy and unwarranted purpose, such as GDP growth for ever, will dominate the absence of purpose. Economists, for all their (our) shallowness and ignorance of the natural world, will continue to dominate ecologists in the policy forum simply because they affirm a purpose while the ecologists do not – and logically cannot as long as they remain faithful neo-Darwinists.

The relevance of the lurking inconsistency to the new subdiscipline of 'conservation biology' should be evident – conservation is, after all, a policy in the service of a purpose. What are we trying to conserve? Biodiversity? Habitat? Why are they valuable, and which parts of the biota are more valuable? Although economists do not know how to value biodiversity, it seems that biologists are even more clueless, having purged their science of the very concept of value because it is tainted with teleology. But the very existence of conservation biology means that some biologists want to affirm purpose at least implicitly. According to economists, preferences are the ultimate standard of value and expression of purpose. Witness economists' attempts to value species by asking consumers how much they would be willing to pay to save a threatened species, or how much they would accept in compensation for the species' disappearance. The fact that the two methods of this 'contingent valuation' give different answers only adds comic relief to the underlying tragedy which is the reduction of value to taste.

8 MORE NEO-DARWINIST FALLOUT

Biologists have taken extreme pains for many years to rid their science of any trace of teleology. As Whitehead (1925) remarked:

> Many a scientist has patiently designed experiments for the purpose of substantiating his belief that animal operations are motivated by no purposes. He has perhaps spent his spare time writing articles to prove that human beings are as other animals so that purpose is a category irrelevant for the explanation of their bodily activities, his own activities included. Scientists animated by the purpose of proving that they are purposeless constitute an interesting subject for study.

Teleology has its limits, of course, and it is evident that mechanism has constituted an enormously successful research paradigm for biology (if for the moment we allow the biologist the implicit purpose whose achievement defines their success). The temptation to elevate a successful research paradigm to the level of a complete worldview is perhaps irresistible. But mechanism, too, has its limits. To deny the reality of our most immediate and universal experience (purpose) because it does not fit the mechanistic paradigm is radically anti-empirical. To refuse to recognize the devastating logical contradictions that result from the denial of purpose is profoundly anti-rational. That people already unembarrassed by the fact that their major intellectual purpose is the denial of the reality of purpose itself should now want to concern themselves deeply with the relative valuation of accidental pieces of their random world is incoherence compounded. If there is objective value then its attainment becomes a public purpose. Even if value is subjective it remains causative for individuals who act on it as a private purpose. Neo-Darwinists who do not accept the reality of purpose in either sense owe it to the rest of us to remain silent about valuation – and conservation as well.

According to biologists the existence of any species is an accident, and its continued survival is always subject to cancellation by random mutation and natural selection anywhere in the interdependent ecosystem. For people who teach this doctrine to sophomores on Monday, Wednesday and Friday to devote their Tuesdays, Thursdays and Saturdays to pleading with Congress and the public to save this or that species is at least surprising. Naturally the public asks these biologists what purpose would be served by conserving certain threatened species? Since most leading biologists claim not to believe in purposes, ends, or final causes, this is not an easy question for them to answer. They reveal the inconsistency that Whitehead saw lurking in the background by the feebleness and wavering half-heartedness of their answers. They tell us about biodiversity, and ecosystem stability and resilience, and about a presumed instinct of biophilia that we who systematically drive other species to extinction are nevertheless supposed to have encoded in our genes.

But the biologists are too half-hearted to affirm any of these descriptive concepts as an abiding purpose, and thereby challenge the fundamental assumption of their science. For example, biophilia could be appealed to as a virtue, a persuasive value, a *telos* rather than a wishfully imagined part of the deterministic genetic code. But that would be to admit purpose. Instead the biologists try to find some overlooked mechanistic cause that will make us do what we suspect we ought to do, but cannot logically advocate without acknowledging the reality of purpose. Absent purpose and value the biologists' appeals to the public are both logically and emotionally feeble. Is it too much to ask the neo-Darwinist think about the 'lurking inconsistency' – to speculate about the possibility that the survival value of neo-Darwinism itself has become negative for the species that really believes it?

9 THE PURPOSEFUL PERPENDICULAR

Why the above excursion into the problems of neo-Darwinism in an essay on valuation and national accounts? The issue under consideration is the omission of purpose and objective value from our cultural world view, and that omission is most evident in and influential through neo-Darwinism. But economics is not far behind in its denial of objective value. It hangs on to purpose only in the attenuated, but still causative, notion of personal preferences. One small but important barrier to this march of insane purposelessness is Hueting's perpendicular social demand curve. This humble perpendicular represents the assertion of objective value and final causation in a world whose plausibility structure recognizes only efficient causation. It is the insertion of a public purpose, a *telos*, an objective value, into both the value-free world of biology and the subjectivistic world of economics. Neither world welcomes it. The perpendicular asserts that sustainability is indeed not derivable from individual preferences, unless individual preferences, like sensitive compass needles, respond to the pull of 'magnetic north', to the lure of objective value. In the latter case it is of course objective value that is luring and persuading preferences, and consequently subjective preferences would not be the ultimate source of value.

The Enlightenment, with its rejection of teleology, certainly illuminated some hidden recesses of superstition in the so-called Dark Ages. But the angle of its cold light has also cast a deep shadow forward into the modern world, obscuring the reality of purpose. To attain the purpose of using the biosphere sustainably we will first have to reclaim purpose itself from the dark shadows.

Those of us who, like Hueting, have in one way or another rediscovered Whitehead's 'lurking inconsistency', are likely to have reason to agree with him, 75 years later, that 'It is not popular to dwell on the absolute contradiction here involved'. But Roefie Hueting has always been more interested in truth than in popularity. For this we honour him.

REFERENCES

Birch, Charles (1990), *On Purpose*, Australia: New South Wales University Press.

Hicks, John (1948), *Value and Capital*, 2nd edn, Oxford: Clarendon Press.

Hueting, Roefie (1980), *The New Scarcity* (More Welfare through Less Production?), Amsterdam: North Holland Publishing Company, (Dutch edition 1974).

Hueting, Roefie (1991), 'Correcting national income for environmental losses: a practical solution for a theoretical dilemma', in Robert Costanza (ed.), *Ecological Economics* (The Science and Management of Sustainability), New York: Columbia University Press, pp. 194–213. The approach there taken was strongly adumbrated already in *New Scarcity* (op. cit.) pp. 142–7.

Hueting, Roefie and Lucas Reijnders (1998) 'Sustainability is an objective concept', *Ecological Economics*, 27, pp. 139–7.

Lewis, C.S. (1944), *The Abolition of Man*, London: The Macmillan Company.
Newbigin, Lesslie (1986), *Foolishness to the Greeks* (The Gospel and Western Culture), Grand Rapids, MI: Wm. B. Eerdmans Publishing Co.
Whitehead, A.N. (1925), *Science and the Modern World*, London: The Macmillan Co.; see p. 76.

6. Values, valuation and valuing processes

Richard B. Norgaard, Astrid J. Scholz and Sarah Fleisher Trainor

1 INTRODUCTION

Roefie Hueting repeatedly argued that 'Society is sailing by the wrong compass, at the expense of the environment' (Hueting, 1992, p. 255). Failing to incorporate appropriate values for nature in critical indicators like gross domestic product affects the economic decisions we make and how we use the environment. Like Roefie, we are suspicious of how economists understand the value of ecosystems as the sum of individual services on the margin. We are equally suspicious of the measurement of value in the context of prices generated by consumers' choices in a market system that is unsustainable. We agree that 'Many environmental losses . . . constitute part of a process which may lead to the disruption of the life-support functions of our planet and endanger the living conditions of generations to come, and therefore cannot be considered separately' (Hueting, 1991, p. 200). Roefie Hueting consistently combined ecological reasoning with a sustainability ethic that precedes market values, an ethic that we share.

An underlying premise of our study is that achieving sustainability is proving difficult precisely because a sustainability ethic is not widely shared. Those who hold a sustainability ethic see protecting the material well-being of future generations as an overarching value, much as Wilfred Beckerman argues elsewhere in this book that justice within generations is an overriding criteria by which we should judge economic development. Political discourse and policy analysis, however, are increasingly dominated by the utilitarian ethics of economic reasoning alone, with fewer and fewer discussions of and appeals to other ethical criteria. In economic theory, this utilitarian ethic is captured by the individual-centric, consequentialist, decision algorithms by which economists currently assign values. Such algorithms are applied to everything from private consumption choices to social welfare considerations, and have been extended to the arena of environmental issues. The increasing dominance of scientific economic reasoning overshadows and largely ignores other forms of valuing such as social, cultural and moral values. (Funtowicz and Ravetz, 1994; Ravetz, 1994). Without a richer discourse on values, the appeals of Roefie Hueting to intergenerational equity, echoed by Herman Daly and other ecological economists, will fall on deaf ears. Through this chapter we seek to help open up and stimulate the richer values discourse on which our more specific efforts to promote sustainability and justice depend.

2 OVERVIEW OF THE ARGUMENT

We begin with an outline of how the economic reasoning that reigns today coevolved with utilitarian moral philosophy in a manner whereby each strengthened the other (Anderson, 1993). We then describe how and why the plural values that necessarily enter into environmental decision making are not adequately accounted for in traditional economic models of valuation. Finally, we suggest discursive, contextual processes as one way to account for plural environmental values. The mutual feedbacks in this coevolutionary process reduced the viability of competing ways of understanding both economic systems and values, leaving us poorly equipped to handle new issues in both the domains of economic reasoning and value theory. After characterizing utilitarianism and its historical influence on values thinking in economics, we describe six interrelated challenges to the dominant approach to thinking about values (or economic utilitarianism for short): the distribution of rights, the aggregation dilemma, the social construction of values, multiple contexts of value, ecosystem complexity and collective values, and the co-evolution of knowledge and value. These problems are especially critical when addressing environmental systems. While economists have certainly confronted each of these problem areas before, they have typically done so each in isolation and have rationalized a utilitarian response that minimizes the challenge to the dominant way of thinking in economics (Wagner, 1995). Taken together, however, these six challenges make apparent the need for valuing processes that account for values pluralism in environmental valuation and decision making. We argue that additional ways of thinking about values should be incorporated more openly. Values pluralism, like methodological pluralism, opens up a multitude of new insights. Rather than propose a meta-framework that resolves the cacophony of values insights that come with multiple ways of valuing, we argue that it will be more realistic if we seek resolution through discursive, democratic approaches to a shared understanding.

3 THE NATURE OF UTILITARIANISM

The utilitarian tradition is too long and intricate to be given full treatment here. Its historical ties and cross-fertilization with economics as a social science are well documented and have been the subject of scholarly debate (see, for example, Sen and Williams, 1982; Scott, 1991; Hausman and McPherson, 1996). The nuanced debate on the foundations and development of economic theory *within* the economic literature notwithstanding, economic valuation shares a number of pertinent features that are rooted in utilitarianism's preoccupation with the individual, and consequences of its actions in terms of units of pleasure and pain, or utils. Economic utilitarianism presumes that the consequences to individuals of public and private decisions can be predicted, that individuals know what gives them pleasure and pain (or their preferences), that these preferences are not culturally constructed through social processes that change, that the utils of different individuals can be weighed and aggregated, and thus that the effects on total utility (or cost and benefit) of a decision can be determined. The inadequacies of each of these premises have been debated for centuries and less stringent assumptions have been proposed (Smart, 1967). Nevertheless, these assumptions continue to underlie many of the debates about 'objective' approaches to environmental valuation.

In economic utilitarianism, values consist of the utils, the net pains and pleasures that follow from specific actions. This has two implications. First, all values reduce simply to facts about individual experience of utils. This is a clear application of the fact – value dichotomy (Schrader-Frehette, 1985; Hausman and McPherson, 1996), for there is simply a factual world right up to the point where pain or pleasure is ultimately felt. Yet, as Anderson (1993) explains, there are different types, or modes, of valuation; she cites use, appreciation, respect, consideration and love as some examples. The dominant economic tradition denies these multiple forms of value and acknowledges only levels of utility. This reduces value discussions to simple questions such as: 'on a scale of "one to ten", how much pain do you feel when you think of the environment and the future of your children?' or 'how much would you be willing to pay to preserve this wild area?' This reductionism that is characteristic of economic valuation, we argue deadens values, making it more and more difficult for values to reproduce across generations and to evolve to fit new problems.

The second implication of equating values with the consequential sum of actions is that in this utilitarian realm, values accord to specific, predictable consequences rather than to general conditions that might lead to a range of possible consequences. One of the shortcomings of consequentialism (of which utilitarianism is a specific form) is that it is very difficult to make value judgements when the consequences are not well known. We argue in subsequent sections that 'not knowing' is more characteristic of environmental problems such as biodiversity loss or climate change than of other problems considered in economic theory. For example, problems such as investment choices, the literature on which forms the basis for many of the valuation models for both biodiversity and climate change are statistically complex yet rely on relatively simple assumptions about probability distributions of outcomes and the arrival of new information each time period. Environmental systems are complex, because our knowledge is frequently only emerging in this area, and because many environmental issues are about consequences over the long term for which prediction is nearly impossible, and probability distributions non-existent. For these reasons, environmental valuation is frequently inconclusive.

A common response to the shortcomings of utilitarianism, and one used occasionally by ecological economists such as Daly (1980) and Daly and Townsend (1993) and Roefi Hueting is to argue that science can determine what we must do when utilitarian valuation fails us. Notions such as carrying capacity, the steady state, and ecological thresholds are frequently invoked to illustrate that there are absolute limits to the economy's relative size to the biotic systems that are the basis for life on this planet. These insights have been formalized for example as vertical demand curves. To the extent that policy-makers and the general public are also wedded to utilitarianism, such an approach has practical value. For much of the twentieth century, furthermore, science has accepted the role of setting thresholds for regulatory purposes, even when no thresholds exist (Jasanoff, 1990). The concepts of environmental and social sustainability frequently entail the assumption that we can scientifically determine what is, and is not, environmentally and socially sustainable. During the latter decades of the twentieth century, however, the public authority of science weakened. This has been, in part, because science has assumed burdens it has not been able to meet including the determination of what is sustainable (Lele and Norgaard, 1996).

Perhaps utilitarianism has served modern people reasonably well overall; no doubt there are specific areas where its application has been effective, such as individual behaviour choices that it was originally designed to describe in moral philosophy. Judging value systems is certainly among the quicker quick sands of philosophy. Yet the persistence of collective environmental problems amid modern life that provides individual material abundance, albeit poorly distributed, suggests that utilitarianism is poorly suited for providing for collective goods. Thus we argue that we need to work with other ethical systems in addition to utilitarianism to enrich the moral bases from which we make values arguments as was historically the case in systems of political economy.

4 MORAL PHILOSOPHY AND ECONOMIC THOUGHT: A HISTORICAL PERSPECTIVE

It is good to remind ourselves that other ethical philosophies were historically not only as common as utilitarianism, but actually underlay systems of political economy. Going back to Thomas Aquinas and the medieval concept of 'just price', early works in political economy were guided by the search for ways to achieve a higher purpose in life. In the past three centuries, economists like Sismondi, Ruskin, Tawney and Hobson all 'looked upon increases in economic activity as a means rather than an end' (Smith, 1993). Economics is widely recognized to have come out of moral philosophy, and though the term encompassed social philosophy as well at the time, early economists, from at least Adam Smith to John Stuart Mill, were well versed in a range of ethical traditions. Adam Smith wrote *The Theory of Moral Sentiments* ([1759] 1976) nearly two decades prior to his more famous *The Wealth of Nations* ([1776] 1976). Bentham's arguments for utilitarianism appeared soon after (1789) but were only slowly incorporated into economic thought over the next hundred years. Thomas Malthus, a clergyman as well as professor of political economy, argued for sexual abstinence over other forms of population control on religious grounds (1789). John Stuart Mill, writing in the middle of the nineteenth century was both a philosopher and an economist and freely moved to a priori ethical arguments when utilitarianism proved inadequate. While holding fast to the fact-value dichotomy, Alfred Marshall carried this tradition forward well into the twentieth century. By the late nineteenth century, however, these other moral bases for economics were being marginalized (pun intended) as a trend towards mathematical analysis aimed to develop scientific credibility and fit with the general spirit of the Enlightenment, and its successor, modernity.

While its utilitarian origins dominate economics today, a priori ethical thought can be found in philosophy and the humanities more generally (Abelson and Nielsen, 1967). In contrast to the strictly consequentialist, or a posteriori, approach of utilitarianism, a priori ethical traditions posit that consequences are difficult to foresee but that prior rules of behaviour can be determined to govern acts which are likely to have different categories of consequences. While deriving broad ethical rules for behaviour is no less presumptuous than adding utils, people share across diverse religious and cultural histories similar ethical concerns about causing suffering and imposing gross injustices. John Rawls (1971) has developed a strong argument as to why we can agree in principle on a priori rules through the use of a hypothetical veil of ignorance. Within the diversity of the broad field of economics, one can still find threads of non-utilitarian moral reasoning. However, environmental economists, partly in an effort to make the pursuit of environmental questions acceptable in the mainstream, have rigorously stayed within the utilitarian tradition (O'Connor and Spash, 1999). Nevertheless a priori ethical traditions fuel the ongoing public debate over whether it is right to adopt instruments of pollution control or methods of environmental valuation which, for example, inherently assume that polluters have the right to pollute (see, for example, Sandel, 1997).

We do not argue that utilitarianism should be dispensed with entirely, either for economics or policy. We are arguing that the value questions we face with respect to our social and environmental future are too complex to be addressed by a single, simple approach to values. The example of biodiversity loss illustrates just how pervasive economic utilitarianism has become. Biodiversity loss is a relatively recent environmental problem that came to prominence when ecologists and biologists began to realize, in the late 1970s, that they were observing an extraordinary array of interlinked, systemic phenomena of species extinctions. When considered globally, these phenomena threaten the very basis for life on this planet (Wilson and Peters,1988). The discourse on biodiversity preservation originated in this scientific realm, and has always been characterized by a plurality of values perspectives and narratives of biodiversity. Yet as the Conference of the Parties to the Convention on Biodiversity went into its fifth session in the summer of 2000, this diversity of narratives stands to be lost. The single voice of economic-utilitarian considerations of the value of biodiversity for agriculture and medicine has by far become the loudest in the policy discourses, with the attendant emphasis on access, benefits and property rights over this new 'resource'. We proceed by mapping a number of key phenomena that utilitarianism is ill equipped to deal with, but that have become particularly pressing with the rise of environmental problems. Addressing these key phenomena requires adoption of policy processes that account for the plurality of narratives, of which economic utilitarianism is just one of many.

5 CHALLENGES TO UTILITARIAN REASONING IN ECONOMIC VALUATION

We proceed by mapping six key phenomena that economic utilitarianism is ill equipped to deal with, but that have become particularly pressing with the rise of environmental problems.

5.1 Values and the Distribution of Rights

Let us begin by considering how economists have dealt with one of the more obvious pitfalls of utilitarianism, that is that we cannot count utils without a common measure. Utilitarianism assumes that the utils of pleasure and pain of different individuals can be added together. Without a common measure of utility between people, however, no such addition is possible. Economists have long dealt with this shortcoming by arguing that economics can determine an efficiency frontier beyond which it is impossible to be and along which it is only possible to increase one person's utility by decreasing that of another person. Where a society 'should' be on such a utility frontier is beyond economic reasoning and requires a social welfare function rooted in another system of valuation. Given such a social welfare function, society can determine how available resources should be distributed between individuals so as to reach the highest level of social welfare (see, for example, Bator, 1957, Sen 1970). By mid-century, Kenneth Arrow (1951) had conclusively shown that a social criterion for distributive decisions could not be derived from individual values. Yet this acknowledgement of the limits of utilitarianism and the need for other bases for making value judgements has not been sufficiently adopted into environmental valuation.

One way to think about the need for other values frameworks in economics is in terms of the distribution of rights and lack of current environmental valuation techniques to account for them. Consider the dominant valuation method today, the contingent valuation method (CVM). Estimates of value of the environment based on willingness-to-accept (WTA), which presume that the respondent has the right to the environmental service in question, is typically on the order of three times larger than willingness-to-pay (WTP), which assumes that the respondent does not have the right to the environmental service (for an excellent review see Hanley and Spash, 1993, especially pages 62–5). By a series of arguments based more on mathematical convenience than on moral consideration of how rights should be assigned, environmental economists have reached a consensus that WTP 'should' be the norm as a measure of value. Furthermore, this convention has been strongly reinforced through the recommendations of a panel of top-ranking economic theorists after the controversy over environmental valuation generated by legal battles over compensation resulting from the Exxon Valdez oil spill (NOAA, 1993). Thus, even in the face of repeated political decisions rooted in moral discourse that has pretty consistently shifted the law towards the rights of those affected by pollution, environmental economists have accepted a measure of environmental value assuming the right to pollute. This they do largely on the grounds that it is empirically easier to get consistent results (Hanley and Spash, 1993, Chapters 3 and 7). This stance is not justified by theory and can only be explained as a product of the historical context in which economics and economists, and environmental economists in particular, were brought into the policy process (Pechman, 1989).

Economists have been quite successful at evading this moral realm concerning the initial endowment of rights through arguments incorporating growth and making markets more efficient such that everyone is made better off. At the end of the twentieth century, however, the situation clearly changed. First, a popular interest in the sustainability of development forced economists to reconsider the adequacy of their models. While many economists responded to the challenge of sustainability by elaborating on the possibilities of technological change, resource substitution, and ever more perfect markets, Howarth and Norgaard (1992, 1995) demonstrated that sustainability is fundamentally about the distribution of rights to resources across generations. Second, Larry Summers wrote a memo while in the World Bank arguing that health-threatening pollution 'ought' to be exported to poor countries where the value of people's lives was lower. Even the editors of the *Wall Street Journal* and *The Economist* argued that this argument violates moral principles (Anonymous, 1992), and their readers agreed. This distributive values problem underlies the vast majority of the debate over how the nations of the world are going to respond to the two major long-term global threats of climate change and biodiversity loss. Third, the poor in both the developed and developing countries initiated environmental justice movements buoyed by documentation that pollution is concentrated among the poor and cleaned up first in the neighbourhoods of the rich (Bryant, 1995). By the same straightforward economic valuation argued by Mr Summers, now President of Harvard University, with respect to pollution between countries, environmental economic reasoning, narrowly defined, rationalizes and contributes to environmental injustices within and between countries (Martinez-Alier and O'Connor 1996; Muir and O'Connor, 1996; Martinez-Alier et al., 1999).

5.2 The Values-aggregation Dilemma

The second limit of economic utilitarianism derives from what we call the values-aggregation dilemma. Values are necessarily embedded in our understanding of the world and in the process of aggregation. Not only does aggregation fail to account for these embedded values, but the process of aggregating embeds a new set of values – and the product is presented as objective reality (Norgaard, 1989). Social and natural scientists face this problem in conveying complex information to policy-makers and the public as well as in refining our own models. When scientists and economists present their 'objective' understanding of reality, numerous details have necessarily already been aggregated together in order to make the information easy to comprehend in a reasonable amount of time. Gross domestic product, for example, is an aggregation representing the state of the economy that weighs goods and service flows by their respective prices. Epidemiologists when presenting health data for policy analysis, for example, might differentiate how an air pollutant affects the mortality of children from that of adults, or how one pollutant interacts with another in different populations. However, only a bare minimum of the details of the different environments and lives of people actually affected can be presented for public understanding before the information overwhelms the public, or even policy-makers. Thus aggregations are necessary. In fact, only a modest amount of detail can be incorporated in the original scientific research itself before analyses become overwhelming. Hence, in the process of doing science and informing the public and the policy process, scientists make decisions on how to aggregate across people and the environmental conditions in which they live. Inevitably, what is presented scientifically as an objective reality for use in economic or democratic valuing processes, in fact, already includes substantial value judgements. Thus, the aggregation of complex information in the valuation process itself is a mechanism for how values get embedded in decisions.

5.3 Values are Socially Constructed

In a third oversight, economic utilitarianism fails to ask where preferences come from, but rather takes preferences as given attributes of individuals. In this view, value is an objective property to be discovered. Yet even pleasures and pains that have clear physiological bases can be felt differently by different people. We contend that values are not inherent to individuals, like their genetic makeup. Nor are values 'out there' to be measured. Rather, values originate in the act of participating in society and these social processes sustain and regenerate values.

Values are socially constructed and sustained through behaviour, interactions, traditions, narratives, music and art. Values are influenced by the decisions we see others make as well as by advertising, social and political institutions, the communities with which we identify and other social relationships. Economic utilitarianism does not acknowledge that valuing and valuation consist of processes, subject to social influence, including through policy. The utilitarian framework is further limited in that its concept of value is static. It allows for the manipulation of rights and incentives through policy while ignoring how the valuing processes are generated, influenced and sustained via social relationships.

While such social constructions of values take different general forms in specific periods and cultures, new constructions also continually arise in the context of particular problems, especially environmental problems (Rosaldo, 1989). Take the example of biodiversity. What is 'out there' is the teeming mass of life, but the value of this biodiversity is constructed. This construction is done by the scientific community, in international conventions and treaties such as CITES (Convention on International Trade in Endangered Species) or the CBD (Convention on Biological Diversity), as well as in popular culture, with for example, marketing and advertising. The value of biodiversity is not there until we create it. Economic utilitarianism does not adequately account for these collective values. Thus, value construction is a constant process. Perhaps more important, values need to be constantly reconstructed – discussed, used and tested, and passed on to the next generation – or they will decay. Furthermore, they need to be updated to apply to new situations, to slice through moral dilemmas heretofore not considered. Thus, values are stagnated in the utilitarian tradition, the values evolution process is hindered and values decay. Furthermore, the utilitarian tradition, by denying how values are sustained and evolve, on the one hand contributes to the demise and unfitness of public and collective values while on the other it gives free rein to the construction of individual, material values through commercial advertising, media campaign and other processes.

5.4 Multiple Contexts and Collective Value

Economic utilitarianism presumes that communities are simply the sum of individuals and hence that community values are simply the sum of individual values. Yet, people do not always perceive themselves as isolated individuals that are combined additively into communities. Rather, most people acknowledge that they can think and value in many social contexts and from various perspectives. We express values and make decisions within a variety of social contexts including as individuals, family and community members, members of particular social groups or organizations, and as state and national citizens. For example, on any given environmental issue, the stakeholders and affected parties may be simultaneously a parent, business owner, elected official and member of a non-profit organization. Working from each of these centres, we participate in efforts to make decisions in the best interest of different allegiances. These allegiances and priorities are dynamic and change with different decision-making contexts. In other words, we have multiple centres of value from which value decisions are made and around which multiple 'conversations' and decisions sustain and evolve values. These processes of collective valuation and decision making are different in significant ways from the utilitarian assumptions of individual valuation and decision-making.

Economic utilitarianism aggregates expressions of individual values to determine a recommendation for action based on the greatest good for the greatest number. While values do exist on the individual level, many values, especially environmental values, operate on a collective level. These individual and collective values operate simultaneously and different aspects of the environment have more or less collective or individual values. There exist crucial elements of the environment that we value in predominantly collective ways. Strict methodological individualists explain our multi-centered nature by portraying arguments of individual utility maximization that are as complex as Ptolemaic explanations of the motions of the planets. By shifting valuing centres, like moving from geocentric to heliocentric perspectives, the picture becomes much simpler.

5.5 Ecosystem Complexity and Collective Values

The fifth limit of economic utilitarianism is that it is simple, but nature is complex. The values associated with nature embody that complexity and cannot be reduced to isolated data. Nature does not break into separable phenomena with discrete consequences on isolated individuals that result in individual utility. Rather, nature occurs as complexly interrelated communities of species that affect people as complexly interrelated communities of people. As we value environmental resources there is a relationship between what is being valued, who is doing the valuing, and the actual values that get expressed and acted upon. Thus, even if we concede a strictly consequentialist framework, not all consequences of human-induced environmental change can be meaningfully expressed as individual values (Anderson, 1993). Sustainability, biodiversity and climate change, are some examples of necessarily collective environmental values. Any given individual's value for these large-scale environmental issues necessarily involves, requires, and depends on the values, valuations, and actions of other people. With its simple aggregate model, utilitarianism overlooks these social relationships and the related inherent complexities in nature.

Furthermore, economic utilitarianism assumes a linear chain of consequences from which values derive. Embedded in utilitarian philosophy is the assumption that value is rooted in the ends achieved, the increase in individual well-being that is a consequence of using or doing something. In this model, the values of environmental and other factors that produce such ends or consequences are derived from the end values. The assumption that we can derive such values in turn relies on the assumption that environmental and other factors are divisible and combine in known, deterministic ways to produce single ends. However, environmental problems arise in effect because environmental systems have multiple indivisible inputs that combine in complex ways to produce numerous joint products (Daily, 1997). Thus, the very nature of nature requires us to value some environmental qualities and services directly; not as something derived from the end happiness they produce; not for their consequences, or at least not their specific consequences; but for something approaching the concept of 'intrinsic' value. Holding too tightly to utilitarianism while trying to derive environmental values for policy decisions means we will always underestimate the value of the environment and degrade it in the process.

While neoclassical economists acknowledge market failure is a result of complexity of interconnected feedback loops, economists still believe that these interconnected entities can be valued separately and that the market can be made to work. The assumption that values attach to 'things' as an objective property has become institutionalized, yet we now recognize that this reduced way of thinking about values is limited, especially with respect to intangible environmental amenities such as clean air, biodiversity and climate change. Consider again biodiversity. Within the utilitarian framework, the value of biodiversity rests on the utility it provides to humans. However, the life support function and other systemic ecological values of biodiversity are, by nature, global and collective values that cannot be ascertained simply by aggregating individual expressions of value. In this way, biodiversity is, in a sense, analogous to a naturally provided public good. Summing up individual WTP for biodiversity cannot capture its collective value. Neither can the value of biodiversity be captured by separating its components and valuing each of them separately. While it is considerably easier to reduce the value of biodiversity to the genetic information it contains this mode of valuation falls short by failing to account for the collective and non-market values.

5.6 The Co-evolution of Knowledge and Values

The assumption that facts and values are distinct has been central to Western science and moral philosophy. This classic dichotomy is critical because some of our most contentious environmental controversies arise at the cusp of what we know and what we can value. We assert that preferences for environmental qualities and services do not exist before we know about and understand the implications of such qualities and services. We argue that the resolution of environmental policy problems is difficult because the outcome of this co-construction process is unclear. Environmental problems and their solutions often arise on the margins of our knowledge, under circumstances of new scientific discoveries, and through the ability of some people to grasp new frameworks for understanding our relations to nature. These situations seem to be the least amenable to maintaining a separation between facts and values.

Again, biodiversity offers a good example. Here we can see how values co-evolve with knowledge. First, scientific knowledge is continually emerging – there is a rising understanding of biodiversity as a scientific concept. Second, the values of biodiversity are also only emerging – as the public consciousness of this new realm and its systemic nature is taking hold. Third, the resolution of the problem of biodiversity loss is as yet unclear. Because of the co-evolution, we never know enough to conclusively solve the problem. While biological diversity as a whole represents a blatant example, most environmental problems to some extent entail discovery, an awareness of new types of ignorance, and competing frameworks of understanding and corresponding values inherent in this knowledge and these frameworks.

From this experience with the rise in our understanding and concern for biodiversity, it is now clear that just as mechanistic frameworks 'value' efficiency *per se*, evolutionary frameworks value diversity *per se*. In both engineering and economics, for example, efficient solutions are valued over all others and it is to difficult to distinguish between the facts about an engineering or economic system assembled within a mechanistic framework and the values we attribute to efficiency. Similarly, it is difficult to distinguish between the facts about biodiversity assembled within an evolutionary framework and the values we attribute to biodiversity.

6 THE WAY AHEAD: FROM VALUES TO VALUING PROCESSES

As noted at the beginning of this chapter, to bring our own argument full circle, the founders of ecological economics including Roefie Hueting and Herman Daly cut through these distributive moral dilemmas before they began their economic reasoning. Daly has long argued that the question of the scale of the economy must be addressed independently, that economic reasoning helps us understand how the weight of the cargo should be allocated fore and aft, port and starboard, but says nothing about how much cargo is safe to carry. Hueting argued at the level of individual environmental services, stressing that it would be immoral to destroy an environmental service for all future generations to come. We argue that environmental economists have avoided addressing redistributing property rights to achieve social ends precisely because to do so begs the question of the value basis as to how such a decision 'should' be made. Ecological economists, on the other hand, see both the natural and social environment as integrally important, rather than marginally important.

We have argued that economists have systematically overlooked the limitations of methodological individualism and utilitarianism. This collective oversight is rooted in the preoccupation with getting valuation right, and the newly found role of experts in the environmental policy process. Environmental problems challenge the status quo and are exemplifying the many ways in which the utilitarian valuation rationale is breaking down, as we have laid out above. It is time to reconsider the actual processes in which people express and act out their values, and to develop a policy framework that allows for multiple, co-evolving values.

We, together with other ecological economists (O'Connor, 1998; O'Connor and Spash, 1999), propose that environmental valuation can best advance at this stage by moving towards discursive, contextual approaches. We can learn from the developments in risk assessment, which is now moving towards the assessment of competing 'objective' analyses of risk through discussion within panels of citizens and through related discursive approaches (NRC, 1996). There are clear parallels between the difficulties of assessing risk and controversies surrounding environmental valuation – in fact, they often go hand in hand, as in the case of global climate change or the loss of biodiversity (Wynne, 1997).

Environmental problems have brought us to the limit of what can be known and understood from a single system of thinking, as was an aspect of the project of modernity. Instead we need to embrace methodological pluralism to make sense of the complexities of reality (Norgaard, 2001; O'Neill, 1997). These different ways of understanding and learning, ranging from traditional single-discipline science models to the experiential knowledges of people close to the system we are trying to understand, can only be brought together through discursive, democratic processes (Norgaard, 2001). Many ecological economists already accept and practise methodological pluralism (O'Hara, 1996). The parallel endeavour, to collectively resolve values conflicts in discursive processes, remains as yet to be fully elaborated (Bingham, 1986; O'Connor and Spash, 1999).

The move towards valuation processes both in theory and practice can be accomplished with help from existing schools of thought as to how environmental policy controversies might be resolved when positive analysis fails. First, 'policy scientists' have long recognized the inseparability of facts and values. They advocate pragmatism and argue for an open, methodologically pluralistic, discursive approach to assure that all the facts are considered and a balanced judgement is reached (Laswell, 1970, 1971; Brunner, 1982; Brunner and Ascher, 1992; Clark, 1992).

Recent work in value theory and environmental policy challenge utilitarian assumptions and point towards a bridging of social, moral and economic valuations by engaging deliberative, participatory methods. O'Neill (1997), for example, challenges the neoclassical assumption that rational choice requires a common monetary unit and argues that rational choices necessarily combine a plurality of values and involve practical judgement beyond objective analysis. Holland (1997) argues that concern for the environment is more effectively expressed via deliberative processes than with contingent valuation or cost–benefit analysis. Beckerman and Pasek (1997) note the incommensurability of natural resource values with ordinary market goods and highlight the disjuncture between economic and philosophic values of natural resources. Sagoff (1988) challenges the utilitarian framework and economic efficiency criterion as basis for policy and challenges the notion that property values exist solely in market value. Hanley and Spash (1993) have drawn attention to the limits of the economic utilitarian concept of value and suggest that protest zeros and extreme bidding responses to willingness to pay questions on contingent valuation surveys reveal that people hold deontological rather than utilitarian values of these resources. Anderson (1993) also objects to the economic assumption that market value, either real or hypothetical, represents the full range of value ascribed to an object or state of affairs. She offers an alternative pluralistic expressive theory of value as more inclusive than the consequentialist, utilitarian framework and advocates a democratic, participatory system of policy making over the dominant cost–benefit, market-based system. Additionally, Glasser (1998) suggests critical rationality as an alternative to the comprehensive rationality of utilitarianism and presents a 'descriptive, participatory approach' for incorporating expert and lay knowledge and plural values into decision making.

Three trends in environmental valuation point towards the inclusion of deliberative methodologies and incorporation of normative judgements to meet this goal. First, Brown et al. (1995) propose the employment of values juries, analogous to grand juries, for environmental decision making. Second, to meet the challenges of incommensurability, uncertainty, irreversibility and consideration for future generations that face economic valuation of the environment, Crowards (1999) integrates moral and economic values into decision making with a combined 'safe minimum standard' and cost–benefit analysis process. While theoretically appealing, he concedes that more work is needed to fill the procedural gap that he calls the 'sociopolitical' decision-making process. A third example of innovation in economic valuation can be found with the VALSE (Valuation for Sustainable Environment) project in Europe. This project has set out a model of plural valuations case studies 'from the point of view of complexity'. Using a form of grounded theory, they explicitly seek to include the 'normative dimensions' of environmental values and frame valuation as a social process rather than a scientific outcome (O'Connor, 1998).

Communicative action theory and consensus-building practice offer numerous case examples of incorporating multiple and conflicting interests, priorities and values into long lasting, mutually agreed upon environmental decisions including the integration of technical, expert input with the opinions and perspectives of the general public (Thompson et al., 1994; Susskind et al., 1999). While the consensus-building process is time consuming, requires incentives for all relevant parties to participate, necessitates commitment and creativity by participants, and requires close attention to issues of co-optation and power imbalance, it is increasingly favoured over litigation as a means of resolving disputes and has been embraced by federal regulators and managers in the USA (Susskind et al., 1999). These collaborative decision-making theories and practices require critical analysis (see, for example, Duane, 1997; Aldred, 1999; Forester, 1999) yet they point to a potentially fruitful new direction in environmental valuation and decision making. While collaborative processes are well under way in environmental decision making on the ground, our economic theories have barely begun to tap these resources.

All the above described approaches have proven successful on their own, in particular cases. Taken together, they and their extensions are radical departures from the individually based, consequentialist, decision algorithm of economics, and will require the concerted effort and commitment of all of us. Ecological economics has arisen out of discontent with the standard vision of economics. It is already well poised to break with the standard process of and approaches to valuation. Now it is time for us collectively to develop the new techniques and encourage the transition in the political and policy process more effectively, away from valuation and towards valuing processes.

REFERENCES

Abelson, R. and K. Nielsen (1967), *History of Ethics*, in Paul Edwards (ed.), *The Encyclopedia of Philosophy*, New York: Macmillan and Free Press.

Aldred, J. (1999), 'Deliberative institutions for environmental policy: some worries', paper presented at the Moral and Political Reasoning in Environmental Practice Conference, Mansfield College, Oxford, UK, June 27–29, 1999.

Anderson, E. (1993), *Value in Ethics and Economics*, Cambridge, MA: Harvard University Press.

Anonymous (1992), 'Let them eat pollution', *The Economist*, February 8–14, 66.

Arrow, K.J. (1951), *Social Choice and Individual Values*. Reprinted, 1963, New York: Wiley.

Bator, R.M. (1957), 'The simple analytics of welfare maximization', *American Economic Review*, **47**, 22–59.

Beckerman, W. and J. Pasek (1997), 'Plural values and environmental valuation', *Environmental Values*, **6** (1), 65–86.

Bingham, G.D. (1986), *Resolving Environmental Disputes: A Decade of Experience*, Washington, DC: Conservation Foundation.

Brown, T.C., G.L. Peterson and B.E. Tonn (1995), 'The Values jury to aid natural resources decisions', *Land Economics*, **71** (2), 250–60.

Brunner, R.D. (1982), 'The policy science as science', *Policy Sciences*, **15**, 115–35.

Brunner, RD. and W. Ascher (1992), 'Science and social responsibility', *Policy Sciences*, **25**, 295–331.

Bryant, B. (ed.) (1995), *Environmental Justice: Issues, Policies, and Solutions*, Washington, DC: Island Press.

Clark, T.W. (1992), 'Practicing resource management with a policy orientation', *Environmental Management*, **16**, 423–33.

Crowards, T.M. (1999), 'Combining economics, ecology and philosophy: safe minimum standards of environmental protection', in M. O'Connor and C.L. Spash (eds), *Valuation and the Environment*, Northampton, MA: Edward Elgar, pp. 223–39.

Daly, H.E. (ed.) (1980), *Economics, Ecology, Ethics: Essays towards a Steady-State Economy*, New York: W.H. Freeman and Company.

Daly, H.E. and K.N. Townsend (eds) (1993), *Valuing the Earth: Economics, Ecology and Ethics*, Cambridge, MA: The MIT Press.

Daily, G.C. (ed.) (1997), *Nature's Services: Societal dependence on natural ecosystems*, Washington, DC: Island Press.

Duane, T. (1997), 'Community participation in ecosystem management', *Ecology Law Quarterly*, **24** (4), 771–97.

Forester, J. (1999), *The Deliberative Practitioner*, Cambridge, MA: MIT Press.

Funtowicz, S.O. and J. Ravetz (1994), 'The worth of a songbird: ecological economics as a post-normal science', *Ecological Economics*, **10**, 197–207.

Glasser, H. (1998), 'On the evaluation of "Wicked Problems"', in D. Borri, A. Barbanente, A. Khakee, N. Lichfield and A. Prat (eds), *Evaluation and Practice and Urban Interplay in Planning*, Dordrecht: Kluwer.

Hanley, N. and C. Spash (1993), *Cost Benefit Analysis and the Environment*, Cheltenham: Edward Elgar.

Hausman, D.M. and M.S. McPherson (1996), *Economic Analysis and Moral Philosophy*, in J. Pencavel (ed.), *Cambridge Surveys of Economic Literature*, Cambridge: Cambridge University Press.

Holland, A. (1997), 'The foundations of environmental decision-making', *International Journal of Environment and Pollution*, **7** (4), 483–96.

Howarth, R.B. and R.B. Norgaard (1992), 'Environmental valuation under sustainable development', *American Economic Review*, **82** (2), 473–77.

Howarth, R.B. and R.B. Norgaard (1995), 'Intergenerational choices under global environmental change', in J. Bromley (ed.), *Handbook of Environmental Economics*, Cambridge, MA: Basil Blackwell, pp. 111–38.

Hueting, R. (1991), 'Correcting national income for environmental losses: a practical solution for a theoretical dilemma', in R. Costanza (ed.), *Ecological Economics: The Science and Management of Sustainability*, New York: Columbia University Press, 194–213.

Hueting, R. (1992), 'Growth, environment and national income: theoretical problems and practical solution', in P. Ekins and M. Max-Neef (eds), *Real-Life Economics: Understanding Wealth Creation*, New York: Routledge, pp. 255–65.

Jasanoff, S. (1990), *The Fifth Branch: Science Advisors as Policy Makers*, Cambridge, MA: Harvard University Press.

Laswell, H.D. (1970), 'The emerging concept of the policy sciences', *Policy Sciences*, **1**, 3–14.

Laswell, H.D. (1971), *A Pre-view of the Policy Sciences*, New York: American Elsevier.

Lele, S. and R.B. Norgaard (1996), 'Sustainability and the scientist's burden', *Conservation Biology*, **10** (2), 354–65.

Martinez-Alier, J. and M. O'Connor (1996), 'Ecological and economic distribution conflicts', in R. Costanza, J. Martinez-Alier and O. Segura (eds), *Getting down to Earth: Practical Applications of ecological economics*, Washington, DC: Island Press.

Martinez-Alier, J., G. Munda and J. O'Neill (1999), 'Commensurability and compensability in ecological economics', in M. O'Connor and C. Spash (eds), *Valuation and the Environment: Theory, Method, Practice*, Cheltenham: Edward Elgar.

Muir, E. and M. O'Connor (1996), 'Rights and liability assignments in the policy valuation of environmental externality: a simple general equilibrium exposition', Cahiers du C3ED, Paris: Universite de Versailles St-Quentin-en-Yvelines.

NOAA (National Oceanic Atmospheric Administration) (1993), *Evaluation of the condition of Prince William Sound shorelines following the Exxon Valdez oil spill and subsequent shoreline treatment*, Hazardous Materials Response and Assessment Division, Rockville, MD : National Ocean Service.

NRC (National Research Council) (1996), *Understanding Risk: Informing Decisions in a Democratic Society*, Washington, DC: National Academy Press.

Norgaard, R.B. (1989), 'Three dilemmas of environmental accounting', *Ecological Economics*, **1**, 303–14.

Norgaard, R.B. (2001), 'The improvisation of discordant knowledges', in Cutler J. Cleveland, Robert Costanza and David I. Stern (eds), *The Nature of Economics and the Economics of Nature*, Cheltenham, UK: Edward Elgar.

O'Connor, M. (1998), *Walking in the Garden(s) of Babylon: an overview of the VALSE project*, C3ED Rapport de Recherche, July 1998, Paris: Université de Versailles St-Quentin-en-Yvelines.

O'Connor, M. and C. Spash (eds) (1999), *Valuation and the Environment*, Cheltenham: Edward Elgar.

O'Hara, S. (1996), 'Discursive ethics in ecosystem valuation and environmental policy', *Ecological Economics*, **16**, 95–107.

O'Neill, J. (1997), 'Value, pluralism, incommensurability and institutions', in J. Foster (ed.), *Valuing Nature: Economics, Ethics, and Environment*, New York: Routledge.

Pechman, J. (ed.) (1989), *The Role of Economists in Government: An International Perspective*, New York: New York University Press.

Ravetz, J. (1994), 'Economics and an elite folk science: the suppression of uncertainty', *Journal of Post Keynesian Economics*, **17** (2), 165–84.

Rawls, J. (1971), *A Theory of Justice*, Cambridge, MA: Harvard University Press.

Rosaldo, R. (1989), *Culture and Truth: The Remaking of Social Analysis*, Boston: Beacon Press.

Sagoff, M. (1988), *The Economy of The Earth*, New York: Cambridge University Press.

Sandel, M. (1997), Op Ed in New York Times in December and subsequent letters to editor.

Schrader-Frehette, K.S. (1985), *Science Policy, Ethics, and Economic Methodology*, Dordrecht: D. Reidel Publishing Company.

Scott, G. (1991), *The History and Philosophy of Social Science*, New York: Routledge.

Sen, A. (1970), *Individual Choice and Social Welfare*, San Francisco: Holden Day.
Sen, A. and B. Williams (1982), *Ultilitarianism and Beyond*, Cambridge: Cambridge University Press.
Smart, J.J.C. (1967), 'Utilitarianism', in Paul Edwards (ed.), *The Encyclopedia of Philosophy*, New York: Macmillan and Free Press.
Smith, A. (1976), *The Theory of Moral Sentiments* (1759), The Glasgow edition of the Works and Correspondence of Adam Smith, Indianapolis: The Liberty Fund, Inc.
Smith, A. (1976), *An Inquiry into the Nature and Causes of the Wealth of Nations* (1776), New York: Oxford University Press.
Smith, G.A. (1993), 'The purpose of wealth: a historical perspective', in H.E. Daly and K.N. Townsend (eds), *Valuing the Earth*, Cambridge, MA: The MIT Press, pp. 183–209.
Susskind, L., S. McKearnan et al. (eds), (1999), *The Consensus Building Handbook*, Thousand Oaks, CA: Sage Publications.
Thompson, R., P.H. Templet et al. (1994), 'A process for incorporating comparative risk into environmental policymaking in Louisiana', *Risk Analysis*, **14** (5), 857–61.
Wagner, A. (1995), 'Communitarianism: a new paradigm of socioeconomic analysis', *Journal of Socio-Economics*, **24** (4), 593–605.
Wilson, E.O., and F.M. Peter (eds), (1988), *BioDiversity*, Washington, DC: National Academy Press.
Wynne, B. (1997), 'Methodology and institutions: valuation as seen from the risk field', in J. Foster (ed.), *Valuing Nature: Economics, Ethics, and Environment*, New York: Routledge.

7. Technical progress, finite resources and intergenerational justice

Wilfred Beckerman

1 INTRODUCTION

This volume bears witness to Hueting's important contribution to environmental economics, in the form of his pioneering work in the area of the valuation of the stock of natural resources and on the conceptual and practical problems of adjusting conventional estimates of economic growth in order to allow for changes in this stock. The widespread view that such estimates are required is based on the assumption that changes in the stock of natural resources are often negative and that depletion of the stock of natural resources means that we are storing up problems for future generations when the stock declines to dangerously low levels. This, it is then argued, means that conventional estimates of economic growth would overstate the true underlying 'net' growth rate, and would also give an exaggerated notion of the feasible rate of so-called 'sustainable development'.

How far this positive assumption is valid and what normative constraints exist anyway on the rate at which current generations should use up the stock of natural resources are two separate questions. The first is a matter of empirical evidence and its interpretation in the light of the related economic theory. The second is a matter of ethics. Having spent most of my life teaching economics at the University of Oxford, which pioneered – at least in Britain – the combined teaching of philosophy and economics, I make no apologies for attempting, in this study, to step outside the boundaries of my own discipline of economics and venture into topics usually left to philosophers. Anyway, since some schools of modern philosophy maintain that the only function of philosophy is to explain what other disciplines are saying I make no apology for trying to explain what I think philosophers are saying.

The structure of the argument in this chapter, therefore, is as follows. First, I shall try to show that the widespread belief that society should adopt some policy of 'sustainable development' on account of considerations of justice or equity between generations and the 'rights' of future generations is false. I am not concerned here with criticisms of the concept of 'sustainable development' as such, and I have published my objections to this concept elsewhere (Beckerman, 1995). In this chapter I try to show that its underlying philosophical premises concerning the rights of future generations are mistaken.

The fact that future generations may not have any rights does not mean, however, that we have no moral obligations to take account of the interests that they will have. Our problem then is to try to predict what their most important interests will be. The chapter goes on to argue that economic growth is likely to continue at a pace that will mean that future generations will be vastly richer than people are today. Furthermore, this growth will not be impeded by any resource constraints. By contrast with the improvement that this will bring in the relief of major problems, such as widespread poverty and environmental pollution, there will be no improvement in the various sources of suffering imposed on the vast majority of the world's population on account of violation of basis human rights or fear of such violation. The most important bequest we can make to future generations, therefore, is to bequeath to them a more decent society than the one in which most people live today, namely a society characterized by tolerance and respect for basic human rights.

2 THE ILLUSION OF INTERGENERATIONAL JUSTICE

One of the results of the growing concern during the last three decades with the impact of economic growth on the environment has been the growing popularity of the concept of 'sustainable development'. There are numerous interpretations of this concept and various ways in which the different versions of the concept have been defended. But a very common feature of most arguments in favour of sustainable development and one that is frequently encountered in environmental discourse is some appeal to notions of justice between generations and the corresponding need to respect the 'rights' of future generations to inherit a certain state of the environment or to receive adequate compensation in some form or other. It is no exaggeration to say that the moral claim of 'sustainable development' is usually alleged to rest largely on its appeal to intergenerational 'equity'. Concern with equity is, in fact, often contrasted with the standard economist's concern with simply maximizing the future stream of utility over some relevant time period. For example, one of the leading authorities on 'green' political philosophy, Robert Goodin, writes that the objective of sustainable development '. . . contrasts with the directive of ordinary expected-utility maximization to go for the highest total payoff without regard to its distribution interpersonally or intertemporally' (Goodin, 1983, p. 1). Or, as an authority on the concept of sustainability, bluntly puts it, 'Sustainability is primarily an issue of intergenerational equity' (Norgaard, 1992).

Whereas the problem of distributive justice within any given society at any point in time has occupied philosophers for over 2000 years, its extension to intergenerational justice is relatively very new. But it is already well known that any attempt to construct a theory of justice between generations encounters special difficulties, such as those set out by Rawls, who believed that the problem of justice between generations subjected ethical theory to 'severe if not impossible tests' (Rawls, 1972, p. 284).

One might well ask, at the outset, therefore, as does Brian Barry (1978, p. 205), whether there is really any need for a theory of intergenerational justice and whether, instead, one could not be satisfied with defining our obligations towards future generations on the basis of common humanity. Barry's view is that in spite of the difficulties such a theory is possible and also that it is necessary. The argument of this chapter is that it may well be impossible and is certainly unnecessary.

The structure of the argument is, first, the major premise that all common theories of justice imply conferring 'rights' on people that give a special status to certain of their interests. The minor premise is that unborn people cannot be said to have any rights. The conclusion is then that the interests of unborn people cannot be protected or promoted within the framework of any common theory of justice. The first of these propositions is the generally accepted (but not unanimous) view of the scope of theories of justice. The second premise is also not new and may be thought to be non-controversial, or even obvious, although some reputable philosophers dissent from it.[1] But taken together the two propositions lead to a conclusion that is less obvious.

As regards the major premise, there are, of course, many different theories of justice. But there is a wide consensus that any theory of justice necessarily implies attributing rights (and hence counterpart duties) to somebody or some group. For example, if it is claimed that people ought to be rewarded in accordance with their need or their merit, once their need or merit has been established they have a right to the corresponding reward. Anybody who claims that some theory of justice does not imply the attribution of rights needs to formulate the theory in such a way that it cannot be transposed in this manner into a proposition about rights.

As regards the minor premise, namely that future generations cannot be said to have any rights, it must be stated at the outset that this chapter is not concerned with overlapping generations. I am abstracting from the rights of small children to be looked after properly by their parents, for example.

Whether or not such categories of people have rights or whether their treatment is to be governed by principles of morality that lay outside the domain of justice is a difficult and debatable issue. But the distinguishing feature of such cases is the *physical* impossibility of the people in question to exercise their rights or to make claims that correspond to their rights. Here, however, I am concerned with the rights of unborn people. In their case it is *logically* impossible for them to exercise their rights or to make claims on behalf of their rights or to delegate those rights to anybody else.

The main reason why future generations cannot be said to have any rights is simply that – as pointed out many years ago by De George – this is implied by the present tense of the verb 'to have' (De George, 1981). Unborn people cannot now be said to have anything, whether it is long hair, a taste for Mozart, or 'rights'. It makes no sense to attribute a property to a non-existent entity. To say that 'X has Y' or 'X is Z' when there is no X is just nonsense.

Similarly, one must also reject the notion that future generations have rights because they have interests. For even if the possession of certain vital interests are believed to carry with it the possession of corresponding rights, this still cannot apply to unborn people since unborn people cannot have interests either, or anything else for that matter. I presume that they *will* have certain interests, notably those that are common to virtually all human beings, such as an interest in material well-being, freedom from fear and persecution, self-respect and immunity from institutional humiliation, and other basic human rights enumerated in various international conventions. And I believe that this imposes certain moral obligations on us. But that is another matter, to which I shall return later on.

The notion that future generations can have rights is presumably based on the fallacy of assuming that unborn people constitute some class of people waiting in the wings to be born. But there is no such class of people. As Hillel Steiner puts it 'In short, it seems mistaken to think of future persons as being already out there, anxiously awaiting either victimization by our self-indulgent prodigality or salvation through present self-denial' (Steiner, 1983, p. 159).

This is not simply a linguistic – if decisive – point. It has substantive aspects. For however widely society wishes to draw the boundary around the rights that future generations *will* have, it cannot encompass rights to something that no longer exists, such as an extinct species. For example, it is surely absurd to say that we have a right to see live dodos. And it would be equally absurd to say that we ever *had* the right to see live dodos.

It may well be true that if somebody steals my property and burns it and then, in a fit of remorse, throws himself on the fire and dies, I still have some rights. But I can no longer say that I have a right to the property in question or that I have a claim against the villain who destroyed it. The right to the property that I had possessed was destroyed when the property was destroyed, and the person against whom I had a claim no longer exists. Any moral (or legal) right that I may well have would be a right to redress in the form of compensation from his family, or friends, or descendants. But this is no longer the same right as the one that was violated. It is a right to something different and is matched by a claim against different people.

This has important implications for our obligations towards future generations. For if we cannot claim that we have a right to see a live dodo it cannot be claimed that the inhabitants of the Mauritius islands three centuries ago violated our rights by failing to save the dodo from extinction. And it would be absurd to claim that we *had* a right to see a live dodo before it was exterminated in the same way that we had a right to some property before some villain burnt it. Before the dodo was exterminated we did not exist. In other words, the people alive at any point of time only have a right to what is available and only have claims against others to respect those rights.

Indeed, insofar as ordinary adults can be said to have a moral right to something or other, it must presumably mean that they have a moral right to choose whether to exercise the right, or claim to exercise it, or complain if they are denied the exercise of that right, or authorize somebody else to exercise the right in their place, or even waive the right. In practice, of course, some of these options may not be open to many people today, particularly in those countries of the world where people live under authoritarian regimes. *In practice* they are unable to exercise their moral rights. But it would not be impossible for them to do so if the regimes in which they live changed. There is no logical obstacle. But given the flow of time it is not *logically* possible for us to insist that inhabitants of Mauritius three centuries ago refrain from hunting the dodo or from taking action to preserve it, on the grounds that its extinction around the end of the seventeenth century deprived us of our right to see it. Nor could we – if we so wished – waive our right to see a live dodo by saying 'OK. Go ahead. Hunt it if you like. We think it is a rather silly bird anyway.'[2] Again, this is a logical impossibility, not a question of whether, in practice, one can exercise some right.

The logical flaw in the notion that future generations have 'rights' outside their relationships among contemporaries cannot be remedied by the assertion that their rights or their interests are being represented today by environmentalist pressure groups and the like. Of course, anybody can claim to represent the interests of future generations, in the same way that one can claim to represent the interests of any existing person or persons, such as a client or a child or a handicapped person. But claiming or believing to represent the interests of any person or person does not mean that one is really doing so, let alone confer rights on them. As it happens I claim to represent the interests of future generations in the sense that I advocate policies that I believe are in their interest. But to do so I have no need to claim that I am representing the 'rights' of future generations.

To recapitulate, therefore, all theories of justice attribute rights (and counterpart obligations). Since future generations (of unborn people) cannot be said to *have* any rights the interests that they *will* have cannot be protected within the framework of any theory of justice.

But the rejection of intergenerational justice does not mean that we have no moral obligations to take account of the interests that future generations will have. For justice does not exhaust the whole of morality.[3] It leaves room for benevolence, or common humanity or virtue. One does not save the life of a drowning child out of consideration of justice any more than one allows one's neighbour to use one's telephone when his or her own is out of order on account of any 'right' that he or she may have to do so.[4] A wider conception of morality goes beyond 'rights' and 'justice' and incorporates what are sometimes known as 'imperfect obligations'. These can be defended in terms of 'virtue', rather than in terms of duties arising out of justice.

It may be asked what difference it makes if we identify our moral obligations to future generations by appeal to some theory of justice rather than by appeal to the interests that they will have and our moral obligation to take account of these interests. The answer is that it makes a great difference to the relative importance we attach to different obligations. For 'rights' are generally regarded as having 'trumping' power over mere interests. The interests approach, which comes more naturally to economists, calls for a balancing of interests. The rights approach, by contrast, imposes a side constraint on any such weighting procedure. In the present context, for example, the rights/justice approach, as embodied in the 'sustainable development' objective, would imply that any weighting of the interests of present and future generations (using a suitable discount rate perhaps) should be subject to the constraint that future generations have a right to inherit the same environment as we have now ('strong sustainability') or corresponding compensation in the form, perhaps, of more man-made capital ('weak sustainability').

Thus switching from a perspective of justice to one of some wider concept of morality changes the relative importance that we should attach to our various moral obligations to future generations. For 'justice' between generations is inevitably a matter of distributive justice. And this must mean justice in the distribution of some scarce resource. Concern with distributive justice between generations, therefore, concentrates on rights to some scarce resource. By contrast, the 'interests' approach invites us to rank our 'imperfect obligations' to future generations according to the strength of the interests that we can safely predict will be experienced by future generations, without any predisposition that this must take the form of scarcity of resources. We have to start from a clean sheet and ask ourselves which of the future generations' most vital interests can be most confidently predicted. When we do this it appears, for reasons given below, that the supply of 'scarce' resources is probably a very minor problem as far as the vital *interests* of future generations are concerned and that the most important bequest we can make to future generations is a radically more just society, characterized by greater respect for basic human rights than those in which most of the world's population now live.

3 HOW MUCH RICHER ARE FUTURE GENERATIONS LIKELY TO BE?

Of course, all long-range predictions of economic growth rates are hazardous. How many people, for example, would have predicted ten years ago that the Japanese economy was soon to enter into a period of prolonged economic stagnation? However, in predicting the likely world growth rate over the next century we do not think we are running any great risks. For the longer the period the more one can abstract from possible medium-term forces, such as the catching-up on wartime dislocation that characterized the 1950s in many Western countries, or the recuperation from the oil shocks that characterized the 1970s, or eccentric bursts of dogmatic monetarism that characterized the 1980s, or the speculative excesses and financial profligacy in some parts of the world that marked the later 1990s. In the very long run these forces can be seen to be relatively transient. To predict growth rates over the next century one must fall back on an appraisal of what are the really fundamental underlying forces determining economic growth potential in the modern world. In my view these are scientific and technological progress and the accumulation of human capital. I believe that these will lead to a growth rate in real world per capita incomes over the course of this new century of somewhere between 1 and 2 per cent per annum.

My reasons for this are as follows. The average growth rate of real income per head in the world over the last 40 years has been 2.1 per cent per annum.[5] And there are two reasons to believe that the future growth rate is likely to be at least as high as this, if not higher. First, in the very long run the main source of growth in incomes per head is technological and scientific progress. This is a function of variables which are all tending to increase, some at a phenomenal rate. In particular, the number of highly educated people in the world, especially those having technological and scientific qualifications, is increasing so rapidly that it far surpasses the corresponding number of people having similar qualifications only two or three decades ago, and is likely to go on expanding rapidly. The main source of current high levels of income and output in the modern world is not so much physical capital or material resources but human capital – that is knowledge, training, skills and attitudes. And there is no physical limitation on the growth of this human capital.

Second, the rate of international diffusion of innovation and technical progress – which many studies have shown to be decisive in determining growth rates – will continue to accelerate. This is partly on account of the increasing 'globalization' of economic activity. This does, of course, bring with it certain problems, but it also means that the technical progress and innovations in one country will spread more quickly than in the past, as already seems to have been the case. This will be intensified by one of the more favourable aspects of the policy revolution of the 1980s, namely the widespread conversion to freer and more competitive markets (including the labour market) than had been the case previously. Some countries – particularly those in the ex-Soviet bloc – are having great difficulty adjusting to a new competitive environment, and it may be decades before they really move into the modern world as far as the operation of their economies is concerned. But, in the longer run, they will no doubt do so. This could unleash vast potential growth rates in many major countries, such as India and Latin America – and even Africa – where, in fact, some signs of this are already visible.

These two underlying forces for *long-run* growth suggest that the average annual long-run growth of output per head over the next century should be above that of the last 40 years. Since this has been 2.1 per cent my projection of between 1 and 2 per cent per annum seems on the cautious side and might be giving excessive weight to the slowing-down during the last decade or so. But to simplify the argument we shall assume a single figure of 1.5 per cent as the annual average growth rate of real incomes per head over the next 100 years. The power of compound interest being what it is this means that world average real incomes per head in the year 2100 would be about 4.4 times as high as they are now!

And it should not be thought that the above guess at the annual average growth rate of (GWP) gross world product over the next 100 years is a fanciful figure. A recent draft report of the IPCC (the UN Intergovernmental Panel on Climate Change) adopted, for purposes of estimating possible levels of energy use and carbon emissions, four possible 'storylines' (to use their terminology describing possible scenarios of rates of growth of population and incomes). These put per capita GWP at between 4.3 times as high as it is today and 20 times as high! In other words, my 'guesstimate' is at the bottom of the range adopted by the IPCC. It is thus a conservative and modest estimate.

And the IPCC scenarios are by no means fanciful. As one of the contributors to their work points out, even on the assumption that world incomes will rise about tenfold over the course of the century, namely to about $300 trillion at present prices, this would be consistent with per capita incomes in the rich countries rising at only 1 per cent per annum and those of the developing countries rising at only 3 per cent per annum.[6] The former figure is well below its long-run trend rate in the twentieth century and almost inconceivably low given the long-run influences on modern economic growth set out above. And given the scope for 'catching up' among developing countries the latter figure corresponds only to their having reached, by the year 2100, merely the average income level enjoyed in the rich countries today. Given the international transmission of technical knowledge and productive techniques it is equally virtually inconceivable that – taken as a whole – they will have failed to achieve this.

4 THE RESOURCES CONSTRAINT

Finally, one popularly perceived threat to the future growth of prosperity is the oft-alleged danger of using up so-called 'finite resources'. A full-scale exposition of the factual and theoretical reasons why one can ignore this possibility would be beyond the scope of this contribution. Some of them have been set out in detail elsewhere (Beckerman, 1995, Chapter 4; Cooper, 1994, Chapter 2; Schelling, 1995). As I have often pointed out we have managed very well without any supplies at all of Beckermonium, the product named after my great grandfather who failed to discover it in the nineteenth century (Beckerman 1972, 1974).

The main reason why we will never run out of any resource, or even suffer seriously from any sudden reduction in its supply, is that whenever demand for any particular material begins to run up against supply limitations a wide variety of economic forces are set up to remedy the situation. These forces start with a rise in price, which, in turn leads to all sorts of favourable feedbacks, notably a shift to substitutes, an increase in exploration, and technical progress that brings down the costs of exploration and refining and processing as well as the costs of substitutes. In the end, of course, the relative prices of the final goods in which the materials in question may be embodied may still rise, which leads to a reduction in demand for them. If, for example, coal were ever to become a very scarce commodity its price would rise to the point where, like other scarce minerals such as diamonds, it would be used only for jewellery or certain very special industrial uses. We would never run out of it. And the process would take place very, very gradually, allowing time for economies to adapt. Key materials only disappear overnight in science fiction stories.

It was this total failure to allow for the way that markets work which led the Club of Rome in 1972 (Meadows et al., 1972) to issue its alarming prediction of the imminent exhaustion of many key minerals. In the event, during the following 20 years the consumption of these materials more or less matched, or exceeded, the levels of 'known reserves' that existed in that year. Yet the known reserves at the end of the period finished up being about as big as or, in some cases, much bigger than they were at the outset. (Beckerman, 1995, p. 53).

In fact the falsification of predictions of rapidly approaching shortages has a very distinguished pedigree, especially in the field of energy predictions. But this does not seem to deter later authoritative bodies from making equally mistaken falsified predictions. For example, the great economist Jevons predicted shortages of coal supply back in 1865 in a very sophisticated piece of applied economics which would still compare favourably with most contemporary applied economics (Jevons, 1865). In spite of the decisive falsification of his predictions during the course of the subsequent decades, 90 years later, in 1955, the 1955 UN Atoms for Peace Conference made estimates of both 'proven' and 'ultimately recoverable' reserves of fossil fuels, which are now seen to be one-quarter and one-twelfth, respectively, of current estimates (Anderson, 1998a, p. 438). The following is a selection out of innumerable equally falsified predictions in later years.[7]

> Countries with expanding industry, rapid population growth . . . will be especially hard hit by economic energy scarcities from now on (Amory Lovins, 1974).

> The supply of oil will fail to meet increasing demand before the year 2000, most probably between 1985 and 1995, even if energy prices are 50 per cent above current levels in real terms (MIT Workshop, 1977).

> The diagnosis of the U.S. energy crisis is quite simple: demand for energy is increasing, while supplies of oil and natural gas are diminishing. Unless the U.S. makes a timely adjustment before world oil become very scarce and very expensive in the 1980s, the nation's economic security and the American way of life will be gravely endangered (Executive Office of the President, *National Energy Program*, 1977).

> The oil-based societies of the industrial world cannot be sustained and cannot be replicated. The huge increases in oil prices since 1973 virtually guarantee that the Third World will never derive most of its energy from petroleum (Worldwatch Institute, 1979).

> What seems certain, at least for the foreseeable future is that energy, once cheap and plentiful but now expensive and limited, will continue to rise in cost (Union of Concerned Scientists, 1980), or

> Conservative estimates project a price of $80 a barrel (in 1985) even if peace is restored to the Persian Gulf and an uncertain stability maintained (National Geographic, 1981).

The falsification of past predictions of energy shortages is the result of three major forces, stimulated in most cases by the economic feedback mechanism outlined above. First, estimates of recoverable energy resources continually increase. Second, continuous technical progress is being made in the efficiency with which conventional energy is used. And, third, there is also substantial progress and innovation in the exploitation of renewable sources of energy.

As regards the first factor, namely supplies of conventional fossil fuels, current expert opinion is that 'In sum, the availability of fossil fuel resources can be measured in units of hundreds – perhaps thousands – of years. The availability of renewable energy resources (including geothermal resources), even if used on an immensely expanded scale has no known time limit (Anderson, 1998b, p. 30). As can be seen in the following table, the number of years' consumption at 1994 rates of consumption that are covered by total resources (including those not yet identified but that are likely to be insofar as prices provide the necessary incentive) varies from 240 years for oil to 1570 years for coal. Combining oil, natural gas and coal in units of oil equivalent 'The total reserves of fossil fuels are currently thought to be around 5000 Gtoe (gigatons of oil equivalent) or about 700 times the current annual rate of world consumption'.

Table 7.1 Consumption rates and aggregate global resources of fossil fuels (giga tons of oil equivalent)

	Consumption p.a. (1994)	Discovered	Further	Total resources
Oil	3.37	333	481	814
Natural gas	1.87	333	537	870
Coal	2.16	1003	2397	3400
Total	7.40	1669	3415	5084

Notes: The figures for oil comprise what are known as conventional and unconventional sources, the latter including oil shales, tar sands and coal bed methane.

Source: Anderson (1998a, p. 437), referring to data in Rogner (1997).

Of course, it may be argued that it is still too soon to claim that the pessimistic predictions will not be fulfilled even in the very long run. The above estimates of oil reserves are admitted to be subject to a significant margin of uncertainty. But some of the major uncertainties are on the favourable side. For example, there are also some unconventional sources of oil that are well known but that are not currently economically and technically viable on a significant scale, but which might well become so as a result of further major cost reductions in mining and processing of these sources.[8]

And we have not yet taken account of the scope for technological progress in renewable energy (especially solar and wind power), or the likely continuation in the trend towards greater efficiency in the use of energy and the declining energy intensity of output in developed countries. Nor have we taken account of geothermal energy.[9]

As for the technical progress in the use of renewable energy it should be born in mind that the total energy received from the sun is about 10000 times total world energy consumption and if only a very small fraction of this can be harnessed in an economically viable manner the whole energy problem disappears. And, indeed, the technical progress in the harnessing of solar energy has been substantial. Already photovoltaic systems and solar-thermal power stations, such as those now operating in California, manage to convert about 10 per cent of the incident solar energy into electricity, and with further developments in the pipeline are expected to be converting about 20 per cent of it.[10] The main constraints, therefore, are costs and storage.

It is true that, given the pace of technical progress especially in fuel cells that can store or produce electricity, there is good reason to believe that their costs will continue to fall. On the other hand, it is possible that some of the recent fast decline in the costs of certain renewable forms of energy will not be maintained into the future and, indeed, there are already signs of this happening. Furthermore, the fossil fuels start with an enormous initial advantage and do not seem inclined to allow it to be eliminated. The advances in gas-fired power generation, in particular, is one of the reasons why even wind power, which is far cheaper than solar, has not yet made much progress outside a few niche markets. And while many major oil producers and automobile manufacturers are spending large amounts on research into renewable fuels for various purposes, they are spending much bigger amounts on finding new resources of fossil fuels and in reducing the costs of exploiting them.

Thus, given the prospects for supplies of fossil fuels summarized above, any significant threat to the market for fossil fuels might simply be met by competitive reductions in their prices. So the future is much more likely to be one of competition between renewable and non-renewables, leading to further long-term declines in (real) energy prices, than one characterized by any shortages on account of an exhaustion of supplies of fossil fuels.

5 OUR REAL OBLIGATIONS TO FUTURE GENERATIONS

I have argued that insofar as future generations cannot be said to have any particular *rights* to anything, the starting point for assessing our moral obligations to distant generations has to be some prediction of what their most important *interests* are likely to be. This should be followed up with some assessment of what effects our policies will have on their interests and how far they conflict with the interests of the present generation.[11] This does not mean, of course, that one can emerge with any 'lexicographic' ordering of priorities in general terms. For example, abuses of human rights can range from horrific behaviour to minor restrictions on peoples' freedom of movement or freedom to dispose of their property. Poverty can range from mass starvation to isolated instances of temporary poverty in generally affluent communities as a result of some transient bad luck or other exceptional circumstances. Environmental problems can range from the elimination of atrocious urban air conditions that were found in major cities of the industrialized countries until relatively recently or the absence of clean drinking water today in most parts of the developing countries at one extreme, to the reduction in noise levels from the occasional neighbourhood street party, at the other.But it is still possible to arrive at some judgement as to which of their interests, taken by and large, will be most important.

We have argued above that future generations will be vastly richer than we are today. So although there will always be pockets of acute poverty – as are found, for example, even in the richest countries today – one can expect that widespread poverty in the world will be eradicated. Furthermore, although there will always be local environmental problems, which may even get worse in the early stages of industrial development in many countries, a much richer world will both permit and stimulate most countries to improve their local environmental conditions and to find ways of adapting to such global environmental problems that may persist. Other problems may prove more persistent and difficult to deal with, such as those associated with the consequences of family breakdown or the problems of crime and drugs in contemporary societies.

But I believe that in the very long run the most important and permanent threat to human welfare will continue to be the violation of basic human rights. For the safest prediction that can be made for the long-term future is that there will always be potential conflict between peoples for all sorts of different 'reasons' and that can all easily lead to horrific violations of basic human rights. At the same time one can predict with great confidence that people will always want life and security, and freedom from fear, discrimination and humiliation.

Except in some Utopian scenarios human wants will always expand more or less in line with what is available, so that, whatever we do now about the future availability of resources and however much technical progress expands our potential for producing goods and services, there will always be conflicting interests in the way that potential output is shared out. Furthermore, conflicts of interest over material possessions are by no means the only causes of conflict, any more than are cultural differences. There is no shortage of other causes. Even within any given culture or civilization there are conflicts of various kinds between interests, objectives and values, which will divide members of any community. The century that has just come to an end has probably seen the most widespread unprecedented savagery on a mass scale of any time in human history (Glover, 1999). There is no reason to believe that human nature will get any better. Human compassion does not seem to keep pace with technological progress.

The greatest contribution that can be made, therefore, to minimize human suffering and promote human welfare will be constant vigilance in the defence of human rights. Our greatest bequest to future generations, therefore, will be a much more 'decent' society than the one that exists in most countries of the world today, namely one in which there is greater respect for basic human rights than is the case today, and, although respect for basic human rights may be in short supply in most countries of the world today, this is not because it is a 'scarce resource' in the same sense as minerals, certain species and so on are often believed to be. Extending respect for basic human rights will also make a major contribution to well-being in most countries today. So there is no conflict of interest between generations as there is believed to be in the case of sharing out finite resources. Hence, on almost any conception of what purpose is served by theories of justice there is no need for a theory of intergenerational justice to guide us as to what an equitable share-out would be. It is indeed paradoxical that many environmental activists attack the materialist obsession to which the defenders of continued economic growth are alleged to be attached, yet seem to be much more concerned with our material legacy to future generations than with other far more important ingredients of human welfare. If the arguments of this study are valid material obstacles will be among the least of the problems that future societies will have to face.

NOTES

1. For example, 'Part Three' of Partridge (ed.) (1981) is entitled 'Can Future Generations be Said to Have Rights?' and the contributions by three philosophers, Feinberg, Pletcher and Baier, to this volume maintain that they can. Kavka, in the same volume, is somewhat ambivalent on this question since although he nowhere claims that future generations have 'rights' he does claim that such of their interests as can be predicted with certainty have equal status with the interests of people alive today. In the same volume Warren is also somewhat ambivalent when she writes 'To say that merely potential people are not the sort of things which can possibly have moral rights is by no means to imply that we have no obligation toward people of future generations, *or that they (will) have no rights that can be violated by things which we do now'* (our italics) (Warren, in Partridge, 1981, *op. cit.*). (See also Beckerman and Pasek, 2001).
2. This point was developed by Hillel Steiner (1983).
3. Recent lucid reminders of this include, notably, Rawls (1972), Raz (1984), and O'Neill (1996).
4. By grounding our concern for future generations in a wider concept of morality we do not need to rely on Gauthier's solution to the problem of intergenerational justice, namely to rely on mutually advantageous contracts between overlapping generations (Gauthier, 1986, pp. 299 *et seq*). In any case, Temkin seems to have refuted this solution (Temkin, 1995, pp. 79ff.)
5. Calculations based on Table D.1a in Maddison (1995).
6. Anderson (1998b), 'Explaining why carbon emission scenarios differ', draft paper for the IPCC special Report on Emission Scenarios, May 1998, Table 1 and p. 8. Anderson's introductory note points out that the scenarios in question are still the subject of discussion in the relevant IPCC group and should not be interpreted as representing any final agreed consensus.
7. Where not otherwise indicated the predictions below are included in many such predictions listed in Mills (1999).
8. These include, in particular, oil shale in the western USA, heavy and extra heavy oil of the kind found in Venezuela, and bitumen (natural tar) such as found in Alberta. If, as seems quite possible, market conditions and their resulting incentives to improved extraction and processing made these sources economically viable, they could add something in the region of a further 15 trillion barrels of oil. And even without some major rise in the price of conventional oil supplies it is quite likely that they would become viable. For example, in Alberta there have been major cost reductions in recent years so that oil production costs from these sources have fallen to about $9 per barrel, which, while much higher of course than the very cheap oil in the Middle East, is below the cost of North Sea oil and much lower than oil costs in most of the USA. If technological and market development brought a large proportion of these 'unconventional' sources into the picture then, of course, at current rates of consumption there would be enough oil to last for several centuries (American Petroleum Institute, 1995).
9. According to a recent review by Mock et al. (1997), estimates for hot dry rock alone 'are orders of magnitude larger than the sum total of all fossil and fissionable resources'. While it is not yet known how much of these resources might be economically viable, the technological capacity for deep drilling already exists so in principle it would be physically feasible to tap this resource. Insofar as the price of conventional fuels rose significantly one can expect that there would be sufficient incentive for technical progress to be made in the exploitation of this source of energy. As Anderson puts it 'To sum up, the availability of fossil fuel resources can be measured in units of hundreds – perhaps thousands – of years. The availability of renewable energy resources, even if used on an immensely expanded scale, has no known time limit' (Anderson, 1998a, p. 443).
10. On conservative assumptions concerning the duration of sunlight and conversion efficiency, only about 0.25 per cent of the area now under crops and permanent pastures would be needed to meet all of the world's primary energy needs. Even if these needs rise – as they

may well do – fourfold over the course of the next century this still means that only 1 per cent of this land area would be needed to supply the whole world demand for energy.

11. To some extent this is a circular procedure, of course. One's prejudices, intuitions and predilections for certain priorities among obligations will naturally colour one's prediction of what one perceives to be the most salient and relevant features of the future evolution of human society. But there is no way of breaking out of the circle by appealing to some external objective formula for ranking the obligations.

REFERENCES

American Petroleum Institute (1995), *Are We Running Out of Oil?* Discussion Paper no. 0181, December, Washington, DC.

Anderson, Dennis (1998a), 'On the effects of social and economic policies on future carbon emissions', in *Mitigation and Adaptation Strategies for Global Change*, Kluwer Academic Publishers, The Netherlands.

Anderson, Dennis (1998b), 'Explaining why carbon emission scenarios differ', paper for IPCC Special Report on Emission Scenarios, May 1998, Geneva.

Barry, B. (1978), 'Circumstances of justice and future generations', in R. Sikora and B. Barry (eds), *Obligations to Future Generations*, Temple University Press, Philadelphia, p. 284.

Beckerman, Wilfred (1972), 'Economists, scientists and environmental catastrophe', *Oxford Economic Papers*, **24** (3), 327–44.

Beckerman, Wilfred (1974), *In Defence of Economic Growth*, Duckworth, London (US edition, *Two Cheers for the Affluent Society*, St. Martin's Press, NY 1975).

Beckerman, Wilfred (1995), *Small is Stupid*, Duckworth, London, (US edition, *Through Green-Colored Glasses*, Cato Institution, Washington, DC, 1996).

Beckerman, Wilfred and Pasek, Joanna (2001), *Justice, Posterity and the Environment*, Oxford University Press, Oxford.

Cooper, Richard (1994), *Environmental and Resource Policies for the World Economy*, Brookings Institution, Washington, DC.

De George, R.T (1981), 'The environment, rights, and future generations', in E. Partridge (ed.), *Responsibilities to Future Generations*, Prometheus Books, NY.

Gauthier, David (1986), *Morals by Agreement*, Clarendon Press, Oxford.

Glover, J. (1999), *Humanity: A Moral History of the Twentieth Century*, Cape, London.

Gooding, R. (1983), Ethical principles for environmental protection', in R. Elliot and A. Garde (eds), *Environmental Philosophy*, University of Queensland Press, Brisbane, p. 1.

Jevons, William S. (1865), *The Coal Question*, Macmillan, London.

Maddison, Angus (1995), *Monitoring the World Economy*, OECD, Paris.

Meadows, Dennis et al. (1972), *The Limits to Growth*, A Report to the Club of Rome, Universe Books, New York.

Mills. M.P., (1999), *Getting it Wrong: Energy Forecasts and the End-of-technology Mindset*, Competitive Enterprise Institute, Washington, DC.

MIT Workshop on Alternative Energy Strategies (1977), *Energy: Global Prospects 1985–2000*, MIT, Cambridge, Mass.

Mock, J.E., Tester, J.W. and Wright, M.W. (1997), 'Geothermal energy from the Earth: its potential impact as an environmentally sustainable resource', *Annual Review of Energy and the Environment*, **22**.

National Geographic (1981), *A Special Report in the Public Interest*, New York.
Norgaard, R. (1992), *Sustainability and the Economics of Assuring Assets for Future Generations*, Policy Research Working Paper WPS 832, World Bank, Washington, DC.
O'Neill, Onora (1996), *Towards Justice and Virtue*, Cambridge University Press.
Partridge, E (ed.) (1981), *Responsibilities to Future Generations*, Prometheus Books, NY.
Rawls, John (1972), *A Theory of Justice*, Clarendon Press, Oxford.
Raz, Joseph (1984), 'Right-based morality', in J. Waldron, (ed.) *Theories of Rights*, Oxford University Press.
Rogner, H-H (1997), 'An Assessment of world hydrocarbon resources', *Annual Review of Energy and the Environment*, **22**.
Schelling, Thomas (1995), 'Intergenerational discounting', *Energy Policy*, **23**, (4/5).
Steiner, Hillel (1983), 'The rights of future generations', in D. Maclean and P. Brown (eds), *Energy and the Future*, Rowman and Littlechild, Totowa, NJ.
Temkin, Larry (1995), 'Justice and equality: some questions about scope', in Paul, Ellen, Fred, D. and Paul, J. (eds), *Social Philosophy and Policy*, **12**, no. 2, Cambridge University Press.

PART THREE

Green Accounting and Sustainable National Income

8. Steering by the right compass: the quest for a better assessment of the national product

Salah El Serafy

1 PROLOGUE

The title of this chapter derives from a phrase that figured at the top of the first section of a joint study Roefie Hueting wrote with Jan Tinbergen (Tinbergen and Hueting, 1992). The subtitle above describes in rough terms the main theme of this study. The Tinbergen–Hueting joint work appeared as a chapter in a book edited jointly by Robert Goodland, Herman Daly and myself (Goodland et al., 1992). All three of us are paying tribute to Roefie's path-breaking achievements in this *festschrift*.

Roefie's monumental opus, *New Scarcity and Economic Growth*, which had been published in Dutch earlier, was still highly original when it appeared in the English language six years later (Hueting, 1980). Perusing it today, with the benefit of hindsight and in the light of later writings, the reader finds *New Scarcity* replete with analytical insights, supported by a genuine caring for the environment. Over the last two decades, participants in international gatherings have noted the special regard with which Hueting was being held, clearly recognized as a founding father of the new discipline of ecological economics. Even his opponents appeared to be impressed by his concern for the environment, imaginative analysis, tenacity in argument and bravery in countering opposing views. We have all come to know and appreciate his multifaceted nature, his sense of humour and his varied cultural interests.

2 TWO EXCEPTIONAL CONTRIBUTIONS

First I would like to state that for me, with my much narrower perspective, at least two contributions by Hueting stand out as of special worth: (a) his identification and elaboration of the concept of *environmental functions*, and contention that environmental services had come to represent a '*new scarcity*' hitherto unrecognized by economics; and (b) his highly practicable method for adjusting the national accounts for pollution, by seeking tolerable standards of impurity and imputing the cost of attaining such standards as a charge against the conventionally estimated gross domestic product. Defining such standards, in fact, is not confined to pollution, but was put forward as a subset of Hueting's 'general theory' aiming at ensuring the sustainability of all environmental functions. As Hueting (1993, p. 53) expressed it:

> Define physical standards for environmental functions based on their sustainable use. Formulate the measures necessary to meet these standards. Finally estimate the amounts of money involved in putting the measures into practice.

If Hueting had contributed nothing else to the topic, these two basic contributions alone will ensure him a place of honour as a founder father of the new discipline of ecological economics.

3 AN INTERPRETATION OF HUETING'S APPROACH

It would be useful at this juncture to offer a brief interpretation of where I think Hueting roughly stands on some of the issues I raise below, and I shall be returning in stages to cast a closer look at some important aspects of his position. We should keep in mind that Hueting would leave the conventional estimates of income unaltered, but would produce alternative estimates intended to show the gap between these and the conventional numbers. Hueting relies on the estimation of a supply curve based on the opportunity costs of sacrificed environmental functions – costs that must be borne to offset the loss of function. He holds that it is always possible to construct such a supply curve, whereas estimating demand, needed to complete the analysis, is trickier. For ascertaining demand, resort would be made in some cases to contingent valuation methods, although these, as he argues rightly, often have grave limitations and yield controversial values. In other cases where environmental functions are so fundamental as to be life-sustaining, such valuations would be inappropriate, if not entirely meaningless. Complete demand curves, according to Hueting, can seldom be constructed, and there is no substitute for making arbitrary assumptions about people's preferences in order to be able to sketch demand curves (Hueting, 1980, Hueting and Boer, 2001)

In this respect, the attention to shadow prices and other theoretical devices implicit in Hueting's approach takes him some distance away from the pragmatism of my own position, and places him, at least at first sight, in the company of other theorists who have been writing, in the context of adjusting the national accounts, about such things as optimal depletion, non-declining utilities and marginal versus average costs and similar nuances which, though certainly interesting, are out of line with the approximations and short cuts which are the stock-in-trade of the accountants, and also requiring data not available to them. Income earners normally seek income under conditions that are far from optimal or ideal, acting with imperfect knowledge in the face of markets that are very often far from perfect. The accountant merely records what had taken place, and if we wish to adjust the accounts *within the framework of national accounting*, we should not insist on idealized and *operationally* impossible adjustments in the hope of grafting them on the rough and approximate base that makes up the national accounts. Such excursions in theoretical subtleties, often related to welfare and conducted under suitably constraining assumptions, have their place in economic analysis, and can provide useful insights. But they do not quite fit with the accountant's methods of estimation. At first sight Hueting's theoretical approach for estimating the loss of functions in value terms may appear similar to the speculations of those theorists, but on closer inspection one realizes that his outlook is rather different, and much more practical. Remember that he would keep his estimates of function losses together with his adjusted income separate from the conventional estimates, and would not integrate the two sets. I return to this aspect of Hueting's work in section 8.

4 ESTIMATING 'WELFARE' OR 'PRODUCT'?

A basic difference separates our approaches, and I shall be elaborating it below. In my writings I have tended to emphasize the role of the national accounts for the estimation of net output, or *product*, whereas Hueting's attention has throughout been trained on *welfare*. Hueting holds that welfare enhancement is a *sine qua non* of 'economic success', a view which he shares with many others (see, for example, Daly and Cobb, 1989). Several national account reformers have also been seeking the adjustment of the accounts, not only to cover welfare losses associated with environmental deterioration, but also other non-environmental elements such as unpaid domestic work and leisure. For me, however, I have been concentrating on getting a better estimate of the product, which I hold to be the accounts' basic function, preferring to leave welfare considerations to a later stage. This is because 'welfare' raises complex issues of interpersonal comparisons, equity of distribution, utility functions, and other factors that are not usually available (or expected) from the standard accounts. Unlike Hueting, I have kept aloof of welfare issues perhaps influenced, in part, by my early training under Lionel Robbins who had strongly cautioned *economists* against getting (professionally) involved in 'ends' (Robbins, 1935).[1] Keeping strictly within the context of national accounting, I was also conscious of the fact that many parts of the environment, which contribute directly to welfare, are not captured in the accounts at all as they are not transacted. How much do we gain then from surmising welfare derived from a product that is incomplete? Welfare considerations appear to me to belong to an 'upper tier' of a basic assessment that needs to be made with force at the ground level, so to speak, before we move on to higher levels involving welfare or satisfactions. Output (or product) which the national accounts indicate cannot be taken as identical with the satisfaction that may be derived from it and which needs further information and analysis.

Before welfare considerations can be contemplated, and in the spirit of Occam's razor, my position has been that we should first raise the fundamental question as to whether the standard accounts deliver what they purport to deliver, namely correct estimates of product or output. If output is wrongly estimated, then any reckoning of welfare based on it is likely to be unreliable. Without minimizing welfare as the ultimate goal of the whole economic discipline, getting the national accounts to yield better estimates of output, in my view, must take precedence over welfare inferences that might or might not justifiably be read from the accounts. If sustainability is a contributor to welfare, then securing a sustainable level of *product* must be seen as a logical first step. By abstracting from welfare, I have been able to claim that in seeking more accurate estimates of output, my endeavour is a 'positive', not a 'normative' one, free from value judgement, and specifically without any conservationist motive.

5 NEW SCARCITIES: HUETING AND ROBBINS

Since I have already invoked the name of Robbins, let me digress a little to note what I believe to be a remarkable insight of Hueting who seems in line with Robbins's position regarding the scope of economics and how it should cover scarcities, old and new. Consider the following passage from Robbins (1935):

> The economist is not concerned with ends as such. He is concerned with the way in which the attainment of ends is limited. The ends may be noble or they may be base. They may be 'material' or 'immaterial' – if ends can be so described. *But if the attainment of one set of ends involves the sacrifice of others, then it has an*

> *economic aspect*. [*Nature and Significance of Economic Science*, p. 25; emphasis added.]

Robbins here seems to retreat from his basic position, qualifying his blanket warning against economists (*qua* economists) involving themselves in ends, and recognizing that the pattern of objectives may shift, indicating 'new scarcities' that should then become the concern of economists. The parallel between Robbins and Hueting in this respect is striking, and leads us to suspect that we may perhaps find in the last sentence in the Robbins passage quoted above the genesis of Hueting's environmental functions as they become a 'new scarcity': environmental functions, while they remain safe and abundant, could justifiably be overlooked by the economists, but under stress they develop into a 'new scarcity' that cannot be ignored in Robbins's economics. The possibility of one function competing against another furnishes a further variation on the same theme, which has also been interestingly developed by Hueting. On reflection there is little doubt that Hueting developed his own ideas independently of Robbins, but what is fascinating to me is that this is yet another demonstration of the acuteness of Hueting's economic intuition, and his firm grasp of the methodological fundamentals of our subject.

6 OTHER DIFFERENCES AND SIMILARITIES

One main purpose of this study (as suggested by one reviewer) is to highlight differences between my views and Hueting's. But there are also many similarities and convergence of outlook that I shall also be noting. Divergence of opinion, however, should be expected since the topic is fairly young and still developing. My own environmental interests have obviously been much narrower than Hueting's wide-ranging concerns. From my perspective since only part of environmental deterioration can be captured in the national accounts the role of the latter must be viewed as limited. Environmental change has to be valued in money terms for it to be married to the economic accounts, and such valuation can be problematic. In some cases even *physical* estimates of environmental change are not possible. Fortunately, however, much can be achieved for securing a healthy environment outside the framework of national accounting.[2]

Although our positions may sometimes differ, they are not basically in conflict, and could in fact be reconciled as representing different emphases and stages along a road leading to a common objective. All along my purpose for reforming the accounts has been *economic* and not *environmental* in realization of the fact that the environment is an essential part of a nation's capital (El Serafy, 1991). As capital, the environment certainly contributes to production, and has to be maintained for the continuation of economic activity, which is the source of income directly, or indirectly. Without any wish on my part to plea for the conservation of the environment, I have been stressing the need for realistic *economic* indicators that would describe realities on the ground more faithfully than the conventional accounts do, thereby serving economic ends better. In the macroeconomic field, such indicators are expected to be provided by the national accounts. As to solving, or even alleviating, the *environmental* problem, the national accounts with their economic focus are in most cases an unsuitable tool of limited utility. But as a device for interpreting and managing economic change, the national accounts have no rival, and are certainly worthy of the effort needed to make them more realistic. Macroeconomic analysis would certainly benefit if the accuracy and realism of the national account estimates are ascertained beforehand particularly in situations where the conventional measurements can be expected to be misleading. The national accounts of primary producing countries are an obvious candidate for reform. In the early 1980s when the World Bank was embarking upon its expanding programme of lending for structural adjustment, economic projections (especially of exports) were required to justify the lending, and country economists would happily make the projections (including primary commodity exports) without considering the resource base from which the projected product must emanate.

7 'WEAK' SUSTAINABILITY

Like Hueting I have been raised in the neoclassical economic tradition, a tradition that is frequently maligned by individuals who do not seem to understand it. You can be both a neoclassical economist and an advocate of economic reform, recognizing 'new scarcities' and wishing to improve the income accounts. In this process neoclassical economic arguments can be made and these are more likely to convince other neoclassical economists. My espousing the cause of a better assessment of product through the medium of the national accounts has earned me the 'epithet' of a 'weak sustainablist', and I suspect that the same appellation might also be extended to Hueting. There is nothing feeble about this position, however, except that it only looks 'weak' from the perspective of the conservationists who favour a 'stronger' sustainbility. So-called 'weak sustainability', as I have argued elsewhere, revolves around getting the income estimates right (El Serafy, 1996). Since the environment must be regarded as part of society's capital, its stock, like other forms of capital, has to be 'kept intact' (to use the accountant's language) for the proper estimation of income. To the accountant, 'keeping capital intact' is only a theoretical device that provides a benchmark against which to assess income. The income-earner may in certain situations deliberately aim at consuming part of his or her capital, and the accountant will show this against the benchmark of 'keeping capital intact'. Income is sustainable by definition, and its sustainability derives from the accountant's concern for capital deterioration and allowing for its restoration out of current receipts before income can be extricated from such receipts. This 'sustainable' income (or income for short) could then be consumed by its recipient without threatening future consumption. In seeking to get the conventional accounts amended, not so much to reflect environmental change as to obtain better indications of sustainable consumption, I have all along argued that we need estimates that would provide a more realistic *description* of the economies concerned, capable of indicating economic performance (or 'success' in Hueting's words), and ultimately serving as guidelines for macroeconomic analysis and policy. Insisting that losses of natural resources must be offset by investment in other forms of capital as a means of 'keeping capital intact' has sometimes been taken by advocates of strong sustainability to mean that I implicitly assume that the two forms of capital are substitutable for each other. A certain degree of substitutability does in fact exist between inputs in the productive process, and also (which is often forgotten) between final demand ends and this, in turn, affects the derived demand for inputs. Needless to say I assume nothing about substitutability when invoking the concept of capital intactness needed for accounting purposes. It is only when my approach is given a *normative* interpretation and applied for the future on a large enough scale and over the long run that the issue of substitutability can arise. It has even been claimed that my proposals (put forward in terms of the 'user cost', see below) involve an implicit assumption of *infinite* elasticity of substitution between natural and produced capital. Such a claim is not warranted as I have argued elsewhere (El Serafy, 1997, 1999).[3]

Estimating output accurately, therefore, should be seen as the primary task of the national accounting reformists, and it should be regarded as no fault of theirs if so early in the process they turn their sight away from welfare considerations. It should also be realized that the accountants work with discrete slices of time that are often a year, and the sustainability they pursue is only a year-to-year sustainability, and not of the environment, but of income. What the accountants certify as product, output or income must be made up entirely of *value added* without a trace of capital contaminating it. National income, it should be remembered, is gross national income less depreciation. And if the environment is viewed as part of a nation's capital, depreciation of the environment should be incorporated in the accounts. I have argued that environmental capital is different in substance from produced capital, and its decline or degradation sometimes requires a different treatment in the accounts. In many instances natural resources are simply being 'used up' (not depreciated like machines), and taking this into account would require reducing the gross product itself, not just the net product, and not by the entire amount of the resource decline either (El Serafy, 1993). If natural capital is sold and the sale proceeds are entered as income, then income would be exaggerated. 'Value added', it can never be overemphasized, is the fundamental brick from which the structure of product is made, and we should keep in mind the fact that the environment is part of the national capital, and should be taken to cover both its roles as 'source' and 'sink': as a source of raw materials and energy, and a sink into which harmful side-effects of production and consumption are poured. There is little doubt that such views are shared by Hueting; in any case I have seen nothing in his writings that might contradict these basic ideas.

8 OPTIMIZATION AND SHADOW PRICING

I return to a topic I raised earlier, namely the proliferation of much writing on adjusting the accounts based on highly theoretical modifications involving optimization. Several writers, especially those whose goal is explicitly the sustainability of 'welfare', have employed precise tools under highly artificial assumptions that can rarely, if ever, be realized in practice. There is no harm in attempting definitions of welfare and its sustainability without giving the impression that these should dictate the way national income should be estimated *in practice*. Exercises based on the optimal use of resources, utility maximization, Pareto prices, smooth and continuous functions, perfect markets and other theoretical subtleties doubtless have their place in economic analysis and can be illuminating for many purposes, but their relevance to the actual estimation of output in the framework of national accounting is often dubious. Hueting's resort to the shadow pricing of environmental functions may appear at first sight to belong to these exercises, but he is very careful not to mix theoretical adjustments with practical estimates of income. As stated earlier Hueting would leave the conventional estimates of income unchanged, and his theoretical estimates are offered only for comparison.

Let me pursue further this comparison between Hueting's position and mine. While I would advocate certain radical changes in the traditional ways of estimating the *gross* national and domestic products (and also their *net* counterparts), I prefer to keep close to the conventions adhered to by the national accountants, including the use of market prices for valuation, and focusing (by and large) on market transactions to the omission of non-transacted activities. In this I realize I am being rather conservative whereas Hueting, by contrast, is more radical. However, in some other respects, he is much less radical than myself. While we are in agreement that the conventional estimates of national income can be misleading (hence his wrong compass metaphor) he seems content with leaving these misleading estimates unadjusted, presumably (and here I am only guessing) for guiding short- and medium-term economic policy. But, for the benefit of longer-term environmental sustainability, identified by him as a welfare objective, Hueting relies on reckoning a parallel set of numbers which would take account of the loss of environmental functions. His valuation departs from the conventional usage in national accounting of prices set by the market, and involves the estimation of shadow prices. The deviation of this new set of 'income' estimates from the conventional ones should, in his view, demonstrate that the latter are not good indicators of 'economic success', success being conflated with welfare enhancement. Unlike myself, Hueting does not seem concerned about the economic implications of using faulty indicators to guide macroeconomic policy. He is content to state that they provide a wrong compass with which to steer economies (Hueting, 1989) but stops short of examining the economic policy consequences of using such a faulty instrument. Hueting's focus throughout is concentrated on the environment, and his emphasis on the wrongness of the compass derives from the fact that the economic success that may be indicated by traditional accounting can be illusory if the loss of environmental functions is not incorporated in the estimates. In other words, *apart from the environment*, and save in general terms, Hueting does not show interest in the economic implications of development when it is being guided by the wrong compass.

In his advocacy of using shadow prices for valuation, Hueting's radicalism is apparent. He intends to show *society* (citizens and politicians alike) how wrong the conventional estimates are as true indicators of 'economic success' in order that something should be done about the environment. His range of environmental functions is very wide, whereas, by contrast, my own environmental focus is much narrower, being confined to those parts that would lend themselves readily to monetized measurement. Besides, since it is the medium of *national* accounting that is being used, those parts of the environment to be incorporated in the accounts would, in my view, vary from country to country depending on the country's resource base that serves its economic activities. Thus coverage would vary from country to country. Adjusting the accounts would be confined to forestry, minerals, water, or soil, or any combination of these, depending on each country's situation since my goal is to obtain macroeconomic magnitudes that would serve the national economic ends better. The adjustment in all cases would be partial and would never aspire to be comprehensive. But, after all, the conventional national accounts themselves are almost never all-comprehensive.

9 RICH AND POOR COUNTRIES

There is great advantage in having systems of national accounting that are universal, applicable to developed and developing countries alike. The special need of the latter countries to have their income and output estimates adjusted to reflect environmental change (not just indicated tentatively in satellite accounts) has been glossed over in the latest revision of the System of National Accounts (SNA), and economic analysts continue to use the conventional estimates for their purposes. I have attributed the coolness observed in the richer countries (albeit with some notable exceptions) towards an *actual* greening of the accounts to the notion that their concern for the environment tends to be concentrated on pollution, whereas the function of the environment *as a source* of raw materials and energy is often underestimated (El Serafy, 1995, 1997). If this notion of mine is correct, and in view of the commanding position of system designers coming from the richer countries, we may not soon expect much change in the SNA beyond the 1993 amendments (Commission of the European Communities–Eurostat et al., 1993; United Nations, 1993). Most of the developed nations had in the course of their industrialisation run down their natural sources and now derive most of their income from secondary and tertiary activities, relying in great measure on importing their raw material requirements from the poorer countries. For them combating pollution does not need the medium of national accounting which, though possibly helpful, is not crucial. That is because pollution, as stated earlier, can be (and has in fact been) fought successfully via physical indicators, fining and taxing perpetrators, and setting tolerable standards (*à la* Hueting) and policing their enforcement. When such efforts are successful, the cost of reducing pollution becomes 'internalized' and the national accounts would come out right.

By contrast, for many developing countries using the conventional estimates of income without adjustment for loss of resources can fundamentally impair understanding their economic problems. On top of the pollution they suffer (which in some cases is so severe as to be life threatening) loss of natural resources is an ever present problem and bears directly on the estimation of their income. Where primary production dominates the conventional estimates of income and its periodic change, the standard macroeconomic magnitudes can be wrongly estimated and thus misleading for economic purposes. Loss of natural resources (forests, fish, minerals, soil, water and so on) in the process of economic activity goes mostly unrecognized in the traditional accounts. Such a loss is in fact 'disinvestment' which is often perversely portrayed in the accounts as a desirable creation of wealth, and referred to wrongly as 'value added'. The faster a country cuts and sells its trees or extracts and exports its petroleum the accounts would show a higher income and indicate faster growth than is warranted. The lack of attention to this elementary fault and its inevitable consequence of diminishing future economic prospects for the economy concerned make a mockery of much economic analysis based on the unadjusted numbers where the needed adjustment is sizeable. 'Experts' on national accounts, including some of those working for the international organizations that have been entrusted with reviewing and amending the United Nations System, have, in my view, tended to underestimate the inadequacy of traditional income reckoning for the poorer countries, and overlooked and continue to overlook the possibility that economic analysis based on such reckoning might be wrong.

If the accounts are wrong, distortion sets in from various directions, affecting the diagnosis of economic weaknesses, and ultimately the prescription of corrective policies. Distortion affects income measurement, the fiscal balance, the price level, the balance of payments, capital formation and many others (El Serafy, 1997). It is striking that obviously sophisticated analyses are worked out by technically skilled economists who do not stop to question the reality of the magnitudes they use as inputs for their analytical work. What is particularly strange is that international institutions, including the International Monetary Fund and the World Bank, which claim concern for the developing countries, would formulate 'corrective' policies based on faulty accounts, and impose with strict conditionality what is euphemistically described as economic 'reform programmes' on some of their helpless borrowers. The record of economic performance over the past three decades of numerous African nations, highly dependent on natural resources, has been dismal, and may be taken to reinforce Hueting's insight (though advanced generally with no specific reference to Africa) that these economies may indeed have been steered by the wrong compass.[4] Needless to add that Hueting shows commendable awareness of the requirements of the developing countries with his attention to environmental functions that lie at the heart of his interests, spanning the whole gamut of resources, sink as well as source.

10 ADJUSTING THE SNA

Hueting's concern for accurate estimates of national income brought us together during the formative years of the 1980s when we were exploring ways and means for changing the United Nations SNA which had remained virtually unaltered since 1968. Our main meeting ground was the joint World Bank–UNEP workshops, some of whose findings have been published (Ahmad et al. 1989). The momentum generated by these workshops led eventually to the 1993 SNA and the introduction of the new concept of 'satellite accounts for the environment' (Commission of the European Community et al., 1993). The new changes have satisfied neither of us, but considering the great variety of opinions proffered by various international 'experts' on how to make the amendments, certain progress should be recognized as having been gained. At least we now have a United Nations-endorsed SNA are offering a window of opportunity in the form of 'supplementary' accounts where various elements of relevant information are shown. Here the interrelationships between the economy and the environment may be recorded and be available for analysis. Simultaneously, and as a complement to the new SNA, the United Nations Statistical Division issued 'guidelines' for compiling the new satellite accounts (United Nations, 1993) although these guidelines have been put forward rather hesitantly as an 'interim version'.

It is obvious that the new system has failed to introduce basic changes, relying, it seems, on the (optional) satellite accounting framework to convey any such changes. In several respects I have found the new proposals unsatisfactory, and for brevity here I lump together both the SNA and UNSD's 'guidelines' since the latter are in effect an application of the SNA. The satellite accounts, because of their complexity, avoidance of indicating a definite course of action, their lack of focus, and emphasis on what I have termed 'stock accounting' (El Serafy, 1997), have remained largely unimplemented despite some valiant attempts at application by a few credulous practitioners. Much interest has been shown in a number of countries for adjusting gross domestic product (GDP) and gross national product (GNP) and some of their sectoral components for environmental deterioration – a fundamental interest for natural resource-dependent countries, but not a central issue in the satellite accounts. Unnecessary attention is given to the valuation of stocks at the beginning and end of the accounting period using current prices and thus indicating a redundant process of 'reconciliation' that is at odds with standard accounting practice. Post-1993, the field sadly remains 'a free for all' for all kinds of experimentation which frequently avoids the satellite accounting format altogether. And the unadjusted conventional measurements have persisted as the only 'valid' ones available for macroeconomic analysis. Some empirical investigations have since 1993 been carried out in different parts of the world, supported sometimes by well-intentioned bilateral assistance, but these efforts tend to propagate different methods often proposed by nationals of the donor countries, thus spreading across the world a bewildering variety of approaches and estimates, and in the process succeeding in spelling confusion about the purpose and function of 'green accounting'. It is remarkable how little effort has been exerted to piece together these trials, compare their methods and results, and cull methodological lessons from them for universal application.

What may have contributed to this unsatisfactory outcome, I believe, is the dichotomy emphasized by the authors of the new SNA and endorsed by the United Nations Statistical Division between the conventional measurements of the national accounts which, I repeat, remained virtually unchanged under the new SNA, and the environmentally adjusted magnitudes worked out (or intended to be worked out) in the satellite accounts. The former, unadjusted estimates, go under the rubric, 'economic accounts', while the latter are merely 'environmental'. Recall the title of the United Nations guidelines for the compilation of the satellite accounts: 'integrated environmental and economic accounting'. This kind of language gave the impression that the conventional estimates could continue to stand unadjusted, being viewed as *economic*, whereas the environmentally amended magnitudes, insulated in satellite accounts, are implicitly held to be extraneous to the economic calculus, bereft of merit for economic description, analysis or policy. A deeper reason perhaps is the bias I have mentioned before in that the designers of the new system, coming from the richer countries, underestimate the macroeconomic need of natural resource-dependent countries for having their accounts corrected. 'Steering by the wrong compass' seems to have become ingrained in the perceptions of many practitioners who remain generally oblivious to the fact that economic performance must rely on a natural base whose state of health is crucial for economic activity and its *ex post* assessment.

Even when faint attempts are made to bring some environmental adjustments into the economic field, the outcome is rarely satisfactory. Thus the belated exercise at the World Bank (World Bank, 1997) to estimate 'genuine savings' as an indicator of sustainability employs questionable methods and produces dubious results including the conclusion that a great majority of the developing countries studied generate negative savings and thus are on an unsustainable path. There is some truth in this but the methods and logic of argument are questionable. These estimates have been properly ignored even by the economists of the very institution where these numbers were concocted. The lack of economic sense underlying such exercises highlights the neglect by their authors of earlier literature that had proposed similar, but perhaps better based, approaches focusing on *investment* rather than saving and indicating the magnitude of the needed adjustment (for example El Serafy, 1992; 1993a). A detailed criticism of the World Bank's work on 'genuine savings' as a guide to sustainability has more recently been cogently put forward by Neumayer (Neumayer, 1999, especially Chapter 5; Neumayer, 2000).

11 DIFFERING RESULTS

Hueting kept a noticeable distance from involvement in the mechanics of the new SNA/satellite account adjustments, and from follow-up work carried out in their wake. This, I guess, was due to an understandable lack of sympathy with the way this initiative was developing, though he remained, I sense, troubled by the fact that different analysts were proposing radically different environmental amendments to the conventional measurements. In the 'Parable of the Carpenter' (Hueting and de Boer, 2001), which was available in draft five years earlier, Hueting expressed dismay over the question why estimators who seemed to have the same concern for the environment were proposing radically different corrections to the conventional accounts. Imagine, he suggested in a figurative comparison, what we would think of a carpenter who set out to measure the dimensions of a room and every time he tried, he came up with vastly differing measurements because he was using a different measuring rod? The same observation impelled others (for example Common and Sanyal, 1998) to go so far as to dismiss all such amendments to the conventional accounts as equally lacking in rigour and recommended that they should be dismissed on the dubious argument that differing adjustments mean that the process cannot be made objective. I have attempted to rebut this position by arguing that different estimates reflected different purposes, outlooks and methods, and that it would have been alarming had the results turned out to be identical (El Serafy, 1999).

Hueting, of course, did not show such iconoclasm, but he continued to seek ways and means to garner consensus for the 'right' approach that might elevate the 'green accountant' to the level of a sensible carpenter. Since one metaphor suggests another, I view myself as one of Keynes's 'dentists', a humble technician seeking (at least initially) to reform income estimates while keeping close to the traditions and limitations of national accounting as they have been developed until now. We may recall that in his *Essays in Persuasion* (Keynes, 1932, p. 373) Keynes looked forward to the time when the economic problem had been largely solved, when humanity began attending to worthier pursuits of culture and refinement, and when the role of the economist became similar to that of a dentist. In my tinkering with national accounts I fancy myself as one of Keynes's dentists, whereas Hueting, by contrast, should be seen as a visionary.

12 A GRADUALIST APPROACH

Perhaps a charitable interpretation of my position is that in *normative* terms I may be viewed as a 'Fabian' seeking gradually and in small steps to wear down the opposition to change (which is formidable). The strength of opposition to change on the part of traditional economists and international organizations is truly amazing. While individuals and institutions may occasionally pay lip service to environmental causes, many of them are adamant against adjusting the national accounts. My objective, at least at this stage, is to seek 'weak sustainability' in the realization that it does not satisfy the higher aim targeted by the more committed environmentalists who have tended to lose patience with my position. Although I have attempted occasionally, and I do not know how successfully, to defend myself against their criticism, I entertain no illusion that weak sustainability would satisfy advocates of strong sustainability. Opposition to my views (and no doubt Hueting's) thus comes equally from the economists and the environmentalists. I have little sympathy with iconoclasts who have doubted the usefulness of the concept of sustainability altogether (El Serafy, 1996). Weak sustainability, I have suggested, is a useful step in the right direction, and it is the only version of sustainability that the national accounting system is capable of delivering, albeit on a limited scale. Opponents of 'weak sustainability' thus abound, and interestingly unite traditional economists reluctant to entertain incorporating environmental change in the macro-measurements, with committed environmentalists eager for radical change.

Economists' reluctance is quite natural to changes that might radically alter previous time series and in retrospect show up past economic policies as inappropriate in the light of the revised estimates. Analysts working in statistical offices around the world tend to be very protective of their old time series and would wish to continue extrapolating them without having to learn new ways. In the poorer countries where sometimes the need is greatest to adjust the conventional income estimates to reflect drastic losses of soil, water, fish stocks, minerals and forests, resources, both material and human, tend to be lacking for statistical offices to undertake serious work on green accounting. But the governments themselves are often equally reluctant to tolerate downward adjustments of what passes as their countries' GDP and per capita income, thereby witnessing their international economic influence reduced as a consequence, and perhaps also facing reduction in their quotas (and hence the little power they enjoy) in international institutions. Politicians with their shorter time perspectives frequently focus on the immediate term and tend to ignore sustainability.

In some of the richer countries, much success has been achieved through resorting to hybrid systems that combine physical measurements with value estimates. In the Netherlands the hybrid system of National Accounting Matrix including Environmental Accounts (NAMEA), which combines economic and environmental indicators, has been developed and this seems to be spreading to other countries also (Keuning and de Haan, 1996). While great steps forward have been made by an exceptional group that includes, besides the Netherlands, Norway, Canada and to some extent also the UK and the USA, where many initiatives have been explored, full integration of the environment in the national accounts for producing altered estimates of *income* have remained incomplete. By contrast, several developing countries' main target for green accounting has been revealed as a re-estimation of *income*, not the reckoning of their total wealth – a task that is rarely, if ever, accomplished even in the most advanced nations through the medium of the national accounts.

13 UNSUITABILITY OF STRONG SUSTAINABILITY FOR ADJUSTING THE ACCOUNTS

Strong sustainability cannot be applied to the national accounts without damaging the flow account estimates. Strong sustainablility views any decline in environmental stock (or degradation of its quality) as a cost that should be charged against the unadjusted product. In parallel with depreciating human-made assets (such as machinery, equipment, buildings) environmental 'depreciation' has to be taken out for reckoning the net product (*NP*) viz:

$$NP = GP - (D_1 + D_2) \tag{8.1}$$

where *GP* is the gross product, and D_1 and D_2 are, respectively, the depreciation of human-made capital and loss of environmental 'capital'.

Applying this strong sustainability approach to an imaginary country that relies totally on the exploitation, at an assumed zero extraction cost, of a stock of a depletable resource we get the following interesting outcome. *GP* is made entirely of asset sales which, under the standard approach, are wrongly counted as value added. Since no human-made capital is involved in extraction, D_1 is zero. Treating the decline in the stock due to extraction as depreciation, D_2 will be equal to the whole value of sale, which is the same as the putative *GP*. So we get the absurd result:

$$NP = GP - D_2 = \text{Zero} \tag{8.2}$$

In other words, this imaginary country has no net income at all, and its 'gross income' is merely revenue from selling its assets. Using this stark example, and treating environmental stock declines as *depreciation* in deference to 'stock accounting' would lead to meaningless estimates such as the above, and indicate that such a country has no net income at all. That is why I believe weak sustainability, based on the 'user cost' approach I have developed, should be preferred when employing the medium of national accounting to reflect natural resource declines. I see that Neumayer (1999, 2000) comes to the same conclusion.

I must add here that my user cost approach does not imply 'perfect' substitutability between natural and produced capital since it is only a year-by-year accounting device. Nor that it involves a constant rate of extraction. It can handle reassessments of reserves with great facility without resorting to valuing them, and it is applicable equally to depletable and to renewable resources to the extent that the latter are being mined. It also discriminates between equal volumes of extraction out of different levels of stocks by raising the issue of sustainability: how many years would the resource last at the current rate of extraction? For there should clearly be a fundamental difference for national accounting between extracting a given volume out of a large or small stock. Extracting the same volume amounting to 5 per cent of the stock has different implications for income and sustainability from extracting the same quantity if it amounts to 50 per cent of the stock.

14 MACROECONOMIC POLICIES

Where significant adjustments have to be made to the conventional accounts to reflect environmental deterioration, the implications of the adjustment can be quite serious. The level of GDP and GNP is bound to come down. Within these quantities, since consumption can be taken for granted, what had passed as capital formation must be scaled downwards. Growth has to be recalculated, and analytical indicators of capital productivity (such as the incremental capital output ratio) have to be reassessed. If natural resources are being extracted in the public sector and the ensuing revenue is mixed with tax revenues, then the fiscal balance and fiscal policy have to be re-examined. Countries selling significant quantities of their depletable resources, including forestry and mineral products, and recording these in the balance of payments as current exports will have to be looked at again to separate such 'capital elements' from current transactions, and assess anew whether there is truly a surplus or deficit in the current account of the balance of payments. Most importantly they should be wary of standard assessments of domestic inflation which indicate whether or not their currency is overvalued in terms of the currencies of trading partners. Currently overvaluation, a reflection of the well-known phenomenon of the 'Dutch disease', can remain obscured by simplistic tests of apparent price stability bought by import surpluses generated by unsustainable natural resource exports of a capital nature.

I have touched on these problems elsewhere, and attempted to bring them to the attention of the Bretton Woods institutions to no avail (El Serafy, 1993a, 1996a, 1997). Resistance to change, as I emphasized before, dies hard, and the IMF, which in many respects shows a greater interest than the World Bank, tries to hide behind the World Bank, allegedly the more expert of the two institutions in matters environmental. The Bank, after all, contains an extensive roster of environmental 'specialists' and is expected to play the role of promoter of long-term development. In my study (El Serafy, 1993a) which began as an internal World Bank document, I attempted to recalculate the adjustments made for Indonesia by the World Resources Institute (Repetto et al., 1989) and presented estimates of downward adjustments to GDP in the period 1971–84 varying annually between 10 and 20 per cent of the unadjusted GDP – a correction that ate up the bulk of the country's apparent gross capital formation. The more recent initiative already mentioned within the World Bank to reassess savings, showing them to be excessively negative in a great number of developing countries, has also been totally ignored by analysts though these dubious numbers make some appearance with all their faults in the Bank's published environmental indicators (World Bank, 2000). The economic analysis, international comparisons and policy advice being made continue to be based on the conventional estimates. It is high time that attention be directed at these powerful institutions that seem impervious to the need to adjust to the era of *New Scarcities*.

15 EPILOGUE

In my judgement, Hueting's extensive writings upon which I lightly touched in this study will be mined by future researchers, and will continue to stimulate genuine drives to integrate the environment fully into national accounting and country macroeconomic analysis. National accounting, of course, is not the only avenue for progress towards a stronger sustainability – an objective that lies at the heart of Hueting's writings. But it deserves to attract the attention of serious analysts who need genuine indicators of progress and reliable measurements that would indicate the directions in which to steer economic development.

The emphasis placed here on environmental capital and its maintenance is crucial, but environmental capital should in this context be viewed only as part of the background, albeit a very important part of the background. It is the *physical* change from year to year in this capital that is relevant, and I have seen very little use in putting a value on its stock as some environmentalists have been eager to do. Since it is the flow accounts (income, savings, investment and so on) that are the main products of national accounting and not the stock of wealth, we should be content with assessing the *physical* changes in the stock that occur periodically, pricing them to the extent possible at the current period market price, which in the first place is being used in the body of the accounts to value the sectoral products.[5] In this, as in many other respects, my views and Hueting's are quite close. But his emphasis on *welfare*, which is paramount in his writings, distinguishes his position from mine.

NOTES

1. Robbins, in his *The Nature and Significance of Economic Science*, Chapter II, proposed that economists, *qua* economists, should not get involved in ends, which they should take as given, but concern themselves with the limited means available for economically attaining such ends. He held that 'economic science' was neutral among and between ends, and that its function should be to inquire how human beings advance towards the realization of their objectives, constrained by the scarcity (and multiplicity of potential uses) of the limited means available to them.
2. It should be stressed that it is the periodic *change* in environmental stocks that needs to be valued for adjusting the accounts, and not the total stock. The physical change may be usefully valued at the current period's prices that are already used for valuing the current period's 'flow accounts'. Putting a value on the whole stock by using any one year's prices (which are liable to fluctuate violently) is often meaningless. Besides, if a resource gets critically scarce and the market puts a higher price on it, the higher value of the remaining stock may in fact obscure the all-important diminished physical dimensions.
3. In the context of accounting the concept of keeping capital intact is an *ex post* device needed as a benchmark for the estimation of income, and is not in any way meant as a 'normative' injunction for a recommended behaviour as some critics have misunderstood it. It is only when the concept is given a normative interpretation as indicating a preferred course of action that it shows signs of weakness. Looked at from this normative angle, investing in produced capital to replace any disinvestment of natural capital is not necessarily a good policy if it is to be observed on a large scale and over the longer term. Year by year, however, and viewed from the limited perspective of individual productive units, replacing one form of capital by another is perfectly justifiable but such replacement should not necessarily be taken to imply any inherent substitutability relationship between forms of

capital as thought wrongly by some critics. *Ad hoc* acts of substitution among assets should not be interpreted as denoting the existence of continuous and stable demand and supply functions from which meaningful and stable elasticity values may be estimated.

4. See my study, 'Natural Resources and Macroeconomic Policy in an African Context' (El Serafy, 1997a) where I have tentatively attributed the failure of development efforts in most sub-Saharan African nations during the past three decades to faulty economic policies based on inaccurate estimation of their national accounts.
5. The accountants usually value end-period stocks at current market prices or at last year's end-period prices whichever is lower. This precautionary valuation rule is basic to income estimation, but its rationale seems often to escape economists.

REFERENCES

Ahmad, Yusuf J., Salah El Serafy and Ernst Lutz (eds) (1989), *Environmental Accounting for Sustainable Development*, (a UNEP–World Bank Symposium), Washington, DC: World Bank.

Collier, Paul and Jan Willem Gunning (1999), 'Explaining African economic performance', *Journal of Economic Literature*, **xxxvii**, 64–111.

Commission of the European Communities–Eurostat, International Monetary Fund, Organization for Economic Cooperation and Development, United Nations and World Bank (1993), *System of National Accounts 1993*, Brussels/Luxembourg, New York, Paris, Washington DC.

Common, Mick and Kali Sanyal (1998), 'Measuring the depreciation of Australia's non-renewable resources: a cautionary tale', *Ecological Economics*, **26**, 23–30.

Daly, Herman E. and John B. Cobb (1989), *For the Common Good: Redirecting the Economy Toward Community, the Environment, and a Sustainable Future*, Boston, MA: Beacon Press.

El Serafy, Salah (1989), 'The proper calculation of income from depletable natural resources', in Yusuf Ahmad, Salah El Serafy and Ernst Lutz (eds), *Environmental Accounting for Sustainable Development* (a UNEP–World Bank Symposium), Washington, DC: World Bank, Chapter 3, pp. 10–18.

El Serafy, Salah (1991), 'The environment as capital', in Robert Costanza (ed.), *Ecological Economics: the Science and Management of Sustainability*, New York, NY: Columbia University Press, Chapter 12.

El Serafy, Salah (1992), ' Sustainability, income measurement, and growth', in Robert Goodland, Herman Daly and Salah El Serafy (eds), *Population, Technology, and Lifestyle: The Transition to Sustainability*, Washington, DC: Island Press, Chapter 5, pp. 63–79.

El Serafy, Salah (1993), 'Depletable resources: fixed capital or inventories?', in Alfred Franz and Carsten Stahmer (eds), *Approaches to Environmental Accounting*, Heidelberg: Physica-Verlag, pp. 245–58. [Proceedings of the International Association for Research in Income and Wealth's Conference on Environmental Accounting, held at Baden, Austria, in May 1991].

El Serafy, Salah (1993a), *Country Macroeconomic Work and Natural Resources*. Environment Working Paper No. 58, Environment Department, Washington, DC: World Bank.

El Serafy, Salah (1995), 'Measuring and evaluating development', *International Social Science Journal*, **143**, 61–74, UNESCO.

El Serafy, Salah (1996), 'In defence of weak sustainability: A response to Beckerman', *Environmental Values*, **5**, 75–81.

El Serafy, Salah (1996a), 'Natural resources and national accounting: impact on macroeconomic policy – Part II', *Environmental Taxation and Accounting*, **1** (2), 38–59.

El Serafy, Salah (1997), 'Green accounting and economic policy' *Ecological Economics*, **21** (3), 217–29.

El Serafy, Salah (1997a), 'Natural resources and macro-economic policy in an African context', paper presented at an international conference organized by the University of Cairo Institute of African Research and Studies in Cairo, May 1997 (mimeo).

El Serafy, Salah (1999), 'Depletion of Australia's non-renewable natural resources: a comment on Common and Sanyal', *Ecological Economics*, **30**, (3), 357–63.

Goodland, Robert, Herman E. Daly and Salah El Serafy (eds) (1992), *Population, Technology and Lifestyle: The Transition to Sustainability*, Washington, DC: Island Press.

Hueting, Roefie (1980), *New Scarcity and Economic Growth: More Welfare through Less Production?* Amsterdam: North-Holland Publishing Company.

Hueting, Roefie (1989), 'Correcting national income for environmental losses: toward a practical solution', in Yusuf J Ahmad, Salah El Serafy and Ernst Lutz (eds), *Environmental Accounting for Sustainable Development*, a UNEP–World Bank Symposium, Washington, DC: World Bank, Chapter 6, pp. 32–9.

Hueting, Roefie (1993), 'Calculating a sustainable national income: a practical solution for a theoretical dilemma', in Alfred Franz and Carsten Stahmer (eds), *Approaches to Environmental Accounting*, Heidelberg: Physica-Verlag, pp. 39–53, [Proceedings of the International Association for Research in Income and Wealth's Conference on Environmental Accounting, Baden, Austria, May 1991.]

Hueting, Roefie and Bart de Boer (2001), 'The Parable of the Carpenter', *International Journal of Environment and Pollution*, **15**, (1), 42–50.

Keuning, Steven J. and Mark de Haan (1996), *What is a NAMEA?* Statistics Netherlands, National Accounts Occasional Paper, Voorburg, The Netherlands.

Keynes, John Maynard (1932), *Essays in Persuasion*, New York, NY: Harcourt, Brace and Company.

Neumayer, Eric (1999), *Weak versus Strong Sustainability: Exploring the Limits of Two Opposing Paradigms*, Cheltenham, UK and Northampton MA, USA: Edward Elgar.

Neumayer, Eric (2000), 'Resource accounting in measures of unsustainability: challenging the World Bank's conclusions', *Environmental and Resource Economics*, **15**, 257–78.

Repetto, Robert, William Magrath, Michael Wells, Christine Beer and Fabrizio Rossini (1989), *Wasting Assets: Natural Resources in the National Accounts*, Washington, DC: World Resources Institute.

Robbins, Lionel (1935), *An Essay on the Nature and Significance of Economic Science* (2nd edn), London: Macmillan and Co.

Tinbergen, Jan and Roefie Hueting (1992), 'GNP and market prices: wrong signals for sustainable economic success that mask environmental destruction', in Robert Goodland, Herman Daly and Salah El Serafy (eds), *Population, Technology and Lifestyle: The Transition to Sustainability*, Washington DC: Island Press, Chapter 4, pp. 52–62.

United Nations (1993), *Integrated Environmental and Economic Accounting*

(Interim Version): Handbook of National Accounting (Studies in Methods, Series F, No. 61), New York, NY: United Nations.
World Bank (1997), *Expanding the Measure of Wealth: Indicators of Environmentally Sustainable Development*, Environmentally Sustainable Development Studies and Monograph Series, No. 17, Washington, DC: World Bank.
World Bank (2000), *World Development Indicators*, Washington, DC: World Bank.

9. Valuing nature

David Pearce, Kirk Hamilton and Giles Atkinson

1 INTRODUCTION

Roefie Hueting's *New Scarcity and Economic Growth* (Hueting, 1980) has a deserved place in the history of environmental economics. Roefie warned that slavish adherence to gross national product (GNP) as an indicator of human well-being was totally misleading because of its exclusion of so many of the factors that contribute to that well-being, not least the quality of the services provided to us by the natural environment. While this observation is today a commonplace, we often risk forgetting the pioneers who drew the issue to our attention. Much the same goes for the other messages of *New Scarcity*: the need to integrate economics and ecology, the distortionary effects of economic policy that neglects non-market values and the need to embrace sustainability as a goal of society. But Roefie has always insisted that, in practice, one of the ways of correcting the failure to account for non-market values is illicit. He has never believed that we can, or even should, measure the shadow prices of many non-market functions. A shadow price in this context is the willingness to pay for securing a change in a non-market value such as clean air, species preservation or a fine landscape. It measures what people are willing to pay indirectly through surrogate markets, or what they would be willing to pay if only there was a market. An example of the former would be the hedonic house price approach, which measures marginal willingness to pay through analysis of the variation of house prices with environmental quality. An example of the latter would be contingent valuation; a questionnaire-based approach, which seeks directly to find hypothetical willingness to pay.

For Roefie, the feasibility of estimating marginal willingness-to-pay (WTP) has always been close to zero, for many, but not all, classes of non-market environmental values. '. . . The construction of shadow prices that are directly comparable with market prices, a prerequisite for a theoretically sound correction of national income, is mostly not possible' (Hueting,

1991). By and large, Roefie's objections to estimating shadow prices have not been theoretical but practical, in that he states that the whole exercise is fruitless because what is at stake are the very life support functions upon which we all depend. Seeking a WTP to conserve those functions would seem fruitless: '. . . asking people how much such a function is worth is pointless' (Hueting, 1991).

Roefie Hueting's solution is to invert the process of estimating a modified or 'green' national income. First, he sets out the requirements for what he regards as sustainability by, in effect, assuming that the world population has very strong preferences for sustaining natural assets at certain levels in perpetuity. These might include, for example, setting pollution levels at rates no greater than the assimilative capacity of the environment, so that there is no net accumulation of pollution or pollution damage. Second, he estimates the costs of achieving those sustainability targets. Third, the gross national product (GNP) consistent with meeting the sustainability targets is compared with actual GNP. The difference measures the 'depreciation' of the environment, which is ignored in current estimates of GNP (Hueting and Bosch, 1990).

We take a different view in this study. We suggest that shadow pricing is essential for the concept of 'sustainable GNP' and that attempts to construct such a concept without shadow pricing are arbitrary.

First, we suggest that much of the view about the 'essentiality' of the environment, based on life support functions, confuses marginal and total willingness to pay, a confusion that is best illustrated by looking at a recent manifestation of the same problem (Costanza et al., 1997). Roefie Hueting's doubts about valuing life support functions are fully justified in light of the misconceptions of this literature.

Second, we suggest that 'sustainable GNP' in the Hueting sense is arbitrary because of the difficulties of measuring sustainability targets and because, even where they can be defined, the marginal cost of achieving the last unit of sustainability is likely to be so large as to make the measure unachievable.

Third, we argue that not only does a correct interpretation of national income require that we estimate shadow prices, but that considerable progress has been made in securing those estimates.

If it seems churlish to appear to take a different route to the author who is the deserved focus of this *Festschrift*, we draw attention to the fact that progress is rarely made without provocation, and it is Roefie Hueting's provocative writings that prompt a constructively critical approach. It is arguable that so much progress could not have been made on valuing nature but for Roefie's contributions.

2 ON THE IMPOSSIBILITY OF VALUING EVERYTHING

In recent years several attempts have been made to measure the economic value of ecosystems at the global level. In terms of Roefie Hueting's concerns, such exercises commit two offences. First, they attempt to derive shadow prices based on WTP. Second, they use those shadow prices for the valuation of life support functions, an illicit application of shadow pricing. Here we argue that shadow pricing *per se* is the right approach, but that the debate over life support functions confuses marginal and total willingness to pay.

Roefie Hueting's own analysis always required the identification of environmental functions, that is what an environmental asset actually does. The most celebrated recent study that tries to value global ecosystem functions is that by Costanza et al. (1997). The study suggests that the economic value of the world's ecosystems is \$33 trillion per annum, within the range of \$16 trillion to \$54 trillion. Since the entire economic output of the world is some \$28 trillion, the world's ecosystems appear to be providing an annual flow of economic value 1.2 times that of world GNP.

Table 9.1 summarizes the economic values estimated in Costanza et al. (1997), taking the central values only and condensing the categories of biome and ecological service. The first part of the table shows that coastal

Table 9.1 The alleged 'global value' of the world ecosystems

Biome		Economic value in 10^{12} \$(1994)
Marine:	Open ocean	8.4
	Coastal	12.6
Total marine		
Terrestrial:	Forests	4.7
	Grass/rangeland	0.9
	Wetlands	4.9
	Lakes/rivers	1.7
	Cropland	0.1
Total terrestrial		
Total		33.3

Source: Adapted from Costanza et al. (1997).

ecosystems provide around one-third of the economic value, with oceans, forests and wetlands also of major significance. The second part of the table indicates that nutrient cycling accounts for over half the value, with 'cultural' and waste treatment values also being significant. Cultural value here refers to non-commercial activity such as gaining aesthetic, spiritual and educational pleasure. Nutrient cycles refer to the ways in which ecosystems acquire, process, store and recycle nutrients, while waste treatment refers to the role played by ecosystems in recovering and modifying nutrients. Both parts compress the greater detail in Costanza et al. (1997) and clearly the relative magnitude of the various categories begs many questions. Indeed, some of the results may not concur with our economic intuition. For example, is the value of cropland in reality likely to be just a fraction of the value of the forests or the open ocean for that matter? Regarding the methods used to estimate each component, a brief example of open oceans illustrates this procedure. Its cultural value (not shown separately in the summarized table) is \$76 per hectare. Multiplied by the hectareage of the open oceans this gives \$2.5 trillion. The \$76 is derived as follows: in California coastal real estate commands a 'premium' of \$10 million hectares over and above the value of similar non-coastal land, and this premium is assumed to reflect the cultural values of living near the ocean. In Alabama the same differential is only \$0.5 million. Taking this as representative of developed country values, and measuring the coastal area in developed countries as 9.7 million hectares, we get (approximately) \$5 to \$105 trillion as the cultural value of ocean land. This is a capital value so it needs to be amortized over the lifetime of the land, taken to be 20 years. When this amortized value is divided by the total ocean area, and combined with a 'guesstimate' for differential land values in developing countries, the resulting value is \$76 per hectare.

It is clear that there are uncertainties inherent in this approach. Each component estimate of ecosystem value entails a range of crude simplifying assumptions, which in turn introduces into the analysis error components of unknown magnitude. Even if this was not the case, an even more basic problem with this approach is that the methodologies for estimating economic value relate to relatively small changes in ecosystem functions, *not to the totality of the functions themselves* (Pearce, 1998). Are the values in Costanza et al. (1997) rooted in WTP, the approach they explicitly espouse, and are they marginal values? Using property price differentials is a well-established procedure for identifying environmental benefits, known as the *hedonic property price* procedure, and this procedure does indeed have its foundations in WTP. But those procedures require, at least, that property price differentials be explained statistically to find the so-called 'implicit' or 'hedonic' prices. This would mean taking representative data and seeing what factors statistically account for the differentials, environmental appreciation, of course, being only one of those factors. That is not the procedure used in Costanza et al. (1997). The defence would be that we lack such statistical studies so that the authors had little to go on and, in any event, they were concerned to get 'first order' estimates, not refined numbers. Nonetheless, this one procedure results in a value which is around 7 per cent of the total ecosystem value in Table 9.1. As it happens, the aggregated numbers are not consistent with WTP for the simple reason that WTP is constrained by world income, $28 trillion. Ecosystem values based on WTP cannot therefore exceed $28 trillion, even if it was valid to 'value everything'.

Nor are the values 'marginal' values. If they were they would relate to small changes in ecosystem services. But the Costanza et al. (1997) values are quite clearly intended to be the value of the totality of the resource. Essentially, a methodology developed for valuation at the margin has been applied to a context where it is not applicable. If we take the oceans away, are we to suppose that $2.5 trillion would compensate for the lost cultural values? In fact, the economic value of the lost totality of oceans either has no meaning or is simply a very large number indeed. The argument for it having no meaning emerges if we take the second measure of economic value, *willingness-to-accept* (WTA) compensation for asset loss. The argument for it being a 'very big' number emerges if we think in terms of WTP. How big could this number be? If we thought we could survive without the oceans, then the absolute maximum must be the world GNP ($28 trillion) less whatever we need just to subsist. As it happens, the entire world's ecological functioning would collapse without the oceans, so the more likely answer is the former – that is the calculation has no real economic meaning.

But if this is true of oceans it will also be true of other ecosystems, for example global atmosphere, stratosphere, the world's forests, wildlife and so on. It follows that there is no economic interpretation of virtually all the aggregated numbers in Costanza et al. (1997).

A more subtle reason for attaching no meaning to the Costanza et al. (1997) numbers lies in the *ceteris paribus* reasoning underlying the WTP concept. WTP values relate to changes in an existing situation, *other things being held equal*. Like ecological systems, economic systems are interdependent – if we make a significant change in one thing it will affect other things. The economist's rationale for not trying to trace these interactions through in many contexts is that the changes in question are very small. The second, third and *n*th order impacts are not likely to change the answer, although there is always an uneasy tension between this 'partial equilibrium' assumption and the need to trace interactions more widely with 'general equilibrium' models. But all economists are clear that once the change is large relative to the status quo, other prices *will* change. In those contexts, WTP for a single change is a misleading indicator. Moreover, one cannot *add* the WTPs for different asset changes. Yet the Costanza et al. (1997) article deals in exactly such a context of wholesale and major change – the presence or absence of entire ecosystems, which incidentally goes way beyond what even a general equilibrium analyst would contemplate modelling.

The 'value of everything' approach adopted by Costanza et al. (1997) does fall foul of Roefie Hueting's warnings about trying to value life support functions, but it does so because it attempts to use marginal concepts for a total value context. In this respect, Roefie's concern about the pointlessness of trying to express WTP for 'everything' is justified.

3 GNP AND THE COST OF ACHIEVING SUSTAINABILITY GOALS

Does Roefie Hueting's approach to 'sustainable GNP' overcome the anticipated problems of finding shadow prices for environmental functions? Our feeling is that it creates an arbitrariness that detracts attention from the theoretically correct (as Roefie acknowledges) solution of estimating a shadow-price-based GNP.

First, the approach assumes that sustainability targets can be established in a fairly robust manner. Roefie's view has been that governments represent a channel of 'revealed preference' so that the targets set by government act like shadow prices. But this presupposes a model of government rationality that it is difficult to sustain. Indeed, it contains a contradiction. The basic rationale for shadow pricing is to measure the true opportunity costs of resource use at the margin. Those costs must be based on individuals' preferences in a democratic society. If government was a perfect 'mirror' and conduit for those preferences we would have no more reason to use WTP as revealed by government target-setting than we have for measuring WTP directly from individual preferences. If government is a perfect reflector of preferences, either approach will do. But governments are well known for not acting in such a way, as the whole of public choice theory points out. Hence, they are at best a very imperfect medium for expressing individuals' preferences. One of the basic tests of this 'distance' between government and the people is the extent to which actual decisions deviate from what individuals' preferences imply is needed. In other words, we use shadow prices, as embodied in cost–benefit analysis, for example, to check on the rationality of government. If we reject shadow prices on the grounds that governments are best placed to reveal preferences then we have no test of that rationality.

The same point can be made by looking at the next stage of the sustainability target approach. To modify GNP we require some monetary estimates (putting to one side the view that one can only construct physical accounts – that is 'satellite accounting'). In the Hueting approach this is achieved by finding the cost of achieving the sustainability target. It is this cost that gives rise to the 'green' GNP estimate. But the cost of reaching a target is (typically) quite different to the benefit of reaching it. The benefit is the damage avoided, and the damage avoided is measured by individuals' WTP to secure that state. The relevant model of government is one where these benefits are compared to the costs of achieving the target to check if government has set the economically optimal target. Once costs are used to measure benefits, this whole structure of rationality is removed. Whatever a government decides is a target is the socially desirable and optimal target (regardless of any benefit estimation), and whatever it costs is the measure of social benefit. The reasoning is entirely circular and the resulting estimates of 'depreciation' are incapable of being falsified, thus failing a most basic scientific test. Yet another way of saying the same thing is that costs and benefits become the same so that the benefit–cost ratio for achieving the sustainability target is always unity.

There is an additional argument against a modified GNP based on the cost of target achievement. In some cases it is possible to define a sustainability target. Take acid deposition from fossil fuel burning, for example. Here we have well-defined 'critical load' maps which indicate the levels of acidic depositions (mainly sulphur and nitrogen oxides) that can be tolerated by ecosystems. In terms of the economic jargon, we define the origin of a damage function. But what we know is that the cost of achieving those critical loads, which vary by geographic area, rises exponentially as we near the critical levels. The marginal cost of achieving the last unit of 'unsustainable' deposition is very large, and it has to be questioned whether it is worth the marginal benefit obtained. The point here is that setting sustainability as a goal is laudable, but its achievement could be extremely expensive, so much so that marginal benefits may be well below marginal costs as the target is approached.

We therefore find the 'distance to targets' approach implicit in the Hueting analysis suspect. We acknowledge, however, that others have found it persuasive, a testimony to the influence that Roefie Hueting has had on real world decision making.

4 A SHADOW PRICED GNP

Finally, we turn to what Roefie Hueting acknowledges is the theoretically sound way of estimating a 'green' GNP (more strictly, a green *net* national product). Elsewhere we have set out the structure of the relevant accounting measure (Hamilton, 1996; Atkinson et al., 1997). The sequence of adjustments to conventional GNP is set out below. First, however, we outline the motivation for these estimates. Given the close linkages that exist between economic activity and environmental change, there is a strong argument for developing indicators that integrate the economy and the environment more closely. While many paths to achieving this are possible, one approach that appears to hold considerable promise is green accounting. At the apex of this accounting work is the attempt to derive 'greener' measures of national income, savings and wealth by expanding the assets and liabilities measured in the standard national accounts to include natural resources and pollutants.

Broadening the asset boundary further, development may usefully be conceived as a process of portfolio management, where the portfolio consists not only of produced assets and natural resources, but of human resources as well. In this paradigm development outcomes are linked to the production of capital goods, the exploitation of natural resources and the accumulation of human skills. Measuring changes in this portfolio provides a means to track development progress and to give a first indication of the sustainability of this progress.

A measure of GNP and 'green' net national product (NNP) in an economy with natural resources, environmental assets and human capital is (see Mäler, 1991; Hartwick, 1993; Hamilton, 1994; Atkinson et al., 1997):

$$GNP = C + S$$
$$NNP^* = C + [S - dK - r(R - G) - p(E - A)]$$

where: NNP^* = modified or 'green' net national product; C = consumption; S = gross saving; dK = depreciation of produced assets; r = unit resource rent (defined as the difference between the price obtained for a unit of extracted or harvested resource and its marginal cost of extraction or harvesting); R = resource extraction or harvest; G = natural growth rate of the resource (zero for non-renewables). For an analysis of the appropriate treatment of discoveries see Hartwick (1993) and Hamilton (1996); p = marginal social damages from pollution; E = emissions; A = natural assimilation (i.e. dissipation) of pollutants. Hence, the terms $r(R-G)$ and $p(E-A)$ are respectively the value of depreciation on natural resources and the value of net pollution damage.

The term in the square bracket is the genuine savings (Sg) rate for this economy. It describes the value of the change in assets over the accounting period. Hence,

$$NNP^* = C + Sg$$
$$Sg = GNP - C - dK - r(R - G) - p(E - A)$$
$$or, \; Sg = S - dK - r(R - G) - p(E - A)$$

In other words, genuine saving is simply gross saving less depreciation on assets (here, produced assets, natural resources and environmental assets). In principle, investment in human capital will be reflected here in a higher rate of gross saving, other things being equal. Hence, there is no need to additionally account for the value of increases in human resources. Of course, a problem with the standard national accounts from the human capital perspective is that, while capital expenditures on education (for buildings and equipment for instance) are treated as investment, current expenditures, both public and private, are not. If this is the case, the creation of human capital through current education expenditures should also be considered to be investment and hence added to our measure of genuine saving.

The link between sustainable development and expanded asset accounting rests on the assumption that flows of income and well-being are ultimately derived from the total stocks of produced, natural and human assets. Declines in the aggregate value of these stocks must lead, eventually, to declines in well-being. Note that it is an indicator of weak sustainability, which assumes there a sufficient degree of substitution between assets. Hence, if $Sg < 0$ there must be a presumption of non-sustainability.

There are several problems with estimating empirically green NNP measures. In particular, there is no 'natural origin' for the resulting indicator. If gNNP is 10 per cent less than conventional NNP we do not know if this indicates non-sustainability. Similarly, rates of change in gNNP are potentially ambiguous in what this says about sustainability. The resulting rate of growth in green NNP may be lower or higher than the rate of growth of conventional NNP: the 'signal' to policy-makers is therefore very weak and may not convey much information at all about the sustainability or otherwise of a given development path. This problem has led us to favour a rearrangement of the above to produce an indicator of 'genuine savings' (Sg) (Pearce et al., 1998).

The advantage of the Sg measure is that it has a natural origin at zero. If Sg is negative then this is prima facie evidence of non-sustainability. The first cross-country estimates of net savings adjusted for resource depletion and environmental damages were published by Pearce and Atkinson (1993). The first consistent cross-country estimates of genuine saving were published in *Expanding the Measure of Wealth* (World Bank, 1997) and Atkinson et al. (1997).

Estimates of genuine saving are now published in the World Bank's *World Development Indicators* (see World Bank, 1999). Table 9.2 presents estimates of genuine saving in the countries of Southern Africa for 1997. The overall accounting structure is relatively straightforward (see, for a detailed review, Hamilton and Clemens, 1999). To reiterate, genuine saving equals gross saving, less depreciation of produced assets, plus investments in human, less pollution damages. Hence, in Table 9.2, reading from left to right, column 1 indicates gross saving from which depreciation of produced assets is deducted. This simple calculation yields net saving, an aggregate familiar from the conventional national accounts. The contribution of the focus on genuine saving is to examine further changes in human and natural assets within an accounting framework. In the case of the former, an estimate of the increase in human capital, as proxied by per annum education expenditures, is added to saving.

Depletion of minerals and energy and net depletion of forests, however, constitute a diminution in assets, other things being equal, and this liquidation of wealth must be subtracted from conventional estimates of saving. Analogous reasoning extends to the accumulation of pollution liabilities. However, it is important to note from Table 9.2, that the only pollutant measured here is carbon dioxide (the contribution to global climate change by a country).[1] For example, while damages from unsafe water are considerable in this part of the world, comparable figures for all countries are not available. The final column in Table 9.2 indicates the genuine savings rate for each country given these calculations. The low or negative savings rates of many countries in this table represent an opportunity not taken. Rather than transforming valuable natural endowments into other forms of capital (produced assets, infrastructure or human capital) these governments have chosen implicitly or explicitly to consume wealth.

The analysis of genuine savings offers a number of policy options for governments aiming for sustainable development. First, it is clear that the major macroeconomic levers, fiscal and monetary policy, will have a major impact on both public and private consumption, with corresponding effects on the gross rate of saving. Second, more optimal natural resource policies, in particular with respect to royalty collection, will boost savings by reducing incentives for excessively rapid depletion. Third, explicit policies to see that resource revenues are invested rather than consumed, as practised in Botswana for instance,[2] will tend to boost savings rates. Finally, the quality of public investments that are made with resource revenues is critically important – in many countries investing in people, through primary education or health care for example, is the highest quality outlet for public investment.

Most, if not all, of the countries in southern Africa have espoused sustainable development as a policy goal. Indicators measuring progress

Table 9.2 Genuine savings in the countries of Southern Africa: per cent of GDP in 1997

Country name	Gross saving	Depreciation	Net saving	Education expenditure	Resource depletion	CO_2 damage	Genuine saving
Angola	27.3%	6.0%	21.2%	2.6%	20.7%	0.4%	2.7%
Botswana	44.7%	13.3%	31.4%	6.9%	0.8%	0.3%	37.2%
Madagascar	3.6%	4.9%	−1.3%	2.3%	0.0%	0.2%	0.8%
Malawi	2.1%	6.4%	−4.3%	3.2%	5.4%	0.2%	−6.7%
Mozambique	13.6%	3.6%	10.0%	3.9%	3.7%	0.2%	9.9%
Namibia	14.2%	13.8%	0.4%	1.7%	0.6%	—	1.5%
South Africa	17.0%	13.8%	3.2%	6.6%	4.0%	1.4%	4.4%
Zambia	9.8%	9.9%	−0.1%	3.8%	1.4%	0.4%	1.9%
Zimbabwe	11.9%	6.0%	5.9%	8.2%	11.1%	1.0%	2.0%

Source: World Bank (1999).

towards or away from sustainability are therefore needed if these policy commitments are to be meaningful. While there is no single, perfect indicator of sustainability, the concept of genuine saving is a useful step in this direction. Measuring rates of genuine saving that are negative can send a clear signal to policy-makers: wealth is being dissipated, and continuing with the current policy regime will eventually lead to falls in welfare.

The remaining issue concerns the reliability of the shadow prices in the measures of genuine savings. Considerable progress has been made in estimating shadow prices. For example, these have been especially researched in the context of energy externalities – primarily air pollution – and it is true that far less progress has been made for other environmental impacts, especially biological diversity. Our view is that it is a matter of time and research before we derive operational shadow prices for these impacts, although we share one doubt about valuation. This relates to the extent to which 'benefits transfer' is feasible in the near future. Energy externalities have been measured in the USA in several studies (Oak Ridge National Laboratory and Resources for the Future, 1994; Rowe et al., 1995) while the ExternE programme in Europe has established similar values (European Commission, 1995). Most of the shadow price estimates suffer the weakness that expert judgement is used to select prices, which are then transferred to contexts for general valuation. This procedure of 'benefits transfer' is known to be illicit in many cases, and it is essential that meta-analysis takes place to explain the variance in estimates of shadow prices (marginal willingness to pay) across the various studies (Garrod and Willis, 1999). At the moment, the process of using single values as if they are applicable across all contexts contains substantial margin for error. But benefits transfer and meta-analysis are also in their infancy so that a reasonable time period is required before we can be sure that estimates are robust. At this stage we can do no more than express our confidence that the prospect for reasonably reliable benefits transfer is a good one.

5 CONCLUSIONS

Roefie Hueting has taken a singular stance of 'green accounting', arguing that it is for society to set its sustainability targets through the political process, and that the resultant cost of achieving those targets is then the true measure of 'depreciation' on conventionally measured GNP. We acknowledge the logic of this view but argue differently. Precisely because we need checks and balances on what politicians decide it is important to keep economic valuation separate from the values implied by the political process. Otherwise there is a risk that whatever politicians decide is for the best is the best of all possible worlds, and that cannot be. Hence, for us, shadow pricing, inclusive of non-market valuation, is paramount. Moreover, we believe that it is a matter of time and resources before we establish reasonable unit shadow prices for pollutants. Nonetheless, we accept that we are not at that stage yet. There is a temptation to adopt a benefits transfer approach when the data and research base are simply not sophisticated enough to support that transfer. But even without that robust transfer database, we would argue that we have already been able to derive important policy conclusions from partial valuation exercises combined with a derivation of the 'green net national product' concept, the concept of genuine savings.

NOTES

1. See Fankhauser (1994).
2. Note that depletion estimates for diamonds are not included in Table 9.2. Genuine savings rates for Botswana and South Africa are therefore overstated.

REFERENCES

Atkinson, G., W.R. Dubourg, K. Hamilton, M. Munasinghe, D.W. Pearce and C. Young (1997), *Measuring Sustainable Development: Macroeconomics and the Environment*, Cheltenham: Edward Elgar.

Costanza, R., R. D'Arge, S. de Groot, S. Farber, M. Grasso, B. Hannon, K. Limburg, S. Naeem, R. O'Neill, J. Paruelo, R. Raskin, P. Sutton and M. van den Belt (1997), 'The value of the world's ecosystem services and natural capital', *Nature*, **387**, May 15, 253–60.

European Commission (1995), *ExternE: Externalities of Energy*, 6 volumes, DGXII, European Commission, Brussels.

Fankhauser, S. (1994), 'Evaluating the social costs of greenhouse gas emissions', *The Energy Journal*, **15** (2), 157–84.

Garrod, G. and K. Willis (1999), *Economic Valuation of the Environment*, Cheltenham: Edward Elgar.

Hamilton, K. (1994), 'Green adjustments to GDP', *Resources Policy*, **3**, 155–68.

Hamilton, K. (1996), 'Pollution and pollution abatement in the national accounts', *Review of Income and Wealth*, **42** (1), 13–33.

Hamilton, K. and M. Clemens (1999), 'Genuine savings rates in the developing countries', *The World Bank Economic Review*, **13** (2), 333–56.

Hartwick, J.M. (1993), 'Notes on economic depreciation of natural resource stocks and national accounting', in A. Franz and C. Stahmer (eds), *Approaches to Environmental Accounting*, Heidelberg: Physica-Verlag.

Hueting, R. (1980), *New Scarcity and Economic Growth*, Oxford and New York: Oxford University Press.

Hueting, R. (1991), 'Correcting national income for environmental losses: a practical solution for a theoretical dilemma', in R. Costanza (ed.), *Ecological*

Economics: the Science and Management of Sustainability, New York: Columbia University Press.

Hueting, R. and P. Bosch (1990), 'On the correction of national income for environmental losses', *Journal of the United Nations*, **ECE 7**, 75–83.

Mäler, K-G. (1991), 'National accounts and environmental resources', *Environmental and Resource Economics*, **1**, 1–15.

Oak Ridge National Laboratory and Resources for the Future (1994), *Estimating Fuel Cycle Externalities*, 8 volumes, Washington, DC: US Department of Energy.

Pearce, D.W. (1998), 'Auditing the earth', *Environment*, **40** (2), 23–28.

Pearce, D.W., K. Hamilton and G. Atkinson (1998), 'The measurement of sustainable development', in J. van den Bergh and M. Hofkes (eds), *Theory and Implementation of Economic Models for Sustainable Development*, Dordrecht: Kluwer.

Rowe, R., C. Lang, L. Chestnut, D. Latimer, D. Rae, S. Bernow and D. White (1995), *The New York Electricity Externality Study*, 2 volumes, New York: Oceana Press.

World Bank (1997), *Expanding the Measure of Wealth: Indicators of Sustainable Development*, ESD Studies and Monographs No. 17, Washington, DC: World Bank.

World Bank (1999), *World Development Indicators 1999*, Washington, DC: World Bank.

10. Natural capital, the greened national product and the monetization frontier

Sylvie Faucheux and Martin O'Connor*

1 ENVIRONMENTAL FUNCTIONS, GREENED GDP AND SUSTAINABLE DEVELOPMENT

It has, by now, become commonplace to refer to ecological goods and services as deriving from existing stocks of 'natural capital'. This involves the simple extension of the well-established economist's and accountant's notions of a firm's capital as the stocks and equipment capable of delivering flows of money or physical services through time. As Daly (1994, p. 30) describes it:

> Natural capital is the stock that yields the flow of natural resource; the population of fish in the ocean that regenerates the flow of caught fish that go to market, the standing forest that regenerates the flow of cut timber; the petroleum deposits in the ground whose liquidation yields the flow of pumped crude oil.

At first sight, the economist's concept of opportunity cost seems to apply quite as well to ecological goods as to economic goods. The biosphere as a habitat and life support system is a finite, and in many respects destructible, reservoir of natural capital. Estimating the severity of trade-offs, and the

* This study was part of the background methodology work in relation to the project *CRITINC (Making Sustainability Operational: Critical Natural Capital and the Implications of a Strong Sustainability Criterion)*, project ENV4-CT97-0561 funded by the European Commission DG Research Environment and Climate, Theme 4 – Human Dimensions of Environmental Change, June 1998 – June 2000. The project has been coordinated by Professor Paul Ekins (Keele University, UK) with the participation of partners also in Sweden, Italy, The Netherlands, Germany and France.

Thanks to our C3ED colleagues Jessy Tsang, Jean-François Noël, Patrick Schembri and Jean-Marc Douguet who have contributed in various ways to the genesis and final form of this text.

Also thanks to our various European colleagues working in the fields of greened national accounting, sustainability and scenario studies methodologies. Responsibility for opinions, arguments and any errors, rests with the authors alone.

redistribution of economic opportunities, access to environmental benefits, financial and ecological costs, and burdens of risks, thus becomes a major task of ecological economics as a policy science. If current patterns of use of natural capital are environmentally unsustainable, this can also threaten economic and social sustainability.

A wide range of proposals and practices have emerged over recent years, seeking to define and estimate indicators of national sustainability prospects via – an environmentally adjusted national product (greened gross domestic product (GDP)); or a 'sustainable national income'; or a 'greened net national product' taking natural capital depreciation into account. This chapter assesses the 'weak' and the 'strong' perspectives on sustainable development as a basis for these putative sustainability indicators.

Section 2 outlines a structural perspective on sustainable development which allows classification of two broad families of 'environmentally adjusted GNP', and then outlines the methods, model frameworks and empirical estimation procedures that correspond to each family. In the framework that we adopt, a general precondition for sustainability is the maintenance of those 'environmental functions' which play a major role in sustaining natural ecosystems and which make a substantial contribution to human welfare. The concept of 'environmental functions' is here defined as the capacity of natural processes and components to provide goods and services which satisfy human needs (see, especially, Hueting, 1980; de Groot, 1992). These natural processes and components can in turn be identified as stocks of natural capitals or flows, provided by these natural capitals.

The 'weak' recipes, discussed in Section 3, involve making subtractions from the conventional gross national product (GNP). The key methodological question is how, in theory and in measurement practice, one can make the jump, first, from GNP as a measure of one period's output level to an 'environmentally adjusted' estimate of 'national net savings', and, second, to an estimate of the *gNNP* as an indicator of prospects for *sustainable future welfare levels* relative to the current level of consumption.

The 'strong' recipes, discussed in Section 4, exploit statistical estimation and modelling procedures for quantifying the long-term economic performance potential based on cost-effectiveness relative to satisfying criteria. The corresponding indicator estimates the performance potential of a 'greened economy GDP', that is, the volume of economic activity (as measured by, for example, final consumption or national income) that a national economy would have been able or might in the future be able to achieve while respecting specified environmental quality, ecosystem integrity and resource husbandry requirements.

Section 5 draws the threads together, explaining how, in reality, the two types of indicators respond to distinct policy questions and they raise distinct issues of measurement and motivation. The 'weak' indicators are most convincing as warning lights about tendencies in a nation's revenue-generating capacity. The 'strong' indicators, by contrast, are signposts about prospects for reaching simultaneous economic and ecological sustainability goals. These latter, while inevitably speculative, are nonetheless 'stronger' for long-term policy guidance, because they are anchored differently in science and policy quality considerations: (a) avoiding 'misplaced concreteness'; (b) the non-substitutable functional importance of natural systems as life support; and (c) the desire for a coexistence in a world of diversity and natural richness.

2 A STRUCTURAL ECOLOGICAL-ECONOMICS FRAMEWORK

First, we outline a structural ecological-economics perspective, and use it to explain two distinct concepts of an environmentally adjusted GNP figure which, as will be explained, correspond approximately to the 'weak' and 'strong' families of sustainability indicators.

2.1 Neoclassical Natural Capital Theory and Sustainability

In our structural perspective (see Faucheux and O'Connor, 1998; Brouwer, et al., 1999), economic resource management for sustainability must fulfil (at least) two complementary functions:

- the delivery of an ecological welfare base through assuring maintenance of critical environmental functions and amenity (lower portion of Figure 10.1), and
- the delivery of an economic welfare base through production of economic goods and services (upper portion of Figure 10.1).

In this perspective, environmental quality is considered to be a primary support for human welfare and for sustainable economic activity. Policies aimed at safeguarding this primary support function – that is, meaning to commit scarce resources in order to maintain or recover the desirable level of environmental quality – correspond to a kind of 'social demand' for maintenance of environmental functions.

The term 'greened national accounts' refers to national accounting systems extended to include information on the state of the environment

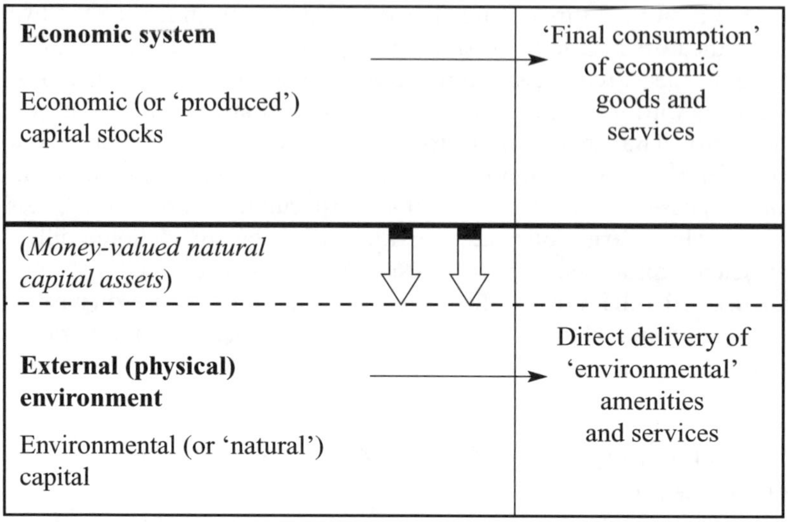

Figure 10.1 *Framework for defining 'environmentally adjusted' macroeconomic aggregates*

and on interactions (for example, 'pressures') between economy and environment. The environmental and interface accounts will include some stock and flow information categories expressed in monetary value terms, and others in non-monetary units of measure. It is, however, crucial to define clearly the respective roles of monetary and non-monetary measures for the various categories of information. In economics it is habitual to ask, is the value of a benefit obtained, or of the loss avoided, worth the investment of economic goods and labour needed to obtain it? Yet the 'demand' for environmental quality, which may include provision for future generations and a demand for protection from environmental harms, cannot easily be expressed as a value in monetary terms. And, even when estimates can be made, the numbers obtained often have very large sensitivity to underlying parameter assumptions concerning possibilities and elasticities of substitution, endowment and income distribution, technological progress prospects, ecological system resilience and so on. These are challenges to be confronted for quality and usefulness of indicators.

As a first step in typology of procedures for defining 'environmentally adjusted' macroeconomic indicators, we refer to Figure 10.1 in order to define two types of adjustment, which are complementary rather than exclusive. There are distinct types of macroeconomic aggregates associated with each adjustment type (and later sections of the chapter will discuss the policy uses, also complementary, of each indicator type).

- The first type of adjustment, relative to standard national accounting conventions, is *a change in the system boundary*, an enlargement of the scope of national accounting to include specified categories of environmental assets. In Figure 10.1, this can be thought of as a shifting of the frontier (the heavy horizontal line) dividing the economy from its external environment. This shift brings some environmental capital (such as minerals, oil and gas, forest or fisheries stocks) into the field of economic accounting, signalled by the fat arrows pointing downwards.
- The second is *adjustment of the economy itself*, that is, an 'adjusted economy' with a new pattern of production processes, levels of production and consumption activity, technologies employed, and so on, which respects specified environmental performance standards. In Figure 10.1, the focus of attention is on the interface between the economic system and its environment, the heavy horizontal line, which is 'crossed' by environmental pressure indicators such as natural resource inputs and pollutant emissions. The volumes of these 'environmental pressures' are to be regulated through adjustments to the economy (technical and structural change).

We now consider how each of these adjustments can be the basis of a useful sort of 'environmentally adjusted national income' figure. Table 10.1 outlines the four combinations of adjustment logically possible, and identifies each combination with established measures and concepts in the green accounting literature.

- The **TOP LEFT** box refers to the 'traditional' macroeconomic indicators based on the 'standard' national accounting conventions for estimating GNP and NNP.
- In the **TOP RIGHT** box, there are 'environmentally adjusted net national income' figures for an existing economy. These are based on using an enlarged asset boundary when assessing *net asset change* for the national economy during the current accounting period. The 'environmentally adjusted national income' or 'green NNP' is then defined as this net asset change (net savings) minus national consumption. Both consumption and asset changes are valued using current prices (or, in the case of some environmental assets for which real prices do not exist, using shadow prices obtained by reference to other goods or costs for the current period). We refer to this as *the 'environmentally adjusted' or 'green' NNP for an unadjusted economy.*
- In the **BOTTOM LEFT** box, there are *the 'unadjusted' GNP and NNP for an 'environmentally adjusted economy'*. These are figures

Table 10.1 Typology of 'environmentally adjusted' aggregates

		System boundary (capital stocks included in the measure of asset value change)	
		Usual set of produced economic assets	*Enlarged to include all produced assets plus specified environmental assets*
Reference economy for estimation	*Statistics for the current really existing economy*	The traditional or 'unadjusted' GNP and NNP (NNP = net savings − consumption)	World Bank 'genuine savings' indicator: An 'environmentally adjusted' indicator for an enlarged portfolio of national assets
	'Shadow aggregates' for a model economy respecting environmental performance standards	The GREENSTAMP approach: GDP and NNP 'volume' measures for an *'environmentally adjusted economy'*	(to be anticipated . . .)

obtained for a hypothetical economic structure, using suitable statistical and analytical techniques, responding to the question: *What would be a feasible macroeconomic performance, is the existing economy were modified so as to respect specified environmental performance standards?* We refer to such figures as *'greened economy GNP'* (or greened economy NNP, as the case may be). Such figures may be obtained in several ways, the most obvious being comparative static and dynamic scenario modelling analyses. (This is the approach developed in the European Commission's *GREENSTAMP* project in 1994–96, which in turn built on experience with 'greened economy' scenarios since the 1970s.)

The top right and bottom left boxes each involve only one of the two forms of 'adjustment' to estimation procedures. The bottom right box provides, logically, for indicator measures that combine both types of adjustment together. As far as we know, estimations of this type of hybrid measure have not yet been developed systematically, but we will return to this idea and its potential policy relevance in our conclusions (Section 5). We first use this schema to discuss the distinction between 'weak' and 'strong' indicators of sustainability.

2.2 Weak Sustainability Indicators: Net Savings, the gNNP and Sustainable National Income

The 'weak sustainability' indicators are obtained by making subtractions from the conventional GNP. The question is how, in theory and in measurement practice, one can make the jump from GNP as a measure of one period's output level to 'net savings' or *gNNP* as an indicator of prospects for *sustainable future welfare levels* relative to the current level of consumption. The usual responses rely on results from neoclassical growth with natural capital theory.

- In general, sustainability is characterized as non-decreasing social welfare over time, the social welfare being defined by an aggregate utility function. The simplest formulation is to represent welfare by final consumption of economic goods and services, but variations are possible where environmental services enter directly the utility function.
- The economic goods and services are produced by three factors of production, which are human capital (labour), produced economic capital and natural capital. Growth paths for the economy depend on the partitioning of produced capital between reinvestment (or 'savings') and final consumption.
- Indicators are then sought concerning (a) the level of final consumption that the economy can deliver on a permanent basis – that is, a sustainable national income, and (b) the 'savings rules' that can ensure that an economy is providing for maintenance of a capacity to deliver non-declining final consumption. Savings and sustainability were conceptually linked through the concept of the *Hicksian national income* as the income flow (or final consumption flow) that can be generated while maintaining the capital stock intact (thus assuring the permanent capacity to continue to deliver this income flow).
- In particular, through an amalgam of theoretical results associated with Weitzman, Hartwick and Solow, it was postulated that (a), the environmentally adjusted net national product (gNNP) defined as the sum of final consumption plus net capital savings *including depreciation of natural capital*, gave a measure of the *Hicksian income* and, hence, the *sustainable national income* (SNI) for the economy in question. This suggestion turned out, upon closer inspection, to be too simplistic and sometimes wrong.

This approach considers welfare as a function of goods and services delivered to households (final consumption). What is important is to understand the opportunity costs of using natural and produced economic capital – the trade-off between present and future consumption. Theoretically, this question is explored using models of intertemporal optimization. The mathematical models are of two main forms. On the one hand are those in the lineage of growth theory, with an aggregate economic capital output that can be used in consumption or invested in economic capital accumulation (see Pezzey, 1992, 1994; Toman et al., 1995; Asheim and Buchholz, 2000 for overviews). On the other hand are overlapping generations intertemporal equilibrium models (see Howarth and Norgaard, 1990; Howarth and Norgaard, 1992; Howarth and Norgaard, 1993), which also consider utility as a function of consumption levels but which characterize the trade-offs as distribution rules for agents living, each with their own consumption preferences, in successive periods.

In Section 3 we give an overview of the development of these literatures since the 1970s, and then a simple example of an overlapping generations equilibrium model (retaken from Faucheux et al., 1997). On the one hand we highlight the important pedagogic messages that can be gleaned. On the other hand we make clear the important 'gap' between the theoretical models and the 'environmentally adjusted GNP' figures that are obtainable in practice. In a theoretical economy, the contributions of natural capital augmentation or depreciation to net savings are defined on the basis of mathematical specifications of stocks, renewal potentials and production functions. But, in any real-world estimation process, there is no such knowledge possible. Many ecological assets and services are excluded altogether from the accounting scheme and, even for those categories included, the sheer complexity of interdependent natural processes (such as atmospheric circulation and hydrological cycles, as bases for agricultural and other ecosystems) makes it very difficult to quantify intertemporal opportunity costs. As Victor et al. (1997) have observed, for the empirical estimates to date:

> By emphasising in their empirical work those aspects of natural capital for which economic measures are more readily available (that is, for resources sold through the market and a few measures of pollution damages), far more has been left out than has been included.

We will conclude that, although environmentally adjusted 'net savings' indicators useful for policy purposes can indeed be defined, they are not silver bullets for the evaluation of sustainability.

2.3 Strong Sustainability and the Economic Opportunity Cost of Ecological Sustainability

The 'strong sustainability' indicators, by comparison, adopt a different approach to the treatment of natural capital. It is argued that the maintenance in the long term of economic welfare levels requires the sustaining, in a functional symbiosis, of economic and natural capital. The physical environment is considered as a complex system, and one may speak of (1) the 'functioning of' natural systems – the internal regulation, cycles of renewal, evolution and transformation by which biosphere activity is maintained, and (2) the specific roles or services provided by natural systems that support economic activity and human welfare – that is, the environment's 'functions for' the human economy.

As will be discussed in Section 4, the 'environmental functions' may be categorized in various ways, such as source of materials and energy, scenic quality and scientific/aesthetic interest, site of economic activity and waste sink. A single ecosystem or natural resource might fulfil a range of economic production input, recreational, biological and pollution absorption functions, for example, forest and river systems. In the 'strong sustainability' perspective it is postulated that, in general, it may not be possible to find full substitutes for this ensemble of functions fulfilled by a given environmental asset. Nor can technological progress be considered to apply in any uniform way to these functions. This leads to the following framework for developing sustainability criteria and rules:

- The identification of categories of 'critical natural capital' whose stocks ought to be maintained at or above some specified minimum levels.
- The problem of resource management for maintenance of essential and desired environmental functions is approached in terms of cost-effectiveness. The requirements are, first, to determine environmental standards or norms, for example, for pollution emissions or natural resource consumption, in physical terms, independently of any notion of economic optimization; and second, to find the least economic cost way of achieving the defined norm.
- A separation is thus maintained between ecological sustainability objectives as such, and the question of economic requirements for attaining them.

In order to give an operational specification to this general framework, supplementary information and analytical propositions must be introduced. These include:

- explanation of the spatial and temporal scales at which the sustainability criteria will be applied;
- the scientific or other justifications for the threshold levels or 'norms' that are proposed;

- explanation of the analytical framework that will be applied to quantify the economic opportunity costs associated with the respect of the specified standards, including whether or not full respect is required immediately or via a transition path over a number of years.

This approach explores the question, what might a 'greened' or 'environmentally adjusted economy' look like that respects the specified sustainability standards? It is thus a scenario-type approach. This distinguishes the approach from the ex post definition of an environmentally-adjusted GNP for the existing economy. The policy relevance of this sort of analysis is also different. Since the question is *how to adjust the economy* (and not how to adjust the accounts), attention can be given to the likely difficulty (in terms of short-term economic costs and social adjustment processes) of satisfying simultaneously a large number of sustainability standards on the basis of available science. This helps to frame policy debates.

We present one example of empirical work carried out in this norm-based cost-effectiveness perspective, using a dynamic multi-sector scenario simulation model (O'Connor and Ryan, 1999; Schembri, 1999a, 1999b). The presentation builds also on some of the methodological results of the research project 'Methodological Problems in the Calculation of Environmentally Adjusted National Income Figures' carried out during 1994–96 for the European Commission Directorate General XII under Contract No. EV5V-CT94-0363. Now known as *The GREENSTAMP Project (GREEned National Statistical and Modelling Procedures)*, this work focused on the development of empirically and theoretically robust methods for quantifying economic opportunity costs associated with meeting specified sustainability standards at sectoral and macroeconomic levels of analysis (see Brouwer and O'Connor 1997a, 1997b; Brouwer et al., 1999). In particular, *GREENSTAMP* investigated prospects for statistical estimation and modelling procedures for quantifying the long-term economic performance potential based on cost-effectiveness relative to environmental pressure criteria in a scenario perspective. The concept of 'greened GDP' recommended was that of a performance potential, namely:

> an estimate of the level of output (or of consumption, or of national income, etc., depending on the exact measure proposed) that a national economy would have been able or might in the future be able to achieve while simultaneously respecting specified environmental quality and resource husbandry requirements.

The value of environmental assets and services is not estimated in monetary terms directly. Rather there is a modular approach. First, information is organized in so-called satellite environmental accounts, which describe the state of the environment according to chosen categories and measures (largely non-monetary) and which establish links between economic activity sectors and environmental change in terms of the pressures acting on each environmental category. Second, cost information is obtained through various levels of analysis (firms and households, sectors and macroeconomic aggregates) about the economic resource requirements – such as investments or consumption foregone – that would be necessary in order to reduce a specified environmental pressure. In this way estimates of the costs of specified improvements in environmental performance can be considered in relation to scientific, political and economic judgements about the importance of the environmental functions, services and assets in question.

3 WEAK NATURAL CAPITAL THEORY

3.1 The Technical and Social Determinants of (Non-)Sustainability

Technological and resource considerations determine whether or not the economy is capable of following a sustainable development time path. We can think of models as expressing 'societal choices', as signified by population growth, individuals' preferences and institutional arrangements governing endowment or income distribution, subject to the defined technical and resource constraints. Population change is usually treated as exogenous, so the emphasis is placed on production feasibility (the intertemporal production possibility frontier) and on the social determinants of investment and consumption over time.

On the feasibility side, the growth and/or sustainability potentials for a model economy depend strongly on the specific assumptions made about natural capital renewal rates, about elasticities of substitution between natural and produced capitals, and about technical progress augmenting productivity of capitals. Where 'technical progress' and/or elasticities of substitution between natural and produced capitals are made high enough, one can obtain models in which the value of the economy's capital stock may grow without limit, and thus the 'sustainable national income' that is attainable 'in the long run' is correspondingly unbounded.

In such instances, just as in the 1950s' literature on growth, achieving sustainability appears as a problem of savings. In any particular period there is a trade-off between consumption and capital accumulation. High consumption in a given period means 'living off capital' during the period in question, but no permanent damage to 'sustainable growth' prospects if this is a transitory phenomenon. The problem becomes serious if the living off capital is repeated period after period, becoming a trajectory of economic decline due to inadequate 'savings propensity'.

The new feature of the modelling work in the 1970s was the introduction of depletable 'natural capital'. Analyses focused on the importance of substitutability and technical progress for relieving growth constraints due to the depletability of the natural capital. Three articles appearing just after the 1973/4 OPEC oil crisis, by Dasgupta and Heal (1974), Solow (1974) and Stiglitz (1974), are among the seminal contributions; much recent work follows directly in their line. (See Faucheux and Noël, 1995 for a detailed exposition.) What was brought out by these early results is the emphasis on feasibility expressed in terms of:

- technical requirements (productivity improvements over time, substitutability between inputs, relative importance of inputs) and
- social parameters (population growth, consumption preferences, savings rules).

By now, a great variety of models have been constructed in which there exists the technological capability for unlimited growth in the value of economic capital over time by substituting away from a renewable or non-renewable natural capital, but where achievement – or not – of consumption sustainability is a social choice. Typically, to investigate this problem of 'social choice', solutions are obtained in these models using the criterion of maximizing the present value of 'society's utility' as defined by some intertemporal social welfare function. The generic result is now well known. Where there is a sufficiently high time preference for present consumption over future consumption, the intertemporal equilibrium path will be characterized, from the outset or after a peak, by monotonically declining values for total capital stock and, correspondingly, per capital utility or consumption levels (see, notably, Howarth and Norgaard, 1990; Howarth and Norgaard, 1992; Howarth and Norgaard, 1993; Norgaard and Howarth, 1991; Mourmouras, 1993; Asheim, 1994, Toman et al., 1995; Pezzey; 1997).

3.2 Characterizing Sustainability in Terms of Consumer and Societal Preferences

In this model framework, consumers' preferences influence sustainability in two respects, along with the 'social distribution rule' that is applied.

First, where more than one good enters into individuals' utility functions at a given moment and these goods have differing natural capital requirements for their production or supply, the relative intensity of preferences for one good over another influences the pressure on natural capital. This expresses one way that lifestyle changes can work for or against sustainability.

Second, individuals' and society's consumption are distributed over time, and this is partly a time-preference phenomenon. We may use the term *subjective time preference* to mean the way that a consumer compares the value (in welfare terms to her- or himself) of consumption at one moment (or period) in time compared with other moments (or periods). But each generation of consumers will have a distinctive, period-based 'preference function', and each consumer's rate of time discounting is determined by his or her particular preference function in conjunction with the consumption opportunity set.

Once the distinction has been made between consumers distributed through time (each with their individual preferences) and 'society' (which decides the 'distribution rule'), the role of savings is seen to be one of influencing the distribution across successive generations of endowments and of consumption opportunities. Thus, for example as Dixit et al. (1980) observed, a programme of investment respecting the Hartwick rule of reinvesting the value of all 'rents' from natural capital, amounts to a policy choice in favour of intertemporal equity.

These issues have been well brought out by models framing the optimal resource use problem as one of intertemporal general equilibrium with utility-maximizing consumers, notably by Howarth (1991, 1992), Howarth and Norgaard (1990, 1992, 1993) and Muir (1996). These authors' usual model form is a closed economy, and the question of time preference is structured by assuming overlapping generations. The example we present is adapted from one by Howarth (Howarth, 1991). Each generation lives for two time periods (say n and $n+1$), and the nth generation maximizes utility:

$$U_n = U_n\,(C_{n,y},\ C_{n+1,old})$$

where $C_{n,y}$ is consumption during period n when the nth generation is young, and $C_{n+1,old}$ is consumption during period $n+1$ when the generation is old. Within each generation, all individuals are identical so we treat them as one. The emphasis thus is on aggregate consumption each period. (The model by Muir, 1996 distinguishes subgroups within each generation and displays interactions between intra- and intergenerational equity.)

Markets for natural capital (resources or environmental amenity), manufactured goods and labour are assumed to be 'competitive' in the sense of equalization of opportunity costs on all margins. Labour is an initial endowment distributed equally across all generations; each generation 'owns' (and thus supplies) labour only while young. Intergenerational transfers are possible through exchange of income for natural capital held as initial endowments.

Technical parameters and initial stock levels determine the intertemporal production possibilities frontier for the economy, and the 'optimal' point on this frontier is then selected as either:

- the equilibrium outcome of utility-maximizing consumers' choices subject to a specified endowment distribution, or
- the optimum of a social welfare function, the latter being formulated in terms of rules about the distribution of consumption or utility levels through time.

The equilibrium obtained will thus be sensitive to, *inter alia*, the choices made explicitly or implicitly about intertemporal natural capital endowment (property rights distribution). First we give a simple model illustration, and then we discuss the significance of these theoretical results.

3.3 A Simple OLG Model of Intertemporal Efficiency and Distribution with Natural Capital

In Faucheux et al. (1997), a simple multi-period overlapping generations (OLG) model was specified, which has the same production function as in Stiglitz's (1974) original problem: three inputs, manufactured capital M, human capital L and non-renewable natural capital R, to a Cobb–Douglas production function which produces manufactured capital as its sole output. The manufactured capital can be used in consumption C or saved for investment S.

The resource management problem is to maximize an intertemporal social welfare function, or in other words an inter-temporal distribution rule, subject to a number of constraints. As in the earlier Howarth–Norgaard models, each generation lives two periods. The nth generation is young in period n, and old in period $n+1$, and obtains utility from consumption specified by the Cobb–Douglas function of the form

$$U_n = \ln(C_{n,y}) + \ln(C_{n+1,old})$$

Note that each generation gives equal weight to its own consumption as 'young' as it does to its own consumption as 'old'. There is no 'subjective' discounting within a generation's life. For the nth period the economic capital output is apportioned between savings S_n and consumption of young and old:

$$M_n^{\alpha_1} L_n^{\alpha_2} R_n^{1-\alpha_1-\alpha_2} = S_n + C_{n,y} + C_{n,old}, \qquad \forall n = 1, 2, \ldots (N-1)$$

The savings of the nth period are the economic capital available in the subsequent period, $M_{n+1}=S_n$. There is a constant endowment of labour $L_1=L_2=\ldots$ for each generation in their 'young' period. If R_{TOT} is the natural resource stock, then the constraint on the total amount of non–renewable natural capital that can be used between the 1st and the Nth period, can be written:

$$\sum R_n = R_{TOT} \qquad \text{where } n=1, 2, \ldots, N$$

The welfare distribution rule is to maximize the present value of utility (henceforth PVU-max), discounting each generation's utility by a constant factor δ, where $0<\delta<1$, relative to the previous generation:

$$\text{Maximize: } \sum \delta^n U_n, \qquad \text{where } n=1, 2, \ldots, N$$

The social discount parameter δ dictates the strength of time-preference (impatience) for the economy overall. The case $\delta=1$ means all generations count equally; but if $\delta<1$ the successive generations count progressively less. The *social discount rate* between generations (which is not the same as the interest rate) is given by ρ defined by:

$$1/(1+\rho)\equiv\delta \Leftrightarrow \rho\equiv(1-\delta)/\delta$$

Having set up the problem in this way, a solution is obtained through specifying values for each of the following parameters:

- N, the number of periods;
- R_{TOT}, the total amount of natural resources;
- L_n, the labour endowment of the nth generation of young (invariant from period to period);
- M_1, the initial level of economic capital in the first period;
- δ, the utility discount factor from generation to generation;
- α_1 and α_2, the output elasticities for economic capital and labour, respectively, in the production function.

It can be seen that this OLG model set-up provides for the direct investigation of the significance of varying any and all of the above parameters. In particular, it puts the focus on:

- the initial stock of natural capital R_{TOT} in comparison with initial economic stock M_1 and labour endowment (set arbitrarily at $L_n=1$ for all periods);

- the *constant* intergenerational discount rate parameter δ or equivalently $\rho \equiv (1-\delta)/\delta$;
- the relative importance of natural capital in production as indicated by the output elasticity coefficient $\varphi \equiv (1-\alpha_1-\alpha_2)$.

The now large body of work on models of growth with natural capital has shown that at least four qualitatively different sorts of PVU-maximizing time paths may be obtained, depending on initial capital stock levels and renewal properties, the technological determinants of production feasibility and the social determinants of the distribution through time of consumption. These are:

- monotonic decrease in utility over time: economic welfare is *non-sustained*;
- increase of utility for a while, then a turning point with monotonic decline after that: *non-sustained economic growth*;
- the special case of exactly constant utility through time: *sustainability as intertemporal economic equality*; and
- monotonic increase in utility through time: *sustainable economic growth.*

Results presented by Faucheux et al. (Faucheux et al., 1997; see also Faucheux and O'Connor, 1999) were obtained with $N=20$, for a number of periods sufficiently 'long' to show the range of solution properties in question. The initial capital stocks and model parameters were deliberately chosen to permit solutions with monotonic decline, growth and decline, and monotonic growth. (The exact equality path requires time variation of δ from period to period, and a different solution procedure would need to be used.) They set $\alpha_2=0.15$ for labour, and looked at two cases for produced capital: $\alpha_1=0.70$ *and* $\alpha_1=0.30$. For the social discount rate, two values were applied:

$$\delta=0.90 \Leftrightarrow \rho \equiv (1-\delta)/\delta = 1/9 \text{ and } \delta=0.70 \Leftrightarrow \rho \equiv (1-\delta)/\delta = 3/7$$

These settings, in combination, yield four 'scenarios', as summarized in Table 10.2. Solution (A) is *sustained growth*; in this case the output elasticity of economic capital is high and the society is sufficiently patient to allow future generations to enjoy a progressively greater utility level. Solutions (B) and (C) are *non-sustainable growth paths* with a boom and decline form. In case (B) the culprit is the high social discount rate $\rho=43$ per cent per generation; in case (C) the main culprit is the heavy dependence of production on depletable natural capital $\varphi=0.55$,

Table 10.2 Parameters for four PVU-max scenarios

	$\delta=0.90 \Leftrightarrow \rho\equiv(1-\delta)/\delta=1/9$	$\delta=0.70 \Leftrightarrow \rho\equiv(1-\delta)/\delta=3/7$
$\varphi\equiv(1-\alpha_1-\alpha_2)$		
0.15	(A) sustained growth	(B) single peak and decline
0.55	(C) single peak and decline	(D) monotonic decline

notwithstanding the lower $\rho=11$ per cent. Solution (D) is monotonic economic decline, due to heavy dependence on the depletable natural capital and high consumption impatience.

3.4 Pareto Optimality, Sustainability and Distribution Rules

What these results immediately bring out is that, *within the framework of this model*, an answer to the question 'sustainable or not?' will be highly sensitive to assumptions about initial capital stock levels, relative output elasticities and the relative weighting of successive generations. More generally, from this literature, we can extract the following theoretical lessons.

First, sustainability and allocative efficiency are clearly distinct. Sustainability, in the sense of indefinitely non-declining consumption from one generation to the next, is an intertemporal equity requirement, which is not guaranteed by the 'competitive' rule of maximizing present value of total consumption over time. When property rights over natural capital are tipped in favour of the 'present' generation (still able to be exchanged between generations to enable the old of each period to consume optimally), the typical result is monotonically declining utility levels beyond some period into the future (see also Dasgupta and Mitra, 1983; Toman et al., 1995; Dubourg and Pearce, 1996).

Second, and conversely, achieving an equilibrium with non-decreasing consumption levels requires that, one way or another, present generations 'care enough' about future generations. This caring for the future can be expressed through a variety of mechanisms, notably:

- a maximin social welfare function;
- intertemporal social welfare maximization subject to non-negative change in representative individuals' welfare from one period to the next;
- the assumption of a sufficiently high level of individual altruism of each generation towards the generation immediately following;
- the assumption of an obligation on the part of each generation to

provide for a utility level of the generation immediately following at least as high as its own, resulting in a 'chain of obligation' indefinitely into the future; and
- the explicit award of property rights over natural capital or the benefits obtainable from it as initial endowments distributed equitably to all generations.

Third, the possible model equilibria are each characterized by distinctive trajectories, not just for capital stocks and consumption, but also for relative prices including the time discount rate (generally itself a function of time, but sometimes time invariant for a given model or class of equilibria). It is often said that, for intertemporal efficiency, the price of natural capital such as minerals or energy resources or fish or forest products, should 'correctly' reflect the intertemporal opportunity cost (namely, the user cost). If sustainability is an objective, we note therefore that this has to be the opportunity costs as evaluated along an intertemporal efficient path that also satisfies the sustainability criterion.

We now turn to the significance of these results for the definition of sustainability indicators based on measures of final consumption and net economic savings.

3.5 Defining Environmentally adjusted Net National Product and Sustainable National Income

Intuitively, the *sustainable national income* (henceforth SNI) for an economy may be defined as the quantity of goods and services, say C^*, that may be consumed (rather than conserved/reinvested) in a given period while the economy system still furnishes the capital stock as the basis for providing (at least) the same level of real consumption C^* in every period through the future. Following Pezzey, it is important to note that (at least) two somewhat different definitions can be offered for an SNI.

- *Immediately and thereafter perpetually obtainable income, SNI(i)*, is the highest level of 'income' that can be attained *immediately*, from some given vector of stocks $X(t=0)$, subject to the constraint that the income level during $t>0$ is permanently non-decreasing. This is a maximin utility path.
- *Later but thereafter perpetually obtainable income, SNI(ii)*, is the highest level of 'income' that the economy can continuously attain *at and after a finite time*, starting from some given vector of stocks $X(t=0)$, subject to the constraint that the income level is permanently non-decreasing.

The *Hicksian definition of a person's (or nation's) income* is the amount he or she (or it) can consume during a specified period, while ensuring that his or her wealth at the end of the period is no less than his or her wealth at the outset (Hicks, 1946). Assume that the value of total capital stocks is K, measured in money units, so let us write: $K \equiv \pi \cdot \mathrm{X}$, where

> $\mathrm{X} = (M, L, R)$ is the vector of stocks in physical units, and
> $\pi = (p_1, p_2, p_3)$ is the vector of relative prices.

Then the *Hicksian national income* will be associated with the rule: $\mathrm{d}K/\mathrm{d}t = 0$. The change in value of capital stock may, generally, be written: $\mathrm{d}K/\mathrm{d}t = \mathrm{d}/\mathrm{d}t\,(\pi \cdot \mathrm{X})$, and this can be split into two parts:

- the current value of savings: $\pi \cdot \mathrm{dX}/\mathrm{d}t$ and
- the 'capital gains' term: $\mathrm{X} \cdot \mathrm{d}\pi/\mathrm{d}t$

Using the above notation, *Hartwick's rule* is written: $\pi \cdot \mathrm{dX}/\mathrm{d} \geq 0$. For a model with constant population we have $\mathrm{d}L/\mathrm{d}t = 0$, so this becomes:

$$p_1\, \mathrm{d}M/\mathrm{d}t + p_3\, \mathrm{d}R/\mathrm{d}t \geq 0$$

The first term refers to the value, in current prices, of the change in manufactured capital stock; the second term refers to the value, in current prices, of the change in natural capital stock.

Now suppose the economy is on a time path that maximizes present value of consumption. Then the *net national product* (henceforth NNP) is defined as value of consumption plus net change in the value of capital stocks. If natural capital stocks are included, we call it a 'green NNP', defined as follows:

$$gNNP = p_1 C + (\pi \cdot \mathbf{dX}/\mathrm{d}t)$$

where, as before, C is the physical quantity of consumption, p_1 is the current price of manufactured capital (which can be saved or consumed) and $(\pi \cdot \mathrm{dX}/\mathrm{d}t)$ is the Hartwick net savings measured in current prices (Solow, 1986; Mäler, 1991).

It can be noted straight away that, because Hartwick's rule does not include the 'capital gains' term, the respect of Hartwick's rule at any moment in time does not necessarily imply non-negative change in the value of total capital stocks. So the Hicksian national income and the net national product (*gNNP*) are evidently not the same thing. Furthermore, the gNNP and the SNI(i) are not the same thing. The work by Asheim and

Pezzey and their colleagues (see Asheim 1994; Withagen and Asheim 1998; Asheim and Buchholz, 2000; Pezzey, 1997; Pezzey and Withagen, 1998) has made plain that, indeed, the gNNP and SNI(i) will coincide only if highly restrictive theoretical conditions are fulfilled.

3.5 The Weaknesses of Net Savings and gNNP as Indicators of Sustainability

Suppose that we seek to give an empirical content to the recipes for obtaining the 'weak' indicators. This means to estimate empirically the components of the formulae above. Two options are open: either to use a model framework with internally consistent shadow prices, or to make estimates on the basis of observed *current period* prices and quantities (or some combination of the two).

According to the formulae, the 'sustainable national income' SNI(i) could be estimated by making subtractions away from *current* GNP ($p_1 C$) of estimates for ($\pi \cdot dX/dt$) representing depreciation during the *current* period, of capital stocks including manufactured capital and natural capital.

But, for valid indicator specification, estimation and interpretation, within the theoretical framework just outlined, three related theoretical points arise. First, the role of capital gains in indicator definition and measurement must be dealt with correctly. Second, the measurements of dK/dt, or of the *gNNP* and the related Hartwickian savings ($\pi \cdot dX/dt$), must be specified in terms of prices (or, as the case may be) shadow prices for the particular moment (or period) in time along the particular equilibrium path being considered. Third, a resulting problem of 'chicken and egg', is that even if we have intertemporarily efficient prices in (say) a market economy, these may not be the right ones for sustainability and, if not, then *within the framework of the model*, the gNNP will misestimate the SNI(i); and the 'net savings' rule will not reliably signal the sustainability potential (or lack of it) – see Box 10.1.

What is at stake here is to specify correctly what is involved, theoretically, in defining the passage from an actual GNP to an estimate for an SNI ? Far more than just some arithmetic with some categories of the national accounts and monetized satellite accounts. The link between gNNP and SNI depends not just on assumptions about efficiency of investment and consumption choices made through time, but also on the underlying model. For example:

- Weitzman (1997) has elegantly illustrated that the link between gNNP and SNI is lost by the introduction of a postulate of secular technological progress. In this latter case, the 'environmentally

BOX 10.1 THE RISE AND FALL OF THE 'GREEN NET NATIONAL PRODUCT' INDICATORS

The theoretical work by Solow, Hartwick and others in the 1970s and 1980s showed that, for a closed economy obeying the PVU-max criterion, a property of the SNI(i) 'maximin' consumption path is that Hartwick's rule is satisfied at all times. It was not initially remarked that respect of Hartwick's rule in this context was a necessary *but not a sufficient* condition. Two complications were not fully appreciated. First, changes in relative prices along a PVU-max path through time will show up in, among other places, the 'capital gains' term. Second, different relative prices are associated with each distinct PVU-max solution. Consider the results that we may obtain if we simply *neglect* price changes. We may write: $gNNP = p_1 C + \pi \cdot d\mathbf{X}/dt$

According to the Hartwick–Solow results, along a path of constant consumption $dC/dt = 0$, Hartwick's rule is necessarily respected in equality form: $\pi \cdot dX/dt = 0$ for all t. Under these conditions we obtain: $gNNP = p_1 C$, and this is the *SNI(i)*. Now, if it were that the prices do not change, the capital gains term would be zero and we could write: $dK/dt = \pi \cdot dX/dt$. Thus *along a PVU-max path where Hartwick's rule is respected at all times and also there are no capital gains (if such a path can be found)*, the net national product *gNNP* is a measure of the immediately and perpetually sustainable welfare delivery potential, the *SNI(i)*, for the economy and its natural capital stock, and this would also be the 'Hicksian national income' at all times. This is the reasoning that has motivated the estimation of ($\pi \cdot dX/dt$) and *gNNP* as sustainability indicators. If the above reasoning were valid (which it is not):

- The $gNNP = SNI(i)$ and so the *gNNP* could be interpreted as an estimate for level of consumption (in money terms) that can be maintained from the present onwards, on a long-term basis, while also maintaining intact the value of the total stock of capital.
- A positive value of the Hartwick term ($\pi \cdot dX/dt > 0$) would signal that the 'net savings' of economic plus natural capital measured in money units, is positive during the period. A negative value ($\pi \cdot dX/dt < 0$) would signal that the 'net savings' is negative, or there is 'net depreciation' during the

period. This yields the Hartwick–Solow *Weak Sustainability Indicator or savings rule* as it emerged from Solow (1986), quickly followed by others such as Mäler (1991) and Pearce and Warford (1993).

The procedures described above had widespread appeal, because they seemed to resolve in an operational way the objections made on environmental grounds to the use of GNP (and, more particularly, of annual increase in GNP) as an indicator of macroeconomic performance. The statistical implementation of the indicator recipes raises, rather obviously, the issue of obtaining monetary measures for the changes in natural capital stocks. But, these recipes are theoretically flawed and cannot, for this reason, guide statistical work on sustainable income indicators with the high hopes originally held out for them.

Take the case of the closed economy. The relevant indicators are *gNNP* and Hartwick 'net savings'. The reasoning is: a positive sign of the Hartwickian 'net savings' $(\pi \cdot dX/dt)>0$ for a PVU-max economy means that the current consumption $p_1C < gNNP$. If it is assumed that $gNNP = SNI(i)$, then the current consumption will be lower than the maximin income and hence the economy is not violating requirements for sustainable consumption. But, estimates will have reliable and transparent 'sustainability' indicator properties, those corresponding to a maximin *SNI(i)* time path, *only if the calculations use the consumption levels, prices and stock variations corresponding to an economy on a PVU-max intertemporal equilibrium path characterized by constant national income.* And yet, as Norgaard (1990) has observed, if the purpose of indicator construction is to learn whether or not an economy is far from a 'sustainable' trajectory, we cannot assume the properties of a sustainable trajectory in the process of making the calculations. Asheim and Pezzey and their colleagues have demonstrated:

- the 'Hartwick income', defined by the *gNNP* when $\pi \cdot dX/dt = 0$, generally is not the same as the *SNI(i)*;
- the equality between *gNNP* and *SNI(i)* holds only for a PVU-max path where Hartwick's rule is respected *at every point in time*;
- the *gNNP* for a PVU-max time path therefore will not, in general, coincide with *SNI(i)*, nor for that matter with *SNI(ii)*. This statement holds even if, *for a particular moment in time*, it happens that $C = gNNP$ is the PVU-max consumption.

- therefore a positive sign of the Hartwickian 'net savings' ($\pi \cdot dX/dt$) for a PVU-max economy is not a reliable indicator that the current consumption p_1C is lower than the *SNI(i)*, and hence that the economy is not violating requirements for sustainable consumption.

As Asheim and Buchholz (2000) summarize, on the one hand a generation may well obey the Hartwick investment rule but nevertheless consume more than the maximum sustainable consumption level, and, on the other hand a generation with a negative value of net investments will not necessarily undermine the consumption possibilities of its successors. For example (as first shown by Asheim, 1994, and Pezzey, 1994), in continuous time infinite horizon models, the 'single peak' consumption paths will necessarily have a portion along which the aggregate wealth – the value of total capital stocks – is rising, prior to monotonic decline. Along the rising aggregate stock portion of such a path, the weak sustainability indicators will fail to signal the consumption 'overshoot' and thus do not signal that the resource use and savings regime is impairing durably the economy's sustainability prospects. An analogous result is obtained in the OLG models (see the scenarios (B) and (C) from Faucheux et al., as presented above), where the economy has a *non-sustainable* PVU-max equilibrium path along which national consumption first rises to non-sustainable levels then falls monotonically. Under these circumstances:

- use of equilibrium prices to estimate natural capital depreciation is a systematic, in the sense that positive Hartwick net savings $\pi \cdot dX/dt \geq 0$ can be obtained even when current consumption is $p_1C > SNI(i)$ and, as such, cannot be sustained indefinitely.
- the *gNNP* obtained from the formula $gNNP = p_1C + \pi \cdot dX/dt$ is higher than the *SNI(i)*, meaning that an estimate for *gNNP* obtained by deducting net capital depreciation from GNP will not correctly indicate the extent to which current consumption overshoots sustainability
- by corollary, a hypothetical reallocation of economic resources away from consumption to investment equal in magnitude to the current value of capital depreciation ($\pi \cdot dX/dt$), would not be sufficient to reduce the consumption to the *SNI(i)* as would be required to put the economy on to a sustainable path.

By the time that aggregate wealth has stopped rising (that is, d*K*/d*t* becomes non-positive), and by the time the sign of the Hartwick 'net savings' ($\pi \cdot dX/dt$) changes from positive to negative, it is too late. Significant damage to sustainability prospects may already have been done.

In short, the Hartwick investment rule cannot serve as a prescription for sustainability. The same applies for the 'Hicksian' rule of non-negative change to the value of a nation's stocks. This latter refers to the suggestion that sustainability is achieved if the value of the nation's capital stock remains intact from one generation to the next, meaning $dK/dt=0$, while providing the Hicksian income as the consumption at any given time. There are two inaccuracies in this idea. First, $dK/dt=0$ is *not* a sufficient condition for a maximin *SNI(i)* time path in a closed economy. The interpretation of Hicksian income as *SNI(i)* would be valid only if the economy is actually on a maximin path and also if there are no capital gains. Second, observing $dK/dt \geq 0$ in a closed economy at a given moment in time does not guarantee that the economy is capable of a non-decreasing Hicksian income. For example, along the boom phase of a boom and decline time path, the Hicksian indicator $\Delta K \geq 0$, signalling a non-negative change in value of total capital stocks from one period to the next, can provide a too weak signal as to whether or not the consumption in the period is compatible or not with the sustainability criterion of non-decreasing utility (see Faucheux et al., 1997). By the time that the sign of the indicator ΔK changes from positive to negative, significant damage has already been done to sustainability prospects.

Note: This box summarizes the main sense of diverse results associated with Asheim, Pezzey, O'Connor and their colleagues. Full sources are listed in the References.

adjusted' gNNP will typically underestimate the sustainability potential of the economy.

- Asheim and Buchholz (2000) show, through a variety of model examples, that 'a judgement on whether short-run behaviour is compatible with sustainable development must be based on the long-run properties of the path and the technological environment', including innovation, bequests, openness or closure of the economy, and so on.

These precise analytical demonstrations reinforce the conclusions of Norgaard (1990) and Faucheux et al. (1997) that, since we do not know what the 'right model' is (in fact, there may be no 'right model'), and since anyway we cannot deduce right model parameters reliably from empirical information, we are in a 'chicken and egg' ignorance situation.

These theoretical defects are compounded by empirical reasons for doubts about 'net savings' as a useful sustainability indicator. The figures presented to date in published literature for 'net savings' are generally admitted to involve 'incomplete' inventories of relevant natural capital stocks (for early examples, see El Serafy, 1991; Peskin, 1991; Pearce and Warford, 1993; Proops and Atkinson, 1996; the recent work by the World Bank is much more up front about the partial character of the assets inventory). Yet, somehow, there has been a tendency to let it be presumed that these 'preliminary' calculations can serve as 'first approximations' with *the same policy relevance as the theoretically specified measures.* This presumption is difficult to defend.

The monetization of natural capital deterioration, in this neoclassical perspective, relies on the ability to estimate opportunity costs associated with resource-use alternatives in economic production, pollution treatment, waste disposal and environmental management. Strictly speaking, these opportunity costs are definable only within the theoretical framework of an inter temporal general equilibrium model. But we do not know the right model (see above!). What we do know is:

- Real trends of economic activity are *ex hypothesi* far from sustainability.
- If one entertains the proposition of a PVU-max interpretation of economic reality, the far-from-sustainability prices and quantities for capital stock variations are systematically wrong for the estimation purposes wanted of them.
- The inventory of natural capital being used in the 'correction' procedures is seriously incomplete.

There is no particular reason to believe that current prices and patterns of resource utilization conform to a PVU-max path. Indeed, the converse is very probably true, given the prevalence of *force majeure*, monopoly and oligopoly market power, high-level bribes, coercion, high commercial discount rates, strategic behaviour, gratuitous and cynical disposal of toxic wastes, state interventions to furnish low-cost access by commercial interests to forest, water, fisheries and agricultural resources, and so on. Many environmental services (including waste disposal) and scarce natural resources (for example, fish, water and forests) are obtained virtually gratis simply because of political and economic power, even when it is known that high opportunity costs and uncompensated environmental damages are involved. Access is determined by social power relations, with or without regard for the future (Martinez-Alier and O'Connor, 1996).

All the omissions and biases push in the same direction. The omissions from the natural capital inventory are tantamount to employing a zero price in the correction calculations. Where these relate to fundamental life support functions such as climate stability drinkable water and ecosystem health, it becomes preposterous to suggest that the empirical figures for 'net savings' supplied in published studies so far, in themselves, furnish any indication of sustainability potential. If they do indeed have some policy relevance (which, we will argue, may indeed be so – see Section 3.6), it cannot be as a 'sustainable national income' indicator, but something else.

3.6 A Modified Use for Enlarged 'Net Savings'?

The neoclassical natural capital theory cannot, we argue, convincingly be employed as a theoretical support for estimation of 'net savings' which, as a correction to *GDP*, yields the *gNNP* as an estimate of the 'sustainable national income'. The proposition is theoretically wrong (except for some special conditions which do not seem very relevant empirically and whose occurrence would, in any case, be difficult to ascertain). This does not mean that there is no value at all of the 'weak' indicator theory. First of all, it has some didactic uses. It allows the construction of parables to alert us to:

- the likely failure of market prices to signal intertemporal opportunity costs of natural resource use and environmental degradation;
- the fact that, even if prices are assumed to be PVU-optimal, they almost certainly do not correspond to anything near a sustainable resource use time path; and if not, then the 'weak' rules for sustainability are logically invalid and wholly unreliable as an indicator of long-run economic performance prospects; and
- the need for quite different non-price-based approaches to the estimation of the severity of economic–ecological 'trade-offs' associated with natural capital use.

The last point will be taken up in Section 4 below. To conclude the present section, we also want to make some suggestions on some appropriate uses as policy guidelines of these adjusted 'net savings' indicators.

As we already outlined in Section 2, the environmentally adjusted 'net savings' indicator is based on making an enlargement of the 'asset boundary' to include changes in a country's capital *stock including specified environmental resources*. In ongoing work by the World Bank, for example, the value of environmental assets such as primary resources (minerals, oil, gas, forests) is, where possible, estimated with market prices. Some results for net change in value of the combined economic and environmental assets have been compiled, in some cases including time series for the past 30 years for selected countries. Evidently, the figures are sensitive to the categories of environmental assets included (see further remarks below). Yet, some rather persistent trends are clear. These include:

- very low or negative 'net savings' over many years for many South countries, for the basket of economic and environmental assets being considered;
- convincing evidence that a large range of environmental assets are being persistently depleted, in many (though not all) of the countries for which figures are produced, without much evidence of investment of the proceeds of this resource exploitation into other productive assets.

The terminology 'genuine savings' has been used to refer to this sort of measure of net change in a country's assets. This label, although by now widely in currency, can be rather misleading for two reasons.

- First, the indicator inevitably takes account only of a small number of 'natural assets' of country – being limited to those for which some sort of money figure for 'change in the asset value' can reasonably easily be obtained. It is unlikely that such monetary evaluations can meaningfully be extended to measure, as asset changes, all the changes to environmental systems and the circumstances of economic activity. (Nor, importantly, is it clearly established that such a generalization is needed for sustainability policy indicator purposes.)
- Second, there is not a direct link from this measure of asset change in the current period to an estimate of the country's long-run wealth creation and income generation capacity.

These two considerations are interlinked. On the one hand, many environmental functions and services that are not readily treated as 'assets' with quantifiable money value are, nonetheless, of great significance for economic vitality and sustainability. Examples are biota, wetlands and other complex ecosystems whose environmental 'functions' may include everything from repose for sore eyes to flood moderation to climate regulation. On the other hand, even where some form of monetary evaluation is possible, the monetary valuations that can be obtained will not necessarily be meaningful to help judge long-run 'sustainability' considerations.

We suggest that a more satisfactory indicator label would be *AICCAN* standing for an *Aggregate Indicator of the Change, during the Current Year, in the Economic Assets of the Nation.* This is not very elegant but it is clear. As a pragmatic measure of net change in the value of assets, the *AICCAN* indicator clearly says something about the country's revenue creation capacity under prevailing conditions (including market, political and institutional as well as environmental conditions).

In order to clarify the relation to the earlier theoretical literature, recall once again that the Hicksian income as usually defined is the permanent revenue stream obtainable while maintaining the total capital stock intact. Evidently, it is tempting to define the 'Hicksian income' figure as the sum of national consumption plus net asset change as measured by the *AICCAN*. But it is to be kept in mind that the empirically measured 'Hicksian' country income, as that for any firm, is basically an accounting result. It gives an evaluation of the performance of the country (or the firm) *during the current year, calculated with present year prices.*

If we continue with the analogy of a firm, the Hicksian income for a firm is 'sustainable' *only if the prevailing prices and external conditions for the firm do not change adversely for the time horizon of interest.* Conversely, if the conditions will or might change in any ways that are not already 'internalized' into these prices and asset valuations, then the Hicksian income as defined for the current period does not work as a reliable guide as to future viability (for better or worse) of the enterprise. For example, if a country is watching the worsening pollution of its waters running in tandem with the stripping of its forest resources, a 'wise use' of the proceeds of forestry production (namely, the re-investment of natural resource rents, in line with the Hartwick rule) may be a helpful, but certainly not sufficient, contribution to the future welfare prospects of the nation. If, in addition, it happens that the deforestation is accentuating some unpriced external effects such as soil erosion, nutrient loss, water-table drop, flood control and water quality degradation, then we can see the sorts of critical 'environmental functions' that are still left out from the accounting.

- The *AICCAN*-type of current account measure of change in assets (valued at current market prices, or similar) can give a useful quick impression of the direction in which a country's asset use is headed.
- However, the diagnosis of an 'asset-stripping' problem – in the case that the *AICCAN* is negative or very small – does not, in itself, tell where a remedy might be found. For this reason, the development of concepts and country capacities for exploring prospects for 'economically and environmentally sustainable' development strategies is also important. Just as a company may undertake a variety of foresight,

forward studies, market research and scenario studies, so a country manager (or, more generally, the policy community) may engage in a variety of forecasting and strategic forward studies exercises to investigate the feasibility of meeting simultaneously specified economic and environmental performance goals (see Section 4).

- It is essential, in order to avoid misunderstandings, to have a clear presentation of what is, and is not, included in the set of economic and environmental assets being considered.
- In complement to the basket of assets included in the asset balance estimation, attention must be drawn to issues of environmental services and environmental change that are not treated as 'country assets' from a monetary point of view.

The latter two recommendations are very important, as they quite change around the sense of the 'net savings' indictor. The emphasis is henceforth placed on careful reflection about where the dividing line is being drawn between a country's money-valued assets and the (probably much larger) set of environmental capital not being included, why the line is being drawn where it is, and what is the significance of the elements on each side of the line. Harking back to our structural perspective on sustainability (Section 2), the emphasis is on the complementary dimensions of economic and environmental system composition and functioning, see Figure 10.2 below.

In Figure 10.2, the economic capital and certain elements constituting the 'natural portfolio capital' are inventoried in monetary terms. The social capital and the supporting physical environment are inventoried with an appropriate variety of quantitative and non-quantitative non-monetary indicators. The heavy vertical line divides monetary asset inventories from

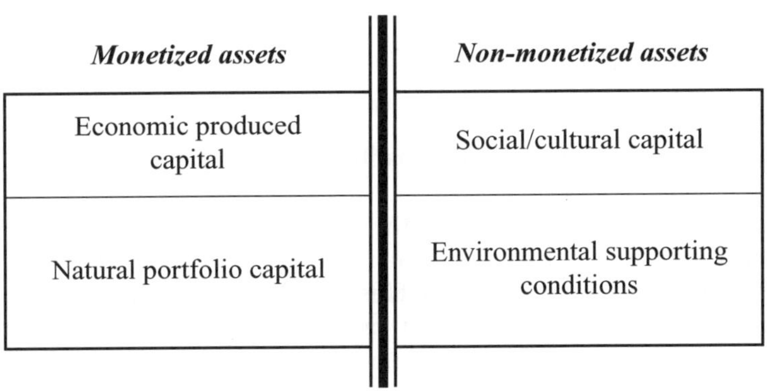

Figure 10.2 *The monetization frontier*

the non-monetized components. (As we have drawn it, social capital is not being monetized but this assumption could be changed for some components of so-called social capital.)

Regarding the question, what is placed in the box of natural portfolio capital and what is left over on the right hand side of the line, the answers may be partly circumstantial. We suggest that there are at least two reasonably general demarcation criteria, as follows:

- whether or not the asset entails monetary or legal liabilities (for example, emissions fees or fines, compensation for damages), or potential for commercial benefits (sale of the asset or derivatives of it). If such liabilities or revenue potential is identifiable, then there will exist some sort of prices, costs, or other fiscal elements that give an indication of the direct economic significance of the asset in question;
- whether or not, taking account of systems complexities, time scales and uncertainties, a meaningful and relevant monetary quantification is possible for the 'asset change' in question.

Given the current state of the art, of work at the World Bank and elsewhere, forests being considered for commercial logging, proven mineral reserves, oil and gas are assets that can fairly easily be brought within the sphere of monetary accounting. On the other hand, fisheries, climate change, health impacts of pollution, and biodiversity/land cover change are cases where the discussion about the usefulness of placement 'in' or 'out of' the asset basket – hence, inclusion or not of money estimates of asset value changes in the current account asset balance indicator – could be very fruitful as explorations of the policy applications, and limitations, of the *AICCAN*-type indicator (see, Concluding Remarks, Section 5.3).

4 STRONG SUSTAINABILITY AND CRITICAL NATURAL CAPITAL

4.1 What do we mean by Strong Sustainability?

The term 'strong' sustainability refers to the maintenance of natural capital stocks, or of important environmental functions as a precondition of economic and ecological sustainability. This perspective is, we suggest, grounded in scientific and ethical preoccupations – on the one hand a conviction about the non-substitutable functional importance of natural systems as life support, on the other hand a will for coexistence in a world of diversity and natural richness.

Ecological economists such as Victor (1991), Daly (1994), and Victor et al. (1997) have long argued, from physical and life sciences perspectives, that ready substitutability between natural and manufactured capitals should not be presumed. For example, thermodynamic irreversibility implies the impossibility of substituting, beyond certain well-defined limits, away from environmental sources of 'free energy' as production inputs. Substitution may be reasonably easy between energy types, but this relative ease applies only within the class of energy sources not between energy and other production inputs (Peet, 1992). Ecological systems have complex spatial structures, and are interlocked with geophysical processes (such as hydrological cycles) that extend over large (sometimes planetary) distances (Passet, 1979). These systems cannot be fragmented and transported in the same way as minerals and manufactured capital inputs. So there is a strong complementarity of 'inputs' in the processes of reproduction and renewal of ecological systems that work against the application of the concept of substitution on the margin.

A simple formulation of strong sustainability, put forward by David Pearce and his colleagues (for example, Pearce and Turner, 1990), refers to natural capital in aggregate terms, separate from manufactured capital, and requires non-negative change in the natural capital stock through time. Where K_N is the natural capital stock, the rule is: $d(K_N)/dt \geq 0$. This formulation is largely impressionistic. There is no meaningful way of aggregating the grand diversity of natural resources, environmental services and ecosystems so as to quantify this rule (see Victor, 1991; Victor et al., 1997). So it serves an essentially symbolic role, signalling the importance of attention to maintaining environmental functions.

4.2 Strong Sustainability and Critical Natural Capital

A more operational approach can be developed through the identification of categories of 'critical natural capital' whose stocks ought to be maintained at or above identified minimum levels. This builds on several decades of work on environmental standards (see, notably, Ciriacy-Wantrup, 1952, Bishop, 1978). The maintenance of environmental functions can be justified by particular ethical or environmentalist attitudes, but is also seen as the functional precondition for economic and social sustainability.

We define *critical natural capital* (henceforth CNC) as that set of environmental resources which, at a prescribed geographical scale performs important environmental functions and for which no substitute in terms of manufactured, human or other natural capital currently exist (Noël and O'Connor, 1998). Making applicable the concept of CNC then requires the following considerations to be addressed:

- identifying the role and significance of different natural capital systems for supporting sustainable economic activity;
- defining the relevant spatial and temporal scales for which natural capital systems may be critical;
- identifying the social and cultural factors which may contribute to making critical any natural capital components; and
- the weight of the precautionary principle when environmental function losses in question are characterized by uncertainty and irreversibilities.

It is important to note that 'strong sustainability' policy targets always have social as well as purely functional (ecological) dimensions. For example, even if the ecological and economic requirements of tropical forest and ocean fish stock maintenance were well known, questions still arise about stewardship of which forests (or fish), where, for whom? Non-built environments are often cherished for recreational, aesthetic and spiritual reasons, in ways that impose strong limits to their substitutability by manufactured goods and services. The conservation and enhancement of ecosystems as habitats for non-human life, and for living biological diversity may be motivated by ethical convictions of respect and coexistence. In the strong sustainability perspective, communities defined by locality or by ethnic or cultural belonging, may identify features of their habitats as 'critical' natural capitals in view of their symbolic or functional significance in defining group identity.

No universally accepted general framework for taxonomy has yet been stabilized. However, it is common to regroup the main types of environmental functions under broad categories such as 'the five S's' – source, sink, scenery, site, life support. Dynamic and spatial features related to the natural capital use can also be used for typology, such as use as a productive input versus degradation through pollution; *in situ* use versus transportation by human agency; localized ecosystem impact versus dispersed impacts (Noël and O'Connor, 1998). Once targets are set, the cost-effectiveness methodology expounded by Baumol and Oates (1971), environmental policy can be formulated by, first, scientific and political work to determine environmental standards or norms, for example, for pollution emissions or natural resource consumption, in physical terms independently of any notion of economic optimization; and second, to find the least economic cost way of achieving the defined norm.

4.3 Sustainability Standards and Macroeconomic Cost-effectiveness Analysis

Although initially framed in terms of subtractions from current GDP, the approach advocated by Hueting for estimating an 'environmentally corrected' national income (see Hueting, 1991; Hueting et al., 1992; Hueting and de Boer, 2001) is actually a good early example of attempts to operationalize the strong sustainability perspective. On the basis of physical and life science analyses, norms are set for ensuring maintenance of key environmental functions. Remedial measures are identified that would be sufficient to ensure that the economy will satisfy these norms. The analytical task is then to obtain estimates of the costs that the society would need to incur to achieve these norms.

This sort of approach leads to the identification of two distinct sorts of measures that can be used as indicators for sustainability (compare Faucheux and Froger, 1994; Faucheux et al., 1994; Ekins and Simon, 1999).

- The first is a measure of the *distance from sustainability*: this is an estimate, in terms of current consumption (money units or percentage of GNP), of the extent to which current economic activity violates the specified sustainability norms and, *ipso facto*, an indication of the magnitude of the reorientation of economic activity that would be required to respect the norms. It is information about the *state of* the sector or of the economy relative to sustainability criteria. Underneath the aggregate figure, of course, there is likely to be considerable variation, from one firm to another, from one industrial sector or consumption category to another. Some sectors may be contributing to major breaches of norms while other sectors may be judged non-offensive.
- The second type of indicator is a *cost of achieving sustainability* measure: in traditional terms, a monetary figure may be sought for the minimum cost that would have to be borne in order, through preservation, prevention, protection or restoration measures, to respect the designated sustainability norms. This would be a quantification of the opportunity cost of achieving sustainability. Since scarce economic resources will have to be engaged to achieve environmental goals (such as restoration activities, pollution abatement or natural capital augmenting but higher-cost alternatives for production), this opportunity cost can, in principle, be expressed in money terms as an amount of consumption that would have to be forgone by the society to achieve or maintain the specified levels of environmental functions. In effect, the analysis aims at quantifying the policy trade-off between: (1) depleting/degrading environmental functions (critical natural capitals) by not making the adjustments required to satisfy the norms; and (2) forgoing consumption and/or using up economic capital if it makes the resource commitments required for achieving the norms.

Since sustainability is the concern, these opportunity costs must usually be estimated in an intertemporal analysis framework. For an individual sector, costs of meeting a sustainability standard through technological improvements, pollution treatment, substitution of inputs, or reductions in volume of activity, can be estimated with partial equilibrium methods (for example, pollutant abatement cost curves, see Radermacher et al., 1999). For a whole economy analysis, however, the comparison must be made between a 'non-adjusted' and an 'environmentally adjusted' economy. The cost-effectiveness concept is applied at a whole-economy level, through comparative static or dynamic scenario modelling approaches, for the definition and estimation of macroeconomic indicators for an 'environmentally adjusted economy' – such as 'greened economy GNP' (Brouwer et al., 1999).

In a scenario context, a comparison can be made between the consumption opportunities associated with a development path of transition towards sustainability, and the consumption opportunities (presumably higher in the short term) associated with a trajectory that depletes or degrades critical natural capital. The respective consumption aggregates can be compared in undiscounted or discounted (present value) terms, or in terms of relative growth/abatement rates for final consumption/environmental pressures (Schembri 1999a, 1999b; Schembri and Douguet, 2000). The comparative scenarios furnish information about opportunity costs, distributed through time, associated with meeting environmental targets.

The key accounting conventions of this 'strong' approach, that distinguish it from the 'weak' sustainability framework, are:

- The 'monetization frontier' is explicitly drawn, being set at the interface between economy and environment where the non-monetary 'environmental pressure' criteria are specified.
- The 'adjustments' being considered in this procedure involve the economy being modelled, not just the accounting conventions.
- The 'greened economy GNP' or NNP measure, or time series, is the level (in money units) of the feasible economic production for the accounting period or periods in question, subject to the condition that the economy is respecting the specified set of environmental standards. This is not an environmentally adjusted measure of actual economic performance. Rather it is an indicator about possible future performance integrating economic output and environmental standards as complementary criteria of performance.
- The 'greened economy GNP' does not set out to measure overall welfare delivery, because it quantifies only one part of welfare delivery (namely, the produced economic output that is or would be

feasible subject to environmental performance constraints). It does not try to include the direct environmental contributions to welfare.

A whole-economy scenario modelling approach must make explicit hypotheses about the timing of various policy and investment responses, where the economic model takes into account the interdependent adjustments between sectors. Many different types of economic change can be considered in analysis. Examples are: expenditures within production sectors to improve efficiency of resource use or to reduce polluting emissions per unit of output, through changes to technologies; shifts between different natural resources or physical locations of environmental exploitation, including exploitation of renewable resources and respect of sustainable yields or assimilation capacities; replacement of products or activities by alternatives less noxious for the environment, that is, changes to products and consumption patterns.

4.4 Climate Stability as a CNC: Illustrating the *GREENSTAMP* Methodology

If the goal is to preserve an identified critical natural capital, then the sustainability commitment must first be made, and feasibility and opportunity costs explored on that basis. This may be explored in scenario terms. In effect, we answer the question, 'how much is it worth?', by identifying the other consumption or investment options that we choose to put aside.

We give the example of carbon dioxide emissions linked to climate change. At the December 1997 Kyoto meeting of country leaders concerned with coordinated targets for reduction of greenhouse gas emissions, a set of (modest) macroeconomic environmental performance goals were agreed for 2010, by comparison with 1990 emissions levels. These reduction targets were based on a provisional political compromise between concerns about possible high disruption costs of climate change, and interests in energy use in industrialized and industrializing countries (including road-based mobility aspirations). They do not indicate the full emissions reductions probably needed to assure climate stability (see van den Hove, 1998, for fuller references and discussions).

Let us consider very rapidly the categories of statistical information and scenario hypotheses needed to implement a dynamic simulation modelling to explore the economic growth–consumption–greenhouse gas emissions trade-offs for a national economy (in our case France). The difference between the asset-accounting base for *AICCAN* or 'net savings' estimation, and this forward-looking scenario simulation exercise, becomes very clear. For illustrative purposes, we refer to the simulation tool *M3ED (Modèle*

Economie Energie Environnement Développement) as it has been developed at the C3ED (Schembri, 1999a, 1999b gives a full mathematical specification). Similar models exist for several country applications around the world (for example, the Netherlands, the UK, Australia, New Zealand). The modular *M3ED* structure is as follows:

- A *population module* (or sub-model) simulates the national population based on three different age groups: those under 35 years, 35–60 years and over 60 years.
- A *household module* uses the output of the population model and assumptions about household structure to calculate the total number of houses of different types.
- A *final consumption module* specifies the demand for each of the different types of good. (Present versions use a disaggregation into 16 categories of final consumption.) The number of houses of each type will affect the demands for each of the types of goods and services. Assumptions can be made about change over time of the pattern of demands for goods from each household type.
- The *production module* relates the demand for the different goods types back to the different production sectors of the economy. This uses an input–output representation of a multi-sector economy. Six main sectors are distinguished, and a modular disaggregation process can then be applied for specific purposes. A matrix describes the proportions in which the different categories of goods are derived from the production sectors.
- For model closure, the domestic production sectors are complemented by *imports and exports*; and household (final) consumption is complemented by *government expenditures*.
- For the quantification of *environmental pressures*, the specification of production sectors and of final consumption is augmented by coefficients specifying average natural resource requirements, and/or pollution emissions from each sector in categories of interest.

In a 1994–96 study, a set of simple scenario themes were developed for *M3ED* analysis of the quantitative relation between household consumption and atmospheric emissions for France and the Netherlands (see Chapters 9–11 of Faucheux and O'Connor, 1998; also O'Connor and Ryan, 1999). In this analysis, scenarios were developed for atmospheric emissions linked to energy use (notably CO_2, NOx, VOCs and SO_2). The four scenario themes were:

- 'Stagnation' (Tendencial Bleak);
- 'Business As Usual' (Tendencial Rosy);

- 'Sustainability through Technological Breakthrough' (Technology);
- 'Sustainability through Reflexive Consumption' (Sus-Cons).

The two 'Tendencial' scenarios give weight to economic liberalization at the expense of social and environmental ideals of sustainability and justice. The two 'utopian' scenarios propose quite different pictures. In the 'Sus-Cons' scenario the choice 'for sustainability' is made by renouncing economic growth as the primary policy priority; in the 'Technology' scenario, the technological progress permits output growth and environmental quality and safety to be achieved simultaneously.

A lot of empirical data are implied in the model specifications, based on national statistics on intersectoral flows (input–output tables) and hypotheses about technological changes prospects for efficiency and mix of primary and refined energy uses. The latter illustrate the sense in which this 'strong' approach seeks to characterize ecological and economic system potentials in physical and technical terms, rather than relying on prices as putative signals of opportunity costs. Assumptions are notably made about improvements in energy use efficiency and about changes in pollution output per unit of fuel over time. The figures up until 2010 were derived from detailed engineering studies together with household and industry use data, integrated in the IER's E^3life model, based on detailed diagnoses for trends from 1990 until 2010 (see Weber et al., 1996; see also discussions in O'Connor and Ryan, 1999). For the subsequent phase of the scenario to 2030, hypotheses had to be formulated beyond mere extrapolations of historical trends, for such categories as: sources of new electricity supplies, sources of thermal fuel requirements, share of thermal fuel demand from coal, gas and oil sources, imports to each sector in the economy, exports from each sector in the economy, assumptions about government consumption. For the *M3ED* demonstration purposes with the France and Netherlands economies, it was assumed:

- new electricity is supplied by thermal, renewable and nuclear power stations in the same ratios as existing power stations (*except in 'Tech Breakthrough' which has new investment in renewable energy sources*);
- increases in thermal fuel requirements are imported;
- share of thermal fuel demand from coal, gas and oil sources are the same;
- a constant fraction of the population is employed;
- imports to each sector increase in proportion to growth of the sector;
- exports are assumed simply to grow as required to balance the books.

Model simulation results for economic output and carbon dioxide emissions for France over a 40-year horizon are shown in Figure 10.3.

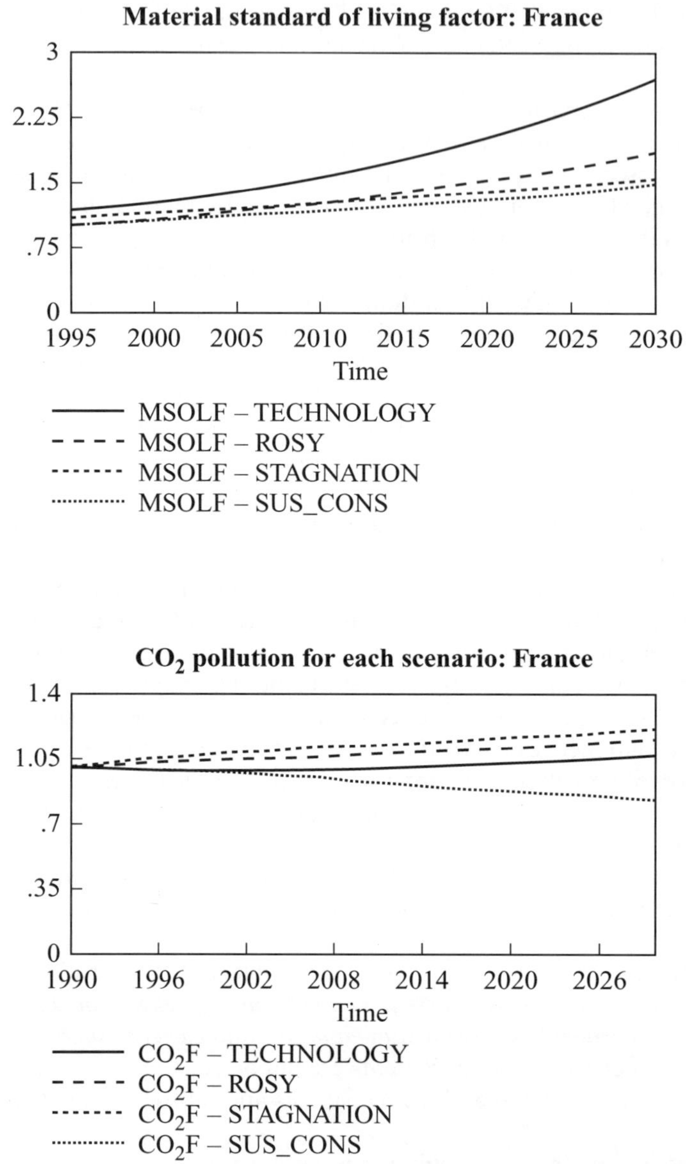

Figure 10.3 *Economic output and CO_2 emissions scenarios for France*

4.4 The Uses of 'Greened Economy GDP' Estimates

The *M3ED* scenarios for 'Technological Breakthrough' and 'Reflexive Consumption' provide estimates of feasible final consumption of economic goods and services in an economy where technical innovation and/or consumption change measures are taking place, motivated by the objective of reducing environmental pressures. We have defined a 'greened economy GDP' as the national final consumption that can be delivered while respecting specified sustainability norms for the scenario time horizon. A 'greened economy GDP' measure, or time series (as obtained with the scenario models), is intended as an indicator about possible future performance integrating economic output and environmental standards as complementary criteria of performance. The definition thus provides for the construction of time series of greened economy GDP figures (on a period-by-period basis), which could, for example, correspond to a scenario of transition towards an environmental performance judged sustainable in the long run. In particular:

- if a complete set of standards sufficient to assure long-run sustainability were specified, and estimations were made of long-term future economic prospects while fully respecting this set, one could speak of scenarios and estimates for *sustainable national income*;
- however, if calculations are made for performance prospects subject to only an incomplete set of standards or only partial compliance, it is more exact to speak only of scenario estimates for an *environmentally adjusted economy's national income*.

Aggregate measures for 'greened' or 'adjusted economies' with differing severity of environmental constraints have obvious policy relevance. Making the distinction just above helps keep visible the question of what really constitutes sustainability. In the case just illustrated, the French economy is being required to meet politically decided standards; these may be only a drop in the global bucket as regards climate stabilization requirements. Nonetheless, the idea of a measurable macroeconomic adjustment cost associated with maintaining environmental standards is clearly illustrated.

The post-Kyoto politically required environmental standard for the France economy is to achieve non-increasing CO_2 emissions (van den Hove, 1998). For a benchmark, take the Tendencial Rosy (Business as Usual) scenario. For France, in Figure 10.3, household aggregate consumption increases by 80 per cent from 1995 to 2030, and CO_2 emissions are rising monotonically to reach about 20 per cent higher than the 1990 level in 2030 (the lightly dashed curves labelled 'Rosy' in the graphs). Relative to this benchmark, the environmental norm of zero per cent increase in French emissions might be obtainable by:

- consumption pattern or lifestyle change measures that reduce consumption of material goods, perhaps in favour of greater appreciation of environmental amenities (thus, in the graphs, the heavy dashed scenario outputs labelled 'Sus-Cons', sustainability through reflexive consumption); or
- natural capital augmenting technological innovation measures that decrease per unit environmental pressure associated with economic production and/or final consumption (thus, in the graphs, the scenario outputs labelled 'Technology', sustainability through technological breakthrough).

The 'adjustment cost for sustainability' is measured as the dynamic trade-off between final consumption and reduction in environmental pressures – namely:

- *the cost* in terms of forgone consumption signalled by the 'gap' between two curves in the upper graph, representing respectively 'Business as Usual' (the Tendencial Rosy scenario) and a path for transition towards sustainability; and
- *the benefit* of achieving the path of reduced environmental pressures signalled by the gap between the 'Rosy' and the specified sustainability scenario emissions curves in the lower graph.

From comparison between 'Rosy' and 'Technology' curves, it appears that, for the next two or three decades, a *win-win* (or double-dividend) policy path might be feasible, where a high pace of natural capital augmenting technological innovation, appropriately targeted, can improve prospects for final consumption while also improving environmental performance to respect sustainability norms. From comparison between 'Rosy' and 'Sus-Cons' scenarios, it appears that a substantially improved environmental performance may be achievable while still achieving modest consumption growth. Indeed, if the benchmark were taken as the more pessimistic 'Stagnation' (Tendencial Bleak) scenario, also shown on the graphs, then it can be suggested that changes in social attitudes plus technological change plus public investment may improve greatly environmental performance without impairing macroeconomic output performance at all.

5 A WORKING PARTNERSHIP ACROSS THE MONETIZATION FRONTIER

This study has tried to bring out contrasting, sometimes complementary sometimes dissenting, insights and policy analysis perspectives offered by 'weak' and 'strong' perspectives on requirements for sustainable development. The divergences revolve around different conceptions of the role of natural capital, associated with different frameworks for establishing appropriate rules for management of natural capital and for accounting of changes in environmental assets and conditions, in the pursuit of long-run sustainability.

5.1 Natural Capital on Two Sides of the Monetization Frontier

The two conceptions of the role of natural capital, with their associated sustainability rules, can be presented as distinctive conceptions of what is meant by taking into account – that is, the internalization of – environmental dimensions of a macroeconomic management problem. The respective formulations are:

- internalization of environmental benefits and damages in a 'weak' sustainability sense, referring to an ideal of intertemporal optimal use or Pareto efficiency in resource allocation,
- internalization in the 'strong' sustainability sense, referring to political processes and institutions establishing policies for maintenance of critical environmental capital (and the associated environmental functions) and for expressing and resolving the associated conflicts.

In the ecological economics literature, sustainability requirements have typically been expressed in terms of three sorts of constraints to be imposed on economic growth paths so as to respect ecological limits (compare Barbier and Markandya, 1990; Costanza and Daly, 1992):

- that the utilization of renewable resources should not exceed their rate of renewal;
- that waste emissions should be less than the assimilation capacity of the environment; and
- that exhaustible resources should be extracted at such a rate as permits their replacement by renewable sources.

The 'weak' sustainability perspective would allow that each of these three constraints might be relaxed by virtue of technological progress that permits (through substitution and/or efficiency improvements) a continuous reduction in dependency on natural capital as a production input or sink for pollutants. In the 'strong' perspective, by contrast, the presumption is that there are not unbounded possibilities of substitution away from environmental sources and sinks. For example, an ecosystems view of natural capital (Berkes and Folke, 1992; Common and Perrings, 1992) focuses on maintenance of ecosystem stability and resilience as a precondition of sustainable economic development. This sort of systems approach emphasizes how ecological and economic systems need to be understood as complementary inputs of dynamic structures that are self-reproducing or self-renewing, and also highlights the need for scientific understanding of ecosystem functioning and change.

This suggests a useful line of demarcation. The 'weak sustainability' precepts can be regarded as applying to the exploitation of non-renewable, and also some renewable resources, to the extent that the latter are not deemed essential and permanent preconditions for durable economic activity. The 'strong sustainability' precepts, by contrast, apply to all components of natural capital that, considered as components of functioning natural systems, are deemed necessary supports for viable economic activity. This refers, notably, to the essential roles of ecosystems in life support services, waste assimilation, renewal of water and biological resources and so on.

One way of highlighting the significance of this demarcation between different zones for application of the 'strong' and the 'weak' precepts is by contrasting the manner in which the question of the value of natural capital is approached in each case. The strong perspective suggests to approach valuation from the point of view of the *economic costs of avoiding depletion or degradation*. This avoids making assumptions about substitutability and preferences on the 'demand side' of the problem, because the policy goal is maintenance of the key features (such as water quality) of the relevant natural systems. A recent analysis by Serôa da Motta (1998) and his colleagues on mineral resource extraction and water resources for Brazil, illustrates. In the case of water resources they describe the way they obtain monetary figures on the basis of a range of different propositions about the desirable levels of industrial and domestic effluent reduction, treatment and water purification. First, they suppose that the marginal damage to society of additional water pollution might be reflected in existing expenditures to partially clean the polluted water. From this they deduce a figure for the 'depreciation' of water natural capital for comparison with GNP in a way that is closely aligned to the 'weak' indicator approach. Second, they estimate the economic costs associated with fully respecting norms of preserving intact the existing capital stock levels and quality. This is closer to the 'strong' sustainability perspective, and suggests an 'economic opportunity cost' for the water quality maintenance that is substantially higher than the figure for the natural capital 'depreciation' obtained through the pricing system.

We now see the usefulness of the notion, introduced in earlier sections, of the 'monetization frontier' as a demarcation between two zones of natural wealth – on the one side the resources and assets that are valued *from the point of view of their potential conversion into commercially priced goods and services* (trees into wood products, for example), on the other side the assets that are valued from the point of view of their roles as *in situ* services as sites, scenery, scientific interest and ecological life support in complement to human economic activity.

5.2 Adjusted National Income Figures: The Hicksian Income Revisited

These two perspectives on the roles of natural capital are, logically, associated with two distinct zones of asset accounting that, in turn, relate to two quite different 'adjustment' concepts for national economic aggregates.

- The first type of adjustment, relative to standard national accounting conventions, is a *change in the system boundary*, an enlargement of the scope of national accounting to include specified categories of environmental assets. This produces an *AICCAN* indicator – an *Aggregate Indicator of the Change, during the Current Year, in the Economic Assets of the Nation.*
- The second is *adjustment of the economy itself*, that is, an 'adjusted economy' with a new pattern of production processes, levels of production and consumption activity, technologies employed and so on, which respects specified environmental performance standards. This produces a 'greened economy GDP' in a comparative scenario framework.

In Figure 10.1 of this chapter, which presents our typology of the two different forms of 'adjustment', these two concepts appear in the top right and bottom left boxes, respectively. We had left empty the bottom right box, which provides, logically, for indicator measures that combine both types of adjustment together. Yet, we now see that there is no fundamental incompatibility between the two types of adjustment concepts. They can be developed as complements, through appropriate specifications of (1) the accounting boundary dividing the enlarged asset set from the external environment and (2) hypotheses about future trends in exploitation and technology change (and so on) in this economy. With care, we could thus develop comparative analyses and scenarios allowing estimates of prospects for *AICCAN* indicators of feasible future economies.

This hybrid concept brings together hypotheses about changes to economic structure or activity patterns to improve environmental performance, together with a shift of the asset boundary in order to include selected categories of natural capital within the 'portfolio' of a nation's economic assets. It allows us to reconcile the two indicator concepts, the 'weak' and the 'strong', by noting *that they ought to be applied to distinct but complementary domains of natural capital.* Appropriately interpreted, they are both concerned with characterizing an economic performance potential while also having regard to the 'external' or 'underlying' environmental conditions that, over time, will bear on this performance capacity.

- The one, 'weak', deals with resources being appraised from the point of view of potential conversion into commercial values;
- The other, 'strong', deals with resources from the point of view of permanent maintenance adjudged essential (or, at least, highly desirable) as a support for durable economic activity.

This reconciliation via complementarity can be seen clearly by reconsidering applications of the Hicksian income concept to a national economy. The Hicksian concept of 'income' for a firm is the revenue stream that, given the available capital stock and prevailing market conditions, is obtainable on a permanent basis. Often this is translated as the revenue that can be obtained while maintaining the firm's capital stock intact. This relies on the presumption that, with an unchanged capital stock the following year, the firm could obtain this level of revenue permanently.

Applying this reasoning, it has been tempting for the case of a country to estimate the 'Hicksian national income' figure as the sum of national consumption plus net asset change, the so-called 'net national income'. But we have shown, in Section 3, that the interpretation of net national income as a sustainable national income is not generally valid, even in theory. There are two reasons for this. First, the current prices are probably 'wrong' for sustainability. Second, the measure of net asset changes is bound to be seriously incomplete.

Plausibly, a negative *AICCAN* means that the nation is probably jeopardizing its future economic welfare prospects. But, the interpretation of *final consumption minus net asset change* as the 'Hicksian' country income has to be given a very limited application. As for any firm, we are dealing here with an accounting result – an indicator of the performance of the country *during the current year, calculated with present year prices.* If we continue with the analogy of a firm, the Hicksian income is 'sustainable' only if, for each successive period, the revenue-generating capacity of the capital stock is unchanged. If not, then the Hicksian income as defined for the current period does not work as a reliable guide as to future viability (for better or worse) of the national enterprise.

We give, as a simple example, a hypothetical country asset manager watching the worsening pollution of its waters, running in tandem with the stripping of its mineral and forest resources. She or he will not be under any illusions. A 'wise use' of the proceeds of her or his national forestry production – for example, reinvestment in manufacturing industry, in conformity with the Hartwick investment rule, may be a help for future revenue generation. But, future revenue generation for whom? If multinational manipulations result in a low price for the minerals and timber products being placed into international markets (because the companies operate transfer pricing regimes and because future generations cannot bid for wood to be held in stock and so on) and only meagre royalties being paid to the host country, then it is company revenues that are being assured. If, moreover, local environmental conditions (such as freshwater quality) and coastal ecological conditions are being disrupted or degraded, without any compensating investments in regional infrastructures being financed by the resource extraction revenues, then no elaborate scenario models are needed to fear that human health, agriculture, coastal fisheries and other aspects of community welfare will suffer.

In the 'strong' approach to sustainability, the focus is placed, precisely, on the danger of adverse changes to underlying environmental conditions. There is a kind of precautionary approach that pushes the policy-maker to draw the line – the monetization frontier – in order to safeguard the ecological basis of durable economic activity. Beyond the frontier, the rule is: 'Try to ensure the permanent maintenance of important environmental functions'.

We can see from this that the 'strong' sustainability approach actually contains its own specific conception of the 'Hicksian income' for a country. Let us adopt the formulation that the Hicksian income can be estimated is the revenue that can be generated while maintaining the firm's (or country's) capital stock intact. Then, in the cost-effectiveness approach to estimating greened economy GNP scenarios, outlined in Section 4, environmental stock maintenance is indicated by respect of pressure and state standards for 'critical' environmental functions. So, if a set of standards is specified that is felt to assure the ecological basis for long-run sustainability, then an estimation of national income prospects durably achievable while respecting the set of standards is, in this specific sense, an estimate for the Hicksian income stream.

It must, however, be emphasized that any such estimates are highly sensitive to model calibration and scenario hypotheses. So they should be treated with caution.

5.3 Concluding Remarks

We arrive at a conclusion that some colleagues may find surprising. The 'weak' and the 'strong' indicator concepts should not be treated as Manicheen opposites. When you look closely at what they can plausibly be measuring, in the real empirical applications, they can be seen as addressing *different but complementary aspects of the sustainability problem*.

This allows us to return to discuss the real purposes of the search for macroeconomic sustainability indicators. The original ambition behind the definitions and estimations of greened economy GNP and NNP figures was to furnish guideposts to policy, helping to chart national economic development paths and to evaluate trade-offs between output growth, final consumption and environmental performance objectives. An indicator of net change in economic assets, enlarged to include commercially valued natural stocks – the *AICCAN*-type indicator – can have a useful role here. But, such indicator work does not reduce the need to specify targets for the ecological aspect of sustainability, the maintenance of critical environmental functions. Work on both sides of the monetization frontier is needed! And, above all, further empirical as well as conceptual work is needed around the question of where (and why) most pertinently to situate the monetization frontier.

One final observation can perhaps help to further reduce futile debates. The information of most value is not found in the aggregate figures and time series themselves – which are always open to alteration through changing assumptions. What matters most is the learning about natural systems, economic systems and policy processes that can take place through construction and comparison of the different aggregates, model outputs and scenarios. As Roefie Hueting has put it, through his 'Parable of the Carpenter' (Hueting and de Boer, 2001), if we get our understanding of the basic problem right, then a rough and ready measure will be enough to help us on our way. This suggests, also, that more investment should be put into processes of two-way communication between researchers of different disciplinary expertise and also between researchers, statisticians and the policy and regulatory communities.

REFERENCES

Asheim, G.B. (1994), 'Net national product as an indicator of sustainability', *Scandanavian Journal of Economics*, 96, 257–65.

Asheim, G.B. and W. Buchholz (2000), 'The Hartwick rule: Myths and facts', Department of Economics, University of Oslo, draft paper, March 2000. Available on http://www.uio.no/~gasheim/hr_m&f.pdf.

Barbier, E.B. and A. Markandya (1990), 'The conditions for achieving environmentally sustainable growth', *European Economic Review*, 34, 659–69.
Baumol, W.J. and W.E. Oates (1971), 'The use of standards and prices for the protection of the environment', *Swedish Journal of Economics*, 73, 42–54.
Berkes, F. and C. Folke (1992), 'A systems perspective on the interrelations between natural, human-made and cultural capital', *Ecological Economics*, 5, 1–8.
Bishop, R. (1978), 'Endangered species and uncertainty: the economics of a safe minimum standard', *American Journal of Agricultural Economics*, 60, 10–18.
Brouwer, R. and M. O'Connor (eds) (1997a), *Summary Report: Methodological Problems in the Calculation of Environmentally Adjusted National Income Figures*, Research Report for the European Commission DG-XII, Contract EV5V-CT94-0363, July 1997.
Brouwer, R. and M. O'Connor (eds) (1997b), *Final Project Report: Methodological Problems in the Calculation of Environmentally Adjusted National Income Figures*, Research Report for the European Commission DG-XII, Contract EV5V-CT94-0363, in 2 volumes, July 1997.
Brouwer, R., M. O'Connor and W. Radermacher (1999), 'GREEned National STAtistical and Modelling Procedures: the GREENSTAMP approach to the calculation of environmentally adjusted national figures', International Journal of Sustainable Development, 2 (1), pp. 8–23.
Ciriacy-Wantrup, S.V. (1952), *Resource Conservation: Economics and Policies*, Agricultural Experiment Station, Berkeley: University of California Press.
Common, M. and C. Perrings (1992), 'Towards an ecological economics of sustainability', *Ecological Economics*, 6, 7–34.
Costanza, R. and H. Daly (1992), 'Natural capital and sustainable development', *Conservation Biology*, **6** (1), 37–9.
Daly, H. (1994), 'Operationalizing sustainable development by investing in natural capital', in A.M. Jansson, M. Hammer, C. Folke and R. Costanza (eds), *Investing in Natural Capital: The Ecological Economics Approach to Sustainability*, Washington, DC: Island Press, pp. 22–37.
Dasgupta, P. and M.G. Heal (1974), 'The optimal depletion of exhaustible resources', *Review of Economic Studies*, 41, 1–23.
Dasgupta, S. and T. Mitra (1983), 'Intergenerational equity and efficient allocation of exhaustible resources', *International Economic Review*, 133–53.
De Groot, R.S. (1992), *Functions Of Nature*, Amsterdam: Wolters-Noordhoff.
Dixit, A., P. Hammond and M. Hoel (1980), 'On Hartwick's rule for regular maximin paths of capital accumulation and resource depletion', *Review of Economic Studies*, 45, 551–6.
Dubourg, R. and D. Pearce (1996), 'Paradigms for environmental choice: sustainability versus optimality', in S. Faucheux, D. Pearce and J. Proops (eds), *Models of Sustainable Development*, Cheltenham, UK and Brookfield, US: Edward Elgar, pp. 21–36.
Ekins, P. and S. Simon (1999), 'The sustainability gap: a practical indicator of sustainability in the framework of the national accounts', *International Journal of Sustainable Development*, **2** (1), 32–58.
El Serafy, S. (1991), 'Sustainability, income measurement and growth', in R. Goodland et al. (eds), *Environmentally Sustainable Economic Development: Building on Brundtland*, Paris: Unesco.
Faucheux, S. and G. Froger (1994), 'Le Revenu National Soutenable est-il un indicateur de soutenabilité ?', *Revue française d'économie*, **9** (2), 3–37.

Faucheux, S., G. Froger and M. O'Connor (1994), 'The costs of achieving sustainability: the differences between "environmentally corrected national acccounts" and "sustainable national income" as information for sustainability policy', *Discussion Papers in Environmental Economics and Environmental Management*, University of York, United Kingdom.
Faucheux, S. and J.F. Noël (1995), *L'Economie des Ressources Naturelles et de l'Environnement*, Paris: Armand Colin.
Faucheux, S., E. Muir and M. O'Connor (1997), 'Neoclassical theory of natural capital and "weak" indicators for sustainability', *Land Economics*, **73** (4), 528–52.
Faucheux, S. and M. O'Connor (eds) (1998), *Valuation for Sustainable Development: Methods and Policy Indicators*, Cheltenham: Edward Elgar.
Faucheux S. and O'Connor M. (1999), 'Natural capital and the national product: a controversial terrain', *International Journal of Development Planning Literature*, **14** (2), 233–74.
Howarth, R. (1991), 'Intertemporal equilibria and exhaustible resources', *Ecological Economics*, **4** (3), 237–52.
Howarth, R. (1992), 'Intergenerational justice and the chain of obligation', *Environmental Values*, **1** (2), 133–40.
Howarth, R. and R.B. Norgaard (1990), 'Intergenerational resource rights, efficiency, and social optimality', *Land Economics*, 66, 1–11.
Howarth, R. and R.B. Norgaard (1992), 'Environmental valuation under sustainable development', *American Economic Review Papers and Proceedings*, 80, 473–77.
Howarth, R. and R.B. Norgaard (1993), 'Intergenerational transfers and the social discount rate', *Environmental and Resource Economics*, 3, 337–58.
Hueting, R. (1980), *New Scarcity and Economic Growth: More Welfare through Less Production*?, Amsterdam: North-Holland.
Hueting, R. (1991), 'Correcting national income for environmental losses: toward a practical solution for theoretical dilemma', in R. Costanza (ed.), *Ecological Economics, The Science and Management of Sustainability*, New York: Columbia University Press.
Hueting, R., P. Bosch and B. de Boer (1992), 'Methodology for the calculation of a sustainable income', *Statistical Essays M44*, Central Bureau of Statistics, Voorburg.
Hueting, R. and B de Boer (2001), 'The Parable of the Carpenter', *International Journal of Environment and Pollution*, **15** (1), 42–50.
Mäler, K.G. (1991), 'National Accounts and Environmental Resources', *Environmental and Resource Economics*, vol. 1.
Martinez-Alier, J. and M. O'Connor (1996), 'Distributional issues in ecological economics', in R. Costanza, O. Segura and J. Martinez-Alier (eds), *Getting Down to Earth: Practical Applications of Ecological Economics*, Washington, DC: Island Press, pp. 153–84.
Mourmouras, A. (1993), 'Conservationist government policies and intergenerational equity in an overlapping generations model with renewable resources', *Journal of Public Economics*, **51** (1), 249–68.
Muir, E. (1996), 'Intra-generational wealth distributional effects on global warming cost benefit analysis', *Journal of Income Distribution*, **6** (2), 193–214.
Noël, J-F. and M. O'Connor (1998), 'Strong sustainability and critical natural capital', in S. Faucheux. and M. O'Connor (eds), *Valuation for Sustainable Development: Methods and Policy Indicators*, Edward Elgar Publisher, Chapter 4, pp. 75–97.

Norgaard, R. (1990), 'Economic indicators of resource scarcity: a critical essay', *Journal of Environmental Economics and Management*, 19, 19–25.

Norgaard, R. and R. Howarth, (1991), 'Sustainability and discounting the future', in R. Costanza (ed.), *Ecological Economics: The Science and Management of Sustainability*, New York/Oxford: Columbia University Press, pp. 88–101.

O'Connor, M. and G. Ryan (1999), 'Macro-economic cost-effectiveness and the use of multi-sectoral dynamic modelling as an environmental valuation tool', *International Journal of Sustainable Development*, **1** (2), pp. 127–63.

Passet, R. (1979/1996), *L'Economique et le Vivant*, 2nd edition 1996, Paris: Economica.

Pearce, D. and K.R. Turner (1990), *Economics of Natural Resources and the Environment*, New York: Harvester Wheatsheaf.

Pearce, D. and J. Warford (1993), *World Without End: Economics environment and sustainable development*, The World Bank, Oxford University Press.

Peskin, H.M. (1991), 'Alternative environmental and resource accounting approaches', in R. Costanza (ed.), *Ecological Economics, The Science and Management of Sustainability*, New York: Columbia University Press.

Peet, J. (1992), *Energy and the Ecological Economics of Sustainability*, Washington, DC: Island Press.

Pezzey, J. (1992), 'Sustainability: an interdisciplinary guide', *Environmental Values*, **1** (4), 321–62.

Pezzey, J. (1994), 'The optimal sustainable depletion of nonrenewable resources', unpublished discussion paper, Department of Economics, University College London, March 1994.

Pezzey, J. (1997), 'Sustainability constraints versus "Optimality" versus intertemporal concern, and axioms versus data', *Land Economics*, **73** (4), 448–66.

Pezzey, J and C. Withagen (1998), 'The rise, fall and sustainability of capital-resource economies', *Scandinavian Journal of Economics*, 100, 513–27.

Proops, J.L.R. and G.D. Atkinson (1997), 'A practical sustainability criterion when there is international trade', in S. Faucheux, M. O'Connor and J. van der Straaten (eds), *Sustainable Development: Concepts, Rationalities and Strategies*, Dordrecht: Kluwer, pp. 169–94.

Radermacher, W., W. Riege-Wcislo and A. Heinze (1999), 'A statistical-analytical methodology for the construction of abatement cost curves', *International Journal of Sustainable Development*, **2** (1), 59–94.

Schembri, P. (1999a), 'Adaptation costs for sustainable development and ecological transitions: a presentation of the structural model M3ED with reference to French energy-economy-carbon dioxide emissions prospects', *International Journal of Environment and Pollution*, **11** (4), 542–64.

Schembri, P. (1999b), 'Environmentally adjusted domestic product and emission control policies: a dynamic simulation modelling approach', *International Journal of Sustainable Development*, **2** (1), 164–84.

Schembri, P. and J.M. Douguet (2000), *CNC: Quantification et Modélisation du Capital Naturel Critique pour la mise en œuvre d'une politique du développement durable en France*, C3ED Rapport de Recherche, April 2000, final report for research contract No. 97085 funded by the French Ministry of Land Use Planning and Environment, 1997–1999.

Serôa da Motta, R.S. (1998), 'Sustainability principles and depreciation estimates of natural capital in Brazil', in S. Faucheux, M. O'Connor and J. van der Straaten (eds), *Sustainable Development: Concepts, Rationalities, Strategies*, Dordrecht: Kluwer.

Solow, R.M. (1974), 'Intergenerational equity and exhaustible resources', *Review of Economic Studies*, 41, 29–46.
Solow, R.M. (1986), 'On the intertemporal allocation of natural resources', *Scandanavian Journal of Economics*, 88, 141–49.
Stiglitz, J.E. (1974), 'Growth with exhaustible natural resources: the competitive economy', *Review of Economic Studies* (Symposium on the Economics of Exhaustible Resources), 41, 123–37.
Svensson, L.E.O. (1986), 'Comment on R.M. Solow', *Scandanavian Journal of Economics*, 88, 153–55.
Toman, M.A., J. Pezzey and J. Krautkraemer (1995), 'L'économie néoclassique face à la soutenabilité', *Economie Appliquée*, **XLVIII** (2), 25–58. English version: 'Neoclassical Economic Growth Theory and Sustainability', in D.W. Bromley (ed.), 1995), *Handbook of Environmental Economics*, Oxford UK and Cambridge USA: Blackwell, pp. 139–65.
van den Hove, S. (ed.) (1998), Special Issue on EU climate policy: The European Commission Policy/Research Interface for Kyoto and Beyond, *International Journal of Environment and Pollution*, 10 (3/4).
Victor, P. (1991), 'Indicators of sustainable development: some lessons from capital theory', *Ecological Economics*, 4, 191–213.
Victor, P.A, J.E. Hanna and A. Kubursi (1997), 'How strong is weak sustainability?', in S. Faucheux, M. O'Connor and J. van der Straaten (eds), *Sustainable Development: Concepts, Rationalities, Strategies*, Dordrecht: Kluwer, pp. 195–210.
Weber, C., A. Perrels, M. O'Connor, G. Ryan et al. (1996), *Consumer's Lifestyle and Pollutants Emissions: Integrated Full Report*, prepared by IER, ECN, C3ED under contract EV5V-CT94-0373 to EC DG-XII, produced at IER, Stuttgart.
Weitzman, M.L. (1997), 'Sustainability and technical progress', *Scandinavian Journal of Economics*, **XCIX**, 1–13.
Withagen, C. and G.B. Asheim (1998), 'Characterizing sustainability: the converse of Hartwick's rule', *Journal of Economic Dynamics and Control*, 23, 159–65.

11. Alternative calculations of a sustainable national income for the Netherlands according to Hueting

Harmen Verbruggen, Rob B. Dellink, Reyer Gerlagh, Marjan W. Hofkes and Huib M.A. Jansen*

1 INTRODUCTION

It is well understood that national income is an inadequate indicator of social welfare. Dependant on the angle, national income is either incomplete or misleading, or both. Hence, there are quite a number of attempts to improve and/or supplement this central statistic of national accounts. One of these attempts is extensively dealt with in this contribution, namely the correction of national income for environmental losses. To be more precise, the aim of this study is to investigate the feasibility of calculating a national income for the Netherlands that takes the environment as a welfare-generating economic good into account, according to the methodology so strongly advocated by Hueting. This methodology would result in a so-called sustainable national income (SNI). Here, Hueting's SNI methodology is briefly summarized, but not discussed.

However, in operationalizing this methodology, an empirical and integrated environment-economy model has to be used. This intermediate step makes the operationalization certainly not a simple exercise. A number of choices have to be made and additional assumptions have to be formulated to make the model run and come up with credible results. Of course, these choices and additional assumptions can be questioned. For that very reason, a number of alternative calculations have been performed to gather insight into the impact of different choices and assumptions, both with

* The research that is reported here is commissioned jointly by the Ministry of Economic Affairs and the Ministry of Housing, Spatial Planning and the Environment of the Netherlands. The useful comments of the editors and anonymous referees are gratefully acknowledged.

respect to the order of magnitude of the corrections and from an analytical perspective. All this will be dealt with in Section 2. Section 3 presents and briefly discusses the so-called cost-effectiveness curves per environmental theme. These curves are needed to translate the costs of meeting the sustainability standards, through model calculations, into corrections of national income. The results of the alternative SNI calculations will be presented and discussed in Sections 4 and 5. Some final remarks are made in Section 6.

It should be pointed out that this study presents preliminary and still incomplete alternative calculations of an SNI. These results should therefore be interpreted with great care. Still a great many improvements and refinements are needed.

2 OPERATIONAL CHOICES AND ADDITIONAL ASSUMPTIONS

According to Hueting, the objective to construct an SNI boils down to a correction of national income for environmental losses. With environmental losses is meant the forgone use of the environment due to competition between the different functions the environment performs to sustain economic activities and human life. As national income is recorded in market prices, the correction for environmental losses should be in comparable terms. Hence, ideally, shadow prices have to be found on the basis of demand and supply curves for environmental functions. Then, environmental losses can be expressed in market prices and deducted from national income to arrive at an SNI.

However, two major problems are encountered. First, supply and demand functions for environmental functions have to be constructed. In principle, it is feasible to discover a supply curve, because the maintenance of environmental functions involves costs. Hence, the supply curve is made up of costs to restore and maintain environmental functions. The sustainability level corresponds with a point on this curve. Hueting denotes this curve as the elimination cost curve, here referred to as the cost-effectiveness curve. The construction of these curves is further dealt with in the next section. By contrast, the construction of a complete demand curve is mostly impossible for various (theoretical) reasons. Hueting's practical solution for this theoretical dilemma is to assume that people have a preference to use vital environmental functions sustainably, since the Dutch and many other governments in the world have officially embraced the concept of sustainable development. Consequently, the officially stated pursuit of sustainable development is interpreted as sustainable use of environmental functions and approximated by sustainability standards. With this interpretation, it is assumed that individual preferences for the sustainable use of the environment are absolute and independent of costs. That is why Hueting's correction of national income is denoted as a *sustainable* national income. Other assumptions about individual and social environmental preferences would result in different green national incomes, not in an SNI.

Hueting's methodology distinguishes itself from other approaches in that it pursues a correction of national income on the basis of assumed preferences for sustainability, that is the sustainability standards, instead of stated preferences for the conservation of the environment through, for instance, the use of a contingent valuation method, or revealed preferences for environmental quality through, for instance, hedonic pricing and production factor methods[1] (Hueting, 1992; Kuik, 1999). According to Hueting and Reijnders (1998), these standards guarantee the indefinite availability of environmental functions and are in this sense objective (see Den Butter and Verbruggen, 1994). Then, it is indeed possible to come up with an imputed value for an environmental loss, that is the costs to meet the sustainability standards. The costs comprise technical measures as well as a shift to less burdening economic activities. All these costs are to be incurred by industry, government and households, and are considered to be intermediate expenditures and should therefore not count as income, or alternatively, deducted from national income.

Then we run into the second difficulty. The environmental losses estimated in this way cannot simply be deducted from national income. For that, the magnitudes of these losses are too substantial. An entirely other economic structure and hence SNI would have resulted if these environmental losses would have been prevented or restored. We then envisage a hypothetical sustainable economy with a hypothetical SNI. This can only be approached through model calculations. For that purpose, an applied general equilibrium (AGE) model for the Dutch economy has been constructed, inclusive of environmental variables (Dellink et al., 1999).

However, the operationalization of this approach, that is the conversion in a model, is definitely not straightforward. This conversion has two levels. The first level is of a more general nature and translates methodological assumptions into general model characteristics. This general conversion will be discussed in this section, because various possibilities arise and operational choices have to be made. At the second level, the general model characteristics have to be translated into technical model specifications, and additional specifications have to be decided upon.

The following methodological assumptions of Hueting's approach need further explanation:

- an instantaneous realization of the sustainability standards;
- this instantaneous realization, however, involves no transition cost;
- the sustainability standards are applied all over the world in order to prevent a reallocation of environmental pressure among countries. This, of course, affects international trade relations;
- the sustainability standards are assumed to be realized at the present state of technological knowledge;
- in addition to technical measures to meet the sustainability standards, reductions in the level of particular economic activities in favour of environment-extensive activities, so-called volume measures, are envisaged;
- national income should also be corrected for double counting;
- there ought to be no effects on the level of employment, at least not negative;
- the SNI should preferably be measured in new, that is sustainable, relative prices;
- consumption patterns will change;
- the role of the government is not supposed to change in a sustainable economy.

Instantaneous Realization

Correcting national income for environmental losses is a strictly static approach. This is not undone by using an AGE model to simulate a sustainable economy that matches with an SNI, because this sustainable economy is brought about instantaneously. Hence, the SNI is a hypothetical construct that results from a comparative static model exercise.

No Transition Cost

The SNI calculations should not be burdened with other cost than environment-related loss of functions. In addition to technical and volume measures to meet the sustainability standards, other costs are very well thinkable. To arrive at a sustainable economy, a drastic restructuring and reallocation of economic activities has to take place. And this inevitably involves a premature write-off of capital goods, and transition or adaptation costs. As these non-environment-related costs should not enter an SNI, it has to be assumed that the (instantaneous) change to a sustainable economy has officially been announced a period in advance, long enough that economic agents are able to integrate this transition in the planning of their investment decisions. Transition costs are then minimized and can be neglected. By this way of reasoning, it is implicitly assumed that the early announcement enhances the substitution possibilities in the economy. This, in turn, should be expressed by applying medium- to long-term substitution elasticities in the model calculations, instead of short-term elasticities, which are common in static modelling. However, long-term substitution elasticities for the sectoral breakdown as well as those pertaining to substitutions among economic and environmental variables are not readily available for the Dutch economy. As it presently stands, elasticities of a rather short- to medium-term nature are applied.

Worldwide Sustainability and International Trade

To calculate an SNI for a particular country, assumptions have to be made with respect to policies in the rest of the world. This is especially relevant for a small and open economy such as the Netherlands, as a unilateral sustainability policy could cause an international reallocation of relatively environment-intensive production activities. To do away with that unwanted effect, it has to be assumed that similar sustainability standards are applied all over the world, taking due account of local differences in environmental conditions. However, it is not feasible to estimate the resulting cost and changes in relative prices in other countries. So, additional assumptions have to be formulated with respect to relative price changes on the world market and the impact on import and export flows to and from the Netherlands.

Two alternative assumptions come to the fore. But before these alternatives are explained, it should be realized that the SNI model calculations have to stick to the standard macroeconomic balance equations. Thus, public and private savings surplus (or deficit) equals trade balance surplus (or deficit). The savings surplus is assumed to constitute a constant share of national income and is set equal to that share in the base situation. This, in turn, determines the relative price level of the Netherlands *vis-à-vis* the rest of the world and the trade balance.

In the first alternative, it is assumed that relative prices on the world market do not change. In the event that the domestic system of relative prices also stays the same, Dutch exports will change in proportion to the level of domestic production per sector. Thus, in the first instance, world market outlet for Dutch exports moves along with sectoral production levels. However, if domestic relative prices do change in response to sustainability standards, exports of goods and services, which become more expensive relative to the world market will decrease more than proportionally and *vice versa*. As regards imports, the standard procedure in

AGE modelling is followed, whereby imports are proportionally linked to the level of domestic demand. If an import product becomes cheaper relative to a domestic substitute, imports will decrease less than proportionally and *vice versa*. In this alternative, it is assumed that sustainability policies all over the world do not influence relative prices on the world market, but are specified through shrinking export and import markets. In addition, as relative prices in the Netherlands do change, it becomes indeed feasible for the Netherlands to partly realize its sustainability standards by importing relatively environment-intensive products, of which the cost of production will increase in the Netherlands, and exporting relatively environment-extensive products, of which the cost of production will decrease in the Netherlands. This is only partly possible, as the sizes of export and import markets move along with domestic sectoral production and demand levels.

Second, it can be assumed that per sector the share of imports in total domestic demand, and the share of export in total domestic production, remain constant compared to the base situation. In economic terms this boils down to the assumption that in reaction to worldwide sustainability policies, all production processes in foreign sectors go through a similar process of adjustment as in the Netherlands. Or again in other words, it is then implicitly assumed that changes in relative prices in other countries and the Netherlands are equal.

The SNI will be calculated for both foreign trade assumptions. It will be clear that the latter assumption of constant import and export shares comes closest to Hueting's methodology. For the sake of clarity, no attention is paid to environmental pressure emanating from transport of internationally traded goods.

Present State of Technology

In estimating the cost of technical measures to meet the sustainability standards, only known technological options can be envisaged. Known technologies comprise options that are already on the market as well as technological options that are indeed technically feasible, but still too expensive or not yet fully applicable and standardized, or both, to apply under present market conditions. These remote options will certainly be considered if more stringent environmental standards are enforced. By broadening the known technological options in this way, some justice is done to the early announcement assumption. For if this really would have been the case, the development of clean technology would have been accelerated. Hence, the cost of technical measures is based on the present state of technological knowledge, and refers to the 1990s.

Volume Measures

In Hueting's methodology, in addition to technical measures to meet the sustainability standards, also a reduction in the production level of relatively environment-intensive sectors is envisaged. These so-called volume measures can be conceived as a shift from environment-intensive to environment-extensive production activities and consumptive expenditures. Instead of going on holiday by air to far remote and exotic destinations, Dutch consumers in a sustainable economy rather prefer a biking holiday or go to France by train. In the SNI model calculations, the cost of technical measures, derived from the cost-effectiveness curve, and the cost of reducing production, approached by value added loss, are weighed against each other. It is very well possible in this trade-off that volume measures are taken before all technical possibilities to reduce emissions are exhausted, namely as soon as the marginal cost of technical measures exceeds the marginal cost of volume measures.

Double-counting

In addition to correcting national income for the cost of technical and volume measures to meet the sustainability standards, national income should also be corrected for so-called double-counting. Double-counting refers to the expenditure on compensatory, restoratory and preventive measures to re-establish or maintain environmental functions, sometimes denoted as defensive measures or asymmetric entering. According to Hueting and many others, these expenditures wrongly enter national income as value added: loss of environmental functions is not written off in the year of origin, whereas restoration is entered afterwards. This line of reasoning can indeed be maintained in case defensive measures are taken in the sphere of consumption, not entering a production process as intermediate input. In our SNI calculations, the cost to reduce dehydration and the clean up of contaminated soils are double-counting cases in point.

However, it is unfeasible to revise the national income accounts for these specific double-countings in a once only correction. Another procedure is therefore followed that is more in line with the overall approach of a comparative static equilibrium analysis. It is assumed that the estimated total cost of soil clean-up amounting to 408 billion guilders (see Appendix) is borne by the government. It is assumed that the soil clean-up activities are spread over a 20-year period. So, each year 5 per cent of the total amount is contracted out for soil clean-up, which will then be entered in the SNI calculations as a yearly deduction. The reduction cost of dehydration is also assumed to be financed out of, and likewise deducted from, the government budget and amounts to 860 million guilders on a yearly basis (see Appendix).

Labour Market and Capital Market

The already mentioned understanding that in the calculation of an SNI only environmental losses have to be considered as relevant corrections and, hence, should not become infected too much by related side-problems, also means the neglect of influences from the labour market on SNI, be it positive or negative. According to Hueting, a sustainable economy will certainly not worsen the employment situation, simply because environmental care in satisfying a particular need will require more labour. Consequently, the labour market can be very simply modelled, whereby the labour force is exogenously given and the labour market is cleared through an adjusting wage rate. In the present calculations, the supply of labour is equated with the level of employment in 1990 and wages are endogenously adjusted such that demand for labour equals supply. It will be clear that SNI will result in downward adjusted wage rates and concomitant productivity levels. The alternative would be labour time shortening at higher productivity levels. This, however, is not in line with Hueting's SNI methodology that envisages a different, sustainable path of economic development.

The arguments that led to the assumptions with respect to the modelling of the labour market also apply to the capital market, which is very simply modelled: there is a fixed rate of return on capital and the capital stock immediately adjusts. This fixed rate of capital return equals 5 per cent in the present calculations, which approaches the average long-term interest rate in 1990. At the demand side of the capital market, both replacement and net investments are assumed to constitute a fixed share of the capital stock. At the demand side, public and private savings make up a constant share of total income. As already indicated, an equilibrium on the capital market is obtained by accommodating a savings surplus or deficit through a compensating surplus or deficit on the balance of payments.

Old and New Prices

It has already been indicated that the correction of national income has to be expressed in directly comparable (shadow) market prices. This is conceivable if as a first approximation the cost of measures to meet the sustainability standards are directly deducted from national income. If, however, SNI calculations are made with the help of an AGE model relative prices change, that is prices of environment-intensive products will generally increase compared to other products. The question now is in which set of prices SNI could best be expressed, such that a comparison with the original national income figure can be ascribed a meaningful interpretation. The literature on empirical welfare economics is in this respect of little help. Several alternative weighting schemes can be defended. For the SNI calculations, two of these alternatives seem acceptable.

In the first alternative, the set of relative prices of the base situation is used to weigh the volumes of the SNI. Intuitively, as the same price sets are used, this alternative would provide an adequate standard of comparison. However, at least two objections can be raised. First, consistency between national income and national product is lost, because the volume shares of an SNI will differ from the original national income. Second, an SNI results in a new set of equilibrium prices and it remains strange to use the old price set. A major objection against the use of a new set of relative prices is the loss of a comparative standard. At least, the new equilibrium prices have to be scaled at the old price level to make this second alternative meaningful. Hence, two price sets will be used to calculate SNI variants.

Private Consumption

Additional assumptions have to be made as to the economic behaviour of consumers in calculating an SNI. More precisely, how would consumers have reacted in case of (substantially) lower income levels of an SNI path of economic development. In Hueting's methodology, it is assumed that a twofold adjustment of consumption patterns have to be envisaged. First, real spendable income will be lower as production factors are employed to keep up environmental functions. In the model calculations, the effects of lower income levels is approached by the use of income elasticities that specify a demand for agricultural products that decreases less than proportional, a demand for services to decrease more than proportional, and a demand for manufactured products which proportionally depends on the stage of economic development. In this way, consumption is thought of as consisting of necessary goods for subsistence and luxury goods. If income falls in the model calculations, the consumption of necessary goods will remain relatively stable, which is compensated by a more than proportional decrease in the consumption of luxury goods. Second, consumption patterns will become more sustainable as a result of relative price changes. Thus, in addition to income substitution effects, the model includes the concept of price elasticities. In general, the consumption of environment-intensive goods and services will decrease, whereas environment-extensive goods and services will show an increase in relative consumption levels. It is assumed that private consumers have more substitution possibilities than the public consumer (the government), which demand is determined by public services that have to be supplied.

Government

In line with the neglect of transition cost and labour market effects, the government is not supposed to have a disturbing impact on the calculation of an SNI. Thus, there is no change in fiscal and income distributional policies. This neutral role of the government implies that environmental functions are owned by the government and that the use of these functions should be paid for. Emissions to the environment are then considered as public endowments, and as these emissions are constrained by sustainability standards, the value that is imputed in the context of the modelling exercise entirely accrues to the government. Put differently, the government sells emission units of which the price is endogenously determined in the model. To guarantee budget neutrality, the revenues from the sale of emission units have to be returned to the producers and consumers by a linearly homogeneous reduction of taxes. In case revenues from emission units exceed the government budget, the surplus will be redistributed to private households through a lump sum.

In addition to the operational choices, decisions had to be reached on a number of technical model specifications. These are dealt with in more detail in the technical model description (Dellink et al., 1999). Specifications related to abatement of emissions are worth briefly mentioning here. In the model calculations, there is one abatement sector in operation that delivers emission reductions to all other sectors. As yet, there is no diversification among sectors in expenditure effect of abatement investment. And, for the time being, environmental emissions are linked to the volumes of production and consumption.

Because no decisive preference can be given to one of the two assumptions on foreign trade as well as on the use of old or equilibrium prices, four SNI variants will be calculated. Of the following variants, variant 2b is most in line with Hueting's methodology.

Variant 1a: constant relative prices on the world market and SNI expressed in relative prices of the base situation (old prices)

Variant 1b: constant relative prices on the world market as in variant 1a, but SNI expressed in new equilibrium prices

Variant 2a: constant shares of imports and exports and SNI expressed in relative prices of the base situation (old prices)

Variant 2b: constant shares of exports and imports as in variant 2a, but SNI expressed in new equilibrium prices

3 COST-EFFECTIVENESS CURVES FOR VARIOUS ENVIRONMENTAL THEMES

Introduction

According to Hueting's methodology, the correction of the traditional national income figures consists of the costs that have to be incurred to meet the sustainability standards. However, costs of pollution reduction consist of costs of technical measures and costs of volume measures. The costs of technical measures are investment costs (recalculated as annual costs) and operation and maintenance costs of changes in the production process. The costs of volume measures are lost value added, due to a reduction in the production volume of a particular economic activity. In this section only the costs of technical measures are treated. These costs are called the costs of reduction of 'avoidable' pollution. Costs of reduction of 'unavoidable' pollution, that is of volume measures, are not dealt with here.

A rational polluter, if faced with the necessity to reduce pollution, will first take the cheapest measures and then, if necessary, turn to the more costly measures. The marginal, and thus also the total cost curve, will therefore be monotonously non-decreasing. As a rule, not all pollution can be prevented by technical measures. Therefore, the cost curve approaches a vertical asymptote, where marginal (and total) costs approach infinity.

A marginal cost curve of reduction will then take the shape of a step function where, from the origin, each time the next cheapest measure is introduced until the last, the most expensive measure is reached and no further reduction is possible with technical means. The integral of the marginal cost function yields the function of total reduction costs. The total cost functions are fitted to a constant elasticity of substitution (CES) function, as schematically pictured in Figure 11.1.

The environmental themes that are included in the SNI calculations are the following: climate change, acidification, eutrophication, dehydration, volatile organic compounds (VOC), zinc in water and soil contamination. For a detailed description of the cost-effectiveness curves for these environmental themes, see the Appendix at the end of this chapter. This section continues with general methodological issues.

Methodology

The methodology for calculating costs of technical measures and resulting reduction of pollution is in line with the methodology that is used by the Netherlands Bureau of Statistics (CBS) and the National Institute for

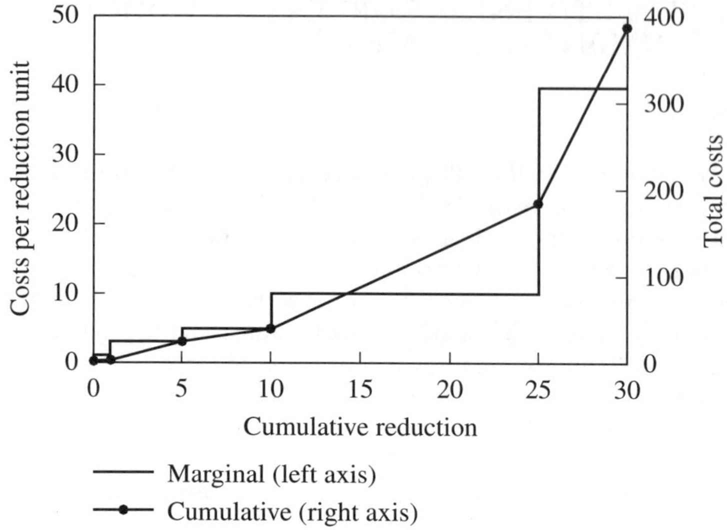

Figure 11.1 *Marginal and cumulative costs of emission reduction*

Public Health and the Environment (RIVM), and described in detail in VROM (1994).

The costs are calculated as seen by the *target groups*. This implies that they include taxes (VAT, for households) and excises (on fuels). The excises play a role in particular, when a measure leads to fuel saving that can be deducted from the reduction costs.

The discount rate, which is used to derive annual figures from investments, amounts to about 5 per cent on average, which consists of the real interest rate plus an additional percentage of 1 per cent for enterprises and 0.4 per cent for lower authorities and households. But in the theme climate change, a discount rate of 9 per cent on average was used. This difference between discount rates in different themes is not consistent, but based on the as yet available studies and databases. It seems that the assumption of a discount rate, as perceived by the *target groups*, of on average 9 per cent is more in line with the most recent insights of environmental policy-makers (VROM, 1998).

Near the origin of the cost curve, the calculated costs of reduction may be negative, meaning that reduction can be achieved with net savings. This is at odds with theory and implies that certain assumptions are violated, be it assumptions on rational behaviour of the target groups, on equilibrium in the economy, on used prices and discount rates, or whatever. In the cost curves, negative net costs of reduction were set equal to zero.

The cost curves are superimposed on the 1990 situation with respect to levels of production and consumption of the various sectors and with respect to the technological state of the art (plus costs and effects) of pollution reduction.

Interaction of Measures

Reduction measures may interact in a number of ways. In the following paragraphs we give a description of how was dealt with interactions. This description is based on Dellink et al. (1997) and does not necessarily apply for the theme of climatic change, which is based on a separate study (de Boer and Bosch, 1995). The possible ways of interactions are exclusiveness, sequentiality, interaction between themes and substances, and interaction between measures.

Exclusiveness of measures

Introduction of one measure may make certain other measures inapplicable. For instance, a fuel switch from coal to gas excludes the measure of coal gasification. The following method was used. The cost-effectiveness of the mutually excluding measures was calculated and the most efficient measure was then introduced in the curve. A drawback of this procedure is that possibly the total effect of the less efficient measure is higher and that therefore the total reduction potential of avoidable emissions is underestimated.

Sequentiality of measures

Sometimes, a measure cannot be taken before another one is introduced. For instance, a third phase water purification cannot be realized before a second-phase purification. This may lead to a situation where a less efficient measure is taken before a more efficient one. This was solved by combining measures into packages. Suppose that we have measure a that reduces pollution from 100 to 50 units, and measure b, that must follow measure a, reducing further from 50 to 35 units; moreover, we have a separate measure c, that reduces pollution from 100 to 40 units. The measures are then redefined as: a; $(a+b)$; and c.

Interaction between themes and substances

Reduction of one substance may lead to a change in the emission of another substance. For instance, improvement of energy efficiency may lead to reduction of CO_2, NO_x and SO_2 emissions. In line with the procedures in RIM^+ (see Appendix), a primary aim of the measure is then identified and the costs of the measure are totally attributed to that primary aim.

If the measure impacts two substances within the same theme (for example, NO_x and SO_2), this procedure does not lead to double-counting of the costs, but if one measure is included in two different themes (for example, CO_2 and NO_x), the measure may well be defined as having a primary aim in both themes, and double-counting of costs may well occur.

Interaction between measures

The combined effect of two measures can be lower than the sum of the effects of the two separate measures. For instance, a fuel switch to lower sulphur fuel and flue gas desulphurisation have, if combined, a lower effect than the sum of the effects of each measure if applied without the other.

This could be solved by combining the measures in packages. However, if many measures interact, the number of packages grows rapidly to unmanageable amounts. The used procedure is that, if measures a and b interact, and if in combination they have the effect of measure c $(=a+b)$, then the measure with the lowest efficiency, say measure b, is redefined as having the effect $c-a$.

4 PRELIMINARY RESULTS: MECHANISMS

Table 11.1 presents the sustainability standards for the various environmental themes that function in combination with the corresponding cost-effectiveness curves as a reference for the alternative SNI calculations.

To gather an understanding of the mechanisms at work in the transition from the ordinary national income to an SNI, Figures 11.2A–11.4B present diagrams for the break-up of national income per expenditure category, per sector and per production factor, respectively. Figure 11.2A shows changes on the way to an SNI in steps of one-tenth of compliance with the sustainability standards, and only refer to variant 1b. Figure 11.2B compares the distribution over different categories for SNI variants 1b and 2b. To simplify

Table 11.1 Sustainability standards for the Netherlands, 1990

Environmental	Units	Base	Sustainability	Required reduction
Climate change	10E9 kg CO_2 equivalents	237	64	173 (83%)
Acidification	10E9 acid equivalents	33.5	10	23.5 (70%)
Eutrophication	10E6 kg P equivalents	318	35	283 (89%)
VOC to air	10E6 kilograms	440	260	180 (41%)
Zinc to water	10E3 kg Zn	975	195	780 (80%)

the comparison, only the results in new equilibrium prices are shown here. The full results for all SNI variants are presented in the next section.

The most noticeable feature that can be learned from Figure 11.2A is that the SNI substantially drops only after about 75 per cent of the sustainability standards are met. In other words, and not unexpectedly, the last 25 per cent of the sustainability standards involves the highest cost and causes the reduction in SNI. Figure 11.2B where SNI variants 1b and 2b can be compared with national income of the base situation clearly shows a substantial lower SNI value for variant 2b than for variant 1b. Apparently, as the specification of imports and exports as constant shares in total domestic demand and production leaves no room for an environmentally extensive specialization of the Dutch economy, the restructuring of the economy has to be more drastic and, hence, SNI is substantially lower.

Of the distinguished expenditure categories presented in Figure 11.2A, net investments, that is investments in addition to replacement investments, decrease most sharply. In the base situation, net investments constitute 8.7 per cent of national income, whereas in SNI variant 1b their contribution is reduced to 5.5 per cent. This can be explained by a reallocation of production from relatively environment-intensive sectors, which are on average also relatively capital-intensive, to cleaner and more labour-intensive sectors, such as services. The lower net investment share in SNI implies that

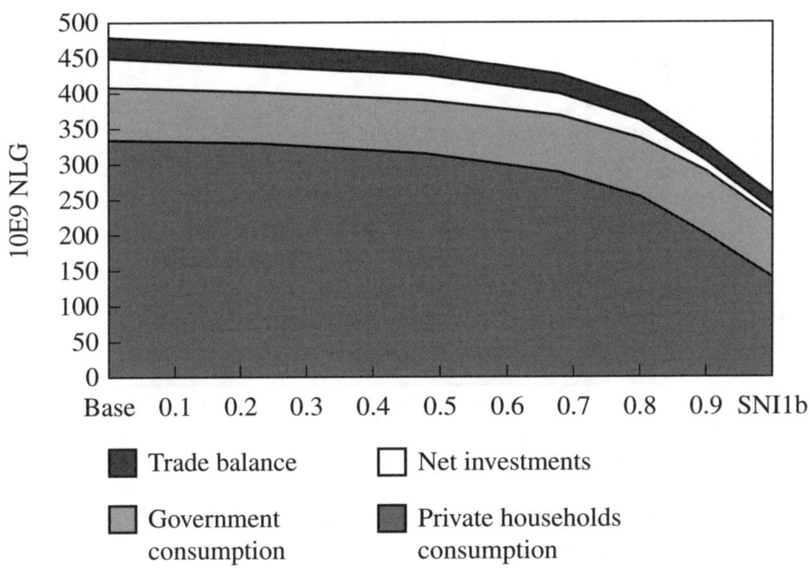

Figure 11.2A *Break-up of national income per expenditure category: from base to SNI (variant 1b)*

the upward pressure on capital demand stemming from increased abatement activities is more than offset by a fall in capital demand due to this reallocation. All this results in a decreasing capital stock. The positive trade balance decreases in proportion, which is due to the general assumption that the trade balance equals a constant share of the savings surplus in national income. The consumption of the private households is most severely affected in an SNI. Its share drops from almost 70 per cent in the base situation to 56 per cent in SNI variant 1b. This is the combined effect of a proportional decrease in spendable income levels and the consumption of relatively cheaper and environmentally more sound goods and services. By contrast, government consumption as share of SNI increases. This can only mean that the so-called other non-commercial services, of which the government is by far the largest client, experience relatively large price increases. The substitution elasticities for these services are close to zero. Relevant examples include infra-structural projects such as roads. In addition, account has also to be taken of the fact that part of the government expenditure is spent on the reduction of dehydration and soil clean-up. These double-countings are not yet corrected for in this figure.

Figure 11.2B facilitates a comparison of the levels of the SNI variants 1b and 2b with national income in the base situation. SNI variants 1b and 2b are 46 per cent and 62 per cent lower than the original national income

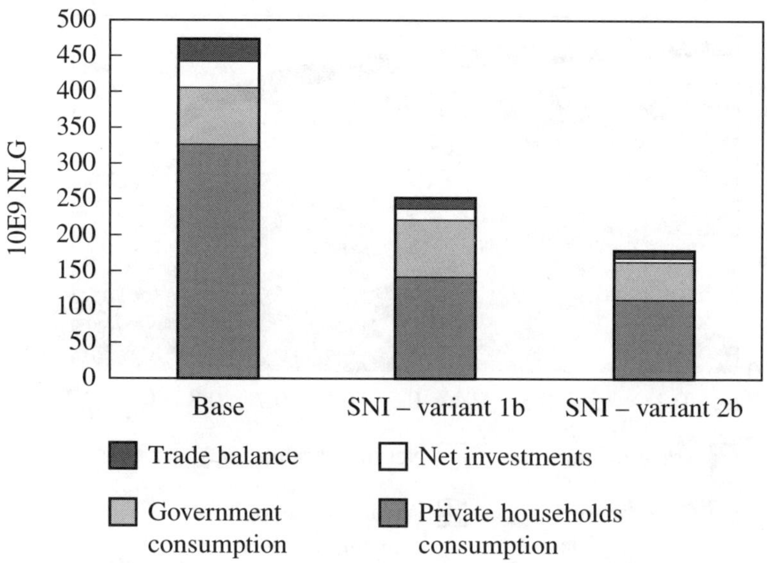

Figure 11.2B *Break-up of national income per expenditure category: distribution over categories (variants 1b and 2b)*

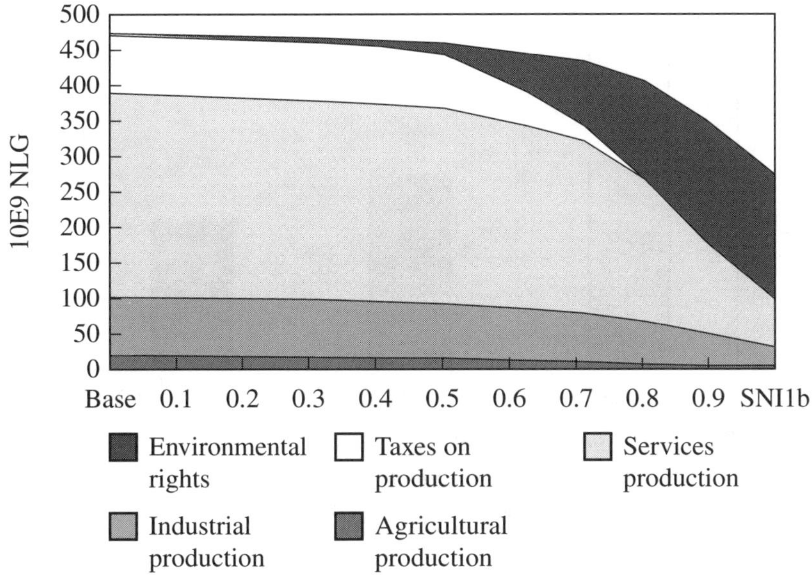

Figure 11.3A *Break-up of national product per sector: from base to SNI (variant 1b)*

figure, respectively. Net investments in SNI variant 2b further decreases to 3.6 per cent of SNI, and government consumption now also declines but proportionally less than other expenditure categories.

The changes in the volumes of total tax income as well as value added in agriculture, manufacturing and services are presented in Figure 11.3A. Clearly, agricultural production is hit hardest, especially after about 60 per cent of the sustainability standards are met. Its share drops from 3 per cent in the base situation to 0.1 per cent in SNI variant 1b. About half of this decline is due to increased imports of agricultural products, which is facilitated in this variant. Apparently, in this SNI variant there is hardly any room for agriculture. The relative shares of manufacturing and services also decline in SNI, but surprisingly, services more than manufacturing. This is particularly due to the more necessary character of manufacturing production, expressed in lower substitution elasticities, compared to services. Put differently, the lower share of services is in line with the lower income level of the SNI. Moreover, in the SNI variants at new equilibrium prices, no compensation takes place in the form of higher prices, as services are generally relatively clean.

The most striking result of the SNI variants in new equilibrium prices is the more than complete greening of the tax system. The government revenues of the sale of environmental rights appear to become higher

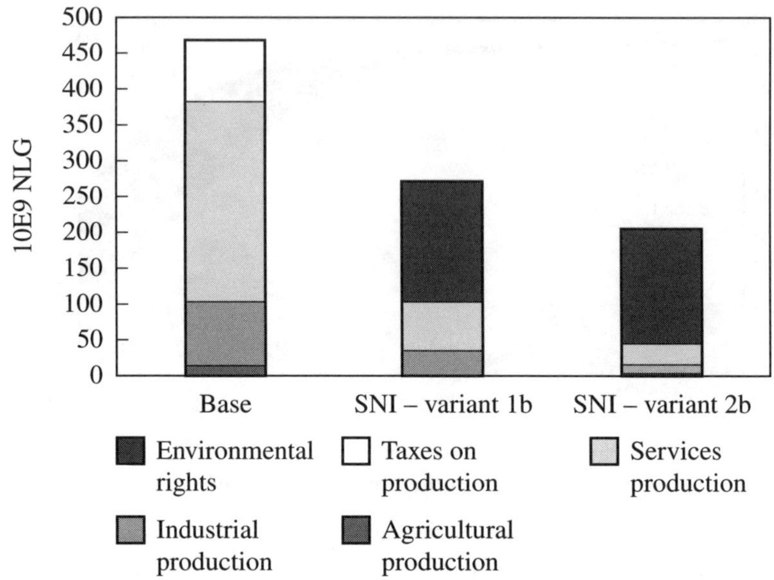

Figure 11.3B *Break-up of national product per sector: distribution over categories (variants 1b and 2b)*

than government expenditure when about 80 per cent of the sustainability standards are met. At that point, all existing taxes are replaced by revenues from environmental rights. The excess revenues that arise in case of full compliance to the sustainability standards are redistributed to private households as lump-sum payments. In SNI variant 1b, no less than about two-thirds of SNI is made up of the value of these environmental rights.

Figure 11.3B shows that the different way of treating imports and exports has a clear impact on the structure of production. Due to the fixed trade shares in SNI variant 2b, the possibilities for changing the structure of production are much smaller. Thus, agriculture can keep up a share in SNI variant 2b of 1.5 per cent as opposed 0.1 per cent in variant 1b, whereas manufacturing and services come out at substantially lower shares. The latter has also to do with the much higher prices for environmental rights in SNI variant 2b than in variant 1b, due to the limited reallocation possibilities of production in variant 2b. Consequently, the share of environmental rights is about two-thirds and 87 per cent in SNI variants 1b and 2b, respectively.

Figure 11.4A gives the development of the various income categories in SNI variant 1b. Income from the production factors capital and labour follow the general trend: a substantial reduction is observed after about three-quarters of the required emission reductions are achieved, especially

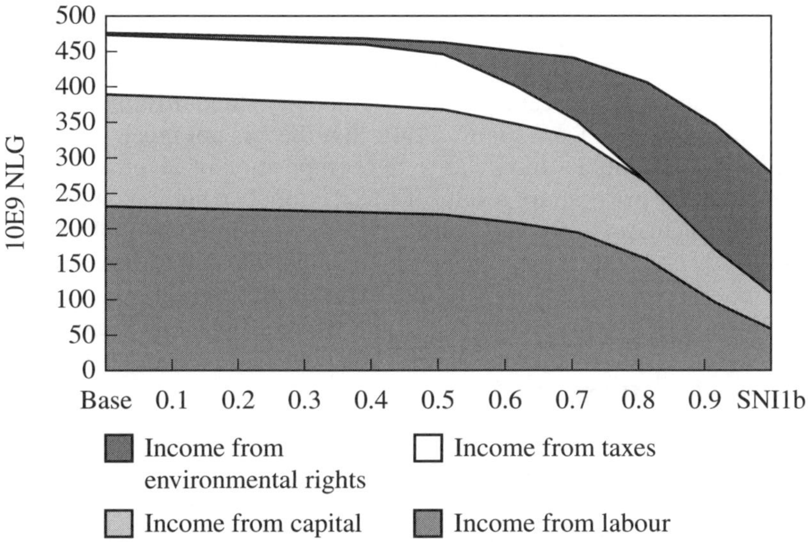

Figure 11.4A *Break-up of national income per production factor: from base to SNI (variant 1b)*

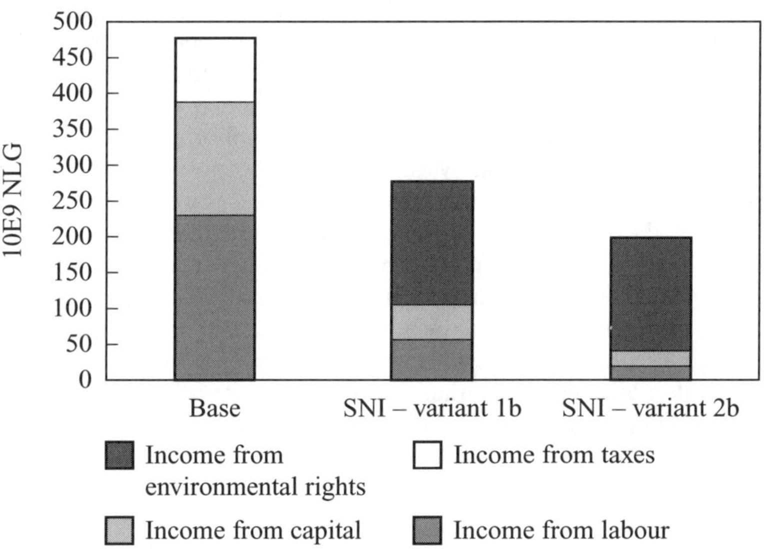

Figure 11.4B *Break-up of national income per production factor: distribution over categories (variants 1b and 2b)*

in labour income. In the SNI equilibrium of variant 1b, both income shares account for about 20 per cent. As already indicated before, existing taxes are more than completely replaced by the revenues from environmental rights after about 80 per cent of the sustainability standards are realized. Finally, it can be seen from Figure 11.4B that there is not much difference between SNI variants 1b and 2b as to the composition of income sources.

To sum up the preliminary results of this section, two findings stand out. First, SNI calculations are very sensitive to the way international trade is specified. Second, the expression in new equilibrium prices has a major impact on the composition of SNI, per expenditure category, the sectoral breakdown as well as per source of income. More insight will be gained by discussing the results of the various SNI calculations in old and new prices in detail in the next section.

5 PRELIMINARY RESULTS: DATA

5.1 Macroeconomic results

Tables 11.2–11.5 present the macroeconomic results of the four SNI variants. In comparing these tables it is quite clear that SNI variants 1a and 1b with constant relative world market prices are about 45–47 per cent lower than national income in the base situation, whereas SNI variants 2a and 2b with constant shares of imports and exports are about 64–66 per cent lower. The extent to which SNI drops is thus largely determined by the specification of international trade. The use of alternative sets of prices is of minor importance. This is not surprising if the scaling of new equilibrium prices on the level of old prices, as discussed above, is taken into account. By contrast, the use of old or new equilibrium prices has a major impact on the composition of SNI. Hence, the composition of the SNI variants 1a and 2a in old prices changes proportionally. SNI variants 1b and 2b in new equilibrium prices show drastic compositional changes. This is particularly due to the imputed prices for environmental rights. In the base situation at old prices these rights have a negligible value. At new equilibrium prices, however, the value of environmental rights outweighs all other SNI categories. It is also noteworthy that if an old set of prices is used to weigh the different components of SNI, national income and national product diverge.

5.2 Sectoral Results

Table 11.6 clearly shows that the changes in the structure of production are much more pronounced in SNI variants 1a and 1b as compared to SNI

Table 11.2 Macroeconomic results in billions of guilders: SNI variant 1a

	Base	SNI	Change (%)
National income	**471.10**	**247.45**	**−47**
Private households consumption	328.20	170.91	−48
Government consumption	74.79	39.15	−48
Net investments	41.19	19.87	−52
Trade balance	26.92	17.52	−35
Exports	*273.26*	*162.73*	*−40*
Imports	*−246.34*	*−145.21*	*−41*
National product	**471.09**	**260.94**	**−45**
Agricultural production	15.11	0.51	−97
Industrial production	86.87	79.43	−9
Services production	284.86	202.09	−29
Taxes on production	84.24	0.00	−100
Environmental rights	0.00	0.17	
Double-counting	0.00	−21.26	

Note: Constant world market prices; variables based on old prices.

Table 11.3 Macroeconomic results in billions of guilders: SNI variant 2a

	Base	SNI	Change (%)
National income	**471.10**	**171.03**	**−64**
Private households consumption	328.20	120.50	−63
Government consumption	74.79	28.12	−62
Net investments	41.19	10.57	−74
Trade balance	26.92	11.84	−56
Exports	*273.26*	*73.74*	*−73*
Imports	*−246.34*	*−61.91*	*−75*
National product	**471.09**	**161.29**	**−66**
Agricultural production	15.11	3.55	−77
Industrial production	86.87	32.26	−63
Services production	284.86	146.61	−49
Taxes on production	84.24	0.00	−100
Environmental rights	0.00	0.13	
Double-counting	0.00	−21.26	

Note: Constant trade shares; variables based on old prices.

Table 11.4 Macroeconomic results in billions of guilders: SNI variant 1b

	Base	SNI	Change (%)
National income	**471.09**	**252.31**	**−46**
Private households consumption	328.21	141.14	−57
Government consumption	74.79	82.23	10
Net investments	41.18	13.98	−66
Trade balance	26.90	14.96	−44
Exports	*273.10*	*138.99*	*−49*
Imports	*−246.20*	*−124.03*	*−50*
National product	**471.09**	**252.31**	**−46**
Agricultural production	15.11	0.31	−98
Industrial production	86.87	33.82	−61
Services production	284.86	73.10	−74
Taxes on production	84.24	0.00	−100
Environmental rights	0.00	166.62	
Double-counting	0.00	−21.55	

Note: Constant world market prices; new equilibrium prices.

Table 11.5 Macroeconomic results in billions of guilders: SNI variant 2b

	Base	SNI	Change (%)
National income	**471.09**	**178.00**	**−62**
Private households consumption	328.21	104.17	−68
Government consumption	74.79	56.40	−25
Net investments	41.18	6.33	−85
Trade balance	26.90	11.10	−59
Exports	*273.10*	*69.17*	*−75*
Imports	*−246.20*	*−58.07*	*−76*
National product	**471.09**	**178.00**	**−62**
Agricultural production	15.11	2.65	−82
Industrial production	86.87	10.99	−87
Services production	284.86	33.21	−88
Taxes on production	84.24	0.00	−100
Environmental rights	0.00	156.37	
Double-counting	0.00	−25.22	

Note: Constant trade shares; new equilibrium prices.

Table 11.6 Changes in the structure of production in SNI variants, in percentages

	Variants 1a–1b	Variants 2a–2b
Agriculture and fisheries	−97	−76
Oil and gas extraction	113	−64
Other mining and quarrying	−18	−81
Food industry	−81	−71
Textiles industry	−90	−71
Wood and furniture industry	29	−79
Paper and graphical industry	−68	−77
Petroleum refineries	166	−61
Chemical industry	−97	−77
Rubber and plastics industry	−82	−81
Building materials industry	−33	−80
Basic metal industry	−99	−86
Other metal industry	−48	−76
Other industries	−91	−75
Electricity supply	−60	−51
Other public utilities	−42	−55
Construction	−44	−73
Transport services	−70	−69
Environmental services	−100	−68
Other commercial services	−49	−67
Other non-commercial services	−51	−63

variants 2a and 2b. In SNI variants 1a and 1b, some sectors virtually disappear out of the Netherlands. These include the relatively environment-intensive sectors – agriculture, chemical industry, basic metal industry and environmental services.[2]

In SNI variants 2a and 2b, the impact of the sustainability standards range for (almost) all sectors between a 60 per cent and 80 per cent reduction. Basic metal industry production decreases most by 86 per cent; Electricity supply and other public utilities (including water and gas distribution) are relatively well off with a decrease of only 51 per cent and 55 per cent, respectively.

Some sectors are among the most severely hit in all SNI variants, such as agriculture, chemical industry, rubber and plastics industry and basic metal industry, whereas other sectors are among the least impacted in all SNI variants, surprisingly including the energy supply sectors and, less surprisingly, the other non-commercial services. However, this trend is certainly not general. As the most stringent environmental themes differ among the SNI variants, the sectors that are the most under pressure also differ. Moreover, the varying possibilities to substitute between goods (including substitution possibilities between domestic and foreign goods) influence the results.

The relatively favourable position of the energy supply sectors (oil and gas extraction, petroleum refineries, electricity supply and other public utilities) depends, among others, on the specific modelling of energy conservation measures. In the current model version, there is no direct link between energy conservation measures and reduced sectoral demand for energy as energy-related emissions could only be linked to output data. In future model versions, the energy-related technical measures will (hopefully) be linked to related energy demand.

Comparing the columns in Table 11.6, it is striking to see that the impact of the trade assumption is huge. In SNI variants 2a and 2b, the differences between the sectors mainly stem from the differences in substitution elasticities and the impact of these differences is clearly less.

The changes in consumption patterns as depicted in Table 11.7 are less substantial than the changes in production structure, especially for SNI variants 1a and 1b, and the differences between the SNI variants are not that great. The specification of international trade has little impact on the consumption pattern, but especially affects the overall decrease in consumption levels: in SNI variants 2a and 2b, the decrease is 15–20 percentage points larger.

There are some noteworthy differences between the sectors. These arise from different emission intensities, substitution possibilities and income elasticities of the various goods and services. The consumption of rubber and plastic products, basic metal products and environmental services is reduced more than average, whereas the consumption of food products, electricity supply and other public utilities decrease less than average. The latter goods and services include some essential expenditures (food, light, gas and water); these products have small income elasticities.

5.3 Environmental Results

This section presents the results for the environmental themes. First, the abatement expenditures are specified per SNI variant. Then the environmental expenditures and corresponding prices and volumes are presented.

In the variant 1a, where old prices are used and constant world market prices, the largest abatement expenditures are paid for reduction of climate emissions, see Table 11.8. These climate measures account for over 80 per cent of all abatement expenditures. On the other hand, the costs of

Table 11.7 Changes in the composition of consumption in SNI variants, in percentages

	Variants 1a–1b	Variants 2a–2b
Agriculture and fisheries	−42	−62
Oil and gas extraction	−70	−80
Other mining and quarrying	−53	−67
Food industry	−39	−59
Textiles industry	−50	−67
Wood and furniture industry	−55	−70
Paper and graphical industry	−45	−62
Petroleum refineries	−52	−65
Rubber and plastics industry	−59	−72
Building materials industry	−60	−71
Basic metal industry	−75	−88
Other metal industry	−56	−70
Other industries	−54	−68
Electricity supply	−39	−56
Other public utilities	−35	−55
Construction	−51	−64
Transport services	−47	−63
Environmental services	−61	−88
Other commercial services	−46	−61
Other non-commercial services	−49	−63

Table 11.8 Abatement expenditures in SNI variants in billions of guilders

Environmental theme	Variant 1a	Variant 2a	Variant 1b	Variant 2b
Climate change	1.15	0	1.17	0
Acidification	0.06	0.01	0.06	0.01
Eutrophication	0.00	0.94	0.00	1.12
VOC to air	0.07	0	0.07	0
Zinc to water	0.09	0.09	0.09	0.10
Total abatement expenditures	*1.37*	*1.04*	*1.39*	*1.23*

eutrophication measures are negligible in this variant. Since the single major source of the eutrophying emissions, the agricultural sector, will virtually disappear from the Netherlands, there is no reason to implement (costly) measures to reduce eutrophication emissions. In other words, the costs of the technical measures to reduce emissions of P and N (the eutrophying emissions) are for most measures higher than the costs of the volume measures to reduce agricultural production (forgone value added).

In variant 2a, the total abatement costs do not differ much from the first variant. However, the distribution of these costs over environmental themes is completely reversed: climate abatement costs are now absent, while the vast majority of the abatement costs are due to eutrophication abatement measures. From Table 11.11 it follows that climate emission in SNI variant 2a come out below the sustainability standard. Consequently, environmental rights are in abundance and the costs of climate rights and the costs of climate abatement is zero. The reason that the climate emissions are below the sustainability standard is that these emissions are reduced as a side effect of the overall drastic reduction in economic activities. This is more likely to occur for climate change than for other themes, as the climate emissions are relatively evenly spread over the various sectors. Consequently, a reduction in the production of one sector to achieve the standard for a particular theme will almost automatically also mean a reduction in greenhouse gases. The costs of reducing VOC emissions are zero for the same reason.

Agricultural production cannot be shifted abroad in SNI variant 2a. Still, the eutrophication standard has to be met. Consequently, costly technical measures have to be implemented, leading to relatively high eutrophication abatement costs.

In SNI variants 1b and 2b, a similar picture emerges: in variant 1b the climate measures constitute the largest cost category, and this appears to be the case for the eutrophication measures in variant 2b. Comparing SNI variants 1a and 2a (abatement measured in old prices) on the one hand and SNI variants 1b and 2b (based on new equilibrium prices) on the other hand, it turns out that the new equilibrium prices are not drastically different from the old prices.

Total environmental expenditures are equal to the total revenues from environmental rights as collected by the government. This can be checked by comparing the last row in Table 11.9 with the rows for environmental rights in Tables 11.2 through to 11.5.

In SNI variants 1a and 2a, environmental expenditures are very small, as old prices are used for valuation.[3] Note that the costs for climate rights are relatively small in comparison to the other themes.

Table 11.9 Environmental expenditures in SNI variants in billions of guilders

Environmental theme	Variant 1a	Variant 2a	Variant 1b	Variant 2b
Climate change	0.01	0.01	22.11	0
Acidification	0.05	0.05	0.35	0.08
Eutrophication	0.04	0.04	0.04	26.34
VOC to air	0.07	0.03	0.89	0
Zinc to water	0.00	0.00	143.24	129.95
Total environmental expenditures	*0.17*	*0.13*	*166.62*	*156.37*

The difference in environmental expenditures between SNI variants 1a and 2a is mainly caused by the lower emissions of VOCs in variant 2a. As already indicated above, the climate and VOC emissions turn out to be substantially below the sustainability standards in SNI variants 2a and 2b; see also Table 11.11.

The new equilibrium prices for environmental rights are a multitude of the old prices. This is not surprising, as the total amount of emission rights is substantially reduced in the SNI equilibrium. In SNI variant 1b, most environmental expenditures go to climate emissions and zinc emissions. The huge costs of the zinc rights can be explained by the relatively strict sustainability standard, especially in comparison with the amount of emissions that can be avoided through technical measures: 80 per cent of emissions have to be reduced while only 36 per cent can be reduced by means of technical measures. Consequently, costly volume measures (economic restructuring) have to be taken to reduce zinc emissions. This will lead to extremely high prices for the emission rights and a substantial loss of national income. For comparison, the expenditures for zinc rights amount to some 30 per cent of SNI variant 1b.

In SNI variant 2b, the expenditures on zinc emissions are still very high. In addition, expenditures on eutrophication are over 26 billion guilders. Expenditures on climate rights are zero in this variant, as the remaining climate emissions are below the standard. In total, the expenditures on environmental rights are slightly lower than in variant 1b, but the distribution over the themes is quite different. Only the dominant position of the zinc emissions remains.

It turns out that the acidification rights are relatively cheap in all SNI variants. Apparently, the acid emissions can be reduced rather cheaply, not in the last instance due to the high portion of acidifying emissions that can be reduced through technical measures.

Table 11.10 Price of environmental theme rights in SNI variants in millions of guilders per theme unit

Environmental theme	Variant 1a	Variant 2a	Variant 1b	Variant 2b
Climate change	0.185	0.185	345.644	0
Acidification	5.233	5.233	35.947	8.514
Eutrophication	1.026	1.026	1.034	753.638
VOC to air	0.280	0.280	3.410	0
Zinc to water	0.011	0.011	734.576	666.394

Table 11.11 Environmental theme emissions in the base year and SNI variants

Environmental theme	Units	Base 1990	Variants 1a–1b	Variants 2a–2b
Climate change	10E9 CO_2 equivalents	237	64	42
Acidification	10E9 acid equivalents	33.5	10	10
Eutrophication	10E6 1 kg P equivalents	318	35	35
VOC to air	10E6 kilograms	440	260	110
Zinc to water	10E3 kg Zn	975	195	195

Table 11.10 shows the prices of the environmental themes in millions of guilders per unit of theme emissions. As these theme units are non-comparable, the price differences between the various themes are not analysed. The huge price differences between most old prices and the new equilibrium prices (compare SNI variants 1a–2a with 1b–2b) clearly demonstrate the impact on relative prices of complying with sustainability standards. For example, in SNI variant 1b, an emission right for one tonne of carbon equivalent amounts to 346 guilders.

The reader can check the revenues from the environmental rights by multiplying the environmental theme emissions reported in Table 11.11 by the price of these emissions reported in Table 11.10. As this product is calculated in millions of guilders, they correspond to the environmental expenditures reported in Table 11.9 in billions of guilders, when divided by thousand.

As already indicated, in SNI variants 1a and 1b, all sustainability standards are exactly met, while in SNI variants 2a and 2b the themes climate change and VOCs are below their targets.

6 FINAL REMARKS

So far, the main emphasis of the research was on the construction of an applied general equilibrium model that is good enough to give reasonably credible results. Although this target seems to be met, many improvements, refinements and sophistications can still be made. Many of these are already indicated in the text. Without being exhaustive, the following points deserve special attention.

1. The coverage of relevant environmental functions (themes) is not complete. Especially land use and solid waste ask for inclusion.
2. The modelling of international trade needs further elaboration.
3. The information on technical options of abatement and their costs, on which the presently used cost curves are based, is not entirely up to date. New material on applicable technologies and costs needs to be incorporated.
4. In the present model, emissions are linked to outputs. It has correctly been argued that part of the emissions could better be linked to certain types of inputs, for instance: CO_2 emissions to fuel imputs. Modelling emissions through links with (fuel) inputs will allow a better reflection of substitution possibilities.
5. Per theme, reduction of emissions through technical measures is now modelled through an abatement sector which 'delivers reduction' to the other sectors. This implies that, per theme, the shape of the cost curve of technical abatement is the same for all sectors. It is necessary to differentiate the cost curves of technical abatement between sectors and to differentiate the expenditure effects of technical abatement
6. A whole gamut of sensitivity analyses can be made by changing and modifying assumptions that underlie the SNI calculations. Among the variables and assumptions that can be modified are: base year, elasticities, assumptions on foreign trade, cost curves and old versus new prices.

Finally, attractive, understandable ways of communication must be found to inform the public and politicians, as well as the scientific community, on the reached results, their meaning and their limitations.

APPENDIX THE COST CURVES PER ENVIRONMENTAL THEME

Data Sources

For climatic change, use was made of a study, so far grey literature, by de Boer and Bosch (1995), and the other themes are based on a study by Dellink et al. (1997).

The database on costs of reduction of greenhouse gases is, with respect to CO_2, mainly derived from the ICARUS database (Blok, 1991; Blok et al., 1991) and from the MARKAL model of ECN (Okken, 1991; Okken et al., 1992); with respect to other greenhouse gases, a variety of data sources was used (see de Boer and Bosch, 1995). For the other themes, the main data source was RIVM's RIM^+ model (RIM^+ is the improved version of RIM, a Dutch acronym for Computation and Information system for the Environment; this system contains emission coefficients and emission factors for various economic sectors, as well as technical reduction measures with their costs and their effects on emissions). The measures, as well as their costs and reduction effects, reflect as much as possible the technological state of the art of the early 1990s.

As already indicated in Section 2, dehydration and soil contamination are special cases, in the sense that they are inheritances from the past, not caused by annual (1990) emissions. The reduction costs are not costs of emission reduction but total costs of cleaning up and/or restoration. The costs consist totally of 'avoidable' costs, for volume measures are not applicable. The databases that were used are the *Nationale Milieuverkenning 2* (National Environmental Reconnaissance 2) (RIVM, 1991) and the *Milieubalans 1996* (Environmental Balance 1996) (RIVM, 1996) on soil contamination, and the *Watersysteem Verkenningen* (Water System Reconnaissance) (RIZA, 1996) on dehydration.

Climate Change

The greenhouse gases (GHG) that cause climatic change are mainly CO_2, methane, nitrous oxide, and CFCs and halons. The effects of these substances on climate change, as well as the duration of their effects, vary. The way in which these GHGs can be aggregated into CO_2 equivalents is not unambiguous, but depend on the mix of emissions (and emission reductions). The coefficients that were chosen to aggregate the GHGs into CO_2 equivalents are described in de Boer and Bosch (1995).

Technical measures and costs to reduce fossil fuel use, and thus CO_2 emissions, were taken from the ICARUS database (Blok, 1991; Blok et al., 1991), which comprises about 300 measures ranging from more efficient energy use and co-generation to local solar power systems, and from ECN's MARKAL model (Okken, 1991; Okken et al., 1992).

Measures to reduce methane emissions were collected from various sources (see de Boer and Bosch, 1995) and comprise changes in the composition of animal fodder, more efficient use of manure, measures in the production and distribution of natural gas, and measures at waste dumps. The measures of changing animal fodder and of more efficient management of manure are also effective for reduction of nitrous oxide. And the measures to reduce CFCs and halons consist of replacing them by HCFCs (with much lower warming potential) or by other substances (VROM, 1990). The resulting marginal cost curve is depicted in Figure 11.A.1.

Many measures have negative net costs (corrected to zero costs, see Section 3). The reason for negative cost figures lies in considerable energy savings. Negative costs options include a number of measures in the energy-intensive greenhouse agriculture, energy efficiency measures in households and transport, energy saving by intensifying aluminium recycling, introduction of co-generation in the chemical industry, the foodstuff industry and other industries, plus a large variety of smaller energy savings in all industrial sectors, in households and in office buildings.

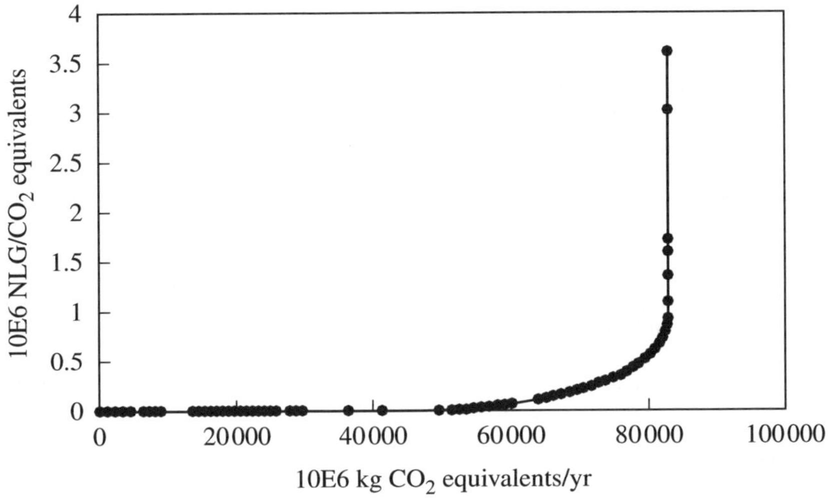

Figure 11.A1 *Marginal costs of reduction of greenhouse gases*

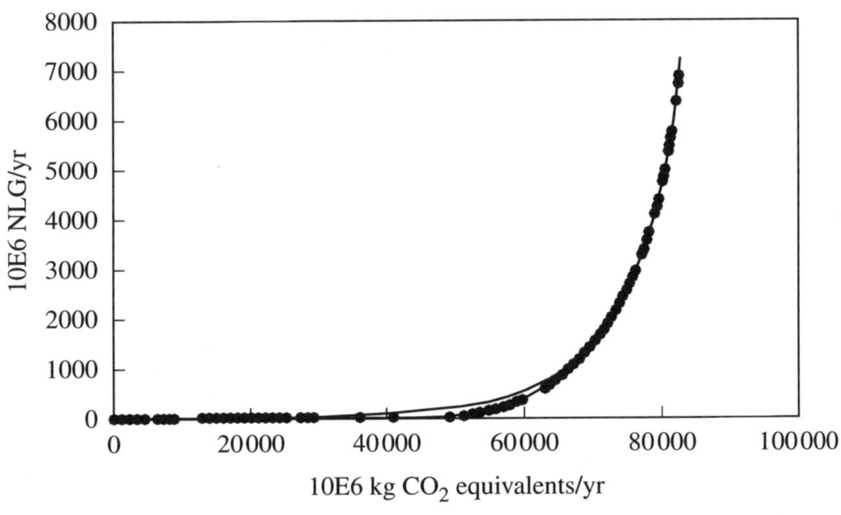

Figure 11.A2 *Total costs of reduction of greenhouse gases*

Measures with small, but positive net costs are situated in the middle of the curve. Apart from additional energy saving measures, they consist of CFC reduction and reduction of methane (CH_4) and nitrous oxide (N_2O).

Marginal costs are gradually rising to guilders 0.40/kg CO_2–eq/yr with measures such as replacement of CFCs and HCFCs in cooling installations, reuse of waste warmth in the ferro metal industry, double glazing and roof insulation in houses, the use of wind and hydro in electricity generation.

Measures with marginal costs between guilders 0.40–0.80/kg CO_2–eq/yr include building of energy efficient houses; wall and floor insulation, and use of biogas from manure.

At the right hand side of the curve, with marginal costs rising steeply from guilders 0.80/kg CO_2–eq/yr, one finds solar energy in houses and the use of reverse osmosis in food industry for saving fossil fuels. The effectiveness of these most expensive options is rather minimal.

The curve of total costs is depicted in Figure 11.A.2, together with the approximation by a CES curve.

Acidification

The substances that cause acidification are NO_x, SO_2 and ammonia (NH_3). The first two are mainly related to the combustion of fossil fuels, the last one to agriculture. Emissions of the three substances can be aggregated into acidification equivalents (AE) as follows: 1 million kg $NO_x = 0.022$ AE; 1 million kg $SO_2 = 0.031$ AE; and 1 million kg $NH_3 = 0.059$ AE. The measures to reduce acidification were taken from the RIM^+ database and comprise about 170 options. The total cost curve for reduction of acidification, and the approximation with a CES function, are given in Figure 11.A.3.

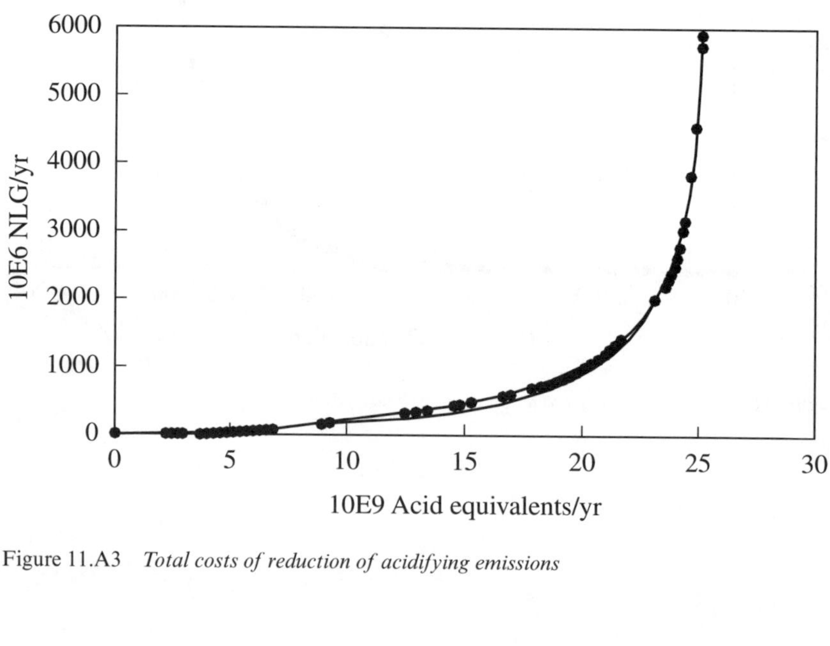

Figure 11.A3 *Total costs of reduction of acidifying emissions*

At the left-hand side of the curve, there are two measures with negative net reduction costs (corrected to zero costs), related to the restriction of maximum speed in traffic. Their effect on acidification is small. The next cost-effective measure is injecting manure in agricultural land, with a very substantial effect of 2.2 reduction in AE at zero costs. Then, after a number of rather insignificant measures with respect to both costs and effects, the next sizeable measures are leanburn and flue gas circulation in gas driven engines; the cost effectiveness is relatively high. Thereafter follows a number of measures in refineries; their costs are actually underestimated as the operation and maintenance costs are unknown and therefore not included. The next sizeable measures relate to emission standards for river-crafts, trucks, diesel buses and tractors. An effective, but more costly measure, with a reduction in SO_2 of 3.3 AE, is the introduction of coal gasification/STAG for electricity generation, costing 143 million guilders. Measures relating to flue gas desulphurization in power plants and the reduction of process emissions of SO_2 in industry are effective, but costly.

Measures that reduce emissions even further than a 25 AE reduction include emission standards for petrol-fuelled cars, reduction of maximum speed of vans and (very high costs and low effects) LowNO_x burners for combi-installations for electricity, and measures to reduce fuel evaporation in LPG and petrol-fuelled cars.

With exclusion of the measures with the highest cost/effect ratio, 25.5 AE can be prevented at a total cost of 5100 million guilders.

Eutrophication

The substances that cause eutrophication are phosphorus (P) and nitrogen (N). They mainly stem from agricultural use of fertilizer and manure in agriculture, but emissions of NH_3 and NO_x contribute as well. The substances can be aggregated

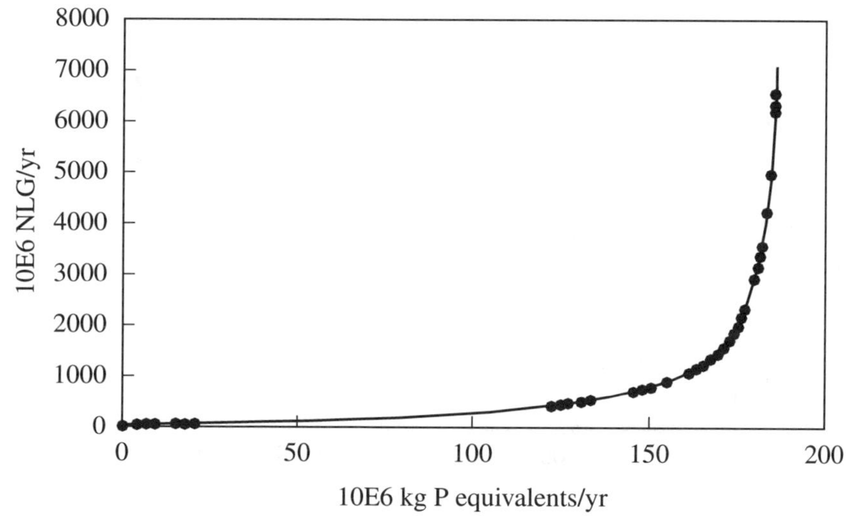

Figure 11.A4 *Total costs of reduction of eutrophying emissions*

into eutrophication equivalents (EE) as follows: 1 kg P = 1 EE; 1 kg N = 0,1 EE. The measures to reduce eutrophication, as well as their costs, are taken from RIM$^+$, and amount to a number of 145 options, of which 125 are also present in the cost curve of reduction of acidification. The curve, together with the CES approximation, is given in Figure 11.A.4.

When the measures for reduction of emissions to air (NO_x, NH_3) are omitted, the total reduction of eutrophication in agriculture, industry and sewerage that can be achieved amounts to about 130 EE, as compared to a total maximal reduction of avoidable emissions of 185 EE. The most important measure consists of elimination of excess manure, which reduces over 100 EE at a yearly cost of about 500 million guilders. Due to lack of data this measure could not be subdivided into its components, which include also dephosphating and denitrification of wastewater from industry and households. Further steps in the reduction relate to additional measures in sewerage and water purification, and the least cost-effective measure at the very end of the curve is relocation of farms: a reduction of 0.02 EE at the fabulous cost of 200 million guilders yearly.

Zinc to Water

Zinc was chosen as an example for water pollution with heavy metals. The number of measures to reduce zinc is limited, only 13, of which 1 had to be omitted as it was excluded by another measure. Of the resulting 12 measures, the costs of 5 are zero, or estimated at zero for lack of data. These are various measures such as adaptation of roof gutters and pipes and of crash barriers (zero costs) and a ban on emissions of phosphorous gypsum (costs unknown). The first measure with positive costs is the use of coatings in the construction sector. Other effective measures are adaptation of greenhouses and a fourth phase in water purification. The total cost curve and its approximation with a CES curve are given in Figure 11.A.5.

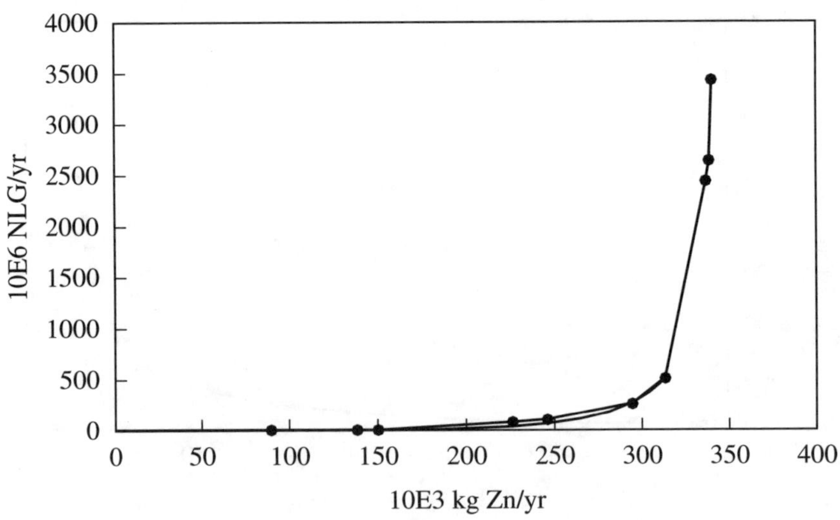

Figure 11.A5 *Total costs of reduction of zinc emissions to water*

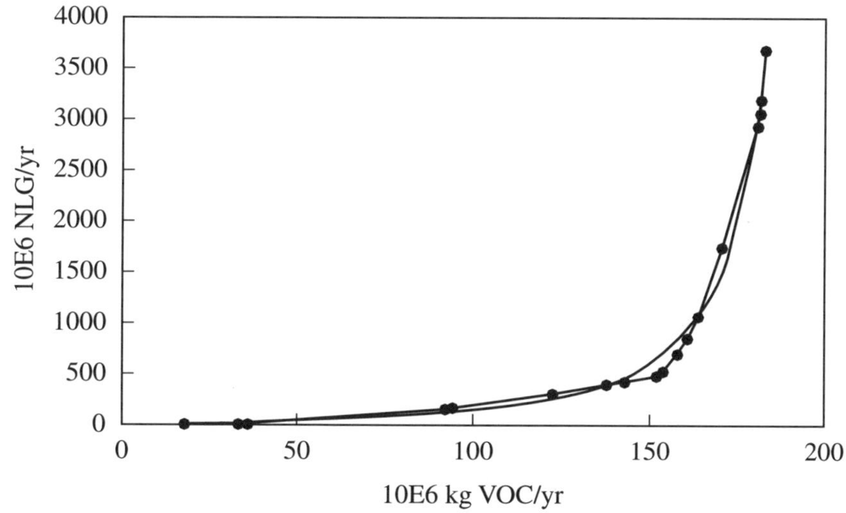

Figure 11.A6 *Total costs of reduction of VOC emissions*

VOC

For the cost curve of VOC (volatile organic compounds, in particular hydrocarbons), 39 measures were identified, of which 8 were deleted because they were excluded by other measures, while twice two measures had to be combined due to sequentiality. This results in 29 points on the curve. The measures with the best cost-effectiveness at the left hand side of the curve relate to households, the construction sectors, industry, services and the energy sector. About 150 kilotonnes can be reduced at relatively low costs of about 500 million guilders yearly. The measures at the right-hand side are mainly within the target group of traffic and transportation, and are mostly not primarily aimed at VOC reduction. They include emission standards for river crafts, locomotives and liquified petroleum gas (LPG) vans and measures to prevent fuel evaporation. The total reduction potential amounts to about. 200 kilotonnes at total costs of about 3500 million guilders. The total cost curve and its approximation by a CES curve are given in Figure 11.A.6.

Dehydration

For the estimation of costs to reduce the arid/dehydrated area, use was made of a study of policy scenarios by RIZA (1996). The scenarios are each composed of a variety of measures, but due to data shortage it was not possible to carry out the analysis on a measure-by-measure basis. Measures of the scenarios include a variety of local small scale projects such as: adaptation of the water system, depoldering, extraction of drinking water, extraction of industrial water and reduction of irrigation water use. The time horizons of the scenarios differ, which leads to smoothing out the cost differences. Table 11.A.1. depicts the annual costs of full and sustained dehydration.

Table 11.A1 Costs for dehydration and soil pollution

	Total costs (10E9 NLG)	Annual costs (10E6 NLG/yr)
Dehydration		861.0
Soil pollution	408.0	20,400.0

Soil Contamination

Estimation of the cost curve of cleaning up soil contamination from the past is a heroic effort. Data are weak or lacking and the estimation should be interpreted, at most, as an indication of the order of magnitude.

The first and possibly largest problem is that no complete inventory of contaminated locations is available. In recent years, the number of suspect locations grew with a factor 200 from about 3000 to 600000. The 600000 locations were, admittedly and necessarily roughly, categorized in three classes: not severely contaminated, severely contaminated (not-urgent) and severely contaminated (urgent).

The bodies involved in cleaning up soil contamination are various, but for estimation of the costs a restriction was made to locations under the responsibility of provinces, with some additional information on private cleaning costs. Not only are the types of contamination different, also the cleaning techniques and their extent of effectiveness differ. The range of costs shows a factor 30 or more between the cheaper and the most expensive techniques. The estimation of costs for total sustainability is in the range of 230–450 billion guilders (total, not yearly costs; see Table 11.A.1.).

Final remarks

The cost curves presented in this Appendix are estimates with weaknesses. They are an approximation to which various improvements can be made. First, the date bases that were used are not complete. Second, the discount rate that is used in the cost curve of climatic change is different from the one that is used for the other themes; this is inconsistent. The basic view behind the choice of the discount rate is that the rate is chosen as perceived by the target groups themselves. This would imply a discount rate that equals the real interest rate plus an additional percentage, which may vary per sector, reflecting risk and uncertainty. It seems to be correct in an AGE model, where each sector is supposed to optimize its position within the market forces as perceived by the sector itself, that this internal interest rate is used, rather than the (lower) social discount rate. But the application of the basic view was not uniform in the studies that were the base of our cost curves.

Third, the costs of some measures were double counted. There is an overlap in measures with respect to climate change and to acidification (in particular energy saving measures) and with respect to acidification and eutrophication (measures on N). A measure can be seen as the primary aim from the perspective of one theme, but the same measure may also be a primary aim in another theme. In the used methodology, the costs of that measure are then double counted. It is by far not obvious how this flaw in the analysis could be corrected for in the stylized modelling structure.

Fourth, excises and (for households) VAT are included in the prices. From a macroeconomic viewpoint one might argue that factor prices should be used. However, the sectors in the model react on prices as perceived by themselves, so including excises and VAT is correct. Moreover, to the extent that revenues of emission charges replace taxes, excises and VAT should diminish. But as excises and VAT are an integral part of the cost curves, they cannot be distinguished. This leads to price distortions that are difficult to justify.

The incompleteness and the double-counting are influences that result in an overestimation of the costs of reduction. Whether the inconsistency in the discount rate and the inclusion of excises and VAT lead to a bias is unclear, but all four points mentioned above lead to inaccuracy. Although the estimated cost curves are based on the best available information, an improvement of the estimates can be achieved in further research. And how to deal correctly with the double-counting requires, in addition, an analytical effort.

NOTES

1. Hueting argues that environmental preferences can only partially be revealed by expenditures to compensate or restore the loss of functions, whereas methods such as contingent valuation cannot yield reliable data (Hueting and de Boer, Chapter 2, this volume; Kuik, 1999)
2. Note that the environmental services sector does not include abatement activities, but consists of waste-handling facilities.
3. To be precise, the prices used here to calculate the environmental expenditures are based on imputed prices for environmental rights, using the actual emission in the base year as the total volume of rights that are distributed.

REFERENCES

Blok, K. (1991), 'On the reduction of carbon dioxide emissions', thesis, Utrecht University, Utrecht.

Blok, K., E. Worrell, R.A.W. Albers and R.F.A. Cuelenaere (1991), *Data on Energy Conservation Techniques for the Netherlands*, Report W. 90008, Department of Science, Technology and Society, Utrecht University.

De Boer, B. and P. Bosch (1995), 'The greenhouse effect: an example of the prevention cost approach', paper prepared for the second meeting of the London group on National Accounts and the Environment, Washington, 15–17 March.

Dellink, R., R. Gerlagh and M. Hofkes (1999), 'An applied general equilibrium model to calculate a sustainable national income for the Netherlands: technical model description, Version 1.0', in H. Verbruggen (ed.), *Interim Report on Calculations of a Sustainable National Income Accounting to Hueting's Methodology*, Institute for Environmental Studies, Vrije Universiteit, Amsterdam.

Dellink, R., F. van der Woerd and B. de Boer (1997), *Kosteneffectiviteit van Milieuthema's*, IVM-R97/10, Institute for Environmental Studies, Vrije Universiteit, Amsterdam.

Den Butter, F.A.G. and H. Verbruggen (1994), 'Measuring the trade-off between economic growth and a clean environment'. *Environmental and Resource Economics*, 4, 187–208.

Hueting, R. (1992), 'Correcting national income for environmental losses: a practical solution for a theoretical dilemma, in J.J. Krabbe and W.J.M. Heijman (eds), *National Income and Nature: Externalities, Growth and Steady State*, Kluwer Academic Publishers, Dordrecht/Boston/London.

Hueting, R. and L. Reijnders (1998), 'Sustainability is an objective concept', *Ecological Economics*, 27, 139–47.

Kuik, O.J. (1999), 'Accounting for the environment – an overview and assessment of approaches', in H. Verbruggen (ed.), *Interim Report on Calculations of a Sustainable National Income According to Hueting's Methodology*, Institute for Environmental Studies, Vrije Universiteit, Amsterdam.

Okken, P.A. (1991), *CO_2 Reduction Consensus? A Conceptual Framework for Global CO_2 Reduction Targets, the Importance of Energy Technology Development*, Report nr. ECN-RX-91-093ECN, Petten.

Okken, P.A., P. Lako, D. Gerbers, T. Kram and J. Ybema (1992), 'CO_2 removal in competition with other options for reducing CO_2 remissions', *Energy Conversion and Management*, 33, 6–10.

RIVM (1991), *Nationale Milieuverkenning 2*, Bilthoven.

RIVM (1996), *Milieubalans 1996*, Bilthoven.

RIZA (1996), *Watersysteem Verkenningen*, mimeo.

VROM (1990), CFK aktieprogramma. Fen samenwerkingsproject van overheden en bedrijfsleven, VROM-rapport, 00301/6–90, The Hague.

VROM (1994), *Methodiek Milieukosten*, Publicatiereeks Milieubeheer 1994/1, The Hague.

VROM (1998), *Kosten en baten in het milieubeleid, definities en berekeningsmethoden*, Publicatiereeks Milieustrategie 1998/6, The Hague.

PART FOUR

Conclusion

12. An appreciation of Dr Roefie Hueting's ecological work

Robert Goodland

1 INTRODUCTION

This chapter honours the ecological contributions made by the economist Dr Roefie Hueting, and constitutes a biographical appreciation of his life work in this field. Hueting's career is long and extraordinarily productive – mainly in economics. His economic contributions are dealt with by other authors in this volume, and are outlined in the bibliography appended to this chapter. On its own, the attached bibliography attests to Hueting's enormous contribution to ecological economics, and reinforces this tribute. Hueting has contributed greatly to the interface between economics and ecology or environment in many spheres. This chapter briefly outlines what, in my opinion, are his main achievements in ecological economics, with emphasis on the former.

Three caveats. First, let me warn readers that I am an ecologist, and possess no background in economics. However, I have had the great fortune of meeting Dr Hueting many times, of reading and using much of his *œuvre*, and have been party to many discussions of his work by himself, Salah El Serafy and Herman Daly over the last 17 years. The second caveat is that this chapter is a personal appreciation by a friend and admirer, and does not pretend to be a comprehensive audit. The third caveat is my lack of familiarity with the Dutch language. This chapter is based only on Hueting's publications in English. Because of this, his contributions are significantly understated in this chapter. Wherever possible, I have lifted passages directly from Dr Hueting's English translations.

2 HUETING'S CONTRIBUTION TO ECOLOGICAL ECONOMICS

In the early 1960s Hueting observed that children could no longer play in city neighbourhoods, because of severe risks of traffic accidents. Medical literature revealed that lack of play could lead to decreased learning capacity and other medical problems. The recommended solutions were medical treatment and playgrounds. Hueting realized that this important loss of welfare was excluded from the System of National Accounts (SNA), whereas medical treatment and playgrounds were included. In addition, he noted that road building is entered in the SNA, but not the loss – by the roads – of environmental and recreational values, as well as peace and quiet. From the ecological literature, Hueting concluded that current market prices provide wrong signals about the relative scarcity of economic goods, leading to misallocation of resources, while the figures of national income provide wrong signals about society's economic success.

In 1969 Hueting founded the Department for Environmental Statistics at the Netherlands Central Bureau of Statistics, a multidisciplinary team which he led until 16 December 1994. The department produces statistics on the whole field of the environment, including species and resources, both in physical and in monetary terms, and makes calculations in order to arrive at alternative national income figures, corrected for environmental losses, alongside traditional official figures. For both the economic and statistical part of this research Hueting introduced the concept of possible uses of our biophysical surroundings, named environmental functions or simply: functions. Hueting insisted that when one function is used at the expense of another function, or threatens to do so in the future, the environment has an economic aspect. This is Hueting's main link between economics and ecology, and an enormous advance in our understanding.

Hueting's seminal work is his 1974 book *New Scarcity and Economic Growth*. Many of his subsequent achievements over the following 25 years can be traced back to passages in that book. Hueting had been cogitating on the ideas formally presented in *New Scarcity* since the 1960s (see 'Chronology'), and had published on the quantification of environmental functions, the flawed concept of throughput growth as a national goal, and the error of excluding environmental values from statistics.

New Scarcity reminded us that economics is the science of scarcity. When something is abundant in relation to wants or needs, economics omits it. Only when something becomes scarce (shortages with respect to wants) does economics admit it for attention. The environment, such as breathable air, potable water, non-human species, had been abundant, hence of no concern to economics. *New Scarcity* made the case that 'environmental functions' had become scarce so that it had become irrational to continue to exclude them from economics, from national accounts and from measurements of national income. I believe Hueting originated the useful term 'environmental function' published in December 1969 and 1970a. This led to great advances in our understanding of substitutability and sustainability. Unfortunately, *New*

Scarcity was not published in English until 1980 because of obstruction and delays for six years after its translation, which had been financed by the World Wide Fund for Nature (WWF). North-Holland had sold the translation to a British publisher, who had been attracted by the publicity around the book. After six years, economics Nobellist Jan Tinbergen and Netherlands Economics Minister Langman felt it was so valuable that they urged North-Holland to buy the manuscript back and to publish it immediately.

I first heard of Hueting through his publications of the 1970s showing that it would be economically rational to clean the Rhine (Hueting, 1978). The 1970s Rhine was similar to the 1970s Lake Erie and to the 1990s Black and Aral Seas. The two latter are dying faster every day and we seem to be accepting that nothing can be done to restore them to health. Hueting's Rhine work was a tremendous boost to ecologists who were harangued that moribund ecosystems, such as Lake Eire, the Rhine, Ohio's Cayuhoga River that used to catch fire many times a year, could not be revived, and that it would be uneconomic to try to do so. Hueting continued to quantify and prove his ideas on the value of environmental functions. Because Hueting showed that under different assumptions than the ones made in the official cost–benefit analyses, it would be economically rational to clean such waterbodies. The Rhine, Cayuhoga and Lake Erie are today vastly improved in water quality.

Hueting had made the important point in *New Scarcity* that all 'environment' falls outside the SNA. Most of his work since then has been to rectify this omission that is so dangerous for human society and the future of our world. He sought to get SNA to include the value of environmental functions by costing the measures that would be necessary to restore and maintain those functions. This became known as 'standards of sustainability'. This was one of the beginnings of Hueting's valuation of environmental functions and expansion of the powerful, but ill-applied, tool of cost–benefit analysis.

3 ENVIRONMENTAL COST–BENEFIT ANALYSIS

Besides his work on statistics and the relation between production growth and environmental conservation, Hueting contributed significantly to the field of cost–benefit analysis (CBA). Always pragmatic and courageous, Hueting applied his improved cost–benefit methodologies to a nationally important environmental controversy. He criticized the official CBA of the construction of a polder in the Balgzand part of the Waddensea, an internationally important estuary. The official CBA of the Waddensea Commission ('s-Gravenhage, 1974) advised the Government to build the gigantic polder. Hueting's main objection was that the official CBA-assigned value of one hectare of the Waddensea estuary was set at the same value as one hectare of marginal agricultural land (the category of land with the lowest revenue/ha). That was the value officially set for nature areas by the Netherlands Government. In his review of the official CBA, Hueting observed: 'This is not valuing at all, because it gives the Government the value which the same Government had already decided upon'. When many values of environmental functions of ecosystems are excluded from economic analysis, of course it appears as though the ecosystems, river, or wetland and so on, are not worth saving. How to value environmental functions or services is a tremendous advance promoted by Hueting. Hueting's criticism led to setting up a new CBA in which he participated,[1] and ultimately to the abandonment of the national polder plan.

He argues that when long-term environmental costs and benefits are involved, the common use of the market interest rate (as the discount rate in CBA) implies that society's preferences for sustainable use of the environment amount to zero. This strong assumption, which cannot be proven, is probably incorrect. Nevertheless most cost–benefit analyses, such as those of the World Bank, are based on this assumption (Hueting, 1991a).

Hueting then made the important point, which originated in *New Scarcity*, that even if the sum total of all standards for breathable air, potable water, healthy soil and so on, were fully achieved, that would still be inadequate; it would not be enough. Although our survival depends on meeting such standards, the world would still be unsustainable. The main category of environmental functions still excluded is biodiversity; the functions provided by non-human species, such as pollination, recycling and resilience. This became formalized as lack of sustainability. Hueting was one of the earliest and remains one of the clearest that the concept of sustainability mandates four goals: (1) a stable human population; (2) stable consumption (decreasing overconsumption of the rich; increasing underconsumption of the poor, both by a stable human population); (3) transition to renewable energies; and (4) recycling. These four goals all seem feasible, although overdue, except for reserving enough physical space, habitat or area for biodiversity. Hueting rightly points out that halting the human pre-emption of non-human biodiversity habitat is the issue most in doubt at the moment.

4 NETHERLANDS NATIONAL SUSTAINABLE INCOME

One of the earliest signs of Hueting's entry into what became known as 'sustainable national income' was the scenario study of Hueting and Theo

Potma in the early 1980s. This scenario study estimated the consequences on the production and employment levels of an economic policy that shifts priority away from production growth, and towards conserving the environment and natural resources. In this exercise, a shift in the direction of environment-conserving activities is achieved by pollution control, both by technological fixes, and by taxing the polluter. The idea of taxing polluters was put forward early on by Hueting. In the early 1970s, Hueting assisted the Ministers of Health and Environment Dr Roelof Kruisinga and Irene Vorrink by providing economic arguments for the first environmental legislation in the Netherlands, introducing the 'the polluter pays principle', later adopted by the whole Organization for Economic Cooperation and Development (OECD), and much of the United Nations, although not yet by the USA. Under this scenario, incomes simultaneously decreased in proportion to the costs of the measures taken.[2] The outcome of the scenario was control of production growth, compared with a traditional growth scenario, increased employment and a substantial slowing of environmental degradation (Hueting, 1987d).

Hueting then spent the next many years estimating 'sustainable national income' for the whole of the Netherlands. This was the first time any nation's accounts were revised through the lens of sustainability. The results of the Netherlands' revised 'sustainable national income' became available for the first time at the April 1999 conference on Hueting's life work. If the value of environmental functions is taken into account in SNA, what would such sustainable national income look like? The results are staggering for three reasons.

First, from Hueting's analysis of the System of National Accounts (SNA) in the early 1980s it emerged that by far the greatest contribution to growth of national income is generated by precisely those activities that harm the environment most, by their use of space, soil and resources, or by the pollution they generate, in both production and consumption.

Second, in terms of the SNA, environment-conserving activities represent a smaller volume (of SNA) than environment-burdening. 'Thus, a bicycle-kilometer, a sweater, an extra blanket, beans, and a holiday by train represent a smaller volume of SNA of environmentally damaging activity than respectively a car-kilometer, heated rooms, heating the whole house, meat, and holiday flights'. Elaboration of this single sentence could be construed as a goal for ecological economics over the next decade or more. Although higher utility bills encourage lifestyle changes, such direct policy guidance also is needed. Losses of functions of renewable and non-renewable resources (= the environment) is not yet charged to national income as costs.

Third, saving the environment requires extra input of labour for restoring and maintaining the functions that are outside the market. The production and consumption of the same amount of market goods requires more labour time with conservation of the environment than without. This makes environment-burdening products much more expensive. Were the opposite true, that is if labour productivity (measured in market terms) would increase by clean production, no environmental problem would exist. The market mechanism then would bring about this situation 'automatically'. For these three reasons the 'green' SNA will be much lower than standard national income.

The thrilling part of this history is that the results of Hueting's decades of work on calculating green SNA were independently corroborated during Hueting's April 1999 conference by Harmen Verbruggen's team. Verbruggen et al. (1999) constructed an applied general equilibrium model that corrected national income for environmental losses thus testing Hueting's methodology, which was fully corroborated for the first time.

5 EXTENDING NATIONAL SUSTAINABLE INCOME OUTSIDE THE NETHERLANDS

In 1983, the United Nations Environment Programme (UNEP), led by Yusuf Ahmad, convened the first international workshop to explore how sustainable national income should be calculated within the whole UN system by modification of traditional SNA. I supported this new and potentially powerful approach and managed later to bring in Salah El Serafy who led the World Bank into green accounting. As Hueting was the only person in the world to have been working on adapting the accounts of any nation up to that point, he contributed greatly to what became known as the 'UNEP–World Bank Working Group on Environmental Accounting'. The World Bank hosted the second workshop in Washington in 1984, the OECD hosted a third workshop in Paris in 1985, and again in Washington in 1986, by which time environmental accounting had become institutionalized.

This group focused mainly on incorporating the exhaustion and depletion of environment and natural resources in national income, notably in developing countries. Their chapters in this book show that Hueting, El Serafy (1981, 1989, 1996), Daly (1988) and Daly and Cobb (1989) continued this work for some years. The results were published in 1989 in *Environmental Accounting for Sustainable Development*.[3] Progress on environmental accounting then slowed down from the early 1990s until the present, and the World Bank Group still relies more on unadjusted national accounts that exclude environmental losses.

Much of Hueting's work originated in developing countries. After having worked on sustainable national income for the Netherlands,

Hueting extended his approach to Indonesia. His proposal to approach sustainability for environmental functions was first made during his visit to Jakarta in 1986, on invitation of H.E. Emil Salim, Minister of Population and Environment (Hueting, 1986b). Hueting then broadened his approach while on the team that produced the 'Taiwan 2000' study.[4]

Hueting observed the causes and consequences of environmental problems first hand in the field: desertification in Sudan, deforestation, erosion and flooding in South India, Java and Cebu (Philippines), mangrove destruction in Ecuador, the richness of the tropical rain forests in Indonesia. Ever the pragmatist, he slept in villages and slums, and personally experienced what it feels like to pedal rickshaws. By doing so he learned that the poor in developing countries are well aware of the causes and consequences of environmental decay, of which they are the victims. He observed that these people tried in vain to stop this process and that they see cheap solutions such as bicycling, family planning and sustainable use of forests as necessary and acceptable. Lack of support, lack of influence on the decision-making process, religious and other traditions, and the subordinate position of women hamper such solutions. Governments even ban rickshaws as clogging roads, and fail to appreciate that this postpones sustainability as more gasoline is imported, more air is polluted and more unemployment is caused.

6 QUESTIONING GROSS NATIONAL PRODUCT (GNP) AS A GOAL

Setting up sustainable national income research for the Netherlands, Indonesia and Philippines led Hueting into his seminal re-evaluation of GNP growth as an economic guide. In 1992, the World Bank decided to devote its annual flagship publication – the *World Development Report* (WDR) – to the topic of 'Development and the Environment' for the first time. Wilfred Beckerman, author of *In Defense of Economic Growth* (1974) was the leading consultant to the WDR team (see this volume). The WDR is produced by a team typically of a dozen economists with a couple of million dollars, over two or three years. It aims at representing current thinking on the selected topic of the year by the world's leading practitioners of economic development, hence it can be enormously influential worldwide. When greener colleagues in the World Bank started to see drafts is was clear that neoclassical economics was overwhelming ecological economics. Three of us, Herman Daly, Salah El Serafy and myself, commented extensively on all available drafts from start to finish seeking to redress this imbalance.[5] However, it soon became clear that our comments and the environmental point of view would be under-represented.

In our spare time, we decided to draft an ecological economic position to counterbalance the traditional and conservative neoclassical stance of the official WDR. As we had a zero budget, we cajoled colleagues into providing us with separate chapters. This modest counterview to the official WDR was surprisingly copyrighted by the International Bank for Reconstruction and Development (IBRD) and United Nations Educational, Scientific and Cultural Organisation (UNESCO) and published as *The Transition to Sustainability* in the same year as the 1992 WDR. Because of their world leadership in questioning the goal of GNP growth, we received a brilliant chapter from economics Nobellist Jan Tinbergen and Roefie Hueting entitled 'GNP and market prices: wrong signals for sustainable economic success that mask environmental destruction'. This was subsequently amplified in Roefie's 1996a paper 'Three myths'. Their stark conclusions were very clear and contrasted with the WDR: (a) promote the transition to renewable energy and recycling, (b) promote the transition from throughput growth to development, starting in rich countries, (c) stabilize global population as soon as possible, and (d) improve international income distribution. Although rarely referred to in official circles, this helped the World Bank and other development workers to question the *idée fixe* of maximizing GNP growth.

7 WEAK AND STRONG SUSTAINABILITY

Hueting (1974a, 1980a, 1980b), Hueting et al. (1992g), and Hueting and Reijnders (1998b) contribute much to the current debate on sustainability. *New Scarcity* (1974a) focuses on renewable resources such as water, air and soil, so Hueting led on this important topic from the earliest days, and also applied his thinking to non-renewables, such as energy. Hueting bases a future acceptable rate of extraction of the non-renewable resource on the historic rate at which improved efficiency, substitution and reuse had become available. Thus Hueting shows the folly of relying on technological optimism, rather than on some historic track record. The only thing that matters in the context of sustainability is that vital functions remain available. The conservation of these functions is critical.

Weak sustainability assumes all or most natural capital is substitutable with other forms of capital, so that restoration of lost elements can be postponed, awaiting cheaper elements provided by future technologies. During that wait, income can be sustained by reserving a sufficient part of the revenues of a resource for investment in consumption goods. This is the wrong and risky advice to get rich first and to attend to the environment later. Now that the ludicrous 'inverted Kuznets environmental curves' or win-wins have been exposed as shams (Maler, this volume), we need to revert to the prudent course advocated by Hueting of restoring and maintaining environmental functions, and preferably not damaging them in the first place. Planetary life support systems are not substitutable, nor are most functions of natural ecosystems. Consequently, Hueting concludes, weak sustainability is impossible for the functions of these systems. With this I agree, although weak sustainability would be a vast improvement as a first step towards a more reliable form of sustainability (Goodland, 1999).

Strong sustainability takes the line, Hueting asserts, that substitution of most elements of the environment is impossible. This implies that the stocks of non-renewable resources should remain integrally intact. This also is impossible and nonsensical, because it would mean that non-renewable resources could never be consumed. Elsewhere, this is normally referred to as 'absurdly strong sustainability'. By substituting non-renewables during the depletion period, the functions of non-renewables remain intact. The prospects for this are hopeful (Goodland and Daly, 1996). Therefore, Hueting correctly concludes that 'there seems to be only one kind of sustainability, in which it is sometimes possible to substitute elements of the environment (resources) by other elements in order to guarantee the availability of functions, and sometimes it is not'.

APPENDIX 1*

Toward a 'Green G.N.P.'

THE NEW YORK TIMES, SUNDAY, DECEMBER 9, 1990

EUROPEANS BEGIN TO CALCULATE THE PRICE OF POLLUTION

In a Spartan office on the eighth floor of the Netherlands Central Bureau of Statistics, a shy man with the stoop of a bookkeeper rather than the bearing of a fire-brand has been quietly plotting a revolution in the way economists look at the environment.

For 30 years, Roefie Hueting has provoked and prodded planners and policy-makers, telling them that they are fooling themselves in the way they measure a country's wealth, the welfare of its citizens, the prices of goods and services. And he has devised his own way, a set of new indicators that would arrive at a 'green' gross national product, accounting for the harm that economic activity does to the environment.

The idea is getting a broader reception in Europe as the environmental debate has heated up, and public opinion now favors more drastic steps to fight pollution.

* Article taken from *The New York Times*, Sunday, December 9, 1990.

By ignoring or disguising the cost of economic production to the environment, Mr. Hueting and other dissident economists argue, the gross national product of many countries has been inflated and sometimes grossly distorted. It is absurd, Mr. Hueting contends, that measures to defend nature or to check or clean damage have been tallied as growth. Mr Hueting, economist and jazz pianist, has been an irritant to people on the left and right. He survived politicians who wanted to close down his department; and he got a reputation as a Don Quixote among economists. Slowly he gained acclaim from his peers. Now governments and international institutions are listening.

The Dutch Government has asked Mr. Hueting to produce an alternative system of national accounting to reflect the damage done to the air, water, soil, and animal and plant life, and to account for the cost of maintaining or restoring them. Planners at the United Nations Environment Program and officials at the World Bank have said that Mr. Hueting's publications got them thinking about the need for 'environmental accounting' in recent years.

Mr. Hueting is far from the only economist contending that the habits of more than 50 years of economic accounting – using the output of goods and services as the only measure of economic and even social success – are outdated and misleading. Arguments that new rules and premises are needed have gained support among researchers in the United States. A bill passed a year ago by Congress directed the Commerce Department to work on a new system of calculating environmental costs and benefits.

In Europe, the idea of 'green' accounting has pried its way into more and more government offices. Sweden's Parliament has sent a delegation to the Netherlands for advice on starting a project. France and Norway have started to compile inventories of their natural resources, a first step to linking the state of the environment to economic activity.

Germany, which is farther along, has responded to pressure from its Green Party and is working out a system to correct the 'double counting' in its national bookkeeping. In a 1989 study, the economist Christian Leipert showed that between 1970 and 1985, West Germany's spending to preserve or restore nature increased from 5 per cent to 10 per cent of its gross national product, and was consistently counted as growth. That meant, said Mr. Hueting, that measures simply to check deterioration were recorded as a significant contribution.

'Take a water treatment plant,' said Mr. Hueting. 'Under the present accounting system, it is booked as a contribution, though it should be entered as a cost. It's built to make up for the loss of usable water. It does not generate growth. You can only count that plant as value added if you have first entered the ruined drinking water as a loss.' It would be equally misleading to count cleaning smog as growth, he said.

Not a Solution

Redefining such costs and correcting the books is useful, he said, but 'it's dangerous if politicians or statisticians present this as the solution, because, as is well known, most environmental destruction is never restored or compensated.'

Ultimately, Mr. Hueting and other ecological economists hope that a new framework for national accounts will lead to a fundamental change of national goals and even a redefinition of progress. 'Green' accounting will show how far the world has drifted from rational behavior, from activities that are not destructive to the biosphere and therefore to society, they argue.

Applying a 'green' G.N.P., Mr. Hueting said, will make polluting products more expensive and consequently will slow growth. But he said this does not have to mean a decline in employment. 'Many activities that protect the environment will have to be more labor-intensive,' he said. 'An economy that protects the environment will create more jobs.'

While he says his work is often complex and frustrating, the political climate for his ideas is far more favorable than in the early 1960s. Mr. Hueting and his team of 30 specialists, among them: biologists, chemists and physicists, reckon that they need at least two years to come up with a draft for a 'green' G.N.P. Even so, the Netherlands seems further along than most nations. The Department for Environmental Statistics, created by Mr. Hueting in 1969, has been collecting data on the environment – all emissions, concentrations of toxic material disappearances of plant and animal species and other changes – over the last two decades. Such an inventory, he said, is a vital prerequisite. The process, he said, involves establishing norms for 'sustainable use' of the environment, that is, leaving intact its capacity to regenerate itself.

Complex Process

The next step, he said, is to decide what measures are needed to attain sustainable use. The costs of these measures must then be subtracted from the current G.N.P. to calculate the 'green' G.N.P. 'It is obviously a very complex process,' said Mr. Hueting, despite the fact that we can apply traditional economic methods.'

Even if governments only use it as a parallel system, he said, it will help to clarify 'our mistaken accounting' and demonstrate how 'we are squandering air, water, ground, trees, spaces, silence, as if they were free goods instead of assets that we are losing.' It will clarify 'that we should abandon the G.N.P. as the main indicator of economic success and not get upset when it drops.'

While many researchers in Europe have agreed that income is not a satisfactory measure of quality of life here, they say a new perspective is even more important for developing nations that are in danger of squandering their assets. Indonesia, Thailand and the Philippines, which have cut their forests and suffered soil erosion, have asked the Netherlands for technical assistance in environmental accounting. At the United Nations, the Statistical Commission is now revising its System of National Accounts, which it does only once every two decades, and it has agreed to set up guidelines for countries that want to draw up their own 'green' G.N.P.s (Marlise Simons, 1990).

APPENDIX 2

Dr Roefie Hueting
Chronology

1929	Born 16 December, The Hague, The Netherlands.
1948	Finished gymnasium A in 1948 and B in 1949.
1949	Sabbatical year to make up his mind whether to choose a scientific career or a career in music. His lifelong friend, Prof. Jan Pen, Economics Emeritus, Groningen University, encouraged him to study economics.

1949	Founded 'The Downtown Jazz Band'.
1951	To 1959, studied economics, University of Amsterdam, while earning his living as a musician.
1957	7 June, married sculptress Erna Jans Postuma; two children: Tanja Kitty Akim (b. 1958) and Bernadine (Narda) (b. 1962).
1959–1962	Short career as an assistant public accountant.
1962–1965	Started in the field of his main interest, labour market research, at the Ministry of Social Affairs.
1965–1968	Labour market research at the Ministry of Housing and Physical Planning.
1960s	In the mid 1960s he started publishing on economic aspects of the environment, mainly in *Economisch-Statistische Berichten*.
1969	Founded the Environment Department at Statistics Netherlands.
1970	In January, he published a collection of his articles as *'Wat is de natuur ons waard?'* (What is Nature Worth to Us?).
1974	Received doctorate (*cum laude*) for his dissertation: *'Nieuwe schaarste en economische groei'*. An updated version in English was published in 1980 under the title 'New Scarcity and Economic Growth'.
1976–1977	Provided environmental prognoses for the Netherlands Scientific Council for Government Policy, published as 'The Next Twenty-five years' (The Hague, 1978).
1991	Decorated Officer of the 'Orde van Oranje Nassau', The Netherlands.
1994	Retired from Bureau of Statistics, 16 December; retained office.
1994	Honoured with the United Nations 'Global 500' award.

Recorded and released 250 tracks on top record labels; First Prize at the 1953 International Jazz Concourse; First Prize at the 1955 AVRO Jazz Competition.

APPENDIX 3 ENGLISH PUBLICATIONS BY DR ROEFIE HUETING*

(1969a), *Functions of Nature: Should Nature be Quantified?* London, World Wildlife Fund.

(1969b), 'The concept of economic growth', note for Dr M.J.J.A. Imkamp, member of Parliament.

(1970a), 'Functions of nature: should nature be quantified? *Economisch-Statstische Berichten*, 21st January (in Dutch). Also in R. Hueting, (1970), *What*

* Further information may be obtained from Dr Roefie Hueting, Statistics Netherlands, P.O. Box 4000, 2270 JM Voorburg, The Netherlands.

is Nature Worth to Us? A collection of articles from the years 1967–1970 (in Dutch).
(1970b), 'Propositions and introduction' The Netherlands Congress for Public Health, 12th November, 'The Price of a Livable Environment', Den Haag.
(1971), 'A statistical system for estimating the deterioration of the human environment, in J.W. Pratt, (ed.), *Statistical and Mathematical Aspects of Pollution Problems*, Symposium International Assococciation for Statistics Physical Sciences (IASPS), Harvard University, 10–20 August, also published in J.W. Pratt (ed.) (1974), *Statistical and Mathematical Aspects of Pollution Problems*, Marcel Dekker, New York.
(1972), 'The set-up of the statistical system within which the deterioration of the human environment will be estimated', in *Problems of Environmental Economics* Organization for Economic Cooperation and Development, Paris, 7.
(1973a), 'A statistical system for estimating the deterioration of the human environment', UN Seminar on Environmental Statistics (Statistical Commission and Economic Commission for Europe), Warsaw, 15–19 October.
(1973b), 'The economic quantification of the environment', in *Planning and Development in the Netherlands*, A Periodical of the Netherlands Universities Foundation for International Cooperation, **VII** (2).
(1974a), *New Scarcity and Economic Growth: More Welfare Through Less Production?* Dutch edition, Agon Elsevier, Amsterdam. English edition, North-Holland Publishing Company, Amsterdam – New York – Oxford (1980).
(1974b), 'Environment and statistics', General Meeting of the International Association of Municipal Statisticians (IAMS), Zürich, May 15–17.
(1974c), 'Environmental statistics in the Netherlands', UN World Health Organization, Seminar on Health Statistics, 5–14 June.
(1975), 'Environmental deterioration, economic growth and national income', 14th General Conference of the International Association for Research in Income and Wealth (IARIW). Aulanko, Finland, 18–23 August.
(1976a), 'Possibilities for environmental improvements in the face of limited availability of national and local means', in: *Papers and Proceedings, Volume II*, Hyogo International Conference of the International Federation for Housing and Planning, Kobe, Japan, 18–22 May.
(1976b), 'Introduction for the conference of the International Cargo Handling Coordination Association (ICHCA), *Loss and Damage in Transport*, Amsterdam, 28–29 October.
(1977a), 'Socio-economic effects of environmental policy', symposium on 'Quality of Life', Universidad de Deusto, Bilbao, 21–23 September.
(1977b), 'The economy and the ecology in the perspective of the motorcar. VIth Congress on Leisure and Touring, *The Motorist and the Environment*, Theme A, 'Ecology, the motorcar and the future', Manila, 5–9 December.
(1978), 'Economic aspects of pollution of the Rhine', in Jessurun d'Oliveira H.U. (ed), *Rhine Pollution: Legal, Economical and Technical Aspects*, Nederlands Juristen Blad, series 5, Tjeenk Willink, Zwolle, The Netherlands.
(1980a), 'Environment and growth, expectations and scenarios', in S.K. Kuipers and G.J. Lanjouw (eds.), *Prospects of Economic Growth*, North-Holland Publishing Company, Amsterdam.
(1980b), 'Scenarios as information for social choice about the environment', in *Sensing the Environment*, International Colloquy, 3–6 June, Council of Europe, Strasbourg.

(1980c), 'The use of environmental data in the economic decision-making process', seminar on *Methodological Problems of Environmental Statistics*, Conference of European Statisticians of the Economic Commission for Europe (ECE) of the United Nations, and the Senior Advisors to ECE Governments on Environmental Problems, Warsaw, 16–19 September.
(1980d), 'Comments on Orio Giarini's paper on welfare and wealth', seminar on *Towards an Ecological Economy*, Ecoropa, Kassel (BRD), 18–20 September.
(1980e), 'Schaarste buiten de markt: van bijzaak tot hoofdzaak', *Maandblad Voor Accountancy en Bedrijfshuishoudkunde*, **3**, 106–15.
(1981a), 'Aspecten van welvaart op lange termijn', *Economisch Statistische Berichten*, 3294, 180–5.
(1981b), Comments on the report 'A low energy strategy for the United Kingdom', in G. Leach et al. (eds), *The International Institute for the Environment and Development (IIED)*, Working Party on Integral Energy Scenarios, The Hague, 20 May.
(1982), 'The context of environmental data when used in making decisions on the environment', OECD Group: *The State of the Environment*, Stockholm, 1–4 June.
(1983), 'Environment-saving economy is feasible', introduction for the *International Water Tribunal*, Rotterdam, 4 October.
(1984a), 'Note on the acquisition of statistical material for projections of environmental burdening and environmental costs', Paris, OECD Group: *The State of the Environment*, May.
(1984b), 'Economic aspects of environmental accounting', *Environmental Accounting Workshop*, UNEP and World Bank, Washington, DC, November.
(1984c), 'Results of an economic scenario that gives top priority to saving the environment and energy instead of encouraging production growth', in Sören Bergström (ed.), *Economic Growth and the Role of Science*, Edsbruk, Holms Gårds Tryckeri, Sweden.
(1985a), 'Energy, the environment and employment: the new scenario', in *The Future of the Electricity Supply Industry*, Centre for Energy Studies, Polytechnic of the South Bank, London, 25–27 June.
(1985b), 'An economic scenario that gives top priority to saving the environment rather than encouraging production growth', *The Environmentalist*, **5** (4) 253–62.
(1986a), 'An economic scenario for a conserver-economy', in Paul Ekins (ed.), *The Living Economy, A New Economics in the Making*, London, Routledge.
(1986b), 'A note on the construction of an environmental indicator in monetary terms as a supplement to national income with the aid of basic environmental statistics', Report to Prof. Dr E. Salim, Minister of Population and Environment, Indonesia, Jakarta, March.
(1986c), 'Framework for a cost–benefit analysis for different uses of a humid tropical forest area', Tropenbos, 22–24 September, Baarn, Netherlands.
(1986d), 'Uitkomsten Van Een Economisch Scenario Dat de Hoogste Prioritiet Geeft Aan Millieubehoud in Plaats Van Aan Produktiegroei', Universiteit Antwerpen, V. Liber Amicorum, Professor P.H. Virenque, 327–52.
(1987a), 'The use of environmental data in the decision-making process', Netherlands Official Statistics, Voorburg, Heerlen.
(1987b), 'Economic aspects of environmental accounting', *Journal of Interdisciplinary Economics*, **2** (1). Also published in *Societat Catalana d'Economia*. 7 Anuari, Barcelona, 1989.

(1987c), 'Energy, the environment and employment: a new scenario', Futures **19** (3), 343–5.
(1987d), 'An economic scenario that gives top priority to saving the environment', *Ecological Modelling*, **38** (1/2), 123–40.
(1988), 'Collective survival and the fallacy of national income as a measure for economic growth', 19th World Conference, Society for International Development on *Poverty, Development and Collective Survival, Public and Private Responsibilities*, New Delhi, 25–28 March.
(1989a), 'The implications for the Taiwan 2000 study of the Netherlands Scenario Study 1980–2000', in *Taiwan 2000. Balancing Economic Growth and Environmental Protection*, The Steering Committee Taiwan 2000 Study (ed.), Taipei.
(1989b), 'Correcting national income for environmental losses: towards a practical solution', in Y. Ahmad, S. El Serafy, E. Lutz (eds), *Environmental Accounting for Sustainable Development*, The World Bank, Washington, DC.
(1989c), 'Design of the cost–benefit analysis of the lower Guayas Flood Control Project', *Economic Evaluation of Environmental Impact*, HASKONING Royal Dutch Consulting Engineers and Architects, Guayaquil, Ecuador, September 1989. Also published in P.C. van den Noort (ed.), (1990) *Costs and Benefits of Agricultural Policies and Projects*, Wissenschaftsverlag Vauk Kiel K.G.
(1990a), 'Economic growth, national income and the blocked choices for the environment (with Christian Leipert)', *The Environmentalist* **10** (1), 25–38.
(1990b), 'The fallacy of the growth of consumption', introduction for the conference on the occasion of the thirtieth anniversary of the *International Organization of Consumers Unions*, Oegstgeest, 2 May.
(1990c), 'The Brundtland Report: a matter of conflicting goals', *Ecological Economics* 2, 109–17.
(1990d), 'On the correction of national income for environmental losses (with Peter Bosch)', *Statistical Journal of the United Nations Economic Commission for Europe* **7** (2), 75–83.
(1991a), 'The use of the discount rate in a cost–benefit analysis for different uses of a humid tropical forest area', *Ecological Economics* **3** (1), 43–57.
(1991b), 'An economic scenario for the Netherlands: shifting priority from production growth to environmental preservation', in M.J. Garrett et al. (eds), *Studies for the 21st Century*, Institute for 21st Century Studies, Arlington, Virginia, USA.
(1991c), 'National Income and economic growth and the concept of defensive expenditures' (with Christian Leipert), in S. Busuttil and B. Rhode (eds), *Sourcebook: Ecological Economics*, European Coordination Centre for Research and Documentation in Social Sciences and Foundation for International Studies, UNESCO, Vienna.
(1991d), 'GNP and market prices: wrong signals for sustainable economic success that mask environmental destruction' (with Jan Tinbergen), in R. Goodland, H. Daly, S. El Serafy and B. von Droste zu Hulshoff (eds), *Environmentally Sustainable Economic Development: Building on Brundtland*, United Nations Educational, Scientific and Cultural Organization, Paris, 1991, pp. 39–52. Also published in R. Goodland et al. (eds) (1992), *Population, Technology and Lifestyle. The Transition to Sustainability*, Island Press, © The International Bank for Reconstruction and Development and UNESCO, Washington, DC. Also published in *Environmentally Sustainable Economic Development: Building on Brundtland*, R. Goodland et al. (eds) Environment Working Paper 46, The World Bank, Washington, DC.

(1991e), 'Note on the correction of National Income for environmental losses' (with Peter Bosch), in O. Kuik and H. Verbruggen (eds), *In Search of Indicators of Sustainable Development*, Kluwer Academic Publishers, Dordrecht.
(1991f), 'Correcting National Income for environmental losses: a practical solution for a theoretical dilemma, in R. Costanza (ed.), *Ecological Economics, The Science and Management of Sustainability*, Columbia University Press, New York, pp. 194–213.
(1991g), 'Calculating a sustainable national income: a practical solution for a theoretical dilemma', Netherlands Official Statistics, Voorburg, Heerlen.
(1991h), 'Calculating a sustainable national income: a practical solution for a theoretical dilemma', in Alfred Franz and Carsten Stahmer (eds.), *Approaches to Environmental Accounting*, Proceedings of the IARIW Conference on Environmental Accounting. Baden, Austria, 27–29 May 1991, Physica-Verlag, Heidelberg, 1993.
(1992a), 'The economic functions of the environment', in P. Ekins and M. Max-Neef (eds) (1992), Real-life Economics: Understanding Wealth Creation, Routledge, London, pp. 61–9. Also published in L.L. Boyer (ed.), *Proceedings of the 5th International Conference on Underground Space and Earth Sheltered Structures*, Delft University Press, Delft, 1992.
(1992b), 'Theoretical problems around growth, environment and national income: a practical solution', in P. Ekins and M. Max-Neef (eds), *Real-life Economics*, Routledge, London.
(1992c), 'Economic evaluation of the environmental impacts: design of a cost benefit analysis of the Lower Guayas Flood Control Project, Equador, *The Environmentalist*, **12** (2), 93–100.
(1992d), 'Methodology for the calculation of sustainable national income' (with Peter Bosch and Bart de Boer), Statistics Netherlands, Statistical Essays, M44, SDU/Publishers, 's-Gravenhage. Also published as WWF International report, Gland, Switzerland, June 1992.
(1992e), 'The calculation of a sustainable national income in the Netherlands, environment statistics and other information requirements' (with Peter Bosch), work session on 'Specific methodological issues in environment statistics', *Conference of European Statisticians (Statistical Commission and Economic Commission for Europe), and Eurostat (Commission of the European Communities)*, Lisbon, 14–17 September.
(1992f), 'Correcting national income for environmental losses: a practical solution for a theoretical dilemma', in J.J. Krabbe and W.J.M. Heijman (eds). *National Income and Nature: Externalities, Growth and Steady State*, Kluwer Academic, Dordrecht, pp. 23–47.
(1992g), 'Het duurzaam nationaal inkomen' (with Peter Bosch and Bart de Boer), *Economisch Statistische Berichten*, **77** (3856), 392–97.
(1992h), 'De relatie tussen milieu en groei' (with Peter Bosch), *Economisch Statistische Berichten*, **77** (3857), 412–6.
(1993a), 'Methodology for the calculation of sustainable national income' (with Peter Bosch and Bart de Boer), in A. Markandya and C. Costanza (eds), *Environmental Accounting: A Review of the Current Debate*, Harvard Institute for International Development and United Nations Environment Programme, Environmental Economics Series, Paper No. 8, pp. 59–63.
(1993b), 'Calculating a sustainable national income: a practical solution for a theoretical dilemma', in J.C. Dragan, E.K. Seifert and M.C. Demetrescu (eds),

Entropy and Bioeconomics: Proceedings of the First International Conference of the European Association for Bioeconomic Studies – EABS, Rome 28–30 November 1991; Milan, Italy, 1993, pp. 322–43.
(1994), 'Sustainable national income in the Netherlands: the calculation of environmental losses in money terms (43–56), in D. Pearce and S. Faucheux (eds) *Models of Sustainable Development: Exclusive or Complementary Approaches of Sustainability? Volume I.* International Symposium, Paris, 16–18 March, Université Panthéon-Sorbonne C3E and AFCET, Paris, pp. 43–56.
(1995a), 'Estimating sustainable national income' (with Bart de Boer, Peter Bosch and Jan Paul van Soest), in Wouter van Dieren (ed.), *Taking Nature into Account: A Report to the Club of Rome*, Springer-Verlag, New York, p 322.
(1995b), 'The economic functions of the environment – valuation of environmental effects', in *Evaluation of Environmental Effects of Transport, Report of an International Roundtable Organized by PTRC Education and Research Services Ltd.*, The Hague (19–20 June) and London.
(1995c), 'The calculation of sustainable national income' (with P. Bosch and B. de Boer), Occasional Papers and Reprints, IDPAD OP&R 1995(2), Indo-Dutch Programme on *Alternatives in Development IDPAD*, New Delhi and The Hague.
(1996a), 'Three persistent myths in the environmental debate', *Ecological Economics*, **18** (2), 81–8.
(1996b), 'Duurzaamheid is een objectief begrip' (with Lucas Reijnders). *Economisch Statistische Berichten*, **81** (04057), 425–7.
(1998a), 'The concept of environmental function and its valuation' (with Lucas Reijnders, Bart de Boer, Jan Lambooy and Huib Jansen), *Ecological Economics*, **25** (1), 31–5.
(1998b), 'Sustainability is an objective concept' (with Lucas Reijnders), *Ecological Economics*, **27** (2), 139–47.
(1999a), 'Uncertainty and sustainability (with Lucas Reijnders)', *Ecological Economics*, **29** (1).
(1999b), 'Green accounting and sustainable national income calculation in the Netherlands' (with Bart de Boer and Mark de Haan), in *From Research to Implementation: Policy-Driven Methods for Evaluating Macroeconomic Environmental Performance*, Proceedings from a workshop, Luxembourg, 28–29 September 1998, European Commission, EU RTD in Human Dimensions of Environmental Change, Report Series 1999/1.
(2001a), 'The Parable of the Carpenter' (with Bart de Boer), *International Journal of Environment and Pollution*, **15** (1), 42–50.
(2001b), 'Sustainable national income in theory and practice' (with Bart de Boer), *International Journal of Sustainable Development*, forthcoming.
(2001c), Some Comments on 'The value of the world's ecosystem services and natural capital' (with Martin O'Connor, Bart de Boer, Huib Jansen, Jan Lambooy and Lucas Reijnders), *International Library of Ecological Economics, Volume 1*. Edward Elgar, Cheltenham.

LITERATURE CITED IN THE TEXT (other than by Roefie Hueting)

Ahmad, Y., S. El Serafy and E. Lutz (eds) (1989), *Environmental Accounting for Sustainable Development*, Washington, DC., UNEP and The World Bank.

Beckerman, W. (1974), *In Defence of Economic Growth*, London, Jonathan Cape.
Daly, H.E. (1988), 'On sustainable development and national accounts', in D. Collard., D.W. Pearce., and D. Ulph (eds), *Economics, Growth and Sustainable Environments*, New York, St. Martin's Press.
Daly, H.E. and J. Cobb (1989), *For the Common Good*, Boston, Beacon Press.
Daly, H.E. (1992), 'Allocation, distribution and scale: towards an economy which is efficient, just and sustainable', *Ecological Economics* 6 (3), 185–93.
Daly, H.E. (1996), *Beyond Growth: The Economics of Sustainable Development*. Boston, Beacon.
El Serafy, S. (1981), 'Absorptive capacity, the demand for revenue and the supply of petroleum', *Journal of Energy and Development*, **7** (1).
El Serafy, S. (1989), 'The proper calculation of income from depletable natural resources' (10–18) in J. Ahmad et al. (eds) *Environmental accounting for sustainable development*. Washington DC, UNEP and The World Bank p. 10–18.
El Serafy, S. (1996), 'In defence of weak sustainability: a response to Beckerman', *Environmental Values*, 5, 75–81.
Goodland, R. and H.E. Daly (1996), 'Environmental sustainability: universal and non-negotiable', *Ecological Applications*, 6 (4), 1002–17.
Goodland, R. (1999), 'The biophysical basis of environmental sustainability' in Jeroen C.J.M. van den Bergh (ed.), *Handbook of Environmental and Resource Economics*, London, Edward Elgar, pp. 709–21.
Verbruggen, H., R. Dellink, R. Gerlagh, M. Hofkes. and H.M.A. Hansen (1999), 'Alternative calculations of a sustainable national income for the Netherlands according to Hueting', Chapter 11 in this book.

NOTES

1. Published as: *'Een haven op het Balgzand?'* (Rotterdam, Arnhem, 1978).
2. The scenario was elaborated with the aid of the SECMON-C model of the University of Amsterdam. The results were published in the report *'Het CE-Scenario, een realistisch alternatief'* (The CE Scenario, a Realistic Alternative) (Centrum voor Energiebesparing, Delft, 1983).
3. Y. Ahmad, S. El Serafy and E. Lutz (eds) 1989, by UNEP and The World Bank.
4. *Taiwan 2000: Balancing Economic Growth and Environmental Protection*, The Steering Committee, Taiwan 2000 Study, Taipei, 1989a.
5. Herman Daly provides an amusing but disturbing account of that vexed process in his 1996 book *Beyond Growth*, Boston, Beacon Press. Daly (1992) had contributed greatly by reminding us that the three goals of allocation, efficiency and scale need three separate tools, rather than the current single goal of 'GNP growth forever'.

13. Rejoinders to symposium authors

Roefie Hueting*

1 INTRODUCTION

Having been writing for 35 years on environmental valuation, growth and sustainable national income, after a five-year incubation prior to putting pen to paper, and having spent 25 years (1969–94) setting up and elaborating a system of environmental statistics, the indispensable raw material for practical calculations, my main desire today is for agreement on theory, that is on method. Agreement among the authors working in this field, who since the 1970s have come to refer to themselves as environmental or ecological economists, and also between them and the vast majority of economists, whose thinking about scarcity and welfare is enacted in an ecological vacuum. My own position lies somewhere in between, perhaps, for my work is regarded by many ecological economists as 'neoclassical' – and they use the term in a clearly pejorative sense. I certainly do not live in an ecological vacuum, though, for the environment is the pivotal focus of my work, because I consider it the principal economic problem facing humankind.

What concerns me most is the enormous differences in the results generated using various methods of environmental valuation and in the associated figures for a national income adjusted for environmental losses, referred to these days as 'green accounting'. Until such time as the reasons for these differences are explained, it will be impossible for serious people to take this work seriously. And until the work of environmental and ecological economists is accepted by a significant proportion of colleagues whose main concern is not with the environment, that work will have only minimal impact in society and on political decision making.

If the mountain will not come to Mohammed, Mohammed must go to the mountain. By 1974 several approaches to environmental valuation had already been published, based on notions of travel costs, willingness to pay

* I am grateful to Bart de Boer, Lucas Reijnders, Wouter Achterberg, Cees Maris and Leontien Tels de Jong (classicist) for their help with certain passages of the text and Nigel Harle for translation.

and to accept, and so on, and in that year I repositioned these within a new theoretical framework, adding some elements of my own. My basic point of departure was the simple notion that without preferences and costs there can be no economic value; my framework was based on the concept of 'competing environmental functions' as economic goods. Although the English edition of that study was held up for six years because of obstruction (I refer the reader to the author's Introduction there and to Robert Goodland's chapter in the present volume), the essentials of my work have been available to readers of the English language since 1971 or 1974, as can be seen from the list of publications appended to Goodland's Chapter 12 (see, in particular, Hueting 1971/1974 and 1975). It is on this 1974 study that all my later work is grounded. It was only after 1974 or 1980 that most authors began publishing on environmental valuation and green accounting. Although it is accepted scientific form to either build on the work of one's predecessors or reject it on the basis of reasoned argument, this was a privilege I was not afforded. Given the crucial importance of agreement on method, in our contribution to this volume Bart de Boer and I have sought to identify the precise differences between our theoretical approach and the methods of other authors. In doing so we have examined the work a number of environmental and ecological as well as general economists, several of whom base themselves on so-called general growth theory. The comforting conclusion is that the differences in results can be traced back either to differences in assumptions (frequently undisclosed) or to anomalous usage of key terms, such as the standard notion of 'production', the sum of values added by labour and 'environmental function', the term I introduced to denote a *possible* (potential) use of our physical surroundings.

In my rejoinders to those authors who were kind enough to contribute to this volume I arrive at the same optimistic conclusion. Although some consider their approach to differ in certain respects, below I hope to demonstrate that in most cases this conclusion is borne of misunderstanding. In Chapter 9 Pearce et al. criticize my work for asserting the exact opposite of what I implicitly intended and, in at least five publications, have explicitly stated. The supposed difference of view thus soon evaporates. Several other contributors do not address my work explicitly. In one case though (Mäler), de Boer and I conclude below that here, too, the (pronounced) discrepancy in results is rooted in making different assumptions.

One final note. Some of the contributors took up the offer of receiving a courtesy copy of the list of references, articles or the 1974a study (*New Scarcity and Economic Growth*), while others declined. In my rejoinders to the latter I have felt free to quote from any or all of my publications, references being given according to the list of publications appended to Robert

Goodland's contribution to the present volume. To facilitate reading, wherever feasible reference has been made to the summary paper by Bart de Boer and myself (referred to as 'H&B' for convenience), which then points readers to my earlier work.

I am very much indebted to the editors for giving me the opportunity not only to present my work on environmental valuation and sustainable national income (SNI) but also to elaborate on specific points of interest in this series of rejoinders to the symposium authors.

2 PAUL EKINS

Paul's study in Chapter 4 perfectly reflects the essence of my work: competing environmental functions – possible uses of our physical surroundings – constitute new scarce goods (Hueting 1969a, 1974a) and sustainability boils down to maintenance of vital functions. From here, the rest of my work follows on logically. For this I am very glad, all the more so because on this point I have not been overindulged (see Introduction). A few comments are nonetheless in order, for on several issues Paul in fact appears to have misinterpreted my work. These relate to: (1) adjustment of the national income for loss of environmental functions, and (2) sustainable use of the functions of non-renewable resources. In addition, he neglects to consider one key element: my statistical studies demonstrating that the bulk of growth is generated by the most environmentally damaging activities; this is discussed below under (1). Together, these factors have led Paul to draw some erroneous conclusions about my work. His study also contains several minor misconceptions, but for the sake of brevity I shall not treat these here.

1. There are a number of misconceptions regarding my position on the adjustment of national income.
   (i) On p. 121 Ekins states that (marginal) damage costs are the theoretically appropriate measure for correcting net national product (NNP), if considered as a measure of welfare. But, as he notes here and on p. 118, citing my work, NNP or production is not a measure of welfare, welfare being a far more complex concept, and consequently national income can never be corrected on this basis. Apart from the fact that solely damage costs are not the appropriate measure for correcting NNP (see below), Paul has misunderstood me here. On many occasions I have written as follows on this point (see H&B, Section 3). Although not amenable to direct measurement, welfare is arguably dependent on a

number of factors which *are* measurable. One of these is the trend in production volume, provided it is constituted in accordance with preferences. As long as environmental functions remain free goods, production represents the sum total of all scarce goods. When functions become scarce this is no longer the case, and a correction must be made in order to restore an important indicator of welfare (see H&B pp. 34–5, including the quotation from Tinbergen and Hueting, 1991d). This correction should not, then, be based exclusively on the damage costs arising, as Ekins posits, but on shadow prices given by the intersection between the marginal elimination cost curve (supply) and an assumed demand curve, which represents (*inter alia*) both actual and anticipated damage. These number as many as the (reasonable) assumptions that can be made about preferences (see H&B, Sections 5.1 and 5.2 and (ii) below). Ekins' argument that correction of national income is impossible because production is not an (all-inclusive) measure of welfare is therefore incorrect.

(ii) It is entirely erroneous to hold, as Ekins does on p. 123, that Hueting et al. (1992d) is based on the maintenance cost approach. H&B (Sections 4 and 5) elaborates why the approaches introduced subsequent to the Hueting 1974a study, which are based solely on costs or solely on preferences, are (already) constituent techniques of the methodology presented in that study: in the absence of costs or preferences, there is no economic value, and these two elements are, moreover, inextricably linked (see (i) above). In the 1974a study I do not employ the term 'maintenance costs', a far later and to my mind rather unhappy notion, but rather 'elimination costs', in which elimination is defined as at-source removal of the environmental burden such as to restore environmental functions.

(iii) In the quotation in the first paragraph of p. 123 the 'burden that has mounted up' relates not to the method but to a particular case that may sometimes arise (Hueting et al. 1992d, p. 14 should be p. 12).

(iv) On pp. 121, 122 and 123 Ekins clearly intimates that I am unaware that internalization leads to changes in prices and consequently to changes in the composition of economic output. Thus, on p. 123 he asserts critically '(. . .) they are static cost calculations (. . .) they cannot simply be deducted from GNP'. This is such a massive criticism that, if it were true, I would be better to pack my bags as an economist. To my relief I found several pertinent statements in earlier publications. In Hueting (1991f, pp. 205–6) we read: 'To be absolutely clear, it should be pointed out that this is a partial equilibrium and static approach. Effects on other sectors of the economy as a result of taking measures and reducing activities are not considered. Neither are future developments (. . .) because in the model to be used, a large number of assumptions would have to be incorporated (. . .) The problem of the environment is a problem of allocation'. The last sentence is in fact almost a literal translation of the title of one of my articles from the years 1967–70, published in the volume *What is Nature Worth to Us?* (Hueting, 1970a, in Dutch). There, I assert that if nature is really that valuable to us, current allocation is suboptimal; reallocation then leads, via internalization, to a lower national income and greater welfare; this is indeed the subtitle of the 1974a study: *More Welfare Through Less Production?* Remarks similar to that cited from Hueting (1991f) are to be found, *inter alia*, in Hueting (1992f, p. 37) and Hueting (1991e, p. 32). Hueting (1995a, p. 223) refers to '(. . .) the intention to investigate whether the assumptions with respect to technical measures and shifts can be validated or improved with the aid of a comprehensive economic equilibrium model'. This intention, for reasons elaborated under (v) below, was realized not at Statistics Netherlands but at the Institute for Environmental Studies (IES) (see Verbruggen et al., Chapter 11, this volume).

(v) As part of his critique under (iv), Ekins states (p. 123) that Hueting et al. (1992d) believed that the values (or costs; see H&B, Section 5) they found can simply be deducted from the standard national income. That is correct, and I still suspect that this is defensible as a rough approximation of sustainable national income (SNI). But this is by no means to say that changes in prices or in the composition of economic output were ignored or that a general equilibrium model approach was rejected (see quotes under (iv)). There was a mix of theoretical and practical reasons for such a rough proxy.

The main theoretical reason was grounded in the insight that a shift towards more environmentally benign activities has a substantial negative effect on national income, because the bulk of production growth is generated by environmentally damaging activities; this is demonstrated by an analysis of the raw material of the Dutch National Accounts (see Hueting 1981d, 1992b, and H&B, p. 21 and p. 57, in conjunction with Section 5, p. 34 and p.35). Most of the economists with whom I had dealings in the early 1990s held this effect to be zero or thereabouts and therefore non-existent (see, for example, Eijgenraam, 1992), so that mere deduction would lead to a substantial underestimate of the level of SNI (there were no fears of too small a correction). A simple example may serve to clarify matters. Assume that environmental measures must be taken for 1000 products, on the production and the consumption side, and that these measures cost $100 per product. According to my critics, if half the consumers are moved by the price rise resulting from internalization to switch to environmentally benign alternatives, the negative impact is then not $100 000 but $50 000. If, as I hold, the effect of the shift is substantial, there is by no means necessarily an underestimation of SNI; the correction may then in fact even exceed the aggregate costs, certainly if direct shifts, forced by levies, have to be applied because technological measures prove insufficient for attaining the sustainability standard (see H&B, p. 57: the new price ratios better reflect a sustainable situation). The Tinbergen–Hueting rough estimate of a sustainable world income (see Hueting, 1991d) was based partly on the 'shift effect'. Tinbergen shared the view that such an effect does indeed exist, because, he said, 'It is based on statistical fact'. In light of the provisional results of the IES modelling exercise, the figure found does not appear extreme: around 50 per cent of world income (see H&B, Section 1, Consequences of the Principles, 11, as well as Verbruggen et al., Chapter 11, this volume). This renders it plausible that a shift effect indeed exists and that it is substantial. I refer the reader, finally, to several arguments in Hueting, 1995a (p. 217).

Another theoretical reason for accepting 'simple deduction' as a rough approximation is that modelling, too, involves major uncertainties, because attaining sustainability entails large changes and a shift in basic priority from production growth to environmental conservation (see (vi) below). This I have stated on repeated occasions: in Hueting (1992d), for example. On p. 18 of the WWF edition (pp. 18–19, CBS edition) I write as follows: 'The labour released by reduction (. . .) will be put to work for the production of alternatives (. . .) a description of future patterns ought to be based on a series of additional assumptions with regard to reactions of consumers (. . .) This will certainly exceed the predictive capacity of the existing econometric models, because a change of priority (. . .) means a trend break in economic behaviour (. . .)

Moreover, a package of measures is involved, the introduction of which will require a long period (. . .)'.

There are additional reasons why an SNI, however it be calculated, can provide no more than an approximate indication of the volume of a sustainable level of production and consumption (national income is an index of *volume* changes). One of these is the insolvable problem of a composite price index, already referred to in the Hueting 1974a study. As stated in the (extensive) footnote 8 on pp. 229–30 of Hueting (1995a), for this and other reasons, not only is computation of an SNI strictly speaking a disputable exercise; the very concept of national income is also impossible. But, again as stated, I choose not to press the point as long as national income figures continue to be calculated and comparison thereof remains the yardstick of economic success, with all the attendant existential risks to future generations that that implies. The latter has to do with the motivation of my work, and that has certainly been well understood by Paul Ekins, witness his words on p. 129.

Following on from here, the following should also be noted. Because preferences can be established only very partially, shadow prices remain unknown and, with them, the value of environmental functions. But this means that the true value of the goods produced and consumed at the expense of environmental functions is equally unknowable. We must therefore weigh two unknown values – and not a known against an unknown (see, for example, Hueting, 1974a and the 'Three Myths' study, Chapter 3, this volume). If information is to be provided, therefore, assumptions must inevitably be made regarding relative preferences for produced goods and environmental functions. It follows that not only are SNI as well as other 'green' national incomes based on assumptions and therefore hypothetical, but also that the volume of the *standard national income*, conceived as the contribution of production to welfare, *is likewise based on assumptions and is therefore hypothetical.* One such assumption is that preferences for sustainability are virtually zero: whether this is true cannot be proven one way or the other. There is, besides, another reason why market prices and the national income constructed from them are to be seen as representing probabilities rather than certainties. This reason is stated in my rejoinder to Herman Daly.

As I mentioned, there was also a practical reason for accepting a 'simple deduction' in order to obtain a rough proxy for an

SNI, which I here briefly (and incompletely) recapitulate. The competence of Statistics Netherlands to undertake an SNI modelling exercise was seriously disputed. In Parliament the government was requested, for a second time, to provide a calculation of a national income adjusted for environmental losses. This led to a meeting between the ministers of Economic Affairs and Environment and the present author. The upshot of the meeting was a grant to IES to elaborate the SNI according to Hueting in a modelling study (see (iv) above).

(vi) Ekins cites, uncritically, the familiar factor four and factor ten, accompanied by a doubling of national income, or more (p. 128). Given (v) above, Ekins appears to have overlooked the following. To bring about a factor two increase in the vast bulk of national income, average labour productivity must be doubled. To achieve this average increase, however, the labour productivity of the approximately 30 per cent of productive activity (in terms of labour volume) that generates the bulk of production growth must far more than double. These are precisely the sectors that burden the environmental most. For this reason, for the approximately 30 per cent of activity having greatest environmental impact, the reduction of environmental burden must be greater than a factor four or ten; how much greater depends on the degree of expansion of the environmentally burdening sectors; this need not be proportional to the increase in productivity, as argued in Hueting (1981b, 1992d): sectoral expansion is something entirely different from sectoral contribution to growth, because (an increase in) added value is not the same as (an increase in) volume; growth of national income refers to a change in volume. To achieve a doubling of national income, moreover, the cost of applying the as yet non-operational technology must be much lower than in the current situation. Furthermore, these prognostications take no account of humankind's ongoing encroachment upon physical space (the principal cause of species extinction), nor of the fact that ongoing growth requires ever greater efficiency to achieve the desired environmental result, which means that with new technologies, too, one ends up in the progressively rising portion of the elimination cost curve (see 'Three Myths' study, Chapter 3, this volume). While sharing Ekins' optimism regarding technological progress, these kinds of 'factor four or ten' recommendations and forecasts are extremely risky for nature and the environment. More in accordance with the precautionary principle of sustainability would seem to be the conclusions of

Tinbergen in Hueting (1991d): '(. . .) accelerate development of new technologies, such as flow energy (. . .) permit no further production growth in rich countries (. . .) stabilize the global population as soon as possible (. . .)'; and H&B, Section 1, Consequences of the principles, 11 and 12: Assuming a preference for sustainability, welfare will increase by pursuing the transition route to a sustainable income level ; this level amounts to about 50 per cent of current income.

2. In order to clear up misconceptions regarding non-renewable resources, let me first briefly recapitulate the essentials of the Tinbergen–Hueting–de Boer–Bosch methodology, focusing on those aspects that tend to be misinterpreted. This methodology has been published on several occasions, including Hueting (1992d, 1995c) and is also summarized in H&B, Section 7. I shall then indicate the main misinterpretations made by Ekins.

As with the renewables, the core of the matter is to derive the appropriate sustainability standard and to estimate the cost of achieving that standard. And, again as with renewables, the sustainability standards for non-renewables represent constant function levels that can be maintained *ad infinitum*. As stated, 'function levels' refers to the availability of possible uses of the resource and its substitutes (that is flows), while 'possible' here means: possible under the constraint of the sustainability standard. One key difference with the renewables is the prognostic element consisting of the assumption that the relative rate of substitution, efficiency improvement and recycling (and thus of technological progress) found in practice will persist into the future. The inescapability of this 'methodological' difference has been argued (see Hueting 1992d, 1995c and H&B, Section 7). Because non-renewable resources must perforce ultimately be entirely replaced by substitutes, an additional adjustment has been incorporated if the relative rate of substitution found is too slow to satisfy this condition (see H&B p. 68 *et seq.*); this raises the costs of achieving the standard; a method is provided for making an approximate calculation of these costs.

The sustainability standards for the use of non-renewables and their substitutes will generally be (substantially) lower than the current use levels. Moving to a lower level will always have a negative effect on national income, regardless of whether this is achieved by technological means or via shifts (see (1)v above). The discovery of new stocks leads to a higher (that is 'milder') standard, because the depletion horizon is extended. But there is still rigid adherence to the requirement that the resource's function(s) must ultimately be taken over by substitutes, in order for the (constant) function level (the flow) determined by the standard to remain available *ad infinitum*. Fulfilment of this requirement is (again) based on the assumption that the relative rate of substitution – generally increased at additional cost – can be maintained in the future. As stated in the aforementioned publications, such assumptions make the standards less 'solid' than in the case of renewables, but, as also stated, rejection thereof has bizarre consequences. The standard for a particular resource in a given country is derived from the global standard, in proportion to the country's share in global consumption of the resource.

Ekins' principal misconceptions regarding our methodology are, now, the following:

1. The method was not 'developed for one particular economy' (Ekins p. 113), but for the countries of the world together.
2. The flow of functions from stock and substitutes need not be maintained at the current level (Ekins p. 112). The level to be sustained may be equal to, higher than or lower than the current level, but is generally lower.
3. Consumption of a particular resource 'in a given period' will never fall to zero, and certainly not if there are 'substantial discoveries' (Ekins p. 112). In our method, resource consumption gradually approximates zero.
4. The Tinbergen–Hueting–de Boer–Bosch method cannot be construed as an application of the strong sustainability principle, for it rejects the distinction between strong and weak sustainability as untenable (see Hueting 1998b as well as H&B, Section 7 and Section 1, Consequences of the Principles, 2). If this distinction is to be made at all, we are here concerned with weak rather than strong sustainability, as posited by Ekins (p. 114).

3 HERMAN DALY

In the debate on nature and the environment there are few people with whom I feel such affinity as Herman Daly. He too deems production growth, as measured in the national income, to be at the heart of the environmental problem. I had therefore expected my rejoinder to Herman to be easy. But Herman has a habit of making people pause for reflection and I indeed prove no exception. In his study he poses a key question that is scarcely ever asked: is there such a thing as objectively good preferences? If the answer is 'yes', then according to Daly this means that alongside subjective preferences there are also objective preferences, since the subjects subordinate their preferences to what is objectively good (or ought to do so). This leads logically to the thesis that objective values exist, alongside subjective.

One of the artefacts used by Daly in defence of this thesis is my perpendicular demand curve, that is to say, perpendicular in the relevant range (see H&B, p. 42). In doing so, he misinterprets this curve. This must have been a conscious move, because in January 1999 we corresponded about the background of the curve, on which occasion I plainly stated my view on the matter. This view has been reported (and clarified relative to earlier formulations) in my publications of 1992 and thereafter: the perpendicular curve is based on an *assumption* regarding *subjective* individual preferences, namely that subjects have an absolute preference for attaining standards of sustainability for vital environmental functions; the absolute character of these preferences is bound up with the nature of a standard; the assumption is inevitable because preferences can be deduced only partially and is legitimate because of the existence of what I have termed 'blockages' (see H&B, p. 42). Daly posits that my perpendicular 'demand curve' is intended to be an expression of objective value, not individual preferences. This is then compatible with Daly's own perspective, in which the attainment of sustainability is an end that is objectively good and one to which the subjects conform their individual ends or wants and thus their preferences (reflecting the relative weights of those wants); these individual preferences are thus objective, for they are derived from an objectively good, generally valid end. This, at least, is how I understand Daly after a close reading of his study in Chapter 5.

With his interpretation, Daly apparently wished to initiate a debate on preferences and the underlying ends or wants (two words for the same notion), and not only those of human beings but also of other organisms. For this I am grateful, although I myself have a different outlook. For the same holds true for perspectives as for assumptions: rendering them explicit improves the quality of the information, because readers then know what they are up against.

Of somewhat less apparent interest are Herman's remarks about a perpendicular supply curve for environmental functions. At the end of the present section I hope to demonstrate that such a curve is an impossibility.

In treating Herman's study, I shall first expound my view on economics, which I shall then confront with his theses. However, these theses in fact imply an outlook on the world that co-determines Daly's perspective on economics: there is thus an underlying perspective or 'vision'. To this I shall turn after discussing point (1) below. Those who dispute the scientific nature of the portion of my rejoinder ensuing from 'vision' and thus from personal experience and beliefs in the widest sense I shall not counter.

My view on economics, by no means unique, can be summarized as follows. Economics rests on assumptions. The basic assumption is that in their dealings with scarce means human beings endeavour to achieve maximum satisfaction of their wants; 'endeavour', because mistakes are possible, and may sometimes be serious. This is a tautology, because the opposite is nonsensical, but it is nonetheless of the utmost importance and all too frequently forgotten. Wants or ends are meta-economic and are not for economists to judge. Ultimately, the economic problem boils down to the problem of choice arising from scarce means and conflicting ends (or 'purposes' in Daly's terminology). The bottom line – the satisfaction of wants, that is welfare – is not amenable to direct measurement. And so we make do with measurable factors which are assumed, by reasoned argument, to have an influence on welfare (see H&B, Section 3, with background literature).

From this it follows that an assumption regarding wants must *always* be made. The assumption must be reasoned through, it must be plausible. In my work and in the summary thereof in H&B, the plausibility and legitimacy of the assumption of preferences for sustainability are defended. In responding to Paul Ekins, I repeat once more that it is not only the prices of environmental functions that are unknown because preferences are unknown; the correct market prices are likewise unknown, and from that I draw the conclusion that the standard national income is also based on assumptions and is therefore just as hypothetical as the SNI. To this I would here add another argument, one that is scarcely ever mentioned in discussions, if at all. To hold market prices and the national income based on these prices for certainties is to assume implicitly that there is absolute consistency between wants and actions. This consistency has been disputed, *inter alia* by Marcuse (1964), who posits that we are caught up in the existing structure of production and consumption and in our actions are consequently hampered in satisfying our true wants. Others have expressed similar views (see footnote on p. 88 of Hueting, 1980a). There is no way to decide this issue one way or the other: it is a question of plausibility, and I myself hold the opposite of Marcuse's thesis to be the more plausible. But I certainly do not reject the thesis as nonsense, when, for example, I see parents, *nolens volens*, driving their children to school or the playground because of the dangers of traffic (see, for example, Hueting 1974a, 1980a). Kuznets would probably characterize these expenditures as intermediate and thus as costs (see Hueting, 1974a). Summarizing: (1) people buy cars, meat and holiday flights because they like them; and (2) the assumption that the positive value of these products is higher than the negative value of the inherent loss of vital functions, which is implicitly made when constructing and using national income figures, is disputable; other assumptions are defensible.

Proceeding from this view, I shall now turn to what I consider to be the principal issues raised in Herman's study.

1. For Daly the only valid definition of (national) income is that of Hicks's *Value and Capital* and it is this that should, he holds, be my basic point of reference. Hicks's concept of national income, says Daly, is 'built around a prudential purpose' and consequently not based on individual preferences. That purpose can be formulated in two ways. The first is: net consumption of capital is to be avoided. If capital is consumed this counts as negative income, for which an appropriate correction should be introduced to arrive at the correct figure. National income, in Daly's view, is therefore by definition sustainable and the term SNI a pleonasm.

But Tinbergen, in the 1930s a chief architect of the system of National Accounts and the concept of national income, and implicitly also Kuznets, for whom the same applies, albeit to a lesser degree, did proceed from individual preferences, with Tinbergen making clearly explicit the assumptions he thereby made (see Hueting 1974a, 1991d). Given that official national incomes are based on this concept and that their growth enjoys top priority in economic politics the world over, to the detriment of the environment, there is an eminently practical reason for conforming to this concept in correcting for environmental loss: comparability. But there is also a theoretical reason for following Tinbergen rather than Hicks, and it is equally important. From the view on economics outlined above, Hicks's income concept rests on an assumption *vis-à-vis* individual preferences: that subjects are prepared to sacrifice a portion of their present consumption, namely up to the time-dependent and therefore variable level required to keep constant the capacity for producing consumption goods, expressed as the aggregate stock of man-made and natural capital. That level (the Hicksian income according to this first formulation) may thus be lower than the level actually realized, even at the start of the year. In Hicks's day the implicit assumption regarding individual preferences was anything but robust: structural, long-term production growth was (and for many still is) an eternal given and the environment was still conspicuously absent in the economic literature (see Tinbergen, in Hueting 1974a, 1991d). Applied to the situation post-1970, however, the assumption is certainly robust.

This can best be clarified with reference to a second, oft-used formulation of Hicksian income: income is what one can spend (consume) in the course of a year without being worse off at year's end. But whether one is better or worse off depends on one's preferences for current consumption relative to future consumption options. If the latter weigh more heavily in a person's preference pattern, then in pursuing Hicks's 'prudential purpose' (Daly's phrase) he or she will be better off, but at a substantially lower level of consumption. If current consumption weighs more heavily, they will be worse off.

Stringing individual years into a long-term time series, it is only the second formulation that yields a constant national income. If preferences for sustainability are moreover assumed to predominate, this yields a national income that is the maximum achievable while securing sustainability; this is then the SNI according to Hueting. (For the reasoning, see my response to Sylvia Faucheux and Martin O'Connor and also H&B, p. 59, for the time horizon taken.) But, in contrast to the Hicksian income, this SNI does rest on a robust assumption regarding preferences: that subjects are 'better off' if, and only if, vital environmental functions remain available *ad infinitum*. Contrary to the situation in Hicks's day, those preferences involve a willingness to accept the sacrifice of a substantial reduction in consumption and a drastically changed consumption pattern. Such willingness and acceptance can be neither proven nor falsified and can therefore only be assumed. To dispute that securing sustainability requires sacrifice is to dispute the existence of the environmental problem.

In addition, the magnitude of this sacrifice, and with it the level of the SNI, can in practice only be estimated with the aid of quantitative sustainability standards established with the greatest scientific rigour (see Hueting 1998b and H&B, Section 7). Again, this is not something to which Hicks attended, because in his day the environment was not an issue. Neither, certainly, did Hicks foresee a substantial sacrifice of consumption. In designing the concept of 'national income' Tinbergen likewise ignored the environment, because it was not then a factor of significance; as from the early 1970s, however, he was a firm advocate of correcting national income for environmental loss (see Hueting 1974a, 1991d). Whether Hicks, too, adopted a similar position in his later life we do not know. Daly as well as Salah El Sarafy, whom he cites, ignore both the assumption regarding preferences and the practical necessity of estimating physical sustainability standards. My conclusion: in the novel situation of a new fundamental category of scarce goods, the established concepts of the economic literature cannot be applied gratuitously (see H&B, pp. 32–3).

2. The second point, more than the first, is concerned with the deep, philosophical questions raised by Herman in our correspondence, which I have interpreted above as his underlying perspective or 'vision'. Herman makes it especially difficult for me here, for when he uses the word 'purpose' he appears to have two entirely different senses in mind, which he does not disentangle: (a) '(human) ends', in the established economic sense of the term, that is meaning wants or needs (fulfilling wants is the same as attaining ends); and (b) the general philosophical or religious meaning of 'object for which a thing exists, final cause' (OXFORD DICTIONARY). What is concerned

in the latter case, as I understand it, are such questions as: Is there a purpose to life, to existence, or is it without purpose? What is the meaning or purpose of existence? This impression is reinforced by Daly's use of the term to encompass all other organisms on the planet, too.

Daly answers the question whether human beings and other organisms have a purpose unshakingly in the affirmative. As an agnostic, my own answer must be: I do not know. On the sole basis of Daly's text I cannot deduce what exactly he holds to be the purpose, but my interpretation is that conservation of nature and the environment, and thus sustainability (or, more religiously coloured, 'stewardship'), are certainly part of it.

I use this interpretation to bridge the gap to the strictly economic sense of the term 'purpose'. Daly addresses my concerned question: If individual preferences are rejected, by whom or by what are our preferences determined? Not, evidently, by government. Neither is that indeed feasible, of course, certainly not in the case of sustainability. Although many governments have rallied behind 'sustainability', following the Brundtland Report, they still continue to give top priority to the conflicting goal of 'production growth': governments build roads, fill in estuaries to construct harbours, open up natural areas to development and neglect to make the market operate in a legislative framework that might lead to sustainability (internalization). The Brundtland Report is itself a matter of conflicting goals, it should be added (see Hueting, 1990c). Daly's answer to my question, now, is the following: 'purpose' is an objective value, a moral compass ('magnetic north'), a generally valid goal which is objectively good and to which both individual subjects and governments (should) subordinate their other objectives.

But this answer begs new questions, such as: (1) How do such 'objectively good' goals arise, and in particular that of 'sustainability'? (2) Alternatively, do they not arise but simply exist? (3) In that case must they be 'eternal' and therefore immutable? (4) How do individuals recognize the objectively good goals to which they (should) conform? From a close reading of Daly's text I distil the following answers to these questions. These objectively good goals are simply there. They are immutable over time. The subjects are well aware what these goals involve. They also know they should (really) show the courage or willingness to subordinate their other wants or goals accordingly – in the realm of sustainability, the goal of additional consumption or unprotected sex, for example. They should also refuse to allow themselves to be manipulated by governments that give priority to goals that conflict with the objectively good. Sustainability is, for sure, an objectively good goal.

Here we have a view on economics derived from a particular outlook on life, on human existence. Herman Daly is a believer. As an agnostic, I lack such faith. But before the reader rejects as eccentric the notion of a person's faith influencing his or her view on economics (including sustainability), let me recall Adam Smith, often cited as the founding father of economics. For was it not Smith who said: the baker bakes his bread as well as he can, not to serve his fellow man but in his own interest? Herein, too, lies embodied an outlook on the human species that determines the perspective from which economics is practised.

Above, I have stated my own view on economics. In consciously misinterpreting my perpendicular demand curve, Herman is in fact implicitly asking me: What is your underlying view or 'vision'? Challenged thus, and for this reason alone, I shall answer that question. Compared with 50–65 years ago, when I held a firm belief, there remains today but one element: a belief in information. I proceed from the assumption that if individual subjects are in possession of appropriate factual information, they will make fewer and less serious errors in endeavouring to attain their goals or, in other words, maximize their welfare (see above). I make no pronouncement on the virtue of those goals (see *New Scarcity* and H&B, Section 3). In religious terms: it is God (rather than man) who is the judge of motives. I thus assume that when subjects have made their choices on the basis of correct information the outcome thereof is 'good' in the sense just mentioned.

The hardest problems arise in the case of collective decisions concerning collective goods such as the environment (sustainability), democracy, and war and peace. As history shows, it is in these realms, above all, that agreement on the validity of information is often lacking, that information is often manipulated or, worse, supplanted by disinformation. History also shows that subjects experience bitter remorse, after the event, if they have acquiesced unprotestingly, due to ignorance, indifference, impotence (real or imagined) or lack of courage, to decisions which for them have proved disastrous and which were taken by individual subjects constituting government, even if those subjects were elected democratically.

Examples are rife, even restricting myself to what I myself have witnessed (sometimes at close hand). In the democratic elections of 1930, Hitler's NSDAP became Germany's second largest party; in 1933 he was elected Chancellor, by way of the democratic process. A small number of individual subjects informed the world about the lies on which that victory rested and about subsequent turns of event. I was seven when I first heard that information. With my own eyes I saw how the majority chose not to believe that information ('the easy way'?) and how already then, four years prior to the outbreak of war, resistance to an inevitable occupation was therefore mounted by a small group of individual subjects. Today, that information is universally believed, and remorse is bitter. Shortly after the war, the democratically elected individual subjects comprising the Dutch government chose to undertake two 'police actions' in Indonesia. The vast majority of the population acquiesced. From Dutch citizens in Indonesia information was available to the effect that those actions constituted a colonial war against freedom fighters. There were but few who gave credence, however. The vast majority believed the aim was to restore law and order, which had been disturbed by a *small* group of 'terrorists'. That majority also included the *small* group of individuals from whom I had heard what was going on in Germany ten years prior and who had mounted resistance, regardless of personal consequence. Today, remorse is the predominant sentiment.

In India, marked on the constitutional atlas as a democracy, I have seen how (widespread) child labour is accepted by much of the population; in some of its manifestations the term slave labour is closer to the truth. This acceptance is likely to decline, however, when information on the consequences for these children sinks into people and the size of families decreases. In my experience, the latter will only be the case if the status of women is improved. For thousands of years slavery and the denial of women's rights, including passive and active voting rights, were accepted facts. In ancient Greece, where the word and notion of democracy were born, the very concept of suffrage for women was not even raised, even by women; slavery was an accepted fact of life. The same held true in classical Rome. Indeed, denial of women's suffrage was generally accepted in both Europe and the USA until the twentieth century. In those countries, slavery was long accepted by the vast majority of the population and their churches. Today, shame predominates. At any particular time, some groups of individuals consider themselves *genuinely* superior. Herein lies part of the cause of these historical events, and of what is still happening today. But human perspectives and the preferences based upon them are continuously evolving.

All these phenomena, from personal experience or from literature, have led me to a different outlook from that of Herman Daly on a number of issues. Let me mention the principal of these. (1) My faith in such abstractions as 'government objectives' has declined. (2) Democracy, contrary to what Herman holds, certainly does find itself subjected to a popular vote – every day anew. (3) Individuals having different preferences which, contrary to what Herman holds, are not a priori either good or bad, may, again contrary to what Herman holds, most surely engage in dialogue. They may exchange information, validate that information and discuss interpretation thereof. Indeed, democracy requires that they do so as an intensive and ongoing process. (4) Perspectives on good and evil evolve over time and differ from culture to culture, often markedly so. But on one point we can wholeheartedly agree: individuals should not allow themselves to be manipulated by other individuals, whether embodying government or otherwise.

Above, most of what there is to say about preferences for sustainability has, *mutatis mutandis*, already been said. Individual subjects, be they citizens or politicians, are confounded in the extreme by the economic information with which they are confronted. Largely through the media and other coverage of economic affairs, there has evolved an almost universal belief in a conflict between environment and employment and in production growth being able to go hand in hand with environmental conservation – and, indeed, even in the necessity of such growth for conservation, whereas the opposite is true: environmental protection creates jobs and conflicts with production growth (as set out in *Three Myths*, Chapter 3, this volume). There is absolutely no justification for proceeding from individual behaviour, because of the existence of what I have termed blockages (see H&B, p. 42). Scarcely, if ever, can subjects form an conception of the *physical* benefits of extremely complex processes, the physical costs (as negative benefits) of disturbance thereof and the technological (im)possibility of intervention in such disturbance. This is also one of the insurmountable problems of contingent valuation (see Hueting, 1989b, 1992a, 1995b). Although on the scientific side our information is better and more consistent, here too there are still major uncertainties. Let me mention the two examples that to me appear the most important: (1) the forced greenhouse effect and (2) the macro-effect of species extinction. The uncertainty regarding the first I presume to be universally familiar. The latter uncertainty is discussed in Hueting (1974a, pp. 145 and 146, English edition), based on the work of Eugene Odum and also personally validated by him. In short, the continuing burden on the environment may lead to an ecological crisis in which man's continued existence is at stake, but there is no way of indicating at what level of burden such a crisis will occur. In the estimation of SNI according to Hueting, species conservation is nonetheless taken as a sustainability standard. That norm is based on the precautionary principle and on the fact that the rate at which species are becoming extinct today is at least a factor 10000 higher than the rate at which new species are evolving (see H&B, p. 67).

My conclusion: there is considerable scope for improving and debating information *vis-à-vis* sustainability, as well as for debating what preferences for sustainability precisely are, before judgement can be made about those preferences. I conclude, and here I differ with Herman, that an assumption about preferences is inevitable as well as legitimate.

Herman posits that estimation of an SNI is a different matter from designing a policy for attaining sustainability in a market economy. But the opposite is true: estimates of SNI are based precisely on simulated internalization of sustainability costs in market prices (see H&B and Verbruggen et al.,

Chapter 11, this volume). He also posits that introduction of tradable permits leads to a perpendicular supply curve (and thus to an objective value). However, supply curves for environmental functions are made up of increasing costs per unit reduction of environmental burden, and thus per unit function restored or supplied. They are empirically grounded and have been estimated since the early 1970s (see Hueting, 1974a for several examples). Obviously, introduction of tradable permits does not change the characteristic, progressively rising shape of the curves. The sole objective is to achieve a certain level of environmental burden (for example emissions) as efficiently as possible. Any standard of environmental burden, sustainable or otherwise, can be represented as a limit and therefore as a perpendicular. Subsequently preferences, and therefore a *demand*, can be assumed which correspond to the (sustainability) standard (see H&B, p. 42, for the ins and outs of verticality). The degree of availability of environmental functions is determined by the standard (and thus by demand). The cost of supply depends on the shape of the specific elimination cost or supply curve determining the point of intersection with the standard or demand curve. This is shown, *inter alia*, in Figure 2.7 of H&B for a sustainability standard D.

A second objection is that there is no such thing as a perpendicular supply curve for environmental functions. Herman here appears to be making the same error as Constanza et al. (1997). A perpendicular supply curve intersects the abscissa. This means that the function (and its services) can be supplied at zero cost up to the perpendicular, which boils down to the statement that functions (including the vital functions of the world's ecosystems) are free goods, because they are 'supplied' free of charge. This is an inappropriate representation of the opportunity costs associated with provision of a typical environmental function. Consider the graphs A and B in Figure 13.1.

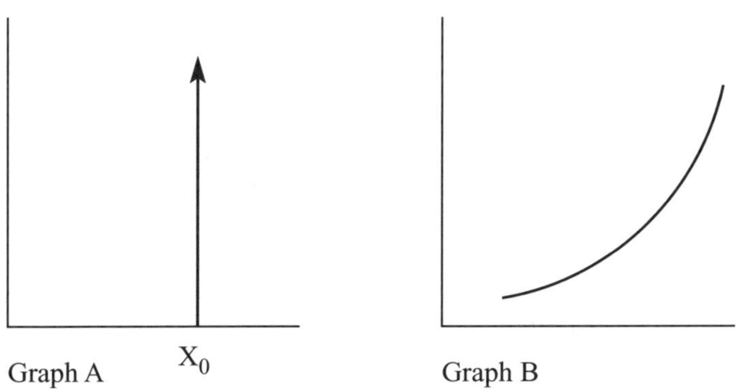

Figure 13.1 *Cost functions for environmental services*

The horizontal axis is some index of quantity and quality (that is: availability) of an environmental function, and the vertical axis is money units. In graph A, a certain amount X_0 of the function is available as a free good, but the cost of increasing the function's availability beyond this level is infinite. This corresponds to the 'indestructible land' of the classical economists, such as John Locke, Jean Baptiste Say and David Ricardo. But it is certainly *not* the typical situation when it comes to environmental functions, including those of the planet's forests, marine ecosystems, wetlands or arable lands, all of which are clearly *destructible* (more or less irreversibly). Now consider the question of how to value this indestructible asset. Say that it is productive land and that the product (say corn) has a money price. If, after every man has taken as much land as he wants, there is still some to spare, then the resource will have a zero price (free good). If, on the contrary, the amount is less than what people would utilize if it were freely available, the land will command a 'rent' as a factor of production, in accordance with established economic theory. However, this rent does *not* measure the cost of producing land, nor is it an opportunity cost in the sense of production having to be sacrificed to obtain more land. There is no question, in this situation, of loss of functions due to depletion of land, nor of marginal cost of an additional unit of land: its supply is fixed. So 'rent' is a value category that arises through imputation back to land as a factor of production, reflecting the usefulness of the land as a source of income through the market value of the goods produced with that land.

Consider by contrast environmental functions from, say, aquatic of forest ecosystems. These are not indestructible, neither is their quantity fixed. The amount of environmental functions available in any period of time becomes an endogenous variable. Today, the functions of ecosystems are no longer free goods (see, for example, H&B) and their supply curves are typically of the form shown in Figure 13.1 (graph B), as demonstrated by research (see, for example, Hueting 1974a; de Boer 1996). Measures must – and can – be taken in order to restore and safeguard the functions that one wishes to maintain, to the extent that irreversible losses have not yet occurred. These measures form (opportunity) costs. So sacrifices in terms of consumption (or family planning: lower national income, more environment) are evidently unavoidable. The costs of the measures form the basis for constructing a supply curve in the normal economic sense of the concept: the supply of a desired economic good through human activity involving the sacrifice of an alternative. The necessary sacrifices are obviously not reflected in the perpendicular that Daly and Costanza et al. (1997) have in mind. Therefore this curve is not a supply curve in the economic sense and cannot consequently be used for economic valuation of environmental functions and their services: all it tells us is that the cost of any quantity of function exceeding that indicated by the perpendicular would approach infinity.

Ecosystems as we find them, the result of hundreds of millions of years of evolution, cannot be quantitatively extended by human action. But they certainly can be – and in fact are – cut back by human (productive and consumptive) action. At the same time, however, these systems can be maintained and restored by human action. It looks as if what Daly and Costanza et al. (1997) have in mind is that irreplaceable goods cannot be supplied. However, it is possible to formulate measures (what has to be done and, above all, from which activities must people refrain?) in order to safeguard (the functions of) irreplaceable ecosystems, and to estimate the (opportunity) costs thereof. This yields an elimination or supply curve: the less risks one wishes to take, the higher the costs (see Hueting 1998a, 2001a).

4 RICHARD B. NORGAARD, ASTRID J. SCHOLZ AND SARAH FLEISCHER TRAINOR

Much of what Richard et al. bring forward in their contribution I can wholeheartedly endorse. In particular, I sincerely support their recommendation to stimulate opinion-forming on collective goods such as environmental functions in 'discursive, democratic processes', thus to arrive at better grounded preferences. Their study does, nonetheless, raise several questions and prompts me to make a few remarks.

1. I cannot comprehend their philippic against utilitarianism. In standard economic theory, utility has a far wider semantic range than in everyday language. Utility derives from anything that can satisfy human wants or – an equivalent statement – can help achieve human ends, to the extent that these depend on our dealings with scarce means. These wants or ends are not for economists to judge. Utility, or welfare, or satisfaction of wants is a psychic category that is not amenable to measurement. Information on the level thereof can be obtained only by introducing (plausible) assumptions. I refer the reader to H&B (Section 3) and my response to Herman Daly. If, for example, a subject deems biodiversity to yield *utility* (satisfaction of wants) in his or her own judgement and conservation thereof involves opportunity costs, in whatever form, then we have a problem of economic choice. In the sense used in standard economic theory, it is entirely irrelevant whether that utility consists of acquiring medicinal drugs and agricultural crops, of the agreeable knowledge that species are being conserved for

their 'intrinsic value', or ditto that future generations are not existentially threatened by disruption of life support systems, including ecosystems, leading to loss of vital environmental functions.

Richard et al. have distinct views on individual preferences, on the dependence of these on culture and historical juncture, and on ethical criteria and normative judgements *vis-à-vis* valuation of vital, indispensable environmental functions, which are collective goods. For my own views on these issues I refer the reader to my rejoinder to Herman Daly.

2. Ultimately, valuation is a question of preferences. Given the existence of scarcity, the bottom line of economics, (individual) preferences necessarily arise out of a process of choice. Which want or need is the more pressing? What alternative is to be sacrificed (opportunity costs)? Because preferences can be identified only very partially (see H&B, Section 5.2), in environmental or ecological economics there are just two 'leverage points': the description of the utility that environmental functions can provide, and the estimated opportunity costs associated with restoration and maintenance thereof, in the form of estimated cost-effectiveness: what reduction in environmental load and thus what increase in function restoration and maintenance is obtained at a certain cost level (see Hueting 1974a, p. 185, English edition)? The latter is a *conditio sine qua non*, for without opportunity costs there is no *economic* value (free goods). I do not therefore understand why even the word 'costs' is absent in Richard et al.'s contribution. When I asked Astrid and Sarah about this after their presentation at the Amsterdam symposium, they responded that they were unaware that such calculations could be made. But such cost-effectiveness estimates have been undertaken since the early 1970s (for some examples, see Hueting, 1974a). In all friendship, I can only conclude that the valuation processes advocated by Richard et al. remain counterproductive in the absence of such essential information as cost-effectiveness data, micro or macro (impact on national income). At the risk of pedantry, let me add one further remark. Contrary to what is commonly held, with opportunity costs money is not, in essence, the point at issue. Although cycling may indeed be cheaper than driving a car, for example, a shift towards cycling in the interests of sustainability does require a sacrifice and will have a negative effect on national income *volume* (see H&B, p. 57, my response to Paul Ekins and *Three Myths*, Chapter 3, this volume).
3. Contrary to Richard et al. I hold that objective, scientific descriptions of a given state of the environment and of sustainability standards are to be strictly distinguished from subjective preferences for such a state,

for sustainability, say (see Hueting, 1998b). If knowledge is lacking, the precautionary principle should be applied and research encouraged. If Richard et al. merely mean that availability of additional information influences preferences, then I am in full agreement with them.

4. On p. 163 the authors hold that I deem it immoral to destroy the vehicles of vital environmental functions, thus depriving future generations of use of those functions. No reference is given, and logically so, for I have never passed judgement on the morality of others. Why I would never consider doing such follows from my response to Herman Daly and, in part, from the above rejoinder.

5 WILFRED BECKERMAN

According to Wilfred Beckerman (Chapter 7, this volume), environmental considerations provide no grounds whatsoever for concern about the physical conditions under which future generations will have to live. In his opinion, an SNI study designed to estimate the distance between actual and sustainable levels of production and consumption is therefore entirely superfluous. The value of such a study rests, moreover, so Beckerman holds, on the erroneous notion that rights can be conferred upon future generations. Any undertaking on behalf of such generations can at best be based on 'imperfect obligations' borne of moral considerations.

Let me start with the second point. Conferring rights has nothing whatsoever to do with the SNI study, nor with any other topic on which I have ever published. The SNI according to Hueting is not based on the rights of future generations, nor on intergenerational equity, but on the *preferences* of the present generation for handing down the vital functions of our physical surroundings (the environment) intact to generations to come. There are two grounds for assuming such preferences. First, the existence of 'blockages' preventing these preferences from being expressed (see H&B, p. 142). Second, the postulate that 'man derives part of the meaning of existence from the company of others. These others include in any case his children and grandchildren. The prospect of a safer future is therefore a normal human need, and dimming of this prospect has a negative effect on welfare' (Hueting, 1987d).

Regardless of these considerations, though, why should one not speak of the rights of future generations? Unlike Wilfred, I am a complete layman in the realm of philosophy (of law). Nonetheless, I do not see how his reasoning can stand up to scrutiny. Wilfred is obviously right in stating that if something no longer exists (an animal species, for example) there is no sense in speaking of rights and obligations. But why should we not be able to confer upon future generations the right to dispose over vital environmental functions that *do* still exist, among them the functions of life support systems, of which natural ecosystems (biodiversity) form an important part? If we assign such rights, surely these would be balanced by our obligation not to destroy those systems? Then surely Beckerman's logical condition is satisfied that rights should always have their counterpart in obligations? Surely the indeed unsatisfiable condition that future generations be able to exercise or waive such rights is not a *conditio sine qua non*?

I put these questions to C.W. Maris, specialized in philosophy of law, and W. Achterberg, specialized in environmental, moral and political philosophy, both at the University of Amsterdam. Their answer: 'yes, indeed'. They had more to say, though.

One's answer depends on how 'rights' are defined. It is, in short, a question of semantics. If rights are defined such that the bearer thereof is to be able to choose whether or not to exercise them – if, in other words, they are defined in terms of the protection of individual autonomy – then there is an identity problem. 'Future persons' cannot, after all, be individually identified. No contract can therefore be concluded with them entailing specific rights and obligations. Beckerman's discourse proceeds from this definition of rights. However, if rights are defined in terms of the protection of interests, there is no problem of identity. Interests are often diffuse and not specifically attached to discrete persons but to groups of persons, such as future generations, for example. In the latter case we can proceed from the reasonable assumption that there will be people in the future and that these 'future persons' will have an interest in being able to dispose over those environmental functions that are indispensable for human life (see, for example, Feinberg, 1974). It is, therefore, surely possible to confer rights of the disposal over those vital functions upon future generations, balancing them with an obligation to hand down these functions undamaged.

Beckerman argues the first point – that there is no need for concern about future generations – solely by extrapolating observed trends *vis-à-vis* technological progress. Two points of criticism can be raised here: (1) his extrapolation is only partial; (2) it is unduly simple.

1. On the first point, Beckerman asserts (p. 170) that my exclusive focus is on stocks of natural resources and in his contesting the need for concern he refers solely to stocks of non-renewables, albeit that renewable energy sources are mentioned in a discussion of fossil fuels. Non-renewables formed in slow geological processes are clearly important natural resources. Wilfred's treatment of these resources is inconsistent and takes inadequate account of the many different functions of the resources. Thus he argues that 'we will never run out of any resource or even suffer seriously from any

sudden reduction in its supply' (p. 178). Further on, though, he approvingly quotes authors who hold that fossil carbon resources will run out in several hundred or thousand years (p. 180).

He asserts, furthermore, that 'if, for example, coal were ever to become a very scarce commodity its price would rise to the point where, like other minerals, such as diamonds, it would be used only for jewellery or certain very special industrial uses' (pp. 178–9). In that case, however, its function as a major source of energy would clearly be lost. Because natural resources formed in geological time should for practical purposes be considered finite and because prices may be expected to soar as resources peter out, ongoing dissipation of these resources will lead ultimately to loss of most, if not all their current functions. With ongoing dissipation, the question is not whether functions will be lost, but when.

Beckerman moreover ignores the fact that burning all fossil carbon stocks would lead to dramatic climatic changes (Graedel and Crutzen, 1993).

Non-renewables are not the only resources on which humankind depends, however. Contrary to Wilfred's assertion, in my work I have always stressed the importance of the life support systems of our planet (for a brief description: H&B, note 2, p. 72). These constitute a key element in the estimation of sustainable national income. Life support systems are not stocks but *processes.* These processes are irreplaceable and non-substitutable; and they are threatened by the ongoing growth of production and consumption by ever more people. Their functioning depends on conditions far up into the atmosphere and probably even beyond. Their equilibrium is vulnerable, extremely complex and as yet only very imperfectly understood. There are already instances in which meddling with those processes has had major deleterious consequences. Cases in point include the recent collapse of a number of fish populations in the North Atlantic and several other important fishing grounds (FAO, 1990–1998; Tolba and El-Kholy, 1992) and, in the more distant past, the collapse of agriculture and a highly evolved culture on Easter Island (due to erosion and the clearcutting of forests) and in what is now southern Iraq (due to salinization) (Reijnders, 1996).

Natural ecosystems are part of the life support systems on which humankind depends. The threat to such ecosystems goes far beyond the extinction of Beckerman's Dodo (Odum, 1971; Lovelock, 1979; Goodland, 1995). Species are currently being lost at a rate exceeding new species formation by several orders of magnitude (see H&B, p. 67, and Hueting, 1998b) and the area of land covered by natural ecosystems is dwindling rapidly. This is fast reducing the availability of resources for plant breeding and pharmaceuticals production and altering the composition of the atmosphere

(Lovelock, 1979; Tolba and El-Kholy, 1992; Graedel and Crutzen, 1993; Goodsland, 1995).

These processes, absolutely vital for future generations, have no part in Wilfred's extrapolations. They are not even mentioned, in fact.

2. My second point of criticism is that Beckerman merely extrapolates historical trends. Attempts to shed light on future economic developments are unfortunately not that straightforward, however. I might well do the same as Wilfred. Consider the following: in estimating the distance between the standard world income and its sustainable counterpart Tinbergen and Hueting arrive at a rough figure of 50 per cent of current world income (see Hueting, 1991d). The provisional results of a modelling exercise show that this estimate is by no means extreme (Verbruggen et al., Chapter 11, this volume). This study also demonstrates that the present 'sustainability gap' cannot be bridged with the technology currently available, implying an additional need for changes in consumption patterns. Not that long ago, on the relevant geological time scale, this gap was virtually non-existent, for environmental functions were then free goods (see H&B., pp. 29, 34 and 35). Despite gigantic technological strides being made, then, with regard to those functions of our physical surroundings that permit our very survival there is an empirical trend of growing scarcity. Entirely in line with Wilfred's method, I might then extrapolate this trend and conclude: if we continue down the present path, humankind as a species is doomed to extinction, regardless of technological progress. Obviously more information can be gained from tracing the development of the gap between SNI and actual national income than from extending lines.

I share Wilfred's optimism about technological progress, although not *in extremo*, particularly when it comes to renewable energy resources to substitute for fossil fuels. However, I would point out a number of errors and omissions that render his extrapolations unduly simple.

(i) In Beckerman's view, scientific and technological progress are the fundamental driving force determining production growth (p. 176). I agree. However, intellect and our physical surroundings are entirely complementary. All produced goods, including human-made capital goods, are a combination of intellect and elements of our physical surroundings. Without the latter, we humans are left empty-handed (see H&B, p. 29 and 'Three Myths', Chapter 3, this volume). The issue is therefore whether the functions of our physical environment remain intact. A number of elements of our environment are irreplaceable and non-substitutable. These Beckerman ignores, as I have already noted. Exhaustible resources must be substitutable (in time) by other elements of our physical surroundings that can provide the same services. Wilfred's assertion that this will remain possible *ad infinitum*, regardless of the levels to which production and consumption soar, is pure speculation and thus at odds with the wisdom of the precautionary principle. He argues this position with almost exclusive reference to energy. But what about the resources required for food production and the world's finite stocks of freshwater? There is no agreement about the adequacy of natural resources to feed an ever-growing world population, particularly given the finite nature of freshwater resources and the ongoing deterioration of land suitable for agriculture due to soil compaction, erosion, salinization and other processes (Tolba and El-Kholy, 1992; Kendall and Pimentel, 1994). For Wilfred, however, all this is absolutely no cause for concern, for his extrapolations assume ever-rising per capita income, *ad infinitum*.

(ii) On p. 178 Beckerman asserts that the price mechanism will ensure that there are no disastrous shocks. There have been serious famines in the recent past, however, in some cases compounded by shortages of drinking water, and new famines are anticipated in the near future (Tolba and El-Kholy, 1992; Kendall and Pimentel, 1994).

(iii) Beckerman's extrapolations are unduly simple, for he overlooks at least six factors of relevance. First, he makes no allowance for the fact that any price rise in real terms means a decline in the volume of national income and therefore a check on production growth (see H&B, pp. 34–5). *Second, Wilfred overlooks the fact that, for a given technology, product costs will rise progressively as the yield (effect) of environmental measures is increased. Technological progress leads to higher yields, of course. As production increases further, however, so too must the yield of the measures in order to maintain the same state of the environment, while the fact of progressively rising costs with rising yield remains unaltered. There is thus a 'race' between environmental technology and production growth, the outcome of which cannot be predicted.* Third, Wilfred neglects the fact that the vast bulk of production growth is generated by the approximately 30 per cent of industries that cause most pollution, utilize the greatest amount of land and deplete natural resources most rapidly (see Hueting, 1981b, 1992d, my response to Ekins and H&B, p. 57). A shift towards environmentally more benign activities therefore implies a substantial check on production growth. Such a shift is already unavoidable if sustainability is to be achieved; see the first paragraph of (2) above. Fourth, Wilfred neglects to consider the impact of increasing land use on, *inter alia*, species extinction, because he ignores the importance of life support systems for human survival.

Fifth, Wilfred does not take into account that in a long historical time series energy consumption (and CO_2 emissions) is found to run parallel to production and that there is negligible substitution by renewable energy sources, that is energy derived from the sun (see Hueting, 1991d). This trend he does *not* extrapolate. Although in the recent past there have been brief periods in which production growth, as measured in national income, was not accompanied by rising energy use, overall in the last 50 years this has been the case (Schipper and Meyers, 1992; Adriaanse et al., 1997; de Bruyn et al., 1998). As a rule, moreover, renewable energy is currently much more expensive than energy generated using fossil fuels. In the case of photovoltaic power, the price may even be far higher than electricity from a coal-fired plant (Johansson et al., 1993). And although I share Wilfred's conviction that the cost of renewable energy will fall substantially in the future, implementation costs will do so far less. The latter will be extremely high, in my estimate, which will check production growth. For this check to be removed and continued production growth achieved, the renewables will have to become *cheaper* than current fossil energy. Whether this will ever be the case we cannot predict. The same holds for substitutes for any other resource.

Sixth, Wilfred makes no allowance for the fact that, for there to be growth of the total mass of production, the productivity of the approximately 30 per cent most environmentally burdening sectors that generate most of that growth would have to rise by far more than the overall average. Consequently, the yield of environmental measures in these sectors would likewise have to increase by far more than the average across the national income in order to maintain the same state of the environment – possibly a factor two or three more, with progressively rising elimination costs and a severe check on production growth as a result (see above). A correct estimate of this factor requires more than a back of the envelope calculation, however (see my response to Ekins).

If due allowance is made for all these factors (and their interrelationships), the growth and other figures predicted by Wilfred may well prove to be a factor ten to twenty too high. But that requires a far more extensive analysis than Wilfred has presented and, as I have said, I have major doubts about the usefulness of such prognostications.

6 SALAH EL SERAFY

Salah El Sarafy (Chapter 8, this volume) shares my concern that the universally accepted compass of economic policy – changes in national income

– is giving us the wrong signals about economic success. Despite irrefutable, or as yet unrefuted, information on the defectiveness of this compass, as detailed by numerous authors for several decades now, there is not one country in the world that has ever published in its official statistics a national income figure amended for natural resource depletion and damage to irreplaceable ecosystems. Economic activity thus continues to be steered by the wrong compass despite steps in the right direction, such as putting physical environmental data into satellite accounts. When it comes to our understanding of economics, too, Salah and I are in basic agreement. With reference to Robbins, Salah states quite rightly that economics is a positivist (descriptive) rather than normative theory. Salah's conjecture, in Section 5, that my introducing competing environmental functions as scarce, and therefore economic, goods is based on Robbins' work is thus correct. I received my training under Hennipman, whose masterful *œuvre* builds on that of Rosenstein and Robbins; see H&B (Section 3), and elsewhere. Finally, Salah states, as I do in the introduction to these Rejoinders, that ecological economists are often unduly dismissive of what they take to be neoclassical economics, and have unnecessarily limited influence as a result.

In Section 6 of his study Salah says he will try and highlight our differences in views, as one reviewer had asked. It is an endeavour in which he has scarcely succeeded, I feel, and given my last paragraph it could hardly be otherwise. To my mind, Salah and I are in agreement on the following essential points:

1. Salah considers my chief concern to be with welfare, giving my work a broader perspective than his own, which he regards as being concerned solely with correct accounting practice. This cannot be the case, for several reasons. From the writings of Rosenstein-Rodan, Robbins and Hennipman and others it follows directly that all economic activity is directed towards the satisfaction of wants and therefore, by definition, towards maximizing welfare (H&B, Section 3). Indeed, what other purpose could it possibly have? The opposite is nonsensical. Data that tell us nothing about welfare, whether directly or indirectly, are therefore devoid of meaning as economic information. Only if welfare increases can there be economic success. Time series of the volume of national income were intended by Tinbergen, Kuznets and the other theoreticians of the SNA to serve as just one indicator of how well a society is succeeding in satisfying its wants, that is achieving welfare, and specifically the indicator of the influence on welfare of scarce goods, under a number of assumptions (Hueting, 1991d; H&B, Section 3). And this is how these time series are still conceived, positive changes

prompting 'flags out' on government buildings and at newspaper offices, and negative changes mourning costumes.

This was perfectly justified as long as all scarce goods were being registered in the national accounts, but became untenable with the widespread emergence of a new category of fundamental, scarce goods – environmental functions. This view was shared by a growing number of authors, including Tinbergen (see Hueting, 1991d) and almost certainly Kuznets (see my rejoinder to Daly). Others, meanwhile, see no reason why the flag-waving and mourning should not continue unabated, the combination of budget and market mechanisms in a democracy being deemed as firm a guarantee as ever of a package of goods – produced goods *and* environmental functions – in perfect conformity with the preferences of the economic subjects (individuals and institutions).

In my work I have argued extensively (in H&B and elsewhere) that this is an *assumption*, an assumption implying that the economy is on an optimum path. That is a legitimate assumption. But no more so than the assumption that there exist overriding preferences for sustainability that are prevented from being expressed by the existence of blockages, implying that the (far) lower-level path on which the SNI lies is optimum (see H&B, Section 5.2). If they are to be providers of impartial economic information, statistical offices therefore have a scientific and moral obligation to publish several national income figures based on different assumptions concerning preferences. Salah can only belong to the former group of authors (preferences not properly reflected, current path suboptimal). Being familiar with his work and his interventions in discussions, neither can I imagine that he regards national income as a mere registration of transactions unrelated to the satisfaction of human needs (welfare), including those of populations of developing countries. Salah's assumptions may be a little more cautious than mine, but the conclusion can never be that my work is broader in perspective.

2. Following Hicks, Salah holds that correct accounting practice involves writing off both human-made capital and non-renewable and renewable resources such as forests at market prices in the current accounting year. (National) income is what remains after depreciation. However, as argued more extensively in my response to Daly, this entails an assumption about preferences which in Hicks's day scarcely merited that name, but today is entirely robust, namely that subjects are prepared to sacrifice a substantial portion of their consumption in order to preserve (the functions of) natural resources. My conclusion once more: Salah and I merely entertain different assumptions.

3. Salah writes that I am seeking consensus on the 'right' approach (p. 202). That is not entirely true, however. What I do see as a minimum requirement is that an explanation be provided for the enormous differences in the results of the 'bewildering variety of approaches and estimates', as Salah puts it on p. 201, and I feel that this should be the concern of us all (see my Introduction, above, and Hueting, 2001a, quoted by Salah. For most authors, including Salah, I feel I have pinpointed the cause of the problems: differences in assumptions that often remain implicit – assumptions about preferences, for example, and about whether or not the economy is on an optimum path. Here, too, we are undoubtedly in agreement.

On the following points, to my mind less crucial, I do see a difference of view:

(i) To my mind no distinction can be made between weak and strong sustainability (Hueting, 1998b; H&B, Section 7). When it comes to environmental sustainability, only one thing matters: preservation of vital environmental functions (that is possible uses of the environment). These functions depend on the state of our physical surroundings (including physical processes), the result of a vast historical process going back many thousands or hundreds of thousands of years. By the same measure, environmental sustainability must also be a very long-term issue. It follows that the only behaviour to be deemed sustainable is that guaranteeing long-term preservation of vital environmental functions. That is why I hold it to be simply unsustainable to expend the funds set aside under 'resource depreciation' on investments in human-made capital (p. 195), unless the explicit aim is to generate substitutes, which is sometimes unfeasible and sometimes essential for attaining sustainability (Hueting, 1998b; H&B, Section 7). Although it may be advantageous for a particular country to invest these funds in the consumer goods industry, if every country does so it will be of no advantage at all. After all, the chief environmental problems – resource depletion, loss of biodiversity, global warming and so on – are global issues. I would like to add that in 'the SNI according to Hueting' the share of a given country in elimination costs is taken proportional to that country's contribution to the exhaustion of renewable and non-renewable resources, thus leaving income ratios unaffected; national contributions to resource depletion are reckoned on the basis of national *consumption* (see Hueting, 1992d, and elsewhere).

(ii) There is absolutely nothing to guarantee that the depreciations at market prices (sums set aside), mentioned in point 2, above, are equal to the sums required to preserve intact the functions of the resources in question – the crucial condition of 'sustainability'. The same applies to the interest rate. Salah's Hicksian income depends on the choice of interest rate. How does one know that the interest figures used are adequate for the measures required to meet sustainability standards?

(iii) Salah says his sole intention is to improve on the registration methods currently being used by national accountants. The System of National Accounts (SNA) records only *transactions*, however, as per international agreement. The corrections that Salah (and many others with him, including this author) would like to see implemented are not based on transactions and – contrary to what he himself suggests – Salah's work is not therefore in accordance with the SNA guidelines. Once more, we are up against underlying assumptions. In the SNA it is assumed – *implicitly* – that the economy is on an optimum path. There would already be major gains in terms of impartiality of economic information if this assumption were rendered explicit. This would automatically mean having to publish more than one national income figure (see point 1, above).

(iv) Salah states (p. 205) that adjusting the national income in deference to strong sustainability 'would lead to meaningless estimates'. This he illustrates with reference to the hypothetical example of a country whose national income consists entirely of the sales revenues of a particular resource extracted at zero cost. According to Salah the required correction then equals the market price of the quantity of the resource extracted and sold in the current accounting period. This is then equal to the national income, which therefore works out at zero. Several comments are in order.

Salah's example is not an illustration but an impossibility. If there is no human-made capital, as Salah assumes, the resource will have to be exploited using bare hands. This labour is value added to the resource. In the SNA it holds that the sum total of values added (to our physical surroundings; see H&B, Section 4) equals the sum total of revenues equals the sum total of costs. In Salah's example the costs are zero, so there is no value added and consequently no labour. Without labour, that is without added value, it is impossible to extract the quantity of the resource in question. The resource then remains intact and cannot be marketed and no correction for depletion can be made. National income (the sum of values added) can therefore never consist solely of rent, as Salah implicitly seems to assume.

Even if we elaborate Salah's example into something physically conceivable, namely bare-handed extraction, his criticism is unjustified. Disregarding any rent, the market value now consists of the value added in manual extraction (equalling the labour costs). In Salah's approach, this value would have to be corrected by the same figure, namely depletion costed at market value (equalling the labour costs). National income once again tallies to zero.

However, the point is that the value added to the resource by labour in the process of extraction (and processing) is precisely *not* the value of the resource's functions (see Hueting, 1998a and H&B, p. 29 and 30). The value of environmental functions and the costs associated with their loss are expressed only imperfectly, if at all, via the market mechanism – and then never as added value. Neither does the value added determine the value of the resource itself, for the latter derives from the value of the functions, or flows, of the resource (the stock), in the same way that human-made capital goods are valued with reference to the value of the consumer goods (the flows) they generate. 'Sustainability' presumes preferences for the future availability of functions (flows) of the resource. In the final count, such can only be guaranteed by replacing the resource by other elements of our physical surroundings (substitution) or, if that is not feasible, by eliminating the environmental burden at source. In either case the associated costs will show up on the elimination cost curve, which simultaneously determines the value, namely at the intersection with the demand curve (see H&B, Section 5.1). These costs have nothing to do with the revenues Salah considers in his example.

Perhaps unnecessarily, I would recall that growth of national income involves a change of *volume*, not of added value (see Hueting, 1992d and H&B, pp. 33, 34, 35 and 36).

My overall conclusion: Salah and I are essentially in agreement. We merely differ in the assumptions we make, with mine going one step further.

7 DAVID PEARCE, KIRK HAMILTON AND GILES ATKINSON

As already noted in Section 1 of these rejoinders, David Pearce et al. (Chapter 9, this volume) are in agreement with me on more issues than their contribution suggests. As was the case with Herman Daly, their study was completed after correspondence in which I clearly stated my position on (individual) preferences. Both Daly and Pearce et al. have ignored this information and in doing so they consciously misrepresent my views on preferences. In Herman's case, I strongly suspect that he was keen to provoke a discussion on crucial issues (see Section 3). Although David et al. undoubtedly also had a reason, I cannot surmise what it might be. Unfortunately, then, I see myself obliged merely to quote, once again, from my work to demonstrate that we are in fact in agreement with regard to basing environment valuation on individual preferences. Subsequently, I shall summarize the points on which we do differ in our understanding, endeavouring to place these in an appropriate perspective; for the good reasons set out in Section 1, I am keener to seek concordance than discord.

David et al. write: '(. . .) the approach assumes that sustainability targets can be established in a fairly robust manner. Roefie's view has been that governments represent a channel of "revealed preference" so that targets set by government act like shadow prices. (. . .) Those costs must be based on individuals' preferences. (. . .) Whatever a government decides is a target is the socially desirable and optimal target. (. . .) The reasoning is entirely circular. (. . .) We therefore find the 'distance to targets' approach suspect'.

It is painful to be criticized for advocating a method of (environmental) valuation that I have for 35 years attacked so vociferously in countless publications. In his contribution to the present volume Robert Goodland quotes as follows from one: 'He criticized the official CBA of the construction of a polder in (. . .) an internationally important estuary. (. . .) Hueting's main objection was that the official CBA-assigned value of one hectare Waddensea estuary was set at the same value as one hectare marginal agricultural land (. . .) That was the value officially set for nature areas by the Netherlands Government. In his review of the official CBA, Hueting observed: "This is not valuing at all, because it gives the Government the value which the same Government had already decided upon." (. . .)' The quote is from 1978 and voices precisely the criticism formulated by David et al.: if the Government perfectly reflected subjects' individual preferences, *quod non*, valuation would be superfluous; economists providing such 'valuation' results make an easy living; it is circular reasoning.

Only recently, in *Economisch-Statistische Berichten* (85, no. 4244), I published an article entitled 'Price the environment, not the policy' in which I criticize derivation of 'shadow prices' for environmental functions from government environmental standards (which had been done in the framework of a transport CBA). After all, in setting those standards the government is implicitly setting the price of the functions in question (the article is being translated and is available on request).

The logic of Pearce et al.'s critique also rather escapes me, since most of the environmental standards set by governments around the world are very far removed from 'sustainability standards'. The standards employed in estimating SNI can therefore never be derived from government targets, as David et al. state. In my *Three Myths* study (Chapter 3, this volume), under Myth 1: 'Environment conflicts with employment', I write: 'The environmental measures taken to date are marginal in relation to what has to be done to arrive at a sustainable use of the environment. Most measures only slow down the rate of deterioration, owing to the persistent character of the burden. No government accepts the unavoidable truth that, given the available technology, more environment means less production (and vice versa); so nowhere is reducing the wage rate taken into consideration'. Obviously, governments may voice their intentions. The voicing of such intentions *vis-à-vis* sustainability worldwide certainly implies that our SNI research enjoys a measure of support in society. At Statistics Netherlands, this is a *conditio sine qua non* for setting up research, and rightly so. However, expressing an intention to act (and a willingness to pay for such action) is of course not the same as actually doing something. Intentions are obviously not revealed preferences.

In Hueting (1994, p.45) I write: '(. . .) the *assumption* is made that the standards reflect the intensity of individual preferences for environmental functions' and (p.46): 'as stated, the calculation is based on the *assumption* that the perpendicular on point D reflects the intensity of individual preferences for environmental functions'. (The italics, like those below, are original. I might add that David was one of the editors of the volume in question.) Hueting (1995a, p.209) puts is thus: '(. . .) any monetary valuation of environmental functions and their loss is based on an assumption about demand. (. . .) assuming that individual economic subjects have a desire to use the environment (including natural resources) sustainably' and (p.226): 'A demand curve (. . .) on the basis of (. . .) assumptions (. . .) that the standard for sustainable use of the environment is a good measure of individual preferences for environmental functions'. Hueting (1995c, p.4) reads: 'The calculation is therefore based on the *assumption* that the perpendicular in Figure 1 reflects the intensity of individual preferences for environmental functions'. Likewise, Figure 1 of Hueting (1995b) is introduced with the words: 'This comes to making the *assumption* that individuals want to use environmental functions in a sustainable way'. On p. 32 of Hueting (1998a), finally, I write: 'Consequently, for finding shadow prices for functions, it is necessary to make assumptions about (individual and social) preferences, in CBA's and green accounting'.

In my rejoinder to Daly (this volume) I have noted my reasons for proceeding from individual preferences. There, I also note that even in a country with high standards of democracy such as The Netherlands, a lack of information can result in fatal decisions being made. Without economic information on the very crux of the environmental problem – the conflict between the environment and production growth as measured in national income (population times volume of economic activity) – well-founded decisions on environmental conservation cannot be made. Besides opportunity cost data, data on (individual) preferences are indispensable for such information. If one takes as an established fact that the latter data can be deduced only very partially from market behaviour or surveys, then making assumptions *vis-à-vis* preferences is inevitable (for example H&B, Section 5.2).

Government decisions do not reflect individual preferences in any a priori sense. On this we are in agreement. Where my difference with David, Kirk and Giles lies is the inescapability of introducing assumptions on preferences as well as on several other points.

1. David et al. believe that, ultimately, WTP will prove an adequate tool for measuring preferences, including preferences for the functions of life support systems of existential importance to future generations. It is merely a question of time, they tell us. In Hueting (1989b, 1992a, 1995b) I have argued why such a quest is very unlikely to succeed. The arguments in these publications overlap one another only partly and are by no means exhaustive.
2. According to David et al., estimation of an SNI is an impossible undertaking. In defence of this position they offer the following arguments:
   (a) In their view, the sustainability standards used in the SNI research are based on government targets or standards, so that the SNI estimate is based on circular reasoning. As already stated, this is a misrepresentation of my work. The sustainability standards used in the SNI are based on independent scientific research (see, for example, Hueting 1992d, 1998b, and H&B, Sections 6.6 and 7).
   (b) The point of estimating the SNI is to attach a value to major changes in the availability of environmental functions, while Pearce et al. maintain that minor changes are all that can be valued. Under the assumption of preferences for sustainability, the marginal costs of environmental measures rise exponentially and it is to be questioned, they hold, whether these costs are worth the marginal benefits obtained. These doubts are obviously legitimate.

   Given preferences for sustainability, however, the benefits consist of the positive effect on welfare of avoiding existential risks to future generations; the costs consist of the negative impact on welfare of (1) abandoning goods that place a major burden on the environment in both the production and consumption phase in favour of environmentally benign alternatives and (2) moving towards smaller families (this may in fact have a positive effect on welfare, especially for women in developing countries). The environmental problem is, after all, an allocation problem. With opportunity costs we are not essentially concerned with money (which, of itself, has no meaning), but with a change in consumption pattern. Whether the reallocation required to safeguard the environment is effectuated by internalizing the costs of elimination measures or by switching directly to ecologically superior products (less meat and more beans, for example) is evidently irrelevant. Once one realizes that this is what is at stake, doubts as to whether the benefits of consuming (ever more) environmentally damaging goods are worth the sacrifices embodied in real and existential risks for the future are equally legitimate (bearing in mind that benefits can be formulated as a reduction of costs and opportunity costs as a sacrifice of benefits). Doubts – either way – are inherent in assumptions. Let me refer once more to *Three Myths* (Chapter 3, this volume) and in particular Myth 3: 'Environmental conservation is not too expensive, for a bicycle is cheaper than a car and raising two children is cheaper than raising eight; naturally, there *is* a sacrifice involved and a negative effect on the volume of national income' (see H&B, pp. 57–8).

As David et al. have well understood, I still stand by the conclusion of Hueting (1974a): shadow prices cannot be constructed on the basis of revealed preferences. However, it has apparently escaped them that in my work post-1985, to be able to provide information on the conflict between production growth and environmental preservation I have introduced assumptions regarding preferences and have since then worked with assumed shadow prices. H&B, Section 5.2, explains that the optimum described in Section 5.1 (which rests on the assumption of fully revealed preferences) remains valid as an assumed optimum (and then rests on a different assumption about preferences); see Figures 2.1 and 2.7. So I do not see how I can possibly be 'detract[ing] attention from the theoretically correct (. . .) solution of estimating a shadow price based GNP', as David et al. write.

The aim of our SNI study is to obtain the best possible information, however crude, on the distance between the current growth path (which is optimum under the assumption that the current package of goods, including environmental functions, is a perfect reflection of preferences) and the sustainable growth path (which is optimum under the assumption of preferences for sustainability); see Figure 2.3 and accompanying text in H&B. This is not the same as estimating the 'total' value of the environment; in their text David et al. wrongly suggest that I am engaged in such a pointless exercise. The distance to sustainability appears to be large, so our work seems to indicate. A decade ago Tinbergen and Hueting gave a rough estimate of about 50 per cent of world income (Hueting, 1991d), by no means an extreme figure given the provisional results of our SNI study (Verbruggen et al., Chapter 11, this volume). One can only conclude that *if* we do not want to jeopardize future generations, we must stop identifying changes in standard national income with economic growth and must indeed abandon the term. What we should then present to politicians and the general public are changes along the sustainable growth path (see H&B, Figure 2.3) as a partial indicator of economic success (that is an increase in welfare). This would encourage the move from the current growth path, via the transitional path (Figure 2.3), to the sustainable growth path. (I would remind readers of the subtitle of my 1974a work: *More welfare through less production?*.) This implies a fundamental shift in economic priorities from production growth to environmental preservation.

I wrote: *if* we do not want to jeopardize the future, we should adopt a certain course of action. However, we can immediately start providing information by *assuming* that we do not wish to roll off serious risks onto future generations. I sincerely hope that David et al. see the point of such an exercise and are willing to cooperate on its realization.

3. I agree with Pearce et al. that the genuine savings approach can provide some kind of (weak) signal *vis-à-vis* sustainability, but only under additional conditions. The two approaches (SNI and genuine savings) can then complement one another, but only under the six conditions stipulated below, which are not presently satisfied.

As Pearce et al. rightly assert, welfare depends on total stocks of produced, natural and human assets. Produced capital, however, is a combination of labour (technology) and elements from our physical surroundings (the environment). In the final count, we are dependent upon but two factors: human and environmental assets (see *Three Myths*, Chapter 3, this volume). The *sine qua non* of *environmentally* sustainable development is a production level that guarantees preservation of vital environmental functions with the available technology (see H&B). From this there follow three conditions for calculation of the 'genuine savings' indicator.

(i) Any increases in human assets must be used exclusively for environmental protection and/or for growth of production that does not (further) damage the environment. This condition is hard to satisfy, because (a) being intermediate deliveries, expenditures on environmental protection check production growth (see, *inter alia*, Hueting, 1974a and H&B) and (b) it is precisely the most environmentally damaging sectors of the economy that account for the bulk of production growth. On the latter point see Hueting (1981b, 1992d), paying due heed, in implementing this condition, to the essential difference explained there between an increase in the size of a sector (expansion) in terms of added value and that sector's contribution to an increase in production volume, as measured in national income; see Hueting (1974a, p. 170, footnote 2, English edition).

(ii) Likewise, increases in stocks of produced assets must be exclusively for the purpose of environmental protection or 'clean' growth. Again, it is a condition that is not easy to satisfy, for the reasons just given under i(a) and i(b). According to David et al., investments in infrastructure contribute positively to genuine savings. From the perspective of sustainability, however, their contribution is surely negative. The fragmentation of the landscape caused by roads and other infrastructure and the consequent loss of habitat and isolation of gene pools are substantially accelerating the rate at which plant and animal species are becoming extinct. Bringing this process to a halt is deemed by many people to be a major first step down the road to sustainability (see H&B). Certainly in the industrialized countries, infrastructure should be demolished rather than constructed if the goal of sustainability is to be realized.

(iii) Resource revenues must be invested in environmental protection or 'clean' growth; see (i) and (ii).

The C in the genuine savings formula is most probably taken from standard national income statistics. So C contains most probably some asymmetric entries (see, *inter alia*, Hueting, 1974a and H&B). This leads to the next condition.

(iv) From C in this formula must be deducted expenditures on elimination of and compensation for loss of environmental functions, to the extent that these are financed by government or private households, as the theory presented by the authors suggests.

Further:

(v) The condition $S_g \geq 0$ must hold for all t to warrant (weak) sustainability, that is for a long time series, not just for a single year or single accounting period, as in the formula presented by Pearce et al.

(vi) Only in the case of non-renewable resources may technology be substituted for nature, as argued in Hueting (1998b) and H&B (Section 7).

As long as these six conditions remain unsatisfied, the genuine savings method certainly cannot serve as an indicator for environmentally sustainable development.

8 SYLVIE FAUCHEUX AND MARTIN O'CONNOR

As Sylvie and Martin's study (Chapter 10, this volume) is so akin to the opening contribution of Bart de Boer and myself (Chapter 2, this volume), the present rejoinder has been written together with my co-author.

Hueting (1974a) proceeds from the principle of possible uses, or functions, of our physical surroundings (the environment, see H&B, p. 29 and 33). From this point of departure no distinction can be made between weak and strong sustainability: in order to attain sustainability some elements of the environment cannot be substituted, while other elements have to be (see Hueting, 1998b, my response to Beckerman, pp. 358–9, and H&B, p. 69–70, and Section 1.2, Consequences of the Principles, 2). We certainly appreciate the breadth of scope and didactic value of Faucheux and O'Connor's Section 3. In our opinion, however, by adopting the above starting point the conclusions of the 'weak theory' (general growth theory) can be readily refuted without conflicting with that theory, allowing the conclusions of their Section 4 to be drawn immediately. We consider ourselves in full agreement with most of these conclusions, while on several others we differ for reasons set out briefly below. We hope that our response will encourage further discussion and publication.

In my introduction to the '*Rejoinders to symposium authors*' I have argued strongly for as much as agreement as possible, because of the pivotal importance of our subject for society and the negligible influence of ecological or environmental economics on the economics of environmental politics in the absence of such agreement. In H&B (Chapter 2, this volume), which represents an attempt to attain such agreement, we conclude that the theory behind the SNI (a term I introduced, I may add) is in accordance with 'general growth theory'. The substantial differences between our results and those of exponents of this theory can be traced back to differences regarding assumptions, one of which is that concerning substitutability; see Chapter 2, (Conclusion 2, H&B). This circumstance has the advantage that it allows the information flow to citizens and policy-makers to be rendered vastly simpler as well as more transparent: assuming a, the conclusion is b, and assuming c, d and so on. Politicians and the public need then no longer be burdened with often very complex theoretical ballast and (apparent) differences in theoretical approach.

Besides substitutability there is another important difference between us and some authors whose work, like ours, rests on general growth theory, discussed by Sylvie and Martin in their Section 3. This other difference pertains to whether or not it is assumed that the economy is currently on an optimum path. We justify our assumption that such is not the case by pointing to the existence of 'blockages' preventing preferences for environmental functions from being expressed. We then draw the conclusion that exponents of general growth theory would arrive at the same results as we do if they admitted the existence of such blockages and at the same time assumed absolute preferences for sustainability, defined as the preservation of vital environmental functions for future generations.

In their Section 3, Sylvie and Martin define a green net national product (gNNP) and argue that within 'weak' or general growth theory Hartwick's rule (applied to all future moments in time) is not a sufficient condition for obtaining an indefinitely constant (or growing) gNNP, which would then be equal to the sustainable national income SNI(i) as defined by them. However, if one proceeds from the more general welfare indicator v (see H&B, p. 48) a different conclusion is reached, provided the availability of each environmental function is included in the analysis right from the start. Constancy of environmental function levels is then found to be a precondition for sustainability. This condition follows – within the weak theory – from Hartwick's rule for the special case of an invariant (that is not explicitly time-dependent) environmental-economic model and human welfare being determined only by the quantities of goods consumed, for the production of which environmental functions are essential. In the more general case of welfare also being influenced directly by such functions (for example, 'air for physiological functioning', that is breathing) the precondition of constant function levels and Hartwick's rule (second condition) do not boil down to the same thing.

Together, though, these two conditions are certainly sufficient for either an indefinitely constant (or rising) welfare indicator v or a ditto *volume* of consumption y_s. *We* define the latter welfare indicator (consumption volume) as the SNI, provided it is maximal and the model is invariant. See, for example, Asheim (1994). If due allowance is made for all preferences, that is including an assumed overriding preference for sustainability, then in theory the welfare indicator v must be maximized. However, calculation of v depends on an (as yet) unsolvable model (see H&B, Section 5.4) and a comparison must moreover be made with the standard national income. In practice, therefore, we have opted to estimate the indicator y_s. As v and y_s are not at a maximum simultaneously, each of these indicators is associated with a path of its own on which, approximately speaking (see H&B, Section 6.6), the assumed predominant preferences for sustainability are optimally satisfied; for each indicator, then, a particular Hartwick condition is valid. Contrary to what Sylvie and Martin state, the prices of manufactured and natural capital goods and human capital (labour) are certainly allowed to vary along that path; see Asheim (1994) and of course the deduction of Hartwick (1978). In fact they must of necessity do so, because non-renewable resources will have to be substituted in order for their functions to be sustained. The authors' conclusion that prices must remain constant to arrive at an SNI is therefore incorrect.

This leaves unaltered the fact that capital gains may indeed play a role, namely outside the path on which the national income is *itself* maximum and sustainable, for example the national income on the path where the welfare indicator v is maximum and sustainable, in other words indefinitely constant or rising. In our contribution to this volume we have therefore defined the SNI as the national income that must be maximum and sustainable and therefore determines the path. Another example is Hicksian income, discussed in my response to Herman Daly.

In their study Sylvie and Martin do not mention the fact that the economy might not in fact be on an optimal path; but their wording does not appear to exclude that possibility. If they can accede to the existence of blockages and a range of different optimal paths, the main disparity between our respective approaches probably vanishes. There remain several other points, which we also feel can be resolved.

In their Section 4.3 Sylvie and Martin state that the opportunity costs involved in achieving sustainability 'usually must be estimated' by comparing the present development path with the transition path from there to sustainability. They make no mention of the fact that the national income on the present path may also be compared with the SNI on the (admittedly unfeasible) sustainable path, just as can be done in the 'weak' theory considered by them earlier. To our mind this unfeasible, unblocked sustainable path provides far more information about sustainability and the distance to it than the feasible transition path with maximum income. The opportunity costs found in this way are a monetary measure of the distance between these two paths. The SNI in question is the 'strong' variant of the volume of the SNI(i) they themselves introduce; see the definition on p. 242. The text of the second full paragraph on p. 244 appears to conflict with this definition, however. The depreciation during the current period certainly does not reflect the distance between the paths on which current GNP, respectively, the SNI are situated, for deduction of this depreciation from current GNP yields a green NNP associated with the same path as current GNP and not the SNI associated with the sustainable path.

We are therefore unclear as to why the authors, in their representation of our work on p. 257, do make a distinction between an indicator for the distance to sustainability and one for the costs of achieving sustainability. In our approach too, we should add, the modelling results include a sectoral breakdown of opportunity costs. On this point see my response to Ekins, pp. 336, 337, 338, 339 and 340 and Verbruggen et al. (Chapter 11, this volume).

We argue (a) that the SNI, the maximum national income associated with an (unblocked) unfeasible path, can be estimated using a general equilibrium model and (b) that none of the points on the transition path satisfies the definition of SNI, even if that path is sustainable to the extent that environmental functions remain preserved at minimum sustainable levels. In that case it is only at its very end that the transition path approximates SNI. See Figure 2.3 (Chapter 2, this volume), in which *f* represents the transition path. We therefore consider Sylvie and Martin's work as *complementary* to our own.

In our calculation of SNI we feel we have resolved the problem of price ratios (H&B, p.34) by using prices in which the opportunity costs involved in achieving sustainability are internalized, just as the charges levied to induce shifts to environmentally more benign activities when further technological improvements become too expensive. The reasoning here is that the price ratios thus obtained approximate those holding in the sustainable situation, in contrast to the current price ratios (see H&B, p.57).

The 'chicken and egg problem' referred to by the authors goes beyond the choice of prices, however, and beyond the feasibility of ascertaining the path of maximum feasible constant (or never-declining) national income in a theoretically all-encompassing environmental-economic model. The problem, rather, lies in extrapolating to a sustainable situation for which the model can be only very partially validated. It is a familiar problem that besets any environmental model used to chart the impact of particular measures on the state of the environment or to assess what measures are to be employed for achieving a particular environment target. The inaccuracy of such projections and the uncertainties surrounding them are often felt to be acceptable, given the elected purpose of indicating the consequences of human activity for the environment and for society within the framework of a decision-making process necessarily involving due improvement of that process.

Our method addresses the unsolvability of the all-encompassing model by breaking it down into two smaller models: one for computing environmental pressure standards, the other for computing the effect on national income of achieving those standards. This does not fundamentally alter the chicken and egg problem posited by Sylvie and Martin, who thereby follow Norgaard. However, introduction of an SNI calculated in this fashion and of the associated economic analyses that implies would certainly render decision making a far more structured process. We are keen to further develop our contribution to these methods in dialogue with kindred researchers like Sylvie, Martin and the other contributors to this volume.

9 HARMEN VERBRUGGEN, ROB B. DELLINK, REYER GERLACH, MARJAN W. HOFKES AND HUIB M.A. JANSEN; ROBERT GOODLAND; KARL-GÖRAN MÄLER

As already mentioned, my responses to Paul Ekins and Herman Daly have been rather more extensive than I first anticipated. There have been no complaints from the editors, however, for they consider this volume first and foremost a record of a debate – and I am in full agreement. After all, it is only in the course of serious debate that misunderstandings come to the surface and theory can be advanced. Still, I am glad my response to this final cluster of authors (Chapters 11 and 12, this volume) can be brief, keeping this rejoinder chapter within reasonable bounds.

I am grateful to all the authors who have contributed to the symposium and to this book. I am sure nobody will be blame me, though, when I say that the most important contribution for me has undoubtedly been that of Harmen Verbruggen and his colleagues. I can do no better here than to reiterate the thoughts expressed in my speech on the occasion of the symposium:

> It goes without saying that special thanks are due to researchers Reijer Gerlagh and Rob Dellink, with Huib Jansen and Marjan Hofkes behind them, and to the man with ultimate responsibility for the exercise with which we are today concerned: Harmen Verbruggen. They have used the model they developed at the Institute of Environmental Studies to produce a provisional estimate of the Sustainable National Income of the Netherlands. They have carried out their work loyally, following the guidelines set out in the 1992 publication '*Methodology for the Calculation of Sustainable National Income*'. The study is being overseen by a broad-based committee chaired by Frank den Butter and received funding from the ministers of the day: Hans Wijers and Margreet de Boer, whom I have already thanked in an interview in the magazine 'Natuur en *Milieu*' (Nature and Environment). [. . . . .] I hope that SNI exercises will be undertaken in other countries, too, particularly in developing countries and particularly for use by the World Bank.
>
> I mention the loyalty of the researchers, and implicitly the committee members and ministers, mainly because in the past they have not all been equally enthusiastic about my ideas concerning the SNI. I am convinced that the frank and friendly exchange of letters between Frank, Harmen and myself prior to the study brought our standpoints much closer. They both understand all too well that when the SNI research was transferred away from Statistics Netherlands, after thirty years, it was not the happiest day of my life. Perhaps that's why Harmen has called his end product 'the SNI according to Hueting'. I value that gesture enormously. Harmen, Frank and others have explained to me that, for obvious reasons, transfer of the research was in fact a blessing in disguise. I believe them and reiterate their words here.

Robert Goodland's perspective on my work is ecological. I value that enormously, and have little more to add. While reading his study I wondered briefly 'What has music got to do with my environmental work?'. But then I realized that Robert, as an ecologist, has understood my work far better than many an economist. Playing the piano is, after all, one of those activities that have a negligible impact on the environment and make no contribution to production growth as measured in the national income (Hueting, 1981b, 1992d).

One of the esteemed speakers at the symposium was Karl-Göran Mäler, whose draft paper was included in the symposium volume along with those of the other speakers. For reasons I fully understand, he has declined to finalize his paper. In our own contribution to the present volume Bart de Boer and I do address his work, however. We thereby conclude that the marked difference between the results of his approach and ours follows from Karl-Göran's assumption that the economy is on an optimum path, while I have consistently assumed that such is not the case. This assumption is justified by the existence of blockages preventing preferences for preservation of the natural environment from being adequately expressed (see H&B).

REFERENCES

As mentioned in the Introduction (Section 1) all references to my published work, alone or with co-authors, are according to the list of publications appended to Robert Goodland's contribution in Chapter 12 of this work. To facilitate reading, wherever feasible reference has been made to the summary paper by Bart de Boer and myself (referred to as 'H&B' for convenience), which then points readers to my earlier work. Other references are listed below.

Adriaanse A., S. Bringezu, A. Hammond, Y. Moriguchi, E. Rodenburg, D. Rogich and H.Schutz (1997), *Resource Flows: The Material Basis of Industrial Economies*, World Resources Institute, Washington, DC.

Asheim, G.B (1994), 'Net national product as an indicator of sustainability', *Scandinavian Journal of Economics*, **96** (2), 257–65.

Boer, B. de, (1996), 'Calculation of sustainable national income in the Netherlands: some results', paper prepared for the workshop *Valuation Methods for Green Accounting: a Practical Guide*, organized by The World Bank, UN Statistical Office and Ecological Economics, Washington, DC, March 20–22.

Bruyn, S.M. de, J.C.J.M. van den Bergh and J.B. Opschoor (1998), 'Economic growth and emissions: reconsidering the empirical basis of environmental Kuznets curves,' *Ecological Economics*, **25**, 161–75.

Costanza, R. et al. (1997), 'The value of the world's ecosystem services and natural captital', *Nature*, **387**, May 15.

Eijgenraam, C.J.J. (1992), 'Reactie op Hueting's stelling dat een verschuiving van één procent arbeidsvolume naar minder milieubelastende activiteiten per saldo een negatief effect heeft op het volume van het nationaal inkomen van tenminste 1,5 %', Centraal Planbureau, mimeo.

FAO (1990–1998), *Yearbooks of Fishery Statistics, Catches and Landings, 1990–1998*, FAO, Rome.

Feinberg, J. (1974), 'The rights of animals and unborn generations', in W. Blackstone (ed.) *Philosophy and the Environmental Crisis*, University of Georgia Press, Athens, pp. 43–68.

Goodland, R (1995), 'The concept of environmental sustainability', *Annual Review of Ecology and Systematics*, **26** 1–24.

Graedel, T.E, and P.J. Crutzen (1993), *Atmospheric Change*, W.H. Freeman and Company, New York.
Hartwick, J.M. (1978), 'Investing returns from depleting renewable resource stocks and intergenerational equity', *Economics Letters*, **1** 85–8.
Johansson, T.B., H. Kelly, A.K.N. Reddy and R.H. Williams (1993), *Renewable Energy*, Island Press, Washington, DC.
Kendall, H.W. and D. Pimentel (1994), 'Constraints on the expansion of the global food supply', *Ambio*, **23**, 198–205.
Lovelock, J.E. (1979), *Gaia, A New Look at Life on Earth*, Oxford University Press, Oxford.
Marcuse, R. (1964), *One Dimensional Man, the Ideology of Industrial Society*, London.
Odum, E.G. (1971), *Fundamentals of Ecology*, 3rd edn, Philadelphia, Penn.
Reijnders, L. (1996), *Environmentally Improved Production Processes and Products*, Kluwer, Dordrecht.
Schipper, L. and S. Meyers (1992), *Energy Efficiency and Human Activity*, Cambridge University Press, Cambridge.
Tolba, M.K. and O.A. El-Kholy (ed.) (1992), *The World Environment 1972–1992*. Chapman and Hall, London.

Index